The Business Skills Handbook
Roy Horn

The Chartered Institute of Personnel and Development is the leading publisher of books and reports for personnel and training professionals, students, and all those concerned with the effective management and development of people at work. For details of all our titles, please contact the publishing department:

tel: 020-8612 6204
e-mail publish@cipd.co.uk
The catalogue of all CIPD titles can be viewed on the CIPD website:
www.cipd.co.uk/bookstore

The Business Skills Handbook

Roy Horn

Chartered Institute of Personnel and Development

Published by the Chartered Institute of Personnel and Development,
151, The Broadway, London, SW19 1JQ

This edition first published 2009
Reprinted 2011, 2012 (twice), 2013, 2015

Typeset by Fakenham Photosetting Ltd, Norfolk
Printed and bound by CPI Group (UK) Ltd, Croydon, CR0 4YY

British Library Cataloguing in Publication Data
A catalogue of this publication is available from the British Library

ISBN 978 1 84398 218 0

Chartered Institute of Personnel and Development, CIPD House,
151 The Broadway, London, SW19 1JQ

Tel: 020 8612 6200
E-mail: cipd@cipd.co.uk
Website: www.cipd.co.uk
Incorporated by Royal Charter
Registered Charity No. 1079797

Contents

List of figures and tables

Preface

Welcome to the *Business Skills Handbook*. If you are a student in further or higher education or in the early years of a business career, this is the book for you. If you are in the school system, this may still be an excellent resource for improving your school work, and I am sure you will soon be in the university system where the ideas in this book will really pay off. The ideas, exercises and approaches will increase your ability to display the skills that are tested at university and those required by employers. I hope it will also lower your anxiety levels.

If you adopt only one or two of the ideas in the book, it will improve your university grades. If you can systematically incorporate all the ideas then you will have a successful and enjoyable time at university. I am not suggesting that reading and using this book will be easy – the techniques and approaches to bring success are varied and often complex. However, I wish you all well on your university journeys. This book is here to make that journey easier and the whole university experience more enjoyable. I hope you find the book useful and I hope you always get great grades.

This chapter is a brief introduction to the book and you should read this first before reading later chapters. It sets out the general approach to each of the chapters and the learning features you will find throughout the book.

WHAT WILL I LEARN IN THIS CHAPTER?

- why this book was written
- understand the level of the book and who can use it successfully
- the learning features of the book
- usage summaries for the different stages of your university journey
- the general layout of the book
- the top ten tips for successfully completing your degree
- the characteristics of excellent and poor assignments and projects.

Why this book was written

I have taught, assessed and assisted many undergraduate and postgraduate students in universities and I have written this book to assist them. I hope it will assist you. On a more selfish note, I tend to have to answer the same questions over and over again; the answers to all the questions I have been asked about business skills are contained in this book. I have tried to make it as friendly and welcoming as possible so it becomes like an old friend to be consulted when you are not sure of how to do something. You will find it most useful if you read it systematically throughout your first year at university and then return to it and reread relevant sections during your studies at levels two and three.

I would advise using the book in the following structured manner:

First reading – When you first start your university course, or before you start, I would advise reading the following chapters:

- Preface
- Chapter 1 – Organising Life and Work
- Chapter 2 – How to Study
- Chapter 3 – Learning and Skills
- Chapter 4 – What are the Key Skills of University Life and the Workplace?
- Chapter 5 – Working in Teams.

The aim at this stage is to get 'switched on' to what is required and to get organised. After just a few weeks of your course you will start experiencing assignment deadlines approaching. If you have not prepared yourself and developed an organised way of working, the deadlines will take over and you will feel stressed and under pressure. Alternatively, prepare to complete your studies and get organised, and you will be able to control the stress and pressure, meet deadlines and be successful.

During year 1 of your degree – Once you have your first assignments I would advise that you read the following chapters:

- Chapter 6 – Effective Reading Skills
- Chapter 7 – Developing Good Writing Skills
- Chapter 8 – Presentation Communication
- Chapter 9 – Business Calculations
- Chapter 12 – Examinations and Assignments
- Chapter 14 – Word Processor Skills.

The aim in this phase is to quickly learn all the skills that contribute to success in the assignments and examinations. There is lots of advice and help in these chapters, but you will need to use them developmentally to get the most from them.

After your first year or at the start of year 2 – The second year of your university course will require you to read and write in a more critical manner. You will also need to display the 'higher-level' skills that are covered in the following chapters:

- Chapter 10 – Critical Reading and Writing Skills
- Chapter 11 – Analysis and Evaluation Skills
- Chapter 12 – Examinations and Assignments
- Chapter 13 – Thinking and Memory Skills
- Chapter 16 – Project Management Skills.

In many undergraduate degrees the marks for modules in the second year of study count towards the classification of degree you will be awarded. If you can display the 'higher-level' skills in assignments and examinations, you will gain higher marks. It is worthwhile getting organised to carry out your dissertation in the second year of your degree so that you can concentrate on doing the research in your third year. The project skills chapter will provide a good grounding in the skills you will need to successfully complete a project or dissertation.

After your second year or at the beginning of your third year – I would advise that you read the following chapters:

- Chapter 15 – Being Effective with Spreadsheets
- Chapter 17 – Social Skills
- Chapter 18 – Leadership, Coaching and Mentoring Skills
- Chapter 19 – Careers and Futuring Skills.

CIPD Students

If you are studying the module Developing Skills for Business Leadership, the following table may be useful in determining how the learning outcomes of that module map to the chapters of this book.

Mapping the learning outcomes of Developing Skills for Business Leadership and the *Business Skills Handbook*

Number	Learning outcome	Mapped to chapters in *Business Skills Handbook*
1	Manage themselves more effectively in the workplace	**Chapter 1 – Organising Life and Work** **Chapter 2 – How to Study** **Chapter 3 – Learning and Skills** **Chapter 4 – What are the Key Skills of University Life and the Workplace?** **Chapter 17 – Social Skills**
2	Manage interpersonal relationships at work more effectively	**Chapter 4 – What are the Key Skills of University Life and the Workplace?** **Chapter 5 – Working in Teams** **Chapter 7 – Developing Good Writing Skills** **Chapter 8 – Presentation Communication** **Chapter 17 – Social Skills**
3	Make sound and justifiable decisions and solve problems more effectively	**Chapter 9 – Business Calculations** **Chapter 11 – Analysis and Evaluation Skills** **Chapter 13 – Thinking and Memory Skills** **Chapter 16 – Project Management Skills** **Chapter 17 – Social Skills**
4	Lead and influence others more effectively	**Chapter 5 – Working in Teams** **Chapter 11 – Analysis and Evaluation Skills** **Chapter 17 – Social Skills** **Chapter 18 – Leadership, Coaching and Mentoring Skills**
5	Interpret financial information and manage financial resources	**Chapter 9 – Business Calculations** **Chapter 10 – Critical Reading and Writing Skills** **Chapter 15 – Being Effective with Spreadsheets**

6	Demonstrate enhanced IT proficiency	**Chapter 8 – Presentation Communication** **Chapter 14 – Word Processor Skills** **Chapter 15 – Being Effective with Spreadsheets** **Chapter 16 – Project Management Skills** **Chapter 17 – Social Skills**
7	Demonstrate an essential people management skill-set	**Chapter 6 – Effective Reading Skills** **Chapter 7 – Developing Good Writing Skills** **Chapter 8 – Presentation Communication** **Chapter 10 – Critical Reading and Writing Skills** **Chapter 11 – Analysis and Evaluation Skills** **Chapter 16 – Project Management Skills**
8	Demonstrate competence in postgraduate study skills	**Chapter 2 – How to Study** **Chapter 4 – What are the Key Skills of University Life and the Workplace?** **Chapter 7 – Developing Good Writing Skills** **Chapter 10 – Critical Reading and Writing Skills** **Chapter 11 – Analysis and Evaluation Skills** **Chapter 12 – Examinations and Assignments**

THE LEVEL OF THIS BOOK

This book has been written with undergraduate and postgraduate business students as the main audience. But, because it follows a logical developmental path, it may be very useful to leisure, tourism, sport and social science students. Throughout the book I have related the chapters and sections to undergraduate and postgraduate (often known as master's) work. Both undergraduate and master's courses require the same skills for success. In many respects there are two major differences between these levels. One is the size and complexity of the university tasks, where more reading and evidence is normally required for master's level. The other is the level of critique and evaluation expected, where a more critical and evaluative stance is expected at master's level.

The book is designed to take you logically through all the major areas of skills development. It will answer many of the questions that will arise as you progress through your degrees. There will be specific areas where you will need guidance from your tutor. I hope this book will provide you with all the support you need to succeed at university and at work.

TOP TEN TIPS FOR SUCCESSFULLY COMPLETING YOUR DEGREE

1 Think and reflect about the learning taking place (Chapters 2 and 3).

2 Be organised from day one (Chapter 1).

3 Follow the pattern of regularly reading, thinking and writing (Chapters 9, 10 and 11).

4 Make the best use of feedback (Chapters 9, 10 and 12).

5 Start writing early, and try to write every day – yes, every day (Chapters 9, 10 and 11).

6 Carefully plan your days and weeks; set and meet deadlines (Chapter 1).

7 Develop work-related skills that will really pay off in the workplace (Chapters 16, 17, 18 and 19).

8 Use electronic methods to reduce your workload (Chapters 2, 12 and 13).

9 Make sure you have a friend or buddy; join or create a study group (Chapters 2, 3 and 4).

10 Try to enjoy the experience – it is possible!

CHARACTERISTICS OF EXCELLENT AND POOR ASSIGNMENTS AND EXAMINATIONS

Excellent assignments will:

- have a clear focus on the questions and will argue precisely these questions
- have a clear, well-planned structure
- display a range of knowledge and understanding of the literature associated with the topic area
- include analysis, critique, synthesis, argument and evaluation, rather than simple description
- display correct referencing and acknowledgement of ideas
- be well written and in the appropriate academic style
- use a range of sources and particularly use journal sources
- use a wide range of sources to create convincing arguments.

A poor assignment will:

- display a weakly focused answer to the question(s) set
- be poorly planned and structured
- be predominantly descriptive
- display little critique, analysis, synthesis and evaluation
- contain inconsistent referencing and acknowledgement of ideas
- display a weak or unconvincing argument
- use a limited range of sources
- be poorly written, with errors of English usage and inappropriate academic style.

RECOGNISING THE DIVERSITY OF LEARNERS AT UNIVERSITY

You will join university as a unique individual; no one else will be exactly the same as you. It is important to recognise and celebrate the uniqueness of you and your fellow students. This may mean that you will be good at some aspects of university life and less good at others. Your skills and attributes may be attributable to learning and history or innate qualities. Most students will have weaknesses in certain areas; three of the most common weak areas are reading, writing and numeracy. Universities have well-developed systems for assisting students with any areas of weakness. When you first enter university you should engage with the student support systems to diagnose any areas where the university can help. If you do not engage with the systems, it will not be possible for the university to assist you.

Most universities will produce a handbook for students with additional needs. You will often find this on the university website. There will be some detailed provisions for the well-known additional needs, such as access issues, dyslexia, dyspraxia. But if you feel you have additional needs, even if it is not one of those listed in the handbook, contact the student support system and discuss those needs.

Learning Features

The Business Skills Handbook has been designed and organised to be friendly and easy to use. Each chapter deals with a separate set of skills. At the beginning of each chapter you will find an introduction and a bullet list of 'What skills will I develop in this chapter?' The main body of each chapter is structured in sections for ease of navigation. At the end of each chapter you will find a short summary, bibliography of sources, further suggested reading and web links.

WHAT SKILLS WILL I DEVELOP IN THIS CHAPTER?

A bullet list of the main aspects covered in the chapter. This is useful for navigating the chapter and as a refresher when you return to a chapter.

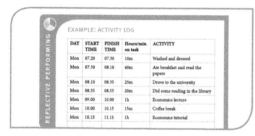

REFLECTIVE PERFORMING

This invites you to pause and reflect on some aspect of the skills development process or invites you to carry out a practical activity to experience an element of the skills development process.

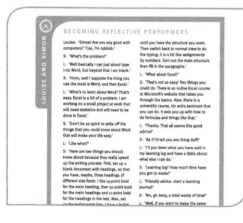

LOUISE AND SIMON 'BECOMING REFLECTIVE PERFORMERS'

This is a running narrative between two students who want to become reflective performers. Reflective performer is a term given to a student or worker who uses reflection to improve performance. The narrative illustrates some of the issues, opportunities, activities and frustrations that occur at university and work.

LEARNING DIARY ENTRIES

These illustrate some of the learning opportunities that might be included in a learning diary. They are essentially reflective statements relating to issues and frustrations of learning and skills development.

TUTOR / STUDENT / MANAGER COMMENTS

Tutor comments represent a tutor view of the skills development process. These are effectively a tutor tip to assist you in your university journey. Student comments represent a student view of the university process related to the chapter topic. It is designed to provide a valuable insight to personal aspects of learning and skills development. Manager represent an insight, approach or thought about workplace practice from experienced managers.

TUTOR COMMENT

I always encourage my tutees to create their work breakdown structures in a spreadsheet, because then it becomes really easy to produce the Gantt charts that display progress. They can also rearrange them for each assignment. I am far more willing to grant an extension for some unforeseen event if I can see how they have planned and developed the work.

WORKED EXAMPLES AND ILLUSTRATIONS

Worked examples occur in various forms and develop the idea in a section with a practical example that illustrates the learning process. Illustrations are provided to display and illuminate important aspects of a chapter.

Figure 1.3 Screenshot of Outlook tasks

SCREEN SHOTS

Where it is important to illustrate a computer-related example, a screen shot will be included. These also help you to carry out practical activities, such as using software, and give you confidence that you are replicating the same technique.

THE 'NIGHTMARE' COLLEAGUE

Susie and Kash had known each other for some time and had worked together on two small projects. They were now co-leaders in a larger and very important organisational project. Kash was about six years older than Susie and she had assumed that he would be the major lead on the new project. She realised that she had never been into his office. This seemed a little strange but did not worry her. She arranged to go out mid-morning for a coffee with Kash to do some preliminary thinking about the

Kash: 'I'm okay. I'm having trouble working out how to tackle the new project. It's quite a large and complex one – I'm just not to sure how to start it.'

S: 'Well, I am here to help and take an equal part in making it work!'

K: 'Sure, that will be a good thing and I know you are really good with these sorts of projects. I am more worried about me. I am a bit disorganised sometimes and this does look complex.'

CASE STUDIES

Each chapter has a case study included to provide you with a practical context to explore ideas and techniques.

SUMMARY

Each chapter has a brief summary at the end. This is to aid recollection of what the chapter covered. It can also provide a top-level summary for note-taking.

EXPLORE FURTHER

This is a list of sources, further reading and website links to help you develop aspects of the chapter.

Walkthrough of the student and tutor support sites

Visit www.cipd.co.uk/bsh to access the following online resources, designed to further enhance the learning and teaching experience.

ONLINE STUDENT RESOURCES

The Business Skills Handbook

CHAPTER 2
How to Study

***Pro forma* page for application action notes**

Subject:	Lecturer:
Topic:	Subject text:
Date:	

Main point	Detailed sub-points	Application	Actions
1.			
2.			

TEMPLATES AND FORMS

All of the templates, forms and checklists from the book are available online as Word files so that you don't have to recreate them.

The Business Skills Handbook

CHAPTER 1
Organising life and work

Study Guide

Chapter overview

How effective you are at university is directly related to how organised you are. This first chapter is all about creating structure in your learning and studying. I would advise you to use it in your first weeks of university to create a sound and effective way of working. Reflective practice is an important part of learning and development and one approach is to reflect each week on how effectively you are organised.

What is covered in this chapter?

☐ How to make effective use of your time
☐ How to be effective by using Work Breakdown Charts
☐ Exploring and using 'time lines'
☐ How to become an effective member of a study group.
☐ How to get help from computer software

Additional chapter activities

Activity 1 - A small survey

Conduct a small survey amongst your new study colleagues at university concerning how long they expect to study each week and how that might change over the length of the course.

You will need to develop a few simple questions such as:

Q1   How long did you spend studying at school?
Q2   How long do you expect to have to study in the first year at university?
Q3   How does this compare to the 3rd year at university?
Q4   What do you think about university/life balance

STUDY GUIDE

For each chapter there is an accompanying online study guide containing:

- A chapter summary, acting as a map and guide to the chapter

- Additional activities, to reinforce your learning

- Multiple choice or short answer questions, to test your understanding of the chapter

- Ideas for learning diary entries, to help you get the most out of this process

- Active web links from the Explore Further sections of the text, for quick navigation

ONLINE TUTOR RESOURCES

All of the tutor resources for this book are also available as a Zip file which can be easily downloaded into your Virtual Learning Environment.

Memory [7]

However, you might have more trouble remembering:

a) Things you don't want to do

b) Things you believe will be difficult to remember

c) Information you consider to be boring or trivial

d) Changes to your daily routine

e) Things you did when you were tired, bored or unwell

LECTURE SLIDES

A set of customisable lecture slides in Microsoft PowerPoint is available for each chapter and can be used as the basis of a lecture presentation. The slides are closely linked to the text through page references and provide a succinct and visual presentation of central themes.

LECTURER'S GUIDE

Each chapter is accompanied by a set of lecturer's notes which will assist both new and experienced tutors in their teaching. Each set of notes includes:

* A chapter summary, acting as a map and guide to the chapter

* Feedback on chapter activities, with guidance answers

* Feedback on chapter case studies, with guidance answers to the related tasks

* A suggested lesson plan and suggested pedagogical approach to the chapter

---

The Business Skills Handbook

CHAPTER 1
Organising life and work

Lecturer's Guide

Chapter overview

Students soon find that there is more to do at university than can be fitted into the time available. This chapter is designed to present a range of ideas and skills to help manage the learning and assessment process. It predominantly deals with organising at university but also covers team organising and work organising.

What is covered in this chapter?

☐ How to make effective use of time
☐ How to be effective by using Work Breakdown Charts
☐ Exploring and using 'time lines'
☐ How to become an effective member of a study group.
☐ How to get help from computer software

Headline chapter points

1. Managing time and the sweet jar theory of time management
2. What is my personal time profile? This section investigates how people use their time.
3. Assignment time line – explores the activities and time required to complete assignments.
4. Task planning introduces the use of Work Breakdown Charts to manage and control activities at university or work.
5. Effective use of time – investigates ways to use time more effectively.
6. Intermittent Parallel Tasking – presents and notion of using time in more effective ways that are compatible with detailed academic and managerial work.
7. Making use of small passages of time – this describes the efficiency benefits of using small passages of time to achieve big things.
8. Using electronic means to get organised – looks at how to use Microsoft Outlook to become an effective organiser.
9. Common habits of high achievers – suggests ten ways that high achievers organise their lives.

Feedback on Activities

CHAPTER 1

Organising Life and Work

What skills will I develop in this chapter?

- how to make effective use of time
- how to be effective by using 'work breakdown charts'
- exploring and using 'time lines'
- how to become an effective member of a study group
- how to get help from computer software

1.1 INTRODUCTION

This chapter is the first chapter because it is the most important. It is possible to survive at university or at work with weak skills in certain areas, but being poorly organised is not one of them. Controlling, planning and organising your life and work are key skills that will significantly contribute to your success. Poor organisation will always affect the class of degree you achieve or the promotion you earn at work. If you accept this point, it follows logically that you need to get organised early. The skill of organisation will also serve you well in the workplace.

It is important to realise there are at least two types of organising. First, there is personal organising, where you control how you use the time available to you. Second, there is group or team organising; in the workplace this is a managerial task. How effective you are in your personal organisation will affect how much productive work you get out of 168 hours each week. If you are managing a small team of 12 people, all at work for 40 hours per week, your organisation skills will determine how much productive work you get out of 480 hours.

The best way to use this chapter is to read it fully and slowly, completing each of the activities as you work through the chapter. It would be ideal if you were able to use this chapter very early in your studies. But, also return to the chapter occasionally and reflect on whether there are any refinements that you can make to your organising and planning and the way you use time. It would also be useful to return to this chapter when you start your first full-time job.

1.2 MANAGING TIME

Time at university and work is exactly the same: you get 168 hours each week, no more, no less. You cannot save it and you cannot buy any more. Therefore, how you use it is vitally important to how effective you will be at work or university.

THE SWEET JAR THEORY OF TIME MANAGEMENT

Imagine a large sweet jar, the kind you find in old-fashioned sweet shops: they are about 400mm high and about 200mm in diameter. Take the jar and put as many chocolate oranges in the jar as will fit (so that you can still get the lid on). Now the jar is full – correct? Nothing else will fit!

Now take the 'full jar' and put as many chocolate M&M's® into the jar as you can, really shake the jar and settle those sweets into it until you cannot get another one in – the jar really is full now, right?

Or is it?

Take a bag of sugar and tip in as much sugar as you can; you may need a second bag. Fill the jar to the brim – now is it full?

Now take that full jar and pour as much water into the jar as you can. The jar is full, so screw on the lid and take a look at that jar.

What does this exercise tell us about time?

Well, the chocolate oranges could represent the important tasks to be completed. We also have a number of other quite important tasks to do each day/week/year; these are represented by the chocolate M&M's®. The sugar represents all the other smaller things that must get done every day/week/year. Finally, the water gets everywhere and gums up the works with a sticky sugary mess; this represents all the things that are not *our* priorities, but are the priorities of other people. The sugar and the water will combine so that you cannot see the sugar; it is dissolved in the water. The sugar represents all the daily tasks that must be done, such as buying food and milk. So when you are busy on the major tasks (chocolate oranges), you may find there is no food in the fridge or milk for a cup of tea.

None of the items in the jar are bad things and we will want a balance of things to do. It would be no use having only large, important things to do. But somehow we have to get the large items completed in order to say we have had a productive and effective day/week/year. It is also important to make use of the small spaces of time to do tasks if we are going to use time effectively – more on this later.

What does this little exercise tell us about time management?

- We only have room for so many chocolate oranges – large, high-priority tasks (your university coursework, study, examinations, work).
- Large tasks can be turned into smaller tasks and fitted more easily into the time available (the chocolate orange is made up of segments that can be separated).
- Low-priority work should fit in around the high-priority work.

- If you don't put the chocolate oranges in first, you cannot get them in at all.
- If you start with water in the jar, you will not be able to get anything else in the jar.
- Some items combine and we lose sight of them, such as the sugar and the water, but they still take time.

If we organise our lives around the sweet jar theory, we must plan to complete the large, high-priority items first, and then be selective about the other things that we choose to do. And we must never, never let our lives be filled with other people's priorities.

WHAT IS MY PERSONAL TIME PROFILE?

There are lots of ways that we can investigate how we use time, but building a personal time profile will indicate your main areas of time use. The first step in this process is to keep an activity log. Next week keep a close track of every activity in every day. You can keep an activity record in any way that works for you, but a common format is shown below. At the end of a week you will have a lot of data about how you spent your time. The next step is to enter the data into a format so that you can see a graphical representation of your time profile. The companion website for this text contains an Excel file marked 'My Time Profile'; this will help you organise your data and give you a visual output of your week. But before you can enter the data you will need a set of categories that reflect the activities you have done in the week you have just 'captured'. You will also need to add up the total hours in any one category.

REFLECTIVE PERFORMING

EXAMPLE: ACTIVITY LOG

DAY	START TIME	FINISH TIME	Hours/min. on task	ACTIVITY
Mon	07.20	07.30	10m	Washed and dressed
Mon	07.30	08.10	40m	Ate breakfast and read the papers
Mon	08.10	08.35	25m	Drove to the university
Mon	08.35	08.55	20m	Did some reading in the library
Mon	09.00	10.00	1h	Economics lecture
Mon	10.00	10.15	15m	Coffee break
Mon	10.15	11.15	1h	Economics tutorial

COMMON CATEGORIES FOR 'MY TIME PROFILE'

- work meetings
- sleeping
- work activities
- studying
- childcare
- travel
- worshipping
- leisure
- formal lectures
- eating
- socialising
- work planning and organising
- exercising
- family time
- shopping (essential)
- shopping (pleasure)
- household chores
- no activity undertaken – spare time

Once you have decided the categories, you need to cover your week of activity. You can enter the detail into the 'My Time Profile' spreadsheet, which can be found on the companion website.

LEARNING DIARY

MY TIME USAGE

Having just carried out a 'My Time Profile' exercise, I just have to record my utter amazement in this diary. When I put my activities into the spreadsheet it seemed that I sleep for nearly half the week. I like to be in bed by about midnight and I don't expect to get up until 10ish. Well, that was nearly half the hours in the week. I am just so amazed!

I also feel a little ashamed! I think I am going to have to do something about this. Although I love being snuggled under the blankets, dreaming away, if I carry on like this I will be asleep for half my life.

1.3 ASSIGNMENT TIME LINE

Many universities hand out assignments at the start of a module and require submission about 8–10 weeks later. How effectively you use this time will affect the grade your work is awarded. Many undergraduate degrees have four modules being taught at the same time or, in the third year, three modules and the project or dissertation. Projects or dissertations commonly run over a period from September to April. At any point in time there will be around four academic tasks to complete; adopting a project approach to each task may be a very effective strategy.

How long will an assignment take to complete? This is a difficult question to answer because of the variation in the nature of assignments. At level 1 of a degree course there are often more numerous, smaller assessments. At level 2 and 3, assignments are often 2,000–3,000 words in length and require extensive research, thinking, analysis and evaluation. The example **below** sets out the time required for a typical range of tasks to complete an assignment. This 'typical' assignment would take between five and eight weeks to complete and would consume 28–43 study hours.

Table 1.1 Estimate of hours and duration of the 'typical' level 3 assignment

Activity	Study hours	Duration
General research around the topic	8–10 hours	1–2 weeks
Develop the body of theory, evidence and cases	8–10 hours	1–2 weeks
Brainstorm 4 or 5 possible arguments and structures	2–4 hours	0.5 week
Write first draft	6–12 hours	1–2 weeks
Check first draft against assessment criteria and assignment brief	1–2 hours	0.5 week
Redraft and discuss with tutor or study group	1–2 hours	0.5 week
Final amendments and proofreading	2–3 hours	0.5 week
Totals	**28–43 hours**	**5–8 weeks**

How much time does the typical level 3 dissertation or project take to complete? There is no such thing as a 'typical' dissertation or project, but the example on page 6 sets out some indicative figures for the 'typical' dissertation or project that gathers primary data using either quantitative or qualitative methods. In this example the total number of hours to complete the dissertation falls in the range 160–280 and the total duration in weeks falls in the range 24–45 (assuming the transcription of any qualitative data is completed by someone else). The imperative for careful planning and execution of the level 3 project is clear from the longer estimate of 45 weeks, which is more time than would be available.

Table 1.2 Estimate of hours and duration of the 'typical' level 3 project or dissertation

Activity	Study hours	Duration***
General research to find a suitable topic	8–12 hours	2–3 weeks
Prepare research proposal	6–10 hours	1–2 weeks
Research and develop a critical literature review (1st iteration)	15–25 hours	2–4 weeks
Research and develop an appropriate methodology (1st iteration)	10–15 hours	2–3 weeks
Further develop the literature review (2nd iteration)	10–15 hours	1–2 weeks
Further develop the methodology (2nd iteration)	8–12 hours	1–2 weeks
Pilot the research instrument, questionnaire or qualitative method	6–10 hours	2–3 weeks
Gather data using a questionnaire*	14–20 hours	3–5 weeks
Gather data using a qualitative process**	20–30 hours	3–5 weeks
Transcription of qualitative data (if required)	30–40 hours	3–4 weeks
Analysis of data (1st iteration)	18–24 hours	2–4 weeks
Further development of the literature review in the light of data	12–18 hours	1–3 weeks
Final development of data analysis (2nd iteration)	12–24 hours	2–4weeks
Developing conclusions and recommendations	8–16 hours	2–3 weeks
Writing up the full dissertation (1st draft)	25–40 hours	2–3 weeks
Writing up the full dissertation (2nd draft)	5–15 hours	1–2 weeks
Proofreading and final development	4–8 hours	2–4 weeks

* assumes the questionnaire is self-administered – 100 questionnaires sent out and 30–40 are returned for data entry
** assumes 15–20 in-depth interviews of 30 minutes' duration
*** some durations will overlap

This overall 'typical' pattern for these tasks takes no account of a number of important issues.

OTHER LIFE AND STUDY COMMITMENTS

The time scale example sets out only the work required for the assignment, project or dissertation, but there will be quite a few commitments related to the taught modules of the course, such as examinations, learning and group work. Many people completing assignments, dissertations and projects will also have family, social, sporting or work commitments; these will limit the time available to spend on developing and completing the assignment, project or dissertation.

UNFORESEEN EVENTS

Even in the best-planned lives there will be any number of unforeseen events that stall or slow the progress of the work. Most research and assignment work will have some delay due to:

- access problems
- illness
- unavailability of resources
- difficult academic areas that need intensive study or thought to solve
- family or work crisis
- rewriting sections of the work that are not effective
- redundancy or, more encouragingly, re-employment or promotion.

Successful university work requires organisation, planning and control. The following sections will investigate ways of organising, planning and controlling.

1.4 TASK PLANNING

Like most work projects, academic work is made up of tasks. When all the tasks are complete, the work is complete. There are many good reasons for investing time to plan your assignments and work projects. The old saying about planning is: 'failing to plan is planning to fail.' The main advantages of careful planning are:

- It creates a proactive approach that can replace a more often found reactive approach.
- It allows you to feel in control.
- It allows you to proactively manage the work of several tasks at once.
- It allows you to initiate and influence outcomes in your favour.
- It allows you to meet deadlines.
- It lowers your stress.
- It adopts a systematic approach, leading to higher grades and more effective work behaviours.
- It improves control of the task.
- It allows for accurate co-ordination of efforts by other projects, persons or contractors.
- It allows the setting of 'milestones' to help control the task.
- It highlights the areas in the assignment or project where planned assistance will be needed, such as data-gathering and proofreading.

A commonly used approach to planning projects is to create a 'work breakdown structure'. This project approach can be adopted for assignments and projects. The work breakdown structure (WBS) or chart (WBC) sets out all the tasks needed to complete the assignment or project. It has an estimate of the amount of time likely to be taken on each task, a note about who will be doing the task and a note about resources or general comments. The example **below** is an excerpt from a WBS showing the detail of these entries.

EXAMPLE: EXCERPT OF A WORK BREAKDOWN STRUCTURE

WBS No.	Task description	Est. hours	Who	Resources/comments
3.1	Research work–life balance assignment	6	Me	
3.2	Find theories and practical examples	3	Study group	Arrange meeting for Thurs., 20 Feb.
3.3	Use Athens to find critical articles related to the main theories	2	Me	
3.4	Brainstorming meeting with my study group	2	SG	Me to prepare a summary
3.5	Attend assignment tutorial	1.5	All	
3.6	Plan the main structure of the assignment	2	Me	Remember to keep a reflective journal exploring the thoughts behind the content and structure
3.7	Write first draft of assignment	6	Me	Discuss with tutor
3.8	Revise and redraft the assignment	4	Me	
3.9	Get Tom to proofread it, then revise	3	Tom	

> ❝ TUTOR COMMENT
>
> I always encourage my tutees to create their work breakdown structures in a spreadsheet, because then it becomes really easy to produce the Gantt charts that display progress. They can also rearrange them for each assignment. I am far more willing to grant an extension for some unforeseen event if I can see how they have planned and developed the work.

The WBS or WBC is a living, dynamic document and will change over time for a number of reasons. Most early attempts at creating a WBS for a project or assignment do not list all the necessary tasks to complete the work. It typically takes about three or four iterations before the WBS covers all the necessary points. As the project or assignment progresses, changes may have to be made to the task list to reflect changes required to complete the work. The WBS can have a further column added, commonly when the work is well under way, to indicate the completion or partial completion of each task. If the WBS is kept up to date, it can be a useful tool to communicate progress.

 TUTOR COMMENT

Some of the students I supervise for projects come from a project management background and often display high levels of planning and organisation. They will often send me their work scheduling spreadsheet with updates on progress included. This is a very fast, easy way for them to keep in touch and let me know what is happening.

A SHORT NOTE ON ESTIMATING THE TIME A TASK WILL TAKE

At the beginning of a project or assignment it is very hard to accurately estimate the time any task will take. There is very little help available from either research or practice about how to accurately estimate the time required to complete 'ill-defined' tasks. This probably means it is a good topic for a project or dissertation. It is known that different motivational beliefs affect the accuracy of estimating the time required to complete tasks. If you are well organised, motivated and a good time manager, you are likely to underestimate how long any task will take; the reverse is also true. Personal experience can be useful in that you will have completed many academic tasks beforehand; use your experience of these tasks to estimate better the time required for university tasks. Most students will have carried out a range of academic tasks at school; these will give you an estimate of the time that the task took. If the school assignment task of 1,500 words took 10–15 hours to complete, then the longer and more involved university task is likely to take three times as long: 30–45 hours. As your academic work progresses you will become much better at estimating the time that tasks take to complete. The examples **above** may be useful in giving you some typical figures for some of the tasks involved in academic work, but these are only typical of general activities. For the planning to be successful, time estimation needs to be as accurate as possible.

1.5 EFFECTIVE USE OF TIME

There are 168 hours in every week; no one gets any more than anyone else and yet some people get more done than others. This section investigates some of the ideas and practices that can help you complete your university work and survive at work when you have a great deal to do. You will, if you completed the time audit, know how you spend your time at the moment, but you may have to make some adjustments to your time usage to enable you to complete all your academic work. When you are employed full-time, around one-third of your 168 hours will be concerned with work activities; how effectively you use the remainder will determine how much enjoyment you get from your leisure time.

PROCRASTINATION

Procrastination is a common problem – we might say it is part of being human. Procrastination is normal: we all put things off, we cannot do all the things we need to do immediately, and yet after a while it does dawn on us that we are deliberately leaving things before we do them or possibly, for the chronic procrastinator, we never do them. University work can have this effect on people; they just put off doing anything until it becomes too late to complete an assignment or project. A similar thing can happen at work, but the added complication is that your boss will be chasing you to complete things. Procrastination can leave you with far too little time to complete an assignment, work task or project, then the quality of the work and the grade suffers. Perhaps if we investigate why we procrastinate we will be able to control it better.

We don't like a task – We all tend to procrastinate more when faced with tasks we don't like or think we are not very good at. Developing the skill to enjoy any task is often the key to enjoying doing that task. Take some time to analyse the skills you need at work and university, such as generating ideas, planning, carrying out practical tasks, carrying out cognitive (thinking) tasks, researching and writing. If you feel any of these areas are not as strong as you would like, seek help from your university skills unit.

We don't like the quality of our work – For most tasks that we do, the outcome will always be less than perfect. The perfectionists among us suffer most with this problem. But ultimately the only way to overcome these feelings is to adopt the saying, 'It is as good as I can get it in the time available,' implying that you will come back and improve it at a later point. You may come back and work on it again, but this little saying allows you to work with some freedom from the feeling that the work is not good enough.

Practical concerns distract us – There are commonly two camps relating to this problem. Either clear all the distractions and then start work on a specific task, or ignore distractions as not as important as getting this task completed. I personally fall into the first camp. I have to deal with all the little chores, emails and other stuff, and then I feel I have a long period to work on something without worrying about any other thing.

Because we are looking for perfection – If you are someone who wants everything to be absolutely right, perfect, then you might think about these seven steps to avoid perfection:

1   First, acknowledge your real goals. Is perfection necessary and appropriate?

2   What is the cost of perfection? Getting one thing perfect invariably means that lots of other things are done very poorly, or not at all.

3   Next, substitute a more realistic, more attainable goal, such as creating good-quality work rather than creating perfect work.

4   Use 'to-do' lists and set priorities but also set maximum allowable times.

5   Review the to-do list daily and adjust the time you are willing to spend on

a task. Don't be afraid to say, 'That is enough time on that task; it is good enough.' It will then drop off the to-do list.

6 Weekly, consider the regular tasks you have to do. Is it really necessary to do all these tasks this often? Could cleaning the kitchen be done every two weeks rather than every week?

7 Learn to delegate a task and accept the quality of the outcome. For example, if you have a number of work tasks to complete, delegate some of them and only comment to say how grateful you are for the help.

Because we are lazy – We are human and, unless you are some sort of super person, we are all lazy to lesser and greater degrees. Sometimes we need to stop and do nothing, go for a walk, sit in front of the television, go for a drink. You may have lazy periods, but make sure they do not last too long. The reward of completing the work and having all the time you are currently spending on university work available for other enjoyments is quite a strong motivator.

WE ARE FEARFUL OF SOMETHING

Fear of failure – If we fear that our work isn't going to be good enough, it can stop us from starting it. Universities and workplaces are very good at the development of skills and people, so be assured that if your work isn't quite good enough there will be help and advice to improve it. Success is often about sticking at a task rather than being successful immediately.

Fear of success – Success brings with it expectations, and if we are successful once, the 'bar' will be raised forever and then we won't be able to achieve it again. We may also fear that success will become addictive; once we have 'tasted' it we will become workaholics to taste it again.

Fear of being alone – The procrastinator who fears being alone will do nothing so that someone or several people will come and help them. So doing nothing ensures help will arrive.

Fear of attachment – Some procrastinators fear being reliant on others, so they fail to progress any work so that the chaotic lack of progress puts other people off helping.

Finally, there can be major problems if you believe that you can do only one thing at a time. Everyone has many things to do in a day, week, month or year, and the ability to carry out these tasks in a planned and sequenced manner is vital to successfully carrying out what is required. Even the one task of completing an assignment has many elements that must be carried out in some sort of sequence. This area is dealt with later under the heading 'The myth of multi-tasking'.

HOW TO AVOID PROCRASTINATION

Work out when you tend to procrastinate. We do not all avoid the same things. If you keep a learning diary (if you don't keep a learning diary – start one), note down in the diary when you think you really should be getting on with a task

WHY I PROCRASTINATE

I have noticed at work that I put off anything to do with spreadsheets. I think for a long time I did this subconsciously, but I noticed when someone asked me to work on an existing spreadsheet – created by a former colleague who had left – that I made all manner of excuses to avoid doing it. Some of my excuses were just embarrassing. I went through 'I am too busy', 'I don't like picking up others' work' to 'I think I am leaving in a week or so' (none of these were true). The manager asking me to do this must have thought I was mad. Anyway, they backed me into a corner and eventually told me to do it and now!

In hindsight I could see that I was just worried that I would not be able to do the job. I did do it but I had to work very slowly and take it home to do on loads of evenings and two weekends. I found I was shaking my head at one stage, saying never again!

I now realise I cannot leave this chronic lack of knowledge of Excel any longer and I have booked myself on a short Excel course. I really don't want to be in that ridiculous situation again.

and what task you are avoiding. I imagine cleaning the student kitchen may be high on most people's agenda for procrastination, but I mean the avoidance of work and academic tasks. A lot of people start to feel that they have other, more important things to do when they have to start on a task. However, by the time I have spent 5–10 minutes on a task I am enjoying it and often carry on with that task until it is complete, or a substantial chunk is complete. I know some colleagues who start their day with the same routine activities just to get warmed up to more challenging tasks. After the warm-up tasks are complete, they are ready for what the day has to throw at them. Once you know the pattern of your procrastination and the tasks you are avoiding, you will be in a better position to control it. If the problem is at certain times, it could well be that you are not doing the quality tasks at your 'prime time'. Everyone has a prime time in a day, week or month. Learn when these times are and use them to do the most demanding work. If the problem is task-related, you need a strategy to encourage you to start, such as:

- a small reward when you get started – mine's chocolate

- a light warm-up technique – as above

- kid yourself – by saying 'I will just review what I did yesterday', invariably when you have done this you carry on with the task

- the promise of a reward at the end of the task – mine's chocolate

- ensure you are intending to work in your prime time

- create a pleasant and welcoming environment.

OTHER TECHNIQUES TO HELP AVOID PROCRASTINATION

Use reminders so that the task cannot be forgotten. Set your phone or computer to remind you, leave notes in prominent places, post electronic sticky notes on your desktop. Create priority lists so that the important tasks feature at the top of the list; Microsoft Outlook or a PDA can help with this. Try to underestimate the amount of time any task will take; it is the idea that maybe you do not have time to complete the task that stops you starting it. Many 'effective' people significantly underestimate how long a task will take, but once started this does not matter.

Writing is a major area for procrastination, so make an outline plan of what you will write, then add the headings to a document so that when you do start it is easy to make progress. This is another 'delusion' strategy, as once the plan and the headings are produced you will often continue on to do some writing. An extension of this idea is to create the headings and paragraph headings and the first line of every paragraph. It then becomes very easy to progress the work quickly by developing the existing material.

Avoid the 'distraction' problem, where the tasks you procrastinate about are left because you carry on doing a task you like. The most common academic 'distraction' task is researching going on and on, when there is no need for more information, while the task of writing is avoided.

 MANAGER COMMENT

The most important advice I give to new starters in our organisation is in relation to avoiding interruptions. We are a friendly and interactive company with informal communications and a lot of shared office space. If you don't have a strategy for avoiding interruptions you will never survive.

There are four key components to this strategy:

First, I have a set time each day for drop-in or open-door inquiries. I use 11.30–12.30, an unproductive time for me anyway, and 4.30–5.30 in the afternoon, the end of the day for 'mop up' problems.

Outside of these times people need to make an email appointment.

Second, control the phone interruptions. I have an answer phone message that indicates that from 9.30–11.30 and 2.30–4.30 I am working on intensive activities and cannot be

disturbed, please leave a message and I will get back to you at the end of these periods.

You'd be surprised how often there is an urgent problem and by the time I ring them back 'the problem has been resolved', mostly by the caller.

Third, get to work early when there is no one else in the building in the period from 7.00–8.30 in the morning or, if people are in, they are like me: trying to make progress before the interruptions start to become a problem.

Fourth, encourage people to contact you by email. This is an asynchronous communication system – they don't expect an immediate reply so I can control when I answer them. Also, having to type out the problem often leads them to figure it out for themselves.

THE MYTH OF MULTI-TASKING

You will often hear people say, in a triumphant sort of way, that they can multi-task. It is true that human rather than computer multi-tasking can be done. Many people can iron and watch the television at the same time, read and talk at the same time, walk and think at the same time. However, work and academic multi-tasking requiring your full attention and thinking is not possible. Yet in life there are many things that must be completed. If you can only work on one task until it is complete and then move on to the next task, your ability to use your time effectively is very limited. Why is this so?

'Task fatigue' becomes a problem after several hours of doing the same thing. We require a varied diet of activity to stop this happening. So if you are only working on one task, when task fatigue occurs, you stop work and do a peripheral task (maybe clean that kitchen).

Creativity works to a cycle of preparation, incubation, illumination and verification; once the cycle has been completed, fatigue sets in and the ideas become poorer.

Personal motivation to continue lessens as we spend time on the task, so after a while we just choose to stop – often described as 'being bored with it'.

If multi-tasking is not possible for important work, how could we organise our time to relieve some of the negative effects attributed to time on the task? In trying to explain this to my own students, I have started to call the approach 'intermittent parallel tasking'. It is founded on two major principles: first, that we can only do one task at a time; second, task fatigue needs to be avoided.

Figure 1.1 uses Monday as an example; the basic principles are:

- Only one task can be carried out at a time.
- The cognitive effort needs to vary throughout the day to avoid fatigue.
- The tasks requiring the highest cognitive effort must be carried out during your 'prime time'.
- Plan the next cycle of activity (days in this case) in the previous cycle.
- Create structures for carrying out activities in the previous cycle so that when you resume work you can progress immediately.

When you look at the cognitive effort chart in the illustration, you can see why the process is described as intermittent. The more difficult cognitive tasks are spread out throughout the day. If you analyse any procrastination that you feel and try to adopt techniques for avoiding it, you will be able to generate and use more productive time. The next section considers ways to use the small spaces of time between the major activities of a day.

Figure 1.1 Intermittent parallel tasking

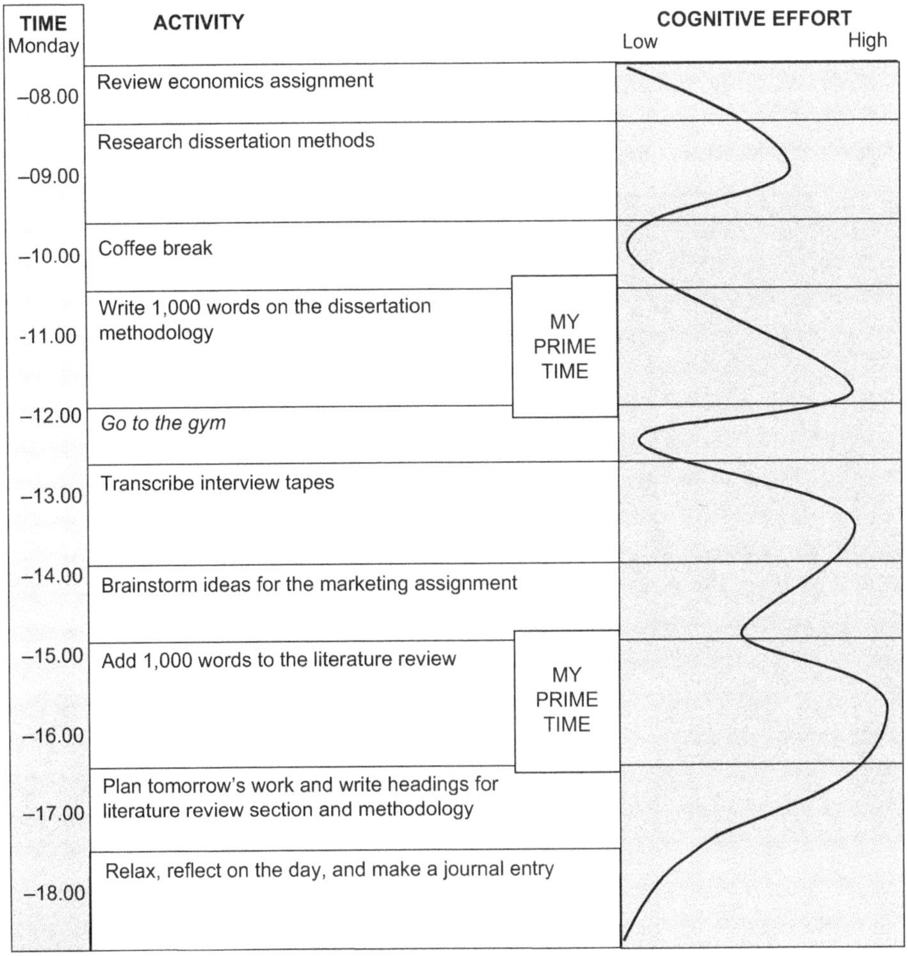

TIME Monday	ACTIVITY		COGNITIVE EFFORT Low High
−08.00	Review economics assignment		
−09.00	Research dissertation methods		
−10.00	Coffee break		
-11.00	Write 1,000 words on the dissertation methodology	MY PRIME TIME	
−12.00	*Go to the gym*		
−13.00	Transcribe interview tapes		
−14.00	Brainstorm ideas for the marketing assignment		
−15.00	Add 1,000 words to the literature review	MY PRIME TIME	
−16.00			
−17.00	Plan tomorrow's work and write headings for literature review section and methodology		
−18.00	Relax, reflect on the day, and make a journal entry		

1.6 MAKING USE OF SMALL PASSAGES OF TIME

University studies are made up of a number of major tasks and a lot of smaller, less time-consuming tasks. The workplace is similar in that you will have major tasks and projects to complete and operational interruptions will break up these tasks. One way to effectively use the time available to you is to become proficient at completing the smaller tasks in the short passages of time between the more major activities. You will need a strategy to facilitate this approach. As most of our work is completed on computers, this is the interface where we need to facilitate the effective use of these small packages of time. In Microsoft Outlook you are able to post notes onto your desktop. At the beginning of each day, arrange to place notes (known as sticky notes) for five small tasks onto your desktop. During the day when you have a few spare minutes, complete one of the small tasks and remove the note. If any tasks remain at the end of the day, you should judge their urgency and either complete them or carry them over to the next day. As you become more effective with this technique, you can increase the number of small tasks to ten per day. A variation of this technique is to split up more major tasks into ten small tasks and then you will be able to complete some larger tasks using time that would otherwise be wasted.

Figure 1.2 Screenshot of five task notes for completion

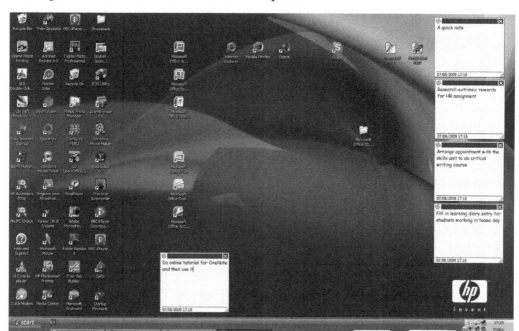

1.7 USING ELECTRONIC MEANS TO GET ORGANISED

There are many electronic devices to help you successfully organise the tasks needed to complete assignments or work projects. The most important point to stress is that arranging some sort of system to ensure tasks are completed on time will go a long way towards being well organised. Broadly, there are two mediums to organise work, assignments and projects. Some people are comfortable and effective using pen and paper methods. If this is your preferred approach, you could create a WBS chart on paper, listing the tasks needed to complete all your academic tasks and work projects, and keep track of progress manually.

Probably the most frequently used organising software is Microsoft Outlook and I will address the organising topics in this section to this software. If your preferred software is different from this, the ideas should transfer into any organising software. Controlling your diary, contacts, setting tasks and dealing with email are all possible with Outlook. This section sets out ways to use these tools to assist with on-time completion.

In the main window of Outlook you will have a menu bar containing inbox, calendar, contacts, task, journal, notes and a waste bin. As versions of Microsoft Outlook vary in the detail of how they operate and how you set up various processes, for each of the sections below you will need to follow the assistance in the help menu.

When you start using Outlook, set up a 'personal folder file'; use these words in the help menu and follow the instructions.

Then set up the 'Remote Mail' setting to access your email account. This will allow you to use the data in Outlook, such as contacts, to speed your email processes. Again, use help and follow the instructions.

You may be using a PDA (personal digital assistant). Most of these come with software that allows you to link to Outlook. You'll need to load that software and synchronise the calendar in Outlook with the calendar on the PDA. You will be working on your computer for long periods while you complete your work, so it will make you more efficient if you use the Outlook programme as the hub of your activity. If you are not using a PDA, then enter the contacts from your diary into the calendar function of Outlook, and then work from this going forward.

If you want to develop Outlook as your main working hub separately from your personal organisation, then add only contacts from your address book that relate to your academic work. If you are using a PDA then you will be able to upload the contact data into Outlook.

After maybe an hour of setting-up work, you will have Outlook functioning in a reasonably practical manner relating to your contacts, email and diary. The next sections will look in more detail at setting and using tasks, the journal and sticky notes.

Controlling tasks, as this chapter has been explaining, is the main issue for on-time completion of assignments, projects and work tasks. You will probably have developed a WBS chart in one of the earlier activities. Now is the time to convert that into a more interactive and controlled set of tasks in Outlook. If you developed a WBS in Excel, open it now so that you can transfer the data into Outlook. Click on the task shortcut on the Outlook menu bar. In the top-left corner click on new task, a window will open. Add a short title name to the box. Set the start date and then the due date from the data in the WBS chart. Set the status, priority and progress made. Set a reminder date and time. Finally, cut and paste the detail of the task and the comments into the main window. The first task is now complete; click save and close.

Now enter each of the other WBS chart entries into an Outlook task. You may find as you enter the data that you want to refine a task, split a task into smaller components, or discover that there are tasks you omitted from the WBS chart. When the data is entered you should have a well-structured set of tasks with built-in monitoring. The tasks will need further refining as the academic year or project progresses, but this should take less than one hour a week.

Figure 1.3 Screenshot of Outlook tasks

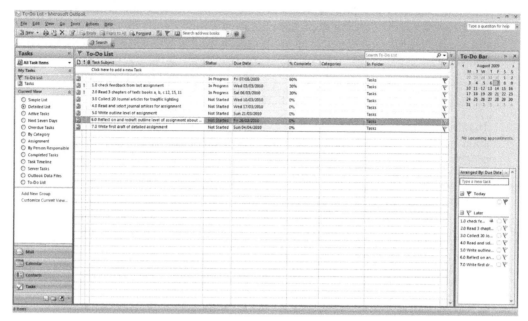

Keeping a learning journal is a valuable technique to record successes, difficulties, thoughts, details of activities and ideas for improvements. Outlook can help with this aspect of your life. The first very useful function in 'journal' is the automatic recording of events in the journal. All the following can be automatically recorded in the journal:

- email message
- meeting request
- meeting response
- task request
- task response
- Microsoft Access
- Microsoft Excel
- Microsoft Office Binder
- Microsoft PowerPoint
- Microsoft Word.

You can set each of these options in the 'Tools', 'Options', 'Journal' menu.

It is important to consider what type of entry you are adding to the journal, as the main access to your entries is by the type of document. The following can be added:

- all Office documents (Word, etc)
- emails

- conversations
- tasks
- notes
- phone calls
- letters
- fax.

You will need to be consistent in your use of journal entry types to enable efficient retrieval of the data.

Finally, the use of sticky notes was covered in section 1.6. The simple sticky note can be a very efficient motivator and organiser. Following the non-procrastination techniques mentioned earlier in the chapter, the final task of each day should be to plan the next day's activities. Using Outlook and posting notes onto the desktop for each activity that has to be completed is very motivational and somewhat addictive. First, having the activities organised the day before assists with an effective start to the following day. It is very motivational because the notes disappear during the day, until at last the final task is complete and you can relax.

At work you will probably be involved in up to ten separate projects and will be the organiser of two or three of those projects. Microsoft Project is a commonly used software tool for organising work-based activities.

1.8 COMMON HABITS OF HIGH-ACHIEVERS

One goal – All tasks, no matter how complicated, are achieved one goal at a time. Setting too many goals and goals that are a long way ahead will end up demotivating you. Set one task at a time, and when that is achieved, set another. You will be surprised how quickly you can achieve big things with little goals.

Start with a small step – Even when you do not feel like doing anything towards a task, start with a very small step. For example, look at the feedback from your last assignment or spend ten minutes planning a task.

Avoid negativity – Negative habits hold us back all the time. You need to recognise the negative behaviour for what it is and turn it around to positive behaviour. Perhaps the worst negative behaviour is procrastination. 'Oh I haven't got enough time to get started on that today.' Whenever you find yourself saying this, stop! Then carry out a very small task towards your goal. You will in a short time stop saying those words and start achieving your goals.

Dream about the benefits – University degrees normally bring huge workplace benefits in the form of new and better-paid jobs. Dream about these new jobs and experiences; they will motivate you. When you are employed, dream about where you want to end up.

LOUISE AND SIMON

BECOMING REFLECTIVE PERFORMERS

Louise: 'Simon! Are you any good with computers? 'Cos, I'm rubbish.'

S: 'What's the problem?'

L: 'Well basically I can just about type into Word, but beyond that I am blank.'

S: 'Hmm, well I suppose the thing you use the most is Word, and then Excel.'

L: 'What's to learn about Word? That's easy. Excel is a bit of a problem. I am working on a small project at work that will need statistics and will need to be done in Excel.'

S: 'Don't be so quick to write off the things that you could know about Word that will make your life easy.'

L: 'Like what?'

S: 'Here are two things you should know about because they really speed up the writing process. First, set up a blank document with headings, so that you have, maybe, three headings of different size fonts. I like 14-point bold for the main heading, then 12-point bold for the main headings and 11-point bold for the headings in the text. Also, set up the bullet point lists. I have a bullet list and a number list. Set these up on a blank document with just headings in it and then save it. Each time you start a new assignment open the document. I call it "blank assignment", and it's all set up ready to go.'

L: 'Wow, I should have known that already.'

S: 'Also, learn how to change the view so that you can see the document normally and in outline view. I am not organised enough to do this, but I know it is good advice. When you are planning the assignment, writing or a project, view the document in outline view. It will show the headings prominently, then you can plan and move things about

until you have the structure you want. Then switch back to normal view to do the typing; it is a bit like assignments by numbers. Sort out the main structure then fill in the paragraphs.'

L: 'What about Excel?'

S: 'That's not so easy! Two things you could do. There is an online Excel course at Microsoft's website that takes you through the basics. Also, there is a university course, six extra seminars that you can do. It sets you up with how to do formulas and things like that.'

L: 'Thanks. That all seems like good advice!'

S: 'As if I'd tell you anything duff!'

L: 'I'll put down what you have said in my learning log and have a think about what else I can do.'

S: 'Learning log? How much time have you got to waste?'

L: 'Friendly advice: start a learning journal!'

S: 'No, go away, a total waste of time!'

L: 'Well, if you want to make the same mistake over and over again, don't give it another thought. Learning logs or journals do what they say on the tin: they help you to learn. Maybe, just maybe, they will stop you making the same mistakes and allow you to progress!'

S: 'Okay, clever clogs, here is some Word practice for you that might help me. Start a Word document and sort out the headings and the bullet lists and format it as a learning journal. I'll check you have all the Word things sorted and then I'll show you some more things in Word. After that I will try to use it for some "learning thoughts" – if I have any.'

L: 'Great. It's a deal.'

Visualise your goal – Your main goal(s) should always be visible to you. Write down your main goal(s) and place a copy of it in all the places you go regularly: your office space, the toilet, your car, the inside of your briefcase or handbag. If a picture can be used to capture your goal(s), then leave these pictures in all the places you go.

Be enthusiastic – Create enthusiasm for your main goal(s) by talking to others about it. You can also create enthusiasm by reading about your goal(s) and how others achieved the same goal.

Find inspiration – Finding inspiration to achieve is about finding and understanding how others have been successful. Talk to successful students and read accounts of successful people. Success breeds inspiration.

Think about your main goal(s) daily – It is easy to forget what you are aiming for. Avoid this by thinking about your main goal(s) every day. Ask the question, 'What can I do to achieve that goal today?'

Create support networks – Academic work and work tasks can be lonely. Create support networks from family, colleagues and friends. These networks will be a source of motivation.

Understand your own ebb and flow – You need to understand your own ebb and flow for each day, week and month. Everyone works best at some point. Find the best times for you and plan the major tasks to coincide with your most effective periods of time.

CASE STUDY

THE 'NIGHTMARE' COLLEAGUE

Susie and Kash had known each other for some time and had worked together on two small projects. They were now co-leaders in a larger and very important organisational project. Kash was about six years older than Susie and she had assumed that he would be the major lead on the new project. She realised that she had never been into his office. This seemed a little strange but did not worry her. She arranged to go out mid-morning for a coffee with Kash to do some preliminary thinking about the project.

When they sat down with two espressos and half a cake, he seemed a bit quiet. Susie thought this was rather unlike his normal bubbly self.

Susie: 'You seem a bit down. Are you okay with the new project? I guess it could be promotion for both of us if it works out well.'

Kash: 'I'm okay. I'm having trouble working out how to tackle the new project. It's quite a large and complex one – I'm just not to sure how to start it.'

S: 'Well, I am here to help and take an equal part in making it work!'

K: 'Sure, that will be a good thing and I know you are really good with these sorts of projects. I am more worried about me. I am a bit disorganised sometimes and this does look complex.'

S: 'Good project planning will get us through that. That's an area I am very experienced in.'

K: 'Good, I think you will need those skills. As I say, this is a big complex project and I am a bit disorganised.'

S: 'I had never noticed any problem. Anything specific or are you just nervous?'

K: 'I am also a bit weak with the computer stuff. I get by, but this is going to be complicated and the total budget is near the £1 million mark.'

S: 'We could finish up the coffees and then go back to the office and throw a couple of hours' work at it.'

K: 'Yea, let's do that. No! Not my office; better go to yours.'

S: 'That's no good. I let them use my office for interviews this afternoon. New Project Manager's job.'

K: [a bit nervously] 'Okay, we'll go back to mine, but it is a bit messy.'

Susie, on entering the office, was a bit surprised. The books on the shelves were all lying down with old coffee cups on top of them – goodness knows what the cleaners made of it. The desk was impossible to miss; there was paper everywhere, piles and piles, some of them tipping into each other and then the papers that could not hold on slipped off onto the floor. In amongst the papers were books and reports and more coffee cups. In amongst the papers there looked to be purchase orders, red-line invoices and delivery notes. It was hard for Susie not to laugh out loud. 'How could anyone work in this mess?' she thought.

S: 'Wow, can you work in here? It's a bit messier than my own office.'

K: 'Yes, I know where everything is. I'll give it a tidy up later in the week.'

Susie was now really worried; her promotion was tied up with a man with a waste tip for an office.

S: 'Do you want me to give you a hand to tidy up?'

K: 'Sure thing. I know it's a bit messy for most tastes.'

S: 'We will also need to start planning our new project and we may need to get more people into the working group.'

K: 'Yes. I normally plan these things on a bit of paper and then use that to control everything. It has worked well in the past.'

S: 'This project is quite large and you said yourself quite complex.'

Susie and Kash had a bit of a clear-up and then decided that they needed to:

- organise meetings
- manage the budget
- plan out the tasks and actions
- get six more members of the project group to handle the workload
- create a way of monitoring progress
- create a reporting framework for Susie and Kash's boss
- create some priorities and work out in which order things need to be done.

Case study tasks:

- Prepare a prioritised action plan that addresses all the necessary tasks.
- Set out the personal issues that Kash must address.
- What areas of the project can participants in the project group complete?
- How should Kash deal with his current workload?
- Suggest a programme of personal measures to ensure Kash is organised in the future.

SUMMARY

To be successful you need to develop effective habits early in your studies and career. Poor organisation will interfere with the quality of degree you achieve and slow your promotion at work.

- Develop effective time use habits:
  - Analyse how you use your time and consider making adjustments.
  - Avoid procrastination.
  - Learn to use your best study times for the most challenging work.
  - Plan and organise.
  - Try out the idea of intermittent parallel tasking.
  - Learn to use small passages of time.

- Consider how long assignments and tasks will take to complete by thinking about:
  - how much time I can set aside for study each week
  - the likely tasks that must be completed
  - how long each task will take
  - if I can get help to complete some of the tasks
  - creating a detailed WBS chart
  - unforeseen distractions and delays.

- Early organisation of some of the key assessment components will lead to success:
  - bibliographic data
  - the reading, writing and note-taking process
  - try to adopt the habits of successful people
  - manage and monitor the completion of tasks.

- Using software will help you towards on-time completion:
  - Microsoft Outlook
  - convert your WBS chart to Outlook tasks with reminders
  - make effective use of Post-It® or sticky notes
  - make use of a learning journal
  - use electronic methods to assist with planning and control.

EXPLORE FURTHER

FURTHER READING

Applegarth, M. and Posner, K. (2008) *The Project Management Pocketbook*. Alresford: Management Pocketbooks.

WEB LINKS

A brief tutorial on Gantt charts: http://www.me.umn.edu/courses/me4054/as

Word 2007 details of bibliography production: http://office.microsoft.com/en-us/word/

Free download of Gantt chart builder for Excel at PC World: http://www.pcworld.com/downloads/file_download/fid,62196-order,2-page,1-c,spreadsheet/download.html#

Gantt chart Excel template from Microsoft: http://office.microsoft.com/en-us/templates/TC300003501033.aspx

CHAPTER 2

How to Study

What skills will I develop in this chapter?

- how to get the most from lectures
- how to take notes from lectures and seminars
- how to use mind maps for notes
- how to use application action notes for lectures and seminars
- how to get the most from seminars
- how to contribute in seminars
- how to get the most from learning resources
- how to use Microsoft OneNote and find everything you ever learned

2.1 INTRODUCTION

For many students their method of studying is already well established when they enter university. However, I would suggest that reviewing your approach to study as you start university would be sensible. The context of university study is very different from school, so the transition point provides an opportunity for change and development. This chapter is designed as a general introduction to the challenge of studying at university. It also conveys a specific software-based approach to recording and organising notes using Microsoft OneNote. Three years of intensive study generates a huge volume of information, ideas, development activities and learning. Unless all these are systematically recorded and organised, much of the information and learning will be lost. Further, excellent organisation will save you time and stress. There is nothing more frustrating than knowing that you have information somewhere but you cannot find it. OneNote provides a structured way to organise notes and more; it can also be used for reflective devices like learning diaries.

2.2 HOW TO GET THE MOST FROM LECTURES

The first major difference between school and university is the nature of lectures. In your A-level studies you will probably have been in relatively small groups and will have had ready access to your teachers. Many universities teach students of business in groupings of 200–400 for lectures. This means lectures will be a one-way form of communication; you won't have much chance to seek clarification or to ask questions. In such large groups you may think that very little learning can occur. You may then be tempted to miss the lectures. This is a major mistake. One-way communication forms can seem a bit boring and uninvolving, so it becomes your job to make them relevant, engaging and interesting.

Study at school is teacher-led but at university the learning model is student-led. In school all that you need to know is covered in your classes. This is not so at university; the lecturer will provide a highly synthesised 'map' of the specific subject area being covered. You will be expected to explore the map in more detail. Lecturers are very often involved as researchers in specific and detailed subject areas. So they will provide a general map of the subject area and very specific and research-focused details of some areas of the subject. Your lecturer may well be at the cutting edge of their specific research area and will be highly involved in creating new knowledge. It is important to identify whether you are being given a general map or a highly specific account of a small area. In some instances their enthusiasm for their 'narrow' subject area can overcome the need to provide an accurate and general map of the wider subject area. For this reason it is always worth reading the appropriate chapter in the module textbook before a lecture and to revisit it after every lecture.

The conduct of any lecture will be highly dependent on the style and approach of the lecturer. This diversity of approach is normal and, I would suggest, provides valuable variation and helps to maintain interest. Some of the key aspects of lectures that vary dependent on the lecturer are:

- speed, pacing and the frequency of pauses for questions
- the issuing of notes or handouts
- the structure and logic of the lecture
- the clarity of expression and ease of understanding
- the amount of depth of detail as opposed to breadth of topic covered
- the balance between visual and oral teaching
- the balance between conceptual and practical teaching
- the variation between the amount of time the lecturer speaks and the amount of time used for student thinking or practical tasks.

As you can see from this list no two lecturers are likely to teach in exactly the same way. You will have to develop techniques and lecturer-specific strategies to get the most out of lectures. In practice some will fire ideas and information at you non-stop for an hour, or more, while others will produce a varied diet of talking, visual aids, practical activities and thinking points. Even in the best and most varied of lectures they can feel very passive. You will enjoy lectures best, and find staying awake easier, if you can turn the passive environment into an active environment. Chapter 3 investigates how to create an active learning environment in detail. My general advice on surviving lectures and learning something from them is as follows.

READ THE MODULE TEXT CHAPTER RELEVANT TO THE LECTURE BEFOREHAND

Reading the module textbook before you attend a lecture primes your thoughts and interest. You do not need to read the chapter in detail; you can use a 'skim and dive' technique. 'Dive' into the subject when you encounter something that catches your interest or is relevant to your work or social life. At this stage your aim should be to have a general understanding of the area; using the map analogy, you need to unfold the map to the right spot and have a general look at the 'lay of the land'. If you are going to use a mind map to record notes during the lecture, you can prepare a 'mind map border' to the page based on the module textbook (see Figure 2.1). If you are intending to use another form of note-taking, prepare a skeleton page of the topic area based on the textbook.

Figure 2.1 Mind map border

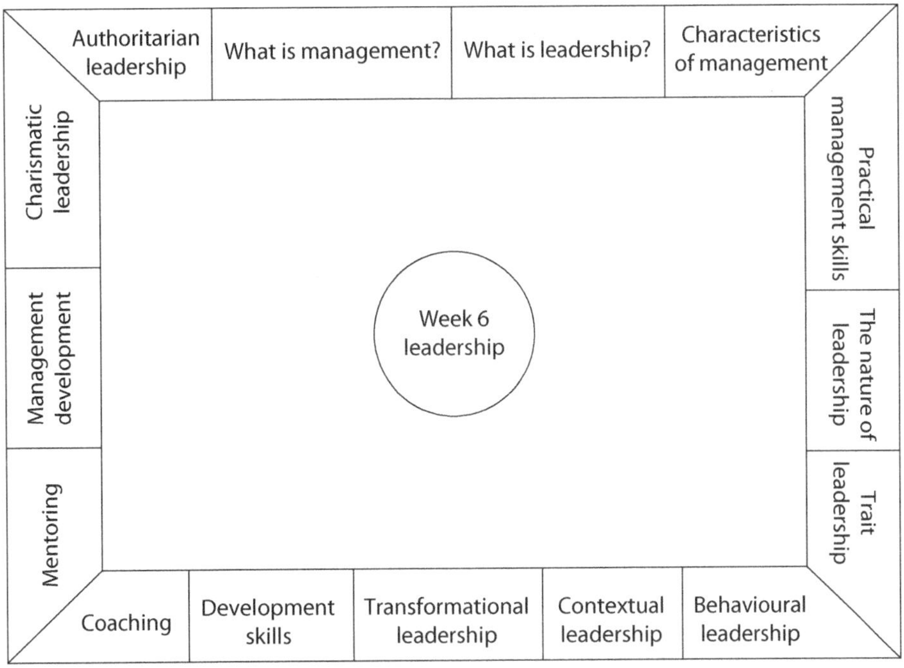

Listen and take notes

It seems a common practice in universities to provide handouts that give the detail of every PowerPoint slide that the lecturer uses. This is not a bad thing as it gives you an accurate record of what the lecture covered. However, it is very passive and encourages students to just sit and not pay attention or even to miss the lecture and copy another student's notes. It gives rise to an old definition of a lecture as 'a system whereby the lecturer's notes are transferred to student's notes without passing through the mind of either'. Active learning requires that the ideas, notions, concepts and information pass actively through the mind of the learner. Incidentally, it also makes lectures much more interesting. Note-taking in one form or another turns the passive into the active. You have to listen carefully and with full attention to be able to make notes.

❝❝ TUTOR COMMENT

I teach organisational behaviour but I also do some study skills teaching. One of my favourite 'Wow' activities is to conduct my first three weeks of lectures using a full set of handouts – this is very much expected at our university. I indicate that the third week lecture topic will come up in the examination. In the fourth week I explain that I will not be giving handouts this week and that this topic is one that will come up in the examination. I suggest that the students take notes on paper using a pen – this leads to much grumbling and a search for a pen and paper. I always bring a large quantity of these items. I also like to make the old Rowan Atkinson joke that goes a bit like this: 'You're a student and you haven't got a pen!! I suppose it is all communication by body language these days.' Anyway, once we are all ready I proceed with my lecture at a sedate pace giving the students time to write down whatever they feel they need to write. At the end of this session I inform them that the next week we will have an in-class test covering the lecture material in weeks three and four – normally met with a very large groan. I do point out it will help with the associated examination questions.

The following week dawns and I sit them down to a medium-length mixed test of short-answer questions, longer analytic questions and some longer evaluative questions – about an hour in all. They grumble, shake their heads and generally do quite poorly. The following week

I talk to them about the results in a general manner:

(one year's results looked like this)

Average of the questions relating to the first week (week 3): 22%

Average of the questions relating to the second week (week 4): 62%

I then discuss with the group why the results should have occurred in this way. I am working round to showing them that when they had to actively engage with the lecture in order to make notes they performed nearly three times as well. Where the notes were simply provided and they were probably poorly engaged and passive, they did very poorly. Indeed, normally a few members of the class claim that some of the topics from the first week were not even covered. Of course I have the PowerPoint evidence to show that the topics were covered. I conclude by making the point that for the lectures to be of any use you have to engage with them in some way.

In later weeks I return to giving out full notes of the slides – although there is something within me that feels I am letting them down by doing this. If they had to think about and record all the material we covered, they would learn much more. Having said that, I notice a much higher proportion of students take notes after this exercise.

ENGAGE WITH THE TOPIC

The above advice is a good way to start turning an essentially passive lecture into an interesting and engaging learning event. The main way to engage the mind is by thinking about the topics and ideas. There are several ways to do this and I feel sure you will quickly develop you own approach. There are some standard ideas for engagement with lecture material:

- Apply the lecture material to a context you know. Ask: 'How would that work at my workplace?'

- Be critical. Ask: 'Is that correct?'

- Think about the consequences. Ask: 'What does that mean in this or that situation?'

- Look for connections. Ask: 'How does this connect with that?'

Hopefully, much of what you hear in a lecture will make sense and you will understand it and be able to engage with it. There will be some ideas, concepts or information that you will not be able to understand when you first hear them. It is important to note these down and investigate them after the lecture. Difficult topics and concepts will often be covered and explored in seminars so you may well have a second opportunity to understand it. It would also be effective to explore areas you do not understand using the module textbook or discussing with your tutor.

CREATE LEARNING ACTIONS

Active learning should inspire action. What you hear and see in a lecture should make you want to investigate and find out more. If you record these inspirations during the lecture you are far more likely to act on them and research further after the lecture. By following up on ideas you have in the lecture, further learning and development will take place. Some of these learning actions will be about asking clarifying questions in seminars; if you don't write them down in an ordered way at the time they will be forgotten. Other actions will be about 'diving' more deeply into interesting or important areas. Yet more actions may be about remembering an important comment that the lecturer may have said, such as, 'This topic is likely to come up in the examination.'

TAKING NOTES IN LECTURES

If you are following the advice above you will need a system for taking notes in lectures. There are lots of ways to do this and the only important point is to use a system that you feel comfortable using and that allows you to recall information and prepare for assignments and examinations.

The standard format of lectures

As we noted above all lectures vary in many respects; however, lecturers are trained to deliver lectures in a standard format or structure. Recognising this format and organising your note-taking around it will make it easier to create effective notes. You might expect a lecture to follow this pattern:

- Entering and settling down – arrive early and collect any lecture notes. Skim-read these before the lecture begins. Underline any important topic areas and highlight any unfamiliar terms or words. Use the notes to provide a skeleton structure for your own notes.

- Lecture introduction – often delivered using a bullet-point list of topics and a set of learning objectives. Write these down, as it marks the start of your active listening. The introduction prepares you for what is to come; it is like a map of the lecture. Knowing this map will make it easier to follow the lecture.

- The main part of the lecture will often be structured as an explanation of a main idea, supported by practical applications and/or research findings. You can tell when a main idea is coming by the lecturer's use of 'signal words', such as 'a major development' and 'the leading author'.

- The lecture summary – as with the introduction, write this down; it symbolises the end of your active listening and involvement. Your notes should 'mirror' the summary.

- Closing the lecture – there is often an opportunity to ask questions at the end of a lecture. The lecturer will normally remain in the room so that one-to-one questions can be asked. Any action note you made requiring an answer could be dealt with in this part of the lecture. If you don't need to ask questions, check and organise your notes before leaving.

General thoughts about note-taking

Learning to make notes effectively and consistently is the most useful device to assist your ability to learn and remember. But, producing notes and understanding the main content of lectures does not allow you to recall the information. Having information ready for recall requires review and reinforcement. Effective note-taking allows for this recall of information. The hardest thing at first is to develop the skill of **selection.** You will not be able to write everything down that is said in lectures. You have to select and record key points and memorable points.

This is my list of important points to do when note-taking:

- Use a title and date on the notes pages.
- Use a paragraph numbering system for easy navigation of the notes.
- Be selective and look out for signal words and record the key ideas.
- Write key words or short sentences – do not try to write everything that is said.
- Leave gaps in the notes for adding extra material as the lecture progresses.
- Use your own words, not the lecturer's, but be careful not to change the meaning of the point being made.
- Write only when you need to record important material – it is easy to just keep note-taking when the lecturer is side-tracked or talking generally.

- Understand that there will be times when you need to listen intensely; at these times it will be difficult to make notes.
- Use indenting to indicate levels of importance.
- Use colour, highlighting and underlining to convey importance and connection.
- Leave half a page at the top of the notes so that you can return and create a top-level summary of the notes.
- Don't worry if you miss a point; just leave some space. You may get the point later or it may be covered in the summary.
- Reflect on the notes as soon after the lecture as possible and add reflective comments if they improve the notes.
- Make it a habit to review your notes regularly as this will aid your recall of the material.

NOTE-TAKING FORMS

As I noted earlier, there are an infinite number of ways to record notes in a lecture. The important thing is to develop a system that works for you. In the following sections I set out a few common methods and one new method that I encourage my own students to use.

Traditional written notes

Every year across the globe millions of students write their lecture notes using short sentences and in chronological form – it is a system that works. As the lecture progresses they record points that the lecturer makes and that seem important. The notes are handwritten using very little structure or emphasis and flow paragraph by paragraph until the end of the lecture.

This system can easily be improved so that the notes are more memorable and easier to understand by the inclusion of colour, underlining and indenting. Leaving a half page space at the top of the notes allows for a summary to be completed after the lecture. The outcome of this method is a file of notes with perhaps two to five A4 pages of notes with a summary at the top of each page for each lecture.

You can enhance this system a bit more by creating an index page as the first page of the file and sequentially numbering the pages in the file. It would be normal to use dividers to separate distinct subjects.

In summary this is a useful, well-tried and effective way to record and store notes from your lectures.

Mind map written notes

Mind map written notes allow for more flexibility in how they are organised. They are still predominantly headings and short sentences but they are arranged in boxes with the writing inside. By using arrows and numbering, the relationships between ideas and the structure of the ideas can be changed. It is a good idea to have a written mind map index as the first page in your file. This lists all the topics week by week with a very short summary of the main points.

You can build a written note mind map with pen and paper or using Microsoft Word or OneNote. OneNote has the added advantage that you can drag and drop all manner of items onto the page, such as screenshots, pictures, webpage images, tables of data, and so on.

Figure 2.2 Written mind map

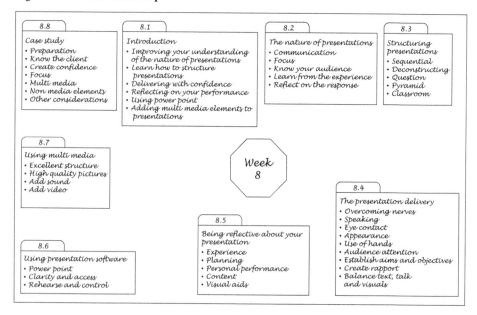

Figure 2.3 Interactive mind map

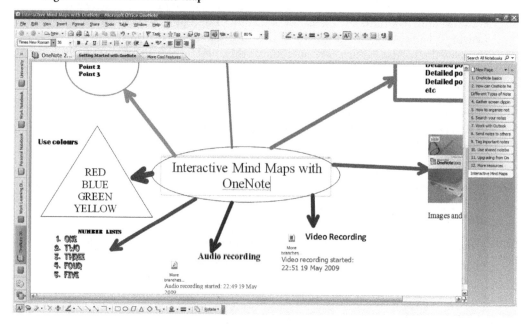

Mind maps

Traditional mind maps contain only top-level ideas and are drawn in a pictorial way. This is a good technique for linking ideas and concepts. It does not work so well in conveying detailed information. Your notes will need to contain detailed information so that you can revise and prepare for examinations. If you are a visual learner, then mind maps may work well for you. You can adapt the technique to include more information alongside the pictorial elements.

Application action notes

This is a specific form of note-taking that works well in business and management courses. It aims to encourage a highly active form of note-taking that encourages learning in lectures by thinking about the application of ideas. It also encourages actions that create more learning after lectures. To note-take using this method you will need a pre-printed form like the one shown below.

Pro forma page for application action notes

Subject:		Lecturer:	
Topic:		Subject text:	
Date:		Chap./page:	

Main point	Detailed sub-points	Application	Actions
1.			
2.			
3.			
4.			
5.			

Example of notes taken using the application action *pro forma*

Subject:	HRM	Lecturer: Roy Horn
Topic:	HR Planning	Subject text: HRM, Beardwell and Clayton
Date:	Tue 20th Oct	Chap./page: 4–122

Main point	Detailed sub-points	Application	Actions
1. Intro	(a) Define HRP – 'a strategy for the acquisition, utilisation, improvement and retention of the enterprise's human resources' (Dept Employment 1974)	What does this translate to in terms of what Tesco does? Well! It is recruitment of staff and how they are used to do useful work. But it is also about training and development.	Investigate some other definitions. Compare definitions to see how the scope changes. How does HRP research define this?
2. Traditional approach to HRP	(a) Often called hard HRP (b) Economics supply demand focus (c) Techniques from an old personnel approach of manpower planning (d) Bramham Model (e) Note – developed by Pilbeam and Corbridge (2002)	What do Tesco do? How is it done?	Find research that uses the Bramham model. Note: Lecturer says this will be an exam topic Is this something I might want to do as a dissertation? Drop figure of the Bramham model into my notes
3. Next main topic			
4. Next main topic			
5. Next main topic			

As the lecture progresses, add each main topic into the first column. Add short notes about the detail of each main point into the second column. There are typically about 5–10 detailed points for each main point. In the third column add your own thinking about what the idea or what the topic means in your workplace or for an organisation that you know – apply it in a context. This column represents your thinking. It is designed to engage your thought process and make the learning active. This third column can also be used to record applications that have already occurred – these are examples. So in the example above about human resource planning, if you have some experience of how this was done in an organisation you would include it here. The fourth column is used to record actions you intend to take. These can take various forms, such as:

- clarify points you did not understand
- areas where you intend to do some more research
- points you would like to bring up in discussion
- critical thoughts about the topic or the application of the topic
- questions that you might ask of the tutor or in the seminar group
- reflections about the topic and its application
- record important notes
- the names of authors who you might want to read
- extra things to add into your notes at a later point.

This type of note-taking makes the lecture a very active and hopefully interesting experience. You will be doing a lot of thinking while you write. This can be a slight problem until you are used to carrying out this many tasks at once. A developmental approach to this is to concentrate at first on taking down clear, accurate notes. You can fill in the application and action columns after the lecture. As you become more skilled you will be able to take notes faster, leaving more time to think about application and examples and the future learning actions you might carry out.

Whatever form of note-taking you use, try to make time soon after the lecture to review the notes for accuracy and add any further thoughts. If you want to be able to recall the information for examinations, you will need to refresh your memory on a regular basis. An effective pattern of review might be to work through the notes after the lecture, reviewing them and adding any extra elements. The following day, reread them and try to recall the detail. Review and try to recall after a week and then review and recall once a month after that. Regularly refreshing your memory does not take very long but can be surprisingly effective in aiding recall.

2.3 HOW TO GET THE MOST FROM SEMINARS

Traditionally seminars are smaller group discussions focused on some aspect of a lecture. In an effort to provide variety and interest and create a more active learning environment, seminars may be different from this traditional form. Business seminars may have a practical nature and be focused on completing a business task, such as creating a marketing plan or carrying out a small piece of research

TRADITIONAL SEMINARS

Traditional seminars focus on creating an interactive environment for discussing a question or a reading. If the seminar is going to be based on a reading, you will get more from the seminar if you have done the reading beforehand; this sounds obvious, but you would be surprised how often students do not read the material before the seminar. Passive reading won't do. You need to read the set material in an active and critical manner. If you do this you will be attending the seminar familiar with the subject matter and with a range of questions or criticisms; that is, you will be in the ideal position to contribute to the seminar and benefit from it.

If the seminar is based on a question or a quotation, you can still carry out some preparation work. Think about the question before the seminar and carry out some research around the concept of the question. Try to synthesise the standard arguments that are generated from the question. If the seminar is based on a quotation, 'Google' it and find the original source document; you can then read about the background to the material. Preparing for a seminar will enhance the learning you can take from it.

❝❝ TUTOR COMMENT

In most universities I have worked in the problem of 'freeloading' students who come to the seminars not having done any prep and then benefit from the preparation of others was never really solved. It drives me mad! More importantly it drives the well-prepared student mad! My solution is simple and I think being applied by more tutors all the time. In the first five minutes I present a simple knowledge test related to the reading (we use traditional reading in my classes); it is only five or six short questions. If students are not able to answer them, or a fair proportion of them, I ask them to leave and do the reading in the library. They are naturally disgruntled about this. I then find that the quality of the seminar discussion is so much better and the 'freeloaders' are thwarted. Most students only need to be turned away once or twice and they then get the message.

Seminars will give you experience of working with others and presenting your ideas orally. While lectures provide the overview of a topic area, seminars provide the opportunity for depth of thought and discussion. Seminars will affect your thinking about a topic area. It is a useful discipline to set out your thoughts and feelings about a topic before you go to the seminar. You can then compare your pre-seminar thoughts with how you feel after the seminar. You will have to become accustomed to having your views challenged; other participants will disagree with what you say. This situation is good practice for the work arena, when convincing other people of the merit of your ideas will be an important skill.

When you first engage with seminars at university you will not be alone if you worry about the following:

- fear of speaking out in a group situation
- not having much to say or contribute
- being attacked for your views by others in the group

- being asked a direct question and not knowing the answer
- fear of being an outsider.

Each of these fears can be overcome by employing social skills. There is a detailed chapter on social skills later in the book, but for now I will look at strategies to avoid or diminish these fears.

Fear of speaking out in a group situation – You have to feel comfortable, to be in your comfort zone, to be able to speak out freely. Do as much preparation as you can so that you feel confident about the subject area. Start by listening carefully and then form some 'ghost' contributions – things you might say but hold back from contributing. Then, gradually, contribute a little at a time. In seminars it is often the people who are shy and slow to engage in discussion that eventually turn out to be the people that contribute the most.

Not having much to say or contribute – If you don't do any preparation before the seminar, you are very likely to have little to say or what you do say will be weak and unhelpful. Knowing the subject area and the likely debates will give you confidence but also allow you to contribute real knowledge or an opinion based in research and evidence. While your personal opinion is useful, your considered opinion based in knowledge, evidence, research and practice is far more valuable.

Being attacked for your views by others in the group – You will need to be comfortable with having your opinions and ideas challenged. However, the tutor will control this interaction to ensure that counter opinions do not turn into attacks on the person. If you are giving a considered and evidenced-based opinion, it is considerably easier to defend what you have said.

Being asked a direct question and not knowing the answer – Some tutors will ask direct questions. This is done to test the foundation of what you are saying. You will also find that the tutor will try to encourage non-participants to engage with the discussion by using direct questions. If you want to avoid being put on the spot, prepare well and contribute.

Fear of being an outsider – Engaging with your peers socially and in classes will ensure that you are accepted as part of the group. Contributing and being seen to have sound opinions will also ensure you are included as part of the group. Displaying inappropriate social skills, such as verbally attacking other students, will ensure you are distanced.

If you prepare well and follow these simple rules you will enjoy seminars and get a lot of learning from them. There is one further action that supports learning in seminars and that is to take notes. It can seem difficult to make notes, listen and contribute, but with practice you will find you gain the most by doing this. Soon after the seminar, go over your notes and review what happened, what was said, what learning happened and what you are going to do now. This is a form of turning passive notes into action notes. You might also want to store those notes for later revision. Seminars seem to generate a lot of learning reflections, so record these in your learning diary.

USEFUL ACTIONS IN SEMINARS

- Be friendly, smile and try to stay relaxed.
- Speak at least once in every seminar.
- Use active listening – see Chapter 17.
- Make notes and follow up on the notes.
- Don't personally attack other students; engage in academic debate about the topic.
- Control your non-verbal cues – see Chapter 17.
- Make preparations to speak by jotting down the point you want to make.
- Understand the natural flow of the seminar as sometimes the point you want to make will be too late – the discussion has moved on, so think about timing.
- Speak a little more slowly than you would usually.
- Make sure you can be heard – speak up, but don't shout.
- Make eye contact with the person speaking.
- When you are speaking, seek out eye contact.
- Use the assertion/premise/conclusion structure to state your argument; you will find details of this in Chapter 10.
- Try to make clear, simple statements.
- If you are looking at the other students, you will see if they are confused by what you say; if they look confused, try restating the point.
- Act confidently but not in an arrogant manner.
- Allow others to finish their points before you speak.

Seminars will generate questions to the person speaking. You will need to develop ways to handle this. First, make sure you know what the questioner is asking. If necessary, ask them to clarify the question. You would be surprised how often in seminars the person speaking does not understand the question and answers a different one. Be prepared to say, 'I don't know the answer to that.' Also be prepared to discuss a question before an answer forms. Be prepared to say, 'I don't know the answer to that one, but if we think about it from this or that position it would seem to suggest that this or that might be the right answer.' Another useful response is to redirect the question to the whole group.

Experiential seminars

Business is concerned with actions and some of your seminars will be about experiencing and practising the skills of business. In these seminars you do not sit around talking; they take a different form:

1 A problem, issue or skill is introduced.

2 The parameters of the problem are set out or the skill is demonstrated.

3 You then process the problem using books, journals or theory and attempt to create an output.

4 If the seminar is based on a skill, you would practise the skill.

5 The seminar concludes with a debrief session where groups feed back their creations, and issues and problems are discussed.

One of the skills of business is presenting ideas to groups. Some experiential seminars would present an issue or idea that is to be presented. You, or a small group, then retire from the seminar to prepare. The conclusion of the seminar would see each person or group deliver their presentation. The tutor would then summarise the good and bad points and any actions that are needed to improve in the future.

The case study is a form of this type of seminar where the problem and the context are presented in written form. You or a small group then retires from the seminar to 'solve' the case study problems, returning at the conclusion of the seminar to deliver your findings. Case studies are predominantly concerned with analysis of business situations and presenting possible solutions. To carry out analysis you need to have a tool or several tools of analysis, and your first action should be selecting a theoretical tool for analysis. Then your group will need to explore what those analyses are displaying about the organisation and the environment. Finally, you will need to generate solutions based on theory, research or best practice.

Computer skills are also developed in this type of seminar. You might, for instance, be given a large volume of research data and asked to analyse it using an Excel spreadsheet. The task is explained at the beginning of the seminar and the tutor guides and helps you to complete the activities. The conclusion of the seminar checks the outputs and presents more skills and actions for further development.

Sections 2.2 and 2.3 have presented some ideas for how to generate the most learning from lectures and seminars. University life will often consist of a much wider range of activities than just lectures and seminars. As you engage with a new learning experience, embrace it fully and record your thoughts and reflections on completion of the activity.

2.4 GETTING THE MOST FROM LEARNING RESOURCES

E-LEARNING

E-learning is a generic term for computer-mediated learning. You will experience virtual learning environments (VLEs) at university. The two main programmes are Blackboard™ and Moodle™. Until recently there was a third system called Web CT, but this has now merged with Blackboard™. A VLE is software that allows the integration of aspects of learning. They have been used in universities for nearly a decade. During this time, rapid development of the way it is used has occurred. This will continue in the next decade. Most universities have a separate VLE 'shell' for each module you study. The 'shell' is the collection of learning resources for that module. VLEs have some unique learning features, such as discussion boards where the student and tutor can post thoughts and observations about aspects or their subject or learning. This tool can be a valuable aid to learning and skills development, but you have to be prepared to join in and contribute. Try to engage with this particular aspect of VLEs. A discussion board is not a substitute for a seminar. But, because of the asynchronous nature and the right of every member to post their thoughts, the dynamics can help those who find it difficult to contribute in seminars to express their thoughts and feelings.

Online tutorials using an interactive white space can allow those who study from a distance to experience a similar learning environment to those students who attend lectures and tutorials. VLEs are more frequently being used for digital submission of assignments. This system allows you to electronically post your assessments into the system. This is normally accompanied by a plagiarism checker like Turnitin™, now more commonly called an 'originality checker'. VLEs also commonly contain a range of course documentation such as course plans, assignment briefs, lists of references and lectures.

Many university module VLEs have a range of formative (not assessed) tests and activities to help you assess if learning has taken place. Short-answer tests are common and help you to check that you have understood specific information. Longer critical and analytic tests will have guideline answers and learning guidance.

In the workplace e-learning is one part of a systematic learning experience. The idea of combining traditional learning activities such as lectures and tutorials with e-learning activities is called 'blended learning'. The e-learning elements in workplace learning are normally more multimedia-focused and are based on interactive tutorials and assessments, and video and audio content. In performance terms you may be required to pass all the elements of a training package before you are allowed to use some part of the work system. For example, if you are a manager you may not be allowed to appraise staff until you have fully completed and passed the appraiser training package. Commercial e-learning software normally actively records your progress and success in completing learning activities. These progress points then contribute to a 'skills matrix' of your authorised areas. These 'performance gatekeepers' are designed to ensure you are competent to carry out a task before you are allowed to engage with that task. Typically this may cover areas of work such as computer software, management skills, leadership skills, financial procedures and all manner of other things that the organisation deems to be important.

Benefits of e-learning

These are some of the benefits of e-learning over traditional approaches:

Cost – E-learning can be easily scaled up to large groups of staff or students, and this makes it a cheaper form of learning, at least for larger groups. In organisations it is also cheaper because staff can complete the training at their desks, so there are no travel costs. Staff can also complete the training when their workload allows, thus using work periods that would otherwise be wasted.

Learner paced – People learn at different speeds. E-learning allows the learner to control the pace of delivery. It is easy to go back and redo sections you did not understand. It also allows learners to 'bite off' chunks of learning that suit them. Some people like 20–30-minute spells of learning and others like to study for hours.

Sequencing – Learning is often sequential where you need to know and understand something before you can add more learning to the foundation. E-learning allows for learning milestones to be set. Testing at the milestone point ensures that you cannot go on to the next learning stage unless you have adequately understood the current stage.

Consistency – E-learning presents a consistent message and does not miss out areas. You will probably know already that different lecturers and tutors teaching the same things deliver slightly different details. E-learning eliminates this variation so that every learner receives an identical experience. This can be vitally important where safety issues are concerned.

Currency – E-learning is structured in such a way that it is easy to keep up to date. Most e-learning resides on a computer server, so any change will be apparent the moment it is made. When legislation or other elements change, it is quick and easy to update the learning package to reflect the change.

Expert knowledge – Corporate e-learning packages are often authored by the leading specialist in an area. Learners therefore benefit form the most up-to-date research and thinking from the most experienced authors.

Global access – Learners can access packages from around the world; whether they are on assignment in a foreign country or on holiday in Wales, they will always be able to learn.

Library

The library is another fantastic resource that you should get to know early in your studies. It can at first seem a daunting place with what seems like millions of books. However, the library is the key resource in more effective and higher-level learning. During your first weeks at university the library will hold induction sessions. You should attend these so that you are familiar with the resources available in the modern university library. After the induction session, try to explore each of the resources that were covered. It will only be a few weeks before you need to use these resources to complete assignments.

The first resource that you need to investigate is the library catalogue. This is where you can search for specific books, place books that are out on loan 'on hold' so they are held for your use when they are returned, and check which books you have out on loan. University libraries impose expensive fines for the late return of books, so be careful and return or renew your books on time.

When you have searched for a book you will be able to see how many copies the library has of the book, whether they are out on loan or on the shelves, and if some of the loan stock is restricted. Restrictions are made on loan stock so that some copies are available for users in the library – reference copies. Books in high demand might be put on short-term loan only – short loan copies.

The library is also the gateway to hard-copy and electronic journals. Journals are a vital part of the written learning resources that you must consult when studying and completing assignments and research. They contain information and research that is far more specific than in textbooks; they are also much more up to date. Hard copies are available on the library shelves and are searchable from the library catalogue. The library website or the VLE site will provide access to electronic journals using a portal called Athens. During your enrolment and library induction, you will have set up an account for Athens or some other portal to access electronic journals. Many electronic journals are 'full text', meaning that you can read the whole journal article online without need to find the paper journal on the shelves. The most up-to-date journals will be searchable for title and abstract but will not be full text. The full-text availability starts about 12–24 months after the journal is published.

Many students use the library space for study. If your hall of residence or home is noisy or otherwise not suited to study, then the library is a great place to work. In every library there will be places that are designated 'quiet study' where you should be able to work undisturbed. Other areas of the library are suited to small group discussion and common working. Most libraries will have group study rooms where you can discuss and present ideas. Libraries will also have facilities for photocopying and printing, most usually these days for a per sheet fee. You will normally be able to use your laptop in a library and there will be WiFi access to the Internet.

Librarians are always willing to help you get the best from the library resources. So if there is something you don't know or cannot find, ask a librarian.

2.5 MICROSOFT ONENOTE

While I don't want to be a salesman for Microsoft products, I do have to accept that at university and work it is the most frequently found office software. Microsoft Office comes in quite a few different packages containing different combinations of software. A typical full application will contain:

- Word 2007: a word processing package
- Excel 2007: a spreadsheet application
- PowerPoint 2007: a presentation programme
- Outlook 2007: an organisation package
- Access 2007: a database application.

Premium software packs also come with other less well-known software, typically:

- InfoPath 2007: data management software
- Groove 2007: team information-sharing package
- OneNote 2007: information organisation software
- Publisher 2007: software to create publications and marketing literature.

The one package that I believe is most valuable to students but also not very well known is Microsoft OneNote. The rest of this section will explain some of the features of OneNote and how you can use it to organise your university notes and learning. At any point in time Microsoft has a discounted version of Office that is available to students and educators. At this point in time (May 2009), this is available to download at a cost of £38.95.

At the basic level OneNote is just like a ring binder for keeping all your notes together. But it is very hard to lose anything and searching the mass of information is very quick and easy. In fact, it is more like ten ring binders. It is a large programme that can easily store three years' worth of lecture and seminar data in a searchable form. When you first open OneNote it may take a short while to become acquainted with the layout.

Figure 2.4 OneNote main window

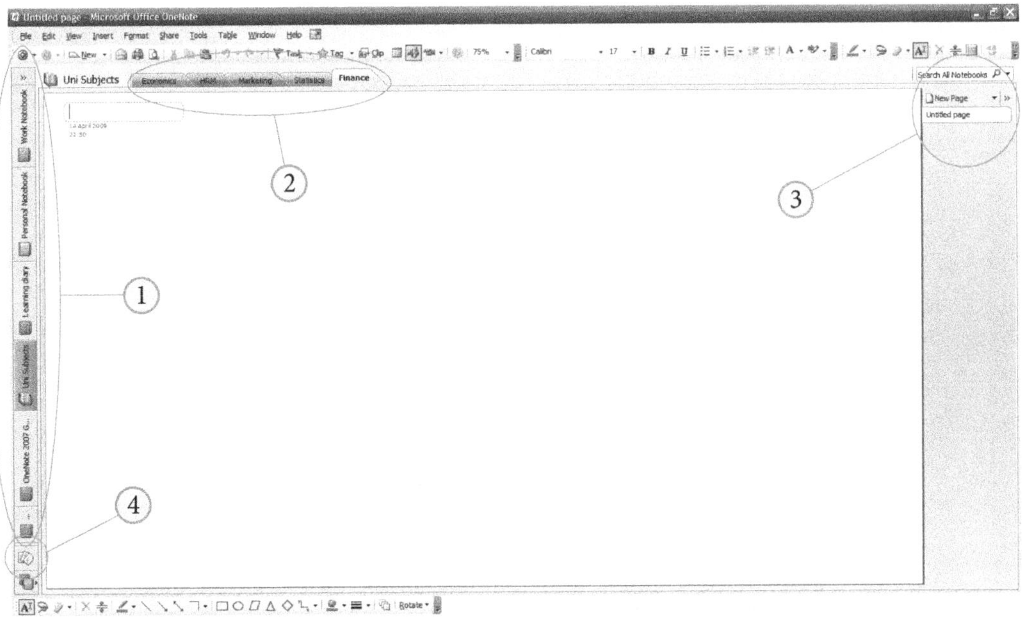

1 Separate notebooks are shown on the left-hand side. In this example they are called: Work Notebook, Personal Notebook, Learning Diary, Uni Subjects and OneNote2007. Each of these can be likened to a separate ring binder.

2   Within each notebook there are Tabs that can be likened to the dividers in a ring binder. The figure shows the Uni Subjects notebook and the tabs different subjects: Economics, HRM, Marketing, Statistics and Finance.

3   These are the pages under each tab and can be likened to the pages in each section of a ring binder.

4   Any unfiled pages are placed in this section and can be filed later.

So the basic structure is to have notebooks listed on the left, section tabs listed across the top, and pages listed on the right. You can add a new page, section tab or notebook by right-clicking in the appropriate space and then clicking new. This will allow you to create one large organised set of notes and other learning-related things. OneNote saves all the changes automatically so you do not have to think about that aspect. OneNote will also save a backup copy of your notes. By default OneNote saves the most recent copy and the one before last. You can set the number of backup copies by: on **Tools** menu click **Options** then in the **Category table** click **Backup** and change the default of 2 to another number. I would advise either 4 or 5. But remember these are backup copies on the same computer, so they are still vulnerable to loss.

Your Notebooks are so important that you cannot rely on this backup method alone. If your computer is lost or stolen then all your notes will be lost as well. This is such an important point that I would advise the following strategy:

You can access the OneNote files by: Right-click the **Start button** then **Explore All Users** then **My Documents** (in Vista click **Start**, then **My Computer**) and you will find a file called OneNote Notebooks; right-click this and **Copy**. You can then paste this to a memory stick. You now have a copy of your notebooks on a mobile memory stick. This is a backup copy but memory sticks are easily lost or damaged, so as soon as you can copy this file to your storage area on the university computer system. These are very secure and should ensure that you can easily get your Notebooks back if they are lost. You will need to do this regularly: I would advise you to do this at least once per week. You would then have three copies of your Notebooks, one on your computer, one on a memory stick, and one on the university server.

STUDENT COMMENT

This is awesome. I've had OneNote on my computer since I got it and never even once opened it, but after looking at it just now, this might be my saviour this semester where I have a whole bunch of difficult modules. Every module generates masses of information and data that is hard to control and then find the bits I need. Looks like this will beat opening Word documents and saving all of them to a folder.

If you want to be totally secure, every month or so copy the OneNote folders to a CD/DVD along with any other important documents, pictures or files and take it or send it home or to another address. This will provide an archive of files that you can return to in the event of any major crisis. I don't think you will lose your computer, the university will burn down and you will sit on and crush your pen drive all in the same day – but you never know! Remember you have a lot to lose!

Creating simple written notes

This could not be easier with OneNote. On your first day and at your first class you will create a new Notebook, maybe called 'University'. You do this by clicking **File**, **New**, **Notebook**, fill in the name as 'University'. It will open with one tab called New Section 1 and One page, and the cursor will be blinking in the title to this new page. Type in your title, let's say 'Course Introduction'. This notebook will now look like Figure 2.5.

Figure 2.5 My first page in OneNote

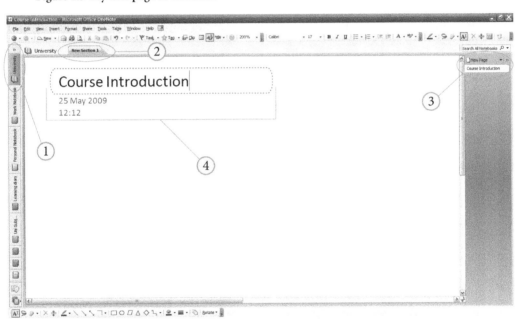

1 Is the name of the current Notebook 'University'. The other notebooks in OneNote are listed down the side. When you create a new notebook it goes to the bottom of this list. Just drag it up the list to place it at the top.

2 This is the only tab 'New Section 1' – you may want to change this to the name of the module, such as Economics, HRM, Marketing. You would then have one tab per subject with multiple pages for each tab. Double-click the tab and it will enter rename; type in the new name. To create a new Tab: right-click just to the right of New Section 1 then click 'New Section'; you will now have another tab called 'New Section 2'. Carry on until you have all the tabs you need for your subjects.

3 The pages of the section tab are listed here. At the moment there is only one called 'untitled page'. Add new pages by right-clicking just below the untitled page and clicking 'new page'. To begin with you may want to have one page for each week's lecture. So that you might have:

Week 1 – Intro

Week 2 – Topic

and so on.

4 The page title is repeated here at the top of each page.

So now the Notebook is structured, what can you add to the page?

Typed notes – Click anywhere in the page and start typing and a text box will open and you can record your notes. You can tab lines to show hierarchy and add bullets. You can scan lecturers' notes into the page or add e-learning resources. In this way you can use OneNote as a traditional set of typed notes. Because OneNote can allow you to move things around after you have typed them, it is not difficult to alter the order of points or change the emphasis of points. You can drag and drop and format the shape of a text box.

You will need to be able to carry out a few extra commands to function effectively in OneNote.

To make the page larger so that you can add more material, use: **Insert, Extra Writing Space**, then when the arrow and line appear draw it down the page to create more space.

As you add notes you can place Smart Tags, which will make it easy to return to the point. The most common tags and their shortcut keys are:

- To Do: Ctrl +1
- Important: Ctrl +2
- Question: Ctrl +3
- Remember for later: Ctrl +4
- Definition: Ctrl +5
- Highlight: Ctrl +6
- Contact: Ctrl +7
- Address: Ctrl +8
- Phone Number: Ctrl +9

The main command is: **Insert, Tag**, then select the required Tag. A logo is added to the page related to the tag used, so a '?' for a question, a star for important.

My general advice is to have a page for each week of a module and one extra page at the beginning for the overall summary for the module. You might like to consider using a clock index, where it can be easier to remember the topics that were covered during each week's lecture.

Figure 2.6 Clock module index in OneNote

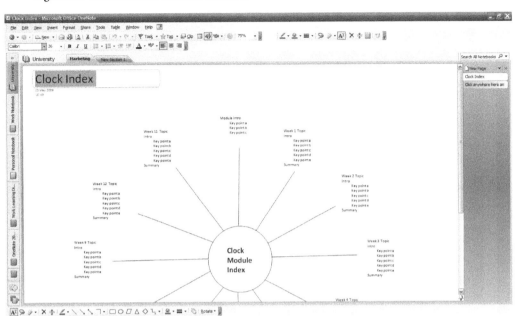

Using a clock index for a module, you would have a small text box for each week that covers the title, a short intro, the main topics covered and a short summary. These are placed week by week around the points of a clock. There will be a corresponding detailed notes page for each week.

Searching

As your notes build up, you will find the search function to be increasingly useful. So if you know that there is a reference to the work of Horn 2009 in a number of weeks of notes, searching on the term will reveal all the incidences of this term. The search box is just above the page listing on the right of the OneNote screen. It can even find words and phrases in pictures.

OTHER OBJECTS IN ONENOTE

It is not just text that you can add to OneNote. You can create fully interactive notes by incorporating some of the following:

- images and screenshots
- tables and data from other Office software
- numbered lists
- simple drawings and shapes
- audio recordings
- video recording
- scanned documents
- handwriting if you have a tablet PC.

Figure 2.7 **Different types of note in OneNote**

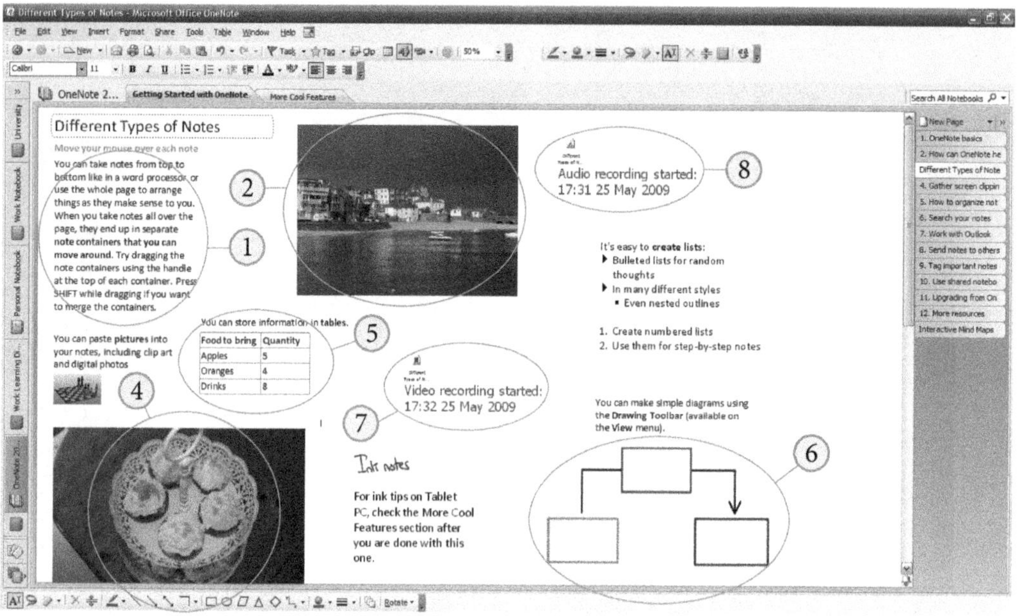

In Figure 2.7 you can see the following types of note:

1 Text note

2 Image as picture file

4 Image from the web

5 Insert tables

6 Simple drawings

7 Video

8 Audio

9 If you look at the image you will also find a list and Ink notes.

Learning diaries

A theme that runs through this book is that learning can occur anywhere. Systematic learning requires some method to trap the learning and the reflective thoughts around that learning. OneNote is an excellent vehicle for recording learning and reflecting on that learning. You can keep a notebook that is solely focused on trapping and reflecting on learning. As you move to the world of work it can be used to record your personal development planning and other work-related learning.

Optical character recognition

OneNote has built-in optical character recognition so that pictures, web sources, audio and video can be searched for specific items. If you have a tablet PC it will also recognise handwriting.

Sharing and emailing

You can share a OneNote notebook with other students or a work team. It is also very easy to email a page of notes to other students who have missed a lecture.

In summary, OneNote is an excellent way to organise and communicate your notes.

LOUISE AND SIMON

BECOMING REFLECTIVE PERFORMERS

Simon: 'Can I use your notes from last week's lecture?'

Louise: 'No way! They're my hard work. Why should I give them to you?'

S: 'Oh come on, help out!'

L: 'Why did you miss it?'

S: 'I overslept.'

L: 'That's pathetic. Go on! This time you can have them.'

S: 'Have them? No, I just need to copy them!'

L: 'What century do you live in?'

S: 'Sorry, I don't get it.'

L: 'I do my notes in OneNote! I'll send you a copy.'

S: 'Sorry! Still not getting it?'

L: 'OneNote is like an electronic filing system. It looks like a paper binder but it has lots of pages and dividers for all your work. You can put anything into it: photos, PowerPoint files, paper documents, video, phone messages etc etc.'

S: 'You said you were rubbish with computers!'

L: 'This isn't about computers; it is about note-taking and being organised. I am really organised.'

S: 'Well I have never heard of it.'

L: 'Really, I bet you have it on that laptop you're carrying.'

S: 'No, I don't think so.'

L: 'Really!'

S: 'Yes, sure.'

L: 'Give me the laptop for a minute.'

S: 'There you are.'

L: 'Aha what's this? "Programs, Office, OneNote".'

S: 'No, I don't believe it!'

L: 'Well, there it is, all nice and new and never been used.'

S: 'Well, I don't know what to say.'

L: 'You don't have to say anything but thank you.'

CASE STUDY

THE TRIPLE LECTURE

This is a case study designed to be carried out in groups of three. If you are doing this in a tutorial, you won't have a problem; if you are studying independently, you will need to engage with two friends.

This case study involves taking notes in different forms from the same lecture. You will need to choose a lecture that is dealing with a substantial topic where information and ideas are conveyed to a large group.

There are three roles to be filled in this case study, so allocate one to each person:

Role one – This person will take notes using the traditional written from of chronological notes.

Role two – Will take notes using a mind map.

Role three – Will take notes using the application action *pro forma*.

If you are using or intending to use OneNote, transfer the notes into that form before the discussion succession. Each participant will need a copy of the three different styles of notes.

After the lecture set aside about 60–90 minutes for discussion.

To think about...

- Each participant needs to spend five minutes explaining how easy or hard it was to take notes.
- Having read each of the forms of notes, discuss the following points:
- How easy are the notes to understand?
- How clear and memorable are the notes?
- Your reaction to the notes, that is, do they make you want to go to sleep or go and study?
- How effective would it be to revise from these notes?
- Which note-taking form would you choose to use from this point onwards?

SUMMARY

Studying at university will be different from school. The main difference is that you are expected to control your own learning. The lecturer will lay out the general map but you must decide the detail of what you learn and how you learn it.

- How to get the most from lectures:
  - Understand the structure, content and purpose of lectures.
  - Appreciate that all lecturers will be different and adjust your approach to their style.
  - Prepare for a lecture by reading 'around' the topic.
  - Take notes in every lecture, even the ones that have full handouts.
  - Turn passive lectures into active lectures.
  - Find and use a note-taking technique that works for you.
  - Review your notes after each lecture.
- How to get the most from seminars:
  - Recognise the difference between traditional seminars and experiential seminars.
  - Prepare for seminars by reading the pre-set material.

- Work to overcome any fears you have of speaking in seminars:
  - fear of speaking out in a group situation
  - not having much to say or contribute
  - being attacked for your views by others in the group
  - being asked a direct question and not knowing the answer
  - fear of being an outsider.
  - Try to develop effective behaviours in seminars.

- Getting the most from learning resources:
  - Make active use of your university VLE.
  - Understand the benefits of e-learning and try to maximise them.
  - Make extensive use of your university library.
  - Attend library inductions.
  - Ask a librarian if you are not sure of how to find anything.
  - Make use of the extensive online resources.

- Microsoft OneNote:
  - Create a systematic way to organise your notes.
  - Use OneNote to organise your notes if you have the software.
  - Develop your skills and creativity with OneNote as you study.

EXPLORE FURTHER

FURTHER READING

Buzan, T. (2004) *Mind Maps at Work: How to be the best at work and still have time to play*. London: HarperCollins.

Preppernau, J., Cox, J. and Frye, C. (2007) *Microsoft Office Home and Student 2007 Step by Step*. Redmond, WA: Microsoft Press Inc.

Weyers, J. and McMillan, K. (2007) *The Smarter Student: Study skills and strategies for success at university*. Harlow: Prentice-Hall.

WEB LINKS

*Microsoft OneNote demonstrations:*http://office.microsoft.com/en-gb/onenote/CH100740841033.aspx

CHAPTER 3

Learning and Skills

What skills will I develop in this chapter?

- how learning and skills improve performance
- using learning styles to enhance learning
- the skills of active learning
- learning in the workplace
- understanding and exploiting university culture
- lifelong learning and the attributes of lifelong learners
- how to 'trap' your learning

3.1 INTRODUCTION

You may have wondered why some students get higher grades than others. You may have at first thought that it is because they are more intelligent, and that may be an explanation. Your level of intelligence remains fairly stable throughout your life, so if intelligence were the only explanatory factor in the grades awarded at university then a simple test at the beginning would determine your grades throughout. Intelligence may be a factor in success, but it is only one factor amongst many. This chapter and the following chapter aim to investigate areas of university and work that will determine how successful you will be.

There are many unknown elements in success; being lucky can be one of them, but to be consistently successful in life you will need to be able to learn and also be able to demonstrate skills. My argument is essentially simple: 'The more open to learning and the more skilful you are the more successful you will be at university and afterwards.'

This chapter investigates what learning is and how to 'trap' it. It also looks at skills and how you can demonstrate them. As with all of these early chapters, I would advise that you work systematically though the chapter and reflect on the activities.

3.2 WHAT IS LEARNING AND WHAT IS A SKILL?

These are fundamental questions relevant to university and to work but prove rather difficult to answer in a definitive manner. There are a lot of different definitions of learning.

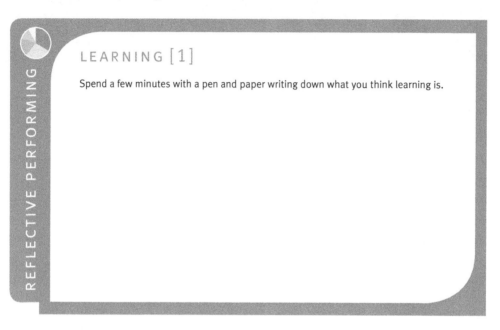

REFLECTIVE PERFORMING

LEARNING [1]

Spend a few minutes with a pen and paper writing down what you think learning is.

The following are just a few definitions of learning for you to consider:

- knowledge gained by studying (Collins Dictionary)
- a relatively permanent change in behaviour brought about by instruction or reinforced practice (anonymous)
- the process of developing a skill or of acquiring knowledge and understanding of a subject (American Accounting Association)
- the acquisition and development of memories and behaviours, including skills, knowledge, understanding, values, and wisdom. It is the product of experience and the goal of education (Wikipedia)
- a person can be said to have learned when they have increased their options for applying, to a specific set of circumstances, new or different behaviours which the person believes will be to their benefit (author).

The definitions above all have some connection to university and studying for a degree. The learning you do in university will be applied in the workplace so we may need to think about what learning would be like in organisations. What follows is the definition of learning in the PacifiCorp organisation:

> Learning as used here, refers to concerted activity that increases the capacity and willingness of individuals, groups, organisations and communities to acquire and productively apply new knowledge and

LEARNING [2]

Having considered the five definitions above, how do you now see learning? Write down your own definition. If your first and second definitions have changed, could this be classed as learning?

skills, to grow and mature and to adapt successfully to changes and challenges. Such learning empowers individuals and organisations to make wise choices, solve problems and break new ground. In particular, it is sustainable, it is a lifelong, renewable process for people and for the institutions that serve people. Learning certainly includes academic studies and occupational training through high school and beyond. But it also encompasses the physical, cognitive, emotional and social development of children in the earliest years of their lives.

It includes the capacity of organisations to anticipate and adapt to evolving values, technologies, performance standards and constituent expectations. And it includes the capacity of geographic communities and communities of common interest to respond with understanding and initiative to broad changes that represent threats or opportunities. (PacifiCorp 2004)

The PacifiCorp definition takes the rather dry and academic definitions earlier and puts them into the organisational context and begins to show the power of learning and the lifelong nature of learning. Twenty-first-century organisations focus on learning and how to encourage it in their organisations. The mantra driving this approach is that learning is vital to success.

We have explored learning, but what is a skill?

Some definitions of skill are:

- refers to a person's ability to perform various types of cognitive or behavioural activity effectively (anonymous)
- ability, proficiency, facility, or dexterity that is acquired or developed through training or experience (Per Johansson)

LOUISE AND SIMON

BECOMING REFLECTIVE PERFORMERS

Simon: 'That was an interesting lecture!'

Louise: 'Yes, it made me think.'

S: 'It was a novel approach to getting us to think about skills.'

L: 'Twelve sentences and I didn't get one correct.'

S: 'Hilarious, I didn't know any of them for sure but I got the highest number right – 4.'

L: 'I just can't work out what is analysis, critique and evaluation – how stupid is that?'

S: 'When she explained what they were it all made reasonable sense.'

L: 'Yea, until she gave us some writing and asked us to classify them.'

S: 'It is all jumbled up; every sentence seemed to contain bits of everything. Or I didn't know what I was looking at.'

L: 'I wonder if it is because I still don't know what they all are, I mean exactly what they are.'

S: 'I guess that is it. But, from what she said if we don't sort out those skills, what they are and how to create them ourselves, we are going to get really low grades.'

L: 'She said she would work on it again, but it really bugs me. It is really difficult to understand what these things are.'

S: 'What are we going to do then?'

L: 'I guess we need more help ... But where from?'

S: 'Wikipedia!'

L: 'Not likely, anyone can write on there...'

S: 'Urg! Evaluation – I recognise that!'

L: 'No, because I didn't present any evidence in support. It was just an unsupported statement.'

S: 'Yes, you got me there.'

L: 'The web's a good idea, though. Type in "what is evaluation?"'

S: 'These sites are about evaluating projects.'

L: 'Change the words; make it "academic evaluation".'

S: 'Okay, now we have nothing of any use. Damn this Internet. Why isn't there anything to help?'

L: 'Try a different form of words...'

After an hour and 22 different forms of words:

S: 'Well, that was a waste of time. Nothing, not a thing of any use.'

L: 'So the web isn't the answer to everything. What shall we try now?'

S: 'The library; it's old fashioned but you never know.'

L: 'Yes, you could be right. Let's get a coffee on the way!'

S: 'Well, no books on evaluation. Stranger and stranger. What is going on?'

L: 'I guess we will need to work this one out for ourselves.'

S: 'Let's throw this at the study group and see how they cope.'

S: 'It is only level one; we could just forget about it until level two.'

L: 'Defeatist, let's get on and sort it out now while we can and it will pay off in our grades later on.'

S: 'As my dad says, don't put off until tomorrow what you can do today.'

L: 'You know I am right. We can then discuss it in a seminar group with the Prof.'

- ability to use knowledge, a developed aptitude, and/or a capability to effectively and readily execute or perform an activity (Mohamed Elashri).

If we analyse the differences between leaning and skills we could conclude that learning is a process of acquisition that leads to change, and skills are the explicit execution of an activity. In university and work you will need to use and demonstrate both of these concepts.

3.3 LEARNING STYLES

The notion of learning styles is widely used and many models represent the ideas. The presumption is that different learners are stimulated by different ways of learning and that most people have a preferred learning style. Short-question tests are used to determine which learning style individuals prefer – see the 'Web Links' at the end of this chapter. These learning style ideas are much criticised and are not universally accepted. But, most teachers and students do find some congruence with the ideas. I will represent the simplest of the models, which has three styles. The other learning style models commonly used are the Kolb Learning Styles Inventory and the VARK model.

VISUAL LEARNERS

Visual learners prefer to learn by seeing and respond best to diagrams, illustrations, images, videos and handouts. You will often find the visual learner taking notes using spider diagrams and other picture forms.

Visual learners tend to:

- take numerous detailed notes
- are usually neat and clean – visually presentable
- often close their eyes to visualise or remember something
- find something to watch if they are bored
- like to see what they are learning
- benefit from illustrations and presentations that use colour
- are attracted to written or spoken language rich in imagery
- prefer stimuli to be isolated from auditory and kinaesthetic distraction
- find passive surroundings ideal.

AUDITORY LEARNERS

Auditory learners prefer to learn from listening and respond best to discussions or the lecturer speaking. They will pick up underlying meanings from the pitch and speed and other nuances in speech. Auditory learners often gain little from written material and may translate this into sound, such as by reading notes into a tape recorder.

Auditory learners tend to:

- sit where they can hear but needn't pay attention to what is happening in front of them
- may not co-ordinate colours or clothes, but can explain why they are wearing what they are wearing and why
- hum or talk to themselves or others when bored
- acquire knowledge by reading aloud
- remember by verbalising lessons to themselves (if they don't, they have difficulty reading maps or diagrams or handling conceptual assignments like mathematics).

KINAESTHETIC LEARNERS

Kinaesthetic learners, also called tactile learners, prefer hands-on learning and respond best to practical learning where they are involved in doing something. They are often fidgety and ill at ease when asked to sit and listen. They will turn dry, paper-based notes into action and practical exercises.

Kinaesthetic learners tend to:

- need to be active and take frequent breaks
- speak with their hands and with gestures
- remember what was done, but have difficulty recalling what was said or seen
- find reasons to tinker with things or move when bored
- rely on what they can directly experience or perform
- use activities such as cooking, construction, engineering and art to help them perceive and learn
- enjoy field trips and tasks that involve manipulating materials
- sit near the door or somewhere else where they can easily get up and move around
- be uncomfortable in classrooms where they lack opportunities for hands-on experience
- communicate by touching and appreciate physically expressed encouragement, such as a pat on the back.

The reason I introduce learning styles here is to assist you in creating the best learning environment for your particular preference. This will not just apply at university but also in the workplace. At university you will have a mixture of activities, lectures (suit visual learners), seminars (suit auditory learners) and practical activities including case studies (suit kinaesthetic learners). You may have wondered why you like the seminars for a subject but hate the lectures, or you like the practical elements but hate the talking. Learning style preferences may in part explain your likes and dislikes. You will have little trouble enjoying the learning that suits your style but how can you make the aspects of learning that you like less more enjoyable? If we look at some practical ideas for learners that prefer the different styles, it may 'spark' ideas for how you can cope with your less preferred style and turn it into a style you do prefer.

Visual learners tend to:

- use visual materials such as pictures, charts, maps, graphs, and so on
- have a clear view of the lecturer when they are speaking so you can see their body language and facial expression
- use colour to highlight important points in text
- take notes or ask the teacher to provide handouts
- illustrate their ideas as a picture or brainstorming bubble before writing them down
- write a story and illustrate it
- use multimedia (for example, computers, videos and filmstrips)
- study in a quiet place away from verbal disturbances
- read illustrated books
- visualise information as a picture to aid memorisation.

Auditory learners tend to:

- participate in class discussions/debates
- make speeches and presentations
- use a tape recorder during lectures instead of taking notes
- read text out loud
- create musical jingles to aid memorisation
- create mnemonics to aid memorisation
- discuss their ideas verbally
- dictate to someone while they write down their thoughts
- use verbal analogies and storytelling to demonstrate their point.

Kinaesthetic learners tend to:

- learn by experimentation and trying something out
- create practical tasks from dry ideas or concepts
- take frequent study breaks
- imagine what it would be like doing the subject of discussion
- move around to learn new things (for example, read while on an exercise bike, mould a piece of clay to learn a new concept)
- act out concepts as role-play
- work at a standing position
- do things rather than read about things

- dress up their work space with posters
- skim through reading material to get a rough idea what it is about before settling down to read it in detail.

A useful approach to learning when you are experiencing a learning mode that does not naturally suit you is to convert it into your preferred learning style. The visual learner when faced with a boring talking lecture with no visuals will draw pictures and make spider diagram notes with pictures at the end of branches. The auditory learner when faced with a predominantly visual presentation will describe the things they see to themselves. The kinaesthetic learner will imagine action and activity and will often make notes that are small action sequences.

❝❝ MANAGER'S COMMENT

We are a small company that needs to be agile in a fast-moving technology sector. It is my belief that we have to be good 'corporate learners' to survive. Every new member of our company is introduced to and takes the Honey and Mumford learning styles questionnaire. Our training provider will then create a bespoke induction programme for the new employee and a development programme for the first six months. All the areas we want to cover at induction can be adjusted and tailored to fit the preferred learning styles of the person. We also introduce them to the other learning styles and use them to a lesser extent.

As a company we aim to 'trap' learning at source and by having an understanding of the different learning styles of our workforce we can more easily understand and adapt the learning that an employee contributes to our organisation.

After the first six months, developmental plans are created that favour an individual's preferred learning style but also offer activities that use the whole range of learning styles.

3.4 ACTIVE LEARNING AT UNIVERSITY

One of the most successful strategies for achieving success at university and in the workplace is to become an active learner. University assessments and workplace activities reflect how much learning you have done and how skilfully you can carry out tasks. If you can adopt an approach that makes you a very efficient learner, your university assessment grades will improve and in the workplace you will achieve more success. This contrasts with the wasteful approach of the passive learners. Passive learners generally receive knowledge and learn things by memorising them and repeating what has been learned. This is a very poor strategy when used with university assessments and will lead to poor grades. At work this passive approach will lead to you being allocated repetitive and boring tasks.

Active learning provides a means to maximise the benefit of the time you spend working, studying and completing assessments. Active learning involves using more than one sensory mode to absorb information and place that information in context. The following is an explanation of how active learning would be used during the assignment process.

ESTABLISH YOUR PERSONAL MOTIVATION AND A SET OF LEARNING GOALS FOR COMPLETING A UNIVERSITY ASSIGNMENT

As an active learner you do not just do an assignment. You must set out reasons for doing the activity and also a set of learning goals that you will achieve along the way. Try to establish this by asking:

- Why have my tutors set this task?
- What will be the focus of my reading?
- What will I get out of this personally?
- What will I learn as I do this task? Be specific and make a list of things to be learned, such as better skills with Excel, being able to apply criticism, and so on.
- How will this learning fit in with the skills I will need in the workplace?

The assignment or activity should not be seen as some task to be done but as a learning opportunity.

READING

Active learners do not just read the words on a page; they engage with the words on the page. They engage by being critical of what has been written. They also engage by placing what they read into a context and asking questions about how useful this idea would be in this or that circumstance. Active readers engage their minds as well as their eyes when they read. When reading for an assignment you will be looking for useful theories, ideas and research that can help you argue the points you want to make. The active learner also writes as they read so that they are using their eyes, brain and hands. Active learners question as they read using these types of question:

- What exactly is the author arguing?
- How is the author supporting their argument?
- Is this argument biased?
- Is the evidence being moulded into the argument?
- Does the author present a clear vision and argument, or is it obscure?
- Does the writing flow logically?
- How can these ideas be applied to my assignment?
- Is the author missing out any important aspects?

WRITING

Writing uses another sense and you should always keep a pen and paper to hand when you read. Include in your notes:

- the main argument
- how good the argument is
- if the argument is convincing or not
- restating the idea in your own words
- 'what if' statements
- draw the argument or idea
- mind maps of the key elements.

TALKING

Active learners verbalise what they have learned by talking about what has been learned in a study group. Alternatively, verbalise to yourself by reading your notes aloud. Verbalising reinforces the learning and improves the retention; it also deepens your understanding of the material.

ACTIVE LISTENING

Active listening involves listening with a purpose. If you have already done some reading before a lecture or tutorial, use your notes as a listening guide. Try to position what is being said into the framework you have already produced. There will always be things that do not fit into the framework, but these can be added as the lecture or seminar progresses. Always listen and make notes; you will engage three aspects: ears, brain and hands.

Active listening will help you get the most out of workplace meetings. Try to do some preparation before the meeting so that you have a framework of ideas or knowledge; these will allow you to engage more positively with the meeting. During meetings make notes about facts, approaches and ideas you have.

ACTIVE LEARNERS CONTINUALLY REVIEW

Active learners don't just read or write once; they continually review what has been done. Create a review strategy so that the material is reviewed on two, three or four occasions. This is a great strategy for examination revision, but is also very useful when preparing to write assignments. You become more familiar with the work but you also become more critical. This constant review approach is also vital at work.

ACTIVE LEARNERS MAKE CONNECTIONS

Before starting on an assignment consider how the assignment and the material fits in with what has already been learned. Also consider how the reading and the assignment fit into a wider structure, maybe a social system. Don't accept the boundaries created by modules; connect information from one module to another and from one year of study to another. Try to make connections between theory and practice.

Try to avoid aspects of passive learning, such as:

- simply reading the words
- just getting a task done
- accepting what you read without question
- trying to remember things
- memorising notes
- recalling information but not being able to use information
- seeing and remembering words, not concepts and ideas
- working on tasks in a linear fashion, completing one task then moving on to the next
- not making connections between material
- not connecting the learning from one project to another.

LEARNING DIARY

ACTIVE LEARNING

I have just been to a university seminar on active learning. I can't believe I didn't know about this before. I have been at school for 13 years and no one ever mentioned this way of learning. I almost feel cheated. If I had known this earlier I might have enjoyed school a bit more and been better at school. Well, now I know about it I am going to change a few things to incorporate an active learning approach.

To start with I will just do a few things differently:

Lecture notes – all of our lecturers give out handouts of the lecture proceedings that I barely look at and certainly don't read.

This is passive and very poor learning. So from now on I will produce my own spider diagram notes while the lecture is going on. At least this will keep me awake.

When I read – I read my textbooks sitting in a comfy chair and quite often fall asleep while reading. Honestly, I hardly read a page before I am asleep. So I am going to use active reading where I write thoughts, ideas and practical applications as I read. I will also keep short notes about what I have read and the main points of that reading.

That will do for a start but I will introduce some other active learning approaches in a week or so.

3.5 WORK-BASED LEARNING

How is learning at work different from learning at university? In university you do a lot of formal learning and very little working. In the workplace you do a lot of working and very little formal learning. At the end of your degree you will move from the university environment to the workplace environment. The workplace is characterised by:

- very little formal learning
- many tasks to be completed – a large workload
- workplace stress and a culture of immediacy
- performance-driven – quality outcomes
- practical problems needing fast, practical solutions
- solutions to problems that must fit within the strategic intentions of the organisation.

As we saw earlier, organisations put great stress on learning, but in this type of environment what sort of learning can be done? Once back in the full-time workplace you will find that most of your learning is what is called experiential. In contrast to university, you will be learning by doing and this takes a particular form which, if you are unfamiliar with it, will mean that you cannot learn anything. If you cannot learn effectively from experience you will be destined to make little progress or improvement.

Figure 3.1 The Kolb Learning Cycle

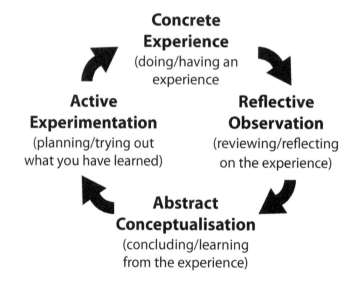

The Kolb Learning Cycle offers a model to explain how to learn from experience. Many learners would follow this approach quite naturally but applying and using the concepts in a conscious manner will lead to improved learning at work. The stages of the cycle are as follows:

Concrete experience – In business contexts this is usually some form of managing. This will be the actual experience of managing a person or a group. But, it could also be task experience. At university it is likely to be the experience of an assessment or presentation, but it could also be the experience of learning or contributing to the learning process, maybe in a seminar.

Reflective observation – This incorporates your thoughts and feelings in relation to the concrete experience you have undergone. People naturally reflect on both good and bad experiences, and this would be called our common-sense reflection. To learn more fully from experience we would need to reflect in a more systematic manner. Keeping a reflective record of your experiences in a diary or logbook facilitates systematic reflection. This approach 'traps' the concrete experience and allows both immediate reflection and reflection after a time, reflection over time and comparative reflection between multiple experiences. As a management example, we may keep a log of our experiences of dealing with a difficult member of our working team. Over time our reflections may suggest patterns of behaviour or trigger events. Reflecting does not of itself lead to learning and change, so the remainder of the cycle must be completed to ensure learning has taken place.

Abstract conceptualisation – This is a way of thinking about experience and reflections of experience. Many of you will have been slightly burned by the steam from a kettle as it boils. Once we have had that experience a few times we reflect that it is unpleasant and should be avoided. Abstract conceptualisation involves using or developing theory to explain what has happened and to change things. Common sense tells us that steam burns so avoid it. So we could theorise that cold drinks are the safest bet; they are, but many people like hot drinks. So conceptualisation is selective; any theory will not do. Theory selection and development needs to lead to changes that still provide the desired output. We could adapt our tea-making experience to wait a few seconds after the water has boiled until the steam goes away. Alternatively, the experience could be changed so that the kettle handle is held in such a way that the steam does not rise and burn our arm. This is a simple example but you can see that theory needs to inform changes.

Active experimentation – The concepts and ideas formed in the previous part of the cycle form the basis for some planned changes when you next experience the situation. You would implement the changes when you next experience the same situation.

Real-world problems are often hard to solve and the experiential cycle will have to be followed many times before a full and satisfactory solution is developed.

I have introduced the Kolb Learning Cycle as a useful tool for workplace improvement, but it is also a very effective approach in understanding and improving learning at university. Assessment experiences such as assignments and presentations can be improved by using the learning cycle: EXPERIENCE – REFLECT – CONCEPTUALISE – EXPERIMENT.

AFTER ACTION REVIEW

I have just come back from a weekend I spent with the Army on a university liaison event. The Army hosts groups of students from various universities and we have a fun weekend of group activities and stuff. I even got to fire a rifle. The food was rubbish, well actually fairly healthy but I didn't like the lack of chips. There is so much to write in here from the weekend that it will take me a couple of weeks. I have made rough notes so I won't forget about all the things we did.

One thing really stood out, though, and I think I will adopt the idea for uni. After every event or activity the group sat down, sometimes outside and on the ground, and carried out an 'After Action Review'. The guy running the weekend said it was standard Army practice after every military engagement and done at all sorts of levels, from a little 'raiding' team to a whole battalion.

The After Action Review follows these principles:

- What was supposed to happen?
- What actually happened?
- Why was there a difference?
- What can you learn from it?

They also use another device at the end of the weekend called a 'Retrospective', the principles being:

- What was the objective of the project?
- What did we achieve?
- What were the successes? Why? How can we repeat the success?
- What were the disappointments? Why? How can we avoid them in future?
- 'Marks out of 10'.

I think I can adapt these two ideas for use in my uni work. I imagine applying the 'retrospective' to assignments I have finished. But I will think out ways to use the ideas.

3.6 UNIVERSITY CULTURE AND LEARNING

You may well be using this book soon after you have entered university from a school environment. The university learning culture is very different from the school culture. Many of these aspects you will enjoy, especially the removal of close control that you may have experienced at school. There are other aspects of the university learning culture that are worth exploring as they can make a big difference to your personal ability to learn. The difference in culture between a work environment and university is also important, where the lack of direction can affect your learning. The following areas of university may present opportunities and difficulties for your learning:

TEACHING METHOD

In business teaching you are likely to experience a wide range of teaching methods; some topics will be taught in large lectures and large seminars. If you don't engage as an active learner and a willing participant in the teaching sessions, you can feel a bit lost and lonely. Active learning approaches (see section 3.4 above) will yield the most learning and improvement.

CONTACT TIME AND PATTERN

Many business courses have four modules taught per semester, and the amount of time in the classroom varies between about 6 hours per week up to 12 hours per week to teach these four modules. This can seem very different from school where you may have been in classes for up to 20 hours per week. At first it can seem very easy and lightweight, but universities expect you to do a lot of independent learning when you are not in class. An old term explains this quite well when we used to describe university education as 'reading for a degree'.

UNIVERSITY TUTORS AND LECTURERS

Culturally you will meet a much wider range of styles and approaches of the teaching staff in universities. Some tutors will spend a lot of time outside classes being helpful and encouraging, but most of your contact with tutors will be in the taught sessions. University teachers generally split their work time into three parts: teaching, research and administration. Culturally you may find it takes some getting used to that the teaching element of their work is not the most important part.

E-LEARNING

A number of aspects of your modules may be taught using e-learning, which is an interactive learning platform that you access using a computer. There is a great deal of variation in the use of e-learning within courses but you can expect that some aspects of your learning will be mediated through this source; in some universities a considerable amount of the content delivered is by e-learning.

INDEPENDENT STUDY

At university no one will 'chase' you to work. If you are not self-motivated then you will fail the course and end up dropping out. The motivation to learn and complete the assessment tasks must come from you. The more effective you are as an independent learner, the more successful you will be.

BEING A GOOD RESEARCHER

You will receive recommended reading lists for each of your subjects but these alone are not sufficient to complete the assessment tasks. You will need to develop good research skills so that you can easily and effectively find information and resources for learning and assessments.

ORGANISATION AND TIME MANAGEMENT

Chapter 1 dealt with being organised at university; this is a cultural element of university life. Assessment deadlines will start to appear within about six weeks of starting university. If you do not plan and organise the learning, research and writing of these, they will soon overtake your life. This is a miserable situation where you can never seem to get ahead of the next deadline. Efficient organisation and ruthless time management is the key to survival.

TEAMWORKING

Many of the academic tasks and assessment tasks you carry out will be in groups or teams. You will need to develop an open and contributing approach to these tasks and develop team skills; these will serve you well in the world of work.

REFLECTIVE, INDEPENDENT THINKER AND LEARNER

Section 3.5 looked at experiential learning and the need to be reflective. You will also need to develop as a critical, independent thinker. The skills of critique and evaluation are highly prized and valued at university. Top grades are only awarded to independent, critical and evaluative thinkers.

3.7 LIFELONG LEARNING

Lifelong learning is a well-used and under-defined phrase. But, it is a phrase that has real meaning and is supported by sound learning theory. The phrase is only two words long, so let's unpack those two words.

LIFELONG

Traditionally most people would do a lot more learning in the early parts of their lives; school and university are the main areas where formal learning has taken place. Changes in the economic climate (globalisation and competition) and in business culture (constant change and improvement) have required a change in the manner of learning and the timescale of learning. Whereas traditionally you could learn all you needed for a whole working life at university, in the current environment that learning is soon superseded by new ideas and ways of doing things. We have already looked at learning from experience and that experience is lifelong, so conceptually and practically techniques are needed that support learning throughout life. Essentially lifelong is a statement of time; the expectation is clear in the name.

LEARNING

We have already investigated learning and found that it comes in several forms. The essence of learning in lifelong learning is towards the less formal methods of learning. There is also a shift towards person-centred learning and organisation-centred learning. This also connects with the reason this book was written, which is to promote learning and skills. Universities also place much greater emphasis on developing a set of learning skills that will serve their students throughout life.

WHAT ARE THE ATTRIBUTES OF LIFELONG LEARNERS?

Lifelong learners are likely to display the following skills:

- organising and planning their own learning
- reflective assessment of their current skills state
- be active learners
- skilled at learning from formal settings
- skilled at learning from informal approaches and particularly experiential learning
- be able to learn from peers, coaches, mentors and colleagues
- integrative thinkers (draw knowledge from various sources to use practically)
- understand and use different learning styles and strategies (be adaptable)
- be good researchers and information-gatherers
- have structured ways to 'trap' learning.

 TUTOR'S COMMENT

I always try to impress on my students that what we do here (university) and how we do it is the real learning that they do. They tend to think that it is the subject material that is important, and to some extent it is. But the really important learning is related to ways of thinking, acting and learning. These are the skills that are valuable in the workplace. They are also the skills that will get them high grades – their ears tend to 'prick up' at that point.

3.8 PERSONAL DEVELOPMENT PLANNING

Personal development planning (PDP) at university is a set of techniques to help you manage the learning process. The same techniques you use at university will be used in the workplace to manage your learning and development. It is essentially a way of recording achievements, successes, weaknesses and a method of reflecting on progress and setting clear, achievable learning goals. By engaging with the process in a systematic way you will improve your ability to learn and will improve the grades you achieve for coursework and examinations.

The benefits of this systematic approach to PDP are:

- gaining greater understanding of how you are learning
- developing a clear view of what you are learning
- improves the skills of study and learning
- improves your ability to be reflective and act on those reflections

- improves your ability to self-diagnose problems in your learning
- gaining skill in setting appropriate goals
- increasing self-awareness of your personal strengths and weaknesses
- leads you towards being an independent learner
- lays the foundations for lifelong learning
- creates a positive 'can do' attitude
- ensures you have a set of learning skills appropriate for the workplace.

PDP is essentially a regular cycle of recording, reflection, planning and monitoring. In university you control the cycle and will need to initiate the required actions at appropriate times. After assignment feedback has been received is a good time to engage in a cycle of PDP. In the workplace the PDP cycle will be controlled by the work environment to a much greater extent; this is normally based on time periods, such as every six months, but can also be at the end of major projects.

One way to view PDP is as a set of steps:

- Stage 1: Understanding
- Stage 2: Developing
- Stage 3: Effectiveness.

These steps lead from understanding what is required in any given circumstance to developing the skills necessary for that circumstance to being an effective performer. The feedback you receive after an assignment is an objective record of your effectiveness. Scores and grades are brutal, but they indicate clearly how well you are able to perform the requirements of any assessment.

Each cycle of PDP should proceed through the following phases.

PHASE 1 – ASSESSMENT OF WHERE I AM NOW

Assess where you are now. Auditing your skills and abilities against a set of criteria can do this. Assignment feedback does this for a range of skills directly related to the assignment. But a wider range of skills (see Chapter 4) will have affected your performance. Eventually you must form a view on your ability in the skill areas related to completing assignments. You must be honest with yourself if you want to progress and improve your performance. A skills matrix (there is an activity to build one in the next chapter) may be a useful way to assess where you are now.

PHASE 2 – REFLECTING ON WHAT THIS MEANS

In the early stages of university the idea and practice of reflection is not an easy thing to grasp. We could think of reflection as: 'a calm, lengthy consideration leading to an expression of personal development'.

Why are we interested in reflection? There are several reasons for focusing on reflection. The completion of your course of study will probably mark the point where you return to the world of full-time work. Many professions regard reflective practice and reflective learning as a vital part of what is called continuing professional development (CPD). Recording your reflective thoughts on the assignment process could be the first entry in your CPD log or file. Reflective logs or diaries aim to trap the personal and emotive feelings of achievement and development. We reflect on our learning and development so that we can learn and develop better in the future. Recording your development throughout the assessment process may have many parallels for your learning at work.

Some universities will ask you to submit a reflective or learning log with your assignments. The following section will consider common ways to be reflective. Reflection records personal thoughts and emotions related to something, in our case assignments; these reflections are often kept in a diary or learning log. A learning diary or learning log is a simple document that records thoughts and emotions over time. Many people simply use a Word document or a paper diary. For some people the reflective account is like a melting pot where bits of emotions, knowledge, feelings, ideas, skills and awareness of things are placed. In the act of writing them there can be recognition of how learning has taken place. Committing thoughts and feelings to paper can make them clearer. Don't expect real reflection to be tidy and linear; it is more often messy and confusing. If you are asked to complete a reflective statement try to tidy up the mess before you submit it.

Let's imagine you are reflecting on the first time you carried out interviews for your project. You might well record your preparations, your anxiety and fears, how effective you thought you had been, what went wrong, what went right, what you would change for next time. Some of these entries may be as reflective questions, such as, 'Why did I do that? It was so stupid.' You might also enter what you thought the interviewee thought of your performance.

Some of the reflective areas that you might cover about the assessment process:

- your fears before starting
- how you decided on a project topic
- what you had to give up to do your course
- what you are still giving up
- the effect on your family
- the skills you started out with
- where you think your skills were weak
- the interaction with your subject tutors
- difficulties you encountered, family, work and university
- how you think you have developed

- career aspirations
- hopes for the outcome of assignments
- what you still feel you are weak on
- time allocation issues
- fears about writing large assignments
- fears about giving presentations.

Questions often encourage deeper reflection, and the following types of questions should help you reflect:

- How well did theory explain what happened?
- Has the nature of the assignment task affected how you reflect?
- What were your motives for doing this thing?
- What were the possible alternatives before you made this decision?
- How did you come to this decision?
- If you had been someone else, a friend maybe, how would you have done this differently?
- Is there another point of view that you could explore?
- Are there alternative interpretations to consider?
- Are others seeing this issue from different points of view that may be helpful for you to explore?
- Does this issue relate to other contexts – how would it relate to these contexts?
- How have your views on this changed over time?
- Do you notice that your feelings about something have changed over time – or in the course of writing?
- Are there ethical / moral / wider social issues that you would want to explore?

 STUDENT COMMENT

I'd been to a couple of seminars on personal development planning, and I liked the ideas and had tried to use them to get better organised and make more of my learning. What I was finding was that I did a lot of thinking about learning (reflection) but didn't change anything much.

It was only when my personal tutor asked to see my learning diary that it was highlighted. She said all the thinking I had done looked great and I had some great ideas, but if I didn't change anything all that reflective effort was wasted.

Reflection will take place randomly in your life. However, systematic reflection is far more useful in improving your grades. There will be points where reflection seems appropriate, such as when assignments are returned with grades and feedback. A more effective way to use reflection is to plan time to reflect every day. Just as there is a time in the day for action and getting things done, there should also be a time for deliberate and considered reflection. The end of the day is a very popular time to reflect on what has been learned today and what could be done differently tomorrow.

PHASE 3 – CHANGE

Reflection without change is daydreaming. Reflection is an important learning activity, but without some planned action nothing will change. So reflection on its own will not improve your grades or your learning. Change needs to be planned; so when you reflect, a good practice is to write down your reflections, but also plan actions at the point of reflecting. If you keep a learning diary for reflective thoughts you could add a column on the right-hand side for action so that reflections lead to change.

Change, even large change, is achieved with small actions. So when you reflect that something is not right or could be improved, investigate actions that will improve the situation. You will need to set objectives of what, how and when. One common way to control objectives is to adopt the SMART objectives idea; it is an acronym for:

- **S**pecific – objectives should specify what they want to achieve.
- **M**easurable – you should be able to measure whether you are meeting the objectives or not.
- **A**chievable – are the objectives achievable and attainable?
- **R**ealistic – can you realistically achieve the objectives with the resources you have?
- **T**ime – when do you want to achieve the objectives?

WHAT SORT OF OBJECTIVES MIGHT YOU SET?

Your reflective activity should have highlighted areas where you are not satisfied with your skills and abilities. These areas are likely to be focused on explicit skills or tacit skills. After you have completed a skills matrix you will have a very good idea of your weakest areas. The SMART objectives you set will be linked to one or more of these skills. Students in a tutorial class expressed their areas for improvement as:

- be better with computers
- read faster
- concentrate more
- get a focus
- spend more time on study and less shopping
- drink less

- do less sport
- plan so that I have enough time to complete assignments well before the deadline
- attend lectures more often
- enjoy things more
- be more critical.

Which ones of the above points are SMART objectives? You guessed it – none of them. But nearly all of them could be turned into SMART objectives and usefully improve performance. Let's just look at the first one: 'be better with computers'. This could become:

- complete the online Word course at MS.com
- score better than 16/20 on the final test
- this should be possible
- this won't cost any money and I have time between assignments to do it
- complete this by next Tuesday.

Remember: without change your reflection is wasted, so try to reflect in ways that lead naturally to actions. PDP is also about keeping a detailed record of your achievements, reflections, failures and development, so devise a method to record all these things. This will often be computer-based, but may also include hard-copy elements. The following types of document are all suitable for inclusion in your PDP profile:

- details about you
- notes about your learning and the modules you attend
- personal assessments such as preferred learning style and personality type
- completed assignment and projects
- practical and portfolio evidence
- details about any study group you attend
- skills you have acquired in the workplace
- your skills matrix
- SMART objectives for improvement tasks
- questionnaires
- semester planners and timetables
- details of your meetings with your personal tutor
- academic and/or personal problems you may have encountered
- your academic targets
- personal records of your progress in course units
- exam results and other achievements
- your career goals.

3.9 KEEPING TRACK OF YOUR LEARNING

Keeping track of your learning both at university and at work is important and you will need to develop a system that suits you. There are several possible ways to do this:

- simple paper diary
- a Word document
- binder of OneNote software
- a spreadsheet
- a database
- MY PDP or other online repositories.

A simple paper diary will suit some people because it is cheap, easy to use and not easy to lose. You would make entries into the diary by simply writing; often the entries are made in chronological order day by day as you reflect about each day. As you go through university you will fill a lot of diary books. There are drawbacks to using a paper system in that the data in them cannot easily be transferred and you cannot easily sort and find entries.

You can transfer a simple paper system to a Word document and this will allow an extensive set of entries to be compiled using no physical space. It is also easily transferred and has some limited searching ability.

What sort of entries would you make in such a system?

- personal details and preferences
- daily reflective notes
- after action reviews
- learning progress files (detailing progress towards larger goals)
- thoughts and feelings
- descriptions of events and activities
- meeting notes
- lecture notes
- bibliography and reading lists
- skills checklist
- PDP entries
- development activities or plans
- assignment and examination feedback and reviews.

It is always a good idea to start simply and then build the complexity that you require into the system. The more technical storage methods of spreadsheets and databases will be featured in the later chapters. Once you start a system and experience the benefits of structured recording of all your learning, you are very likely to extend it beyond the list above.

One final point: if you haven't started a learning diary yet, DO IT NOW!

LEARNING

Vardo is an overseas student who started her studies in September; it is now March and she is in semester two of year one. She is exceptionally hardworking and attends every lecture and tutorial. She studies every evening and most weekends. She doesn't have to work as her father gives her a generous allowance, although it makes her feel guilty and puts pressure on her to succeed. She lives on campus and is well liked although she is not part of any study group, preferring to study alone. Vardo speaks and writes excellent English – better than most of the other students.

Vardo likes to study and reads and rereads her notes all the time. She is friendly with all the lecturers and is well liked by them. When it comes to assignments and exams she puts in a tremendous amount of effort. She really, really wants a first-class degree as she wants to work for a global top 100 company. But, her grades thus far have been really disappointing, always in the range of 41% to 49%; she doesn't understand how this can be so. She is not too worried because the first-year grades will not count towards the class of degree she is awarded. However, she is a little worried about the future because she has to start performing better.

When she gets feedback on her work she often finds it very difficult to understand what the tutors are telling her to do. She sometimes thinks, 'Why don't they just tell me what they want?' She also finds the feedback to be very personal and does not like to be criticised in that manner; now she has stopped reading them because they are just too painful. She is so busy she does not stop to think about the university experience, but she does like being here.

Case study questions:

- Is Vardo bright enough to be at university?
- What do you think is causing her to achieve low grades?
- What needs to be done to improve?
- Set out a SMART action plan for Vardo to follow so that her grades improve.

SUMMARY

The level of learning and the amount of skill you can employ will determine your success at university and work. This chapter has investigated aspects of learning and skills.

- Understand the difference between learning and skills:
  - Learning is the process of acquiring knowledge and the process of change.
  - A skill is the explicit execution of an activity.

- Understanding your preferred learning style should make learning easier and more enjoyable:
  - visual learners
  - auditory learners
  - kinaesthetic learners.

- Active learning at university will maximise the learning you get from the time you spend studying. Active learning can be applied to:
  - reading
  - writing

- – talking
- – listening.

- Work-based learning is characterised by:
  - – very little formal learning
  - – many tasks to be completed – a large workload
  - – workplace stress and a culture of immediacy
  - – performance driven – quality outcomes
  - – practical problems needing fast, practical solutions
  - – solutions to problems that must fit within the strategic intentions of the organisation.

- The Kolb Learning Cycle is one way to think about and analyse workplace learning. It consists of a cycle of activities:
  - – concrete experience
  - – reflective observation
  - – abstract conceptualisation
  - – active experimentation.

- Understand and embrace the university culture relating to:
  - – teaching and learning
  - – university lecturers
  - – e-learning
  - – independent study
  - – researching
  - – time management
  - – teamworking
  - – reflection.

- Lifelong learners tend to display the following skills:
  - – organising and planning their own learning
  - – reflective assessment of their current skills state
  - – are active learners
  - – skilled at learning from formal settings
  - – skilled at learning from informal approaches and particularly experiential learning
  - – are able to learn from peers, coaches, mentors and colleagues
  - – integrative thinkers (draw knowledge from various sources to use practically)
  - – understand and use different learning styles and strategies (be adaptable)
  - – are good researchers and information-gatherers
  - – have structured ways to 'trap' learning.

- Personal development planning is based on reflective practices and is an important development process in professional working environments.

- Develop a system to keep track of your learning:
  - – a paper diary
  - – Word document
  - – OneNote diary.

EXPLORE FURTHER

FURTHER READING

Boud, D., Keogh, R. and Walker, D. (1985) *Reflection: Turning experience into learning*. London: Kogan Page.

Kolb, D.A. (1984) *Experiential Learning: Experience as a source of learning and development*. Upper Saddle River, NJ: Prentice Hall.

Moon, J. (1999) *Reflection in Learning and Professional Development Theory and Practice*. London: Kogan Page.

Schon, D. (1991) *The Reflective Practitioner: How professionals think in action*. London: Avebury.

WEB LINKS

Test that determines your learning style: http://www.usd.edu/trio/tut/ts/style.html

CHAPTER 4

What are the Key Skills of University Life and the Workplace?

What skills will I develop in this chapter?

- academic skills
- key skills
- life skills
- graduate skills
- workplace survival skills
- skills for dealing with stress

4.1 INTRODUCTION

As we have seen in Chapter 3, the key to success is learning and skills. This chapter looks at the skills you need to develop to be successful at university and in the workplace. There is no agreed list of these skills, so this chapter represents my version and interpretation of the skills needed to be successful.

It is arguable that the skills groups can be represented in four ways. The skills you are likely to require first are academic skills. Success at university also requires a set of less focused skills, often called transferable skills. These are now more often known as key skills. University is not solely about studying – there is a set of skills known as life skills. Finally, as you move towards the world of work, you might be interested in graduate skills. There is also a section on stress and how to use it to your advantage.

The skills you can bring to bear in any given circumstance will determine the success you achieve. So, skills are important! Following on from this point I would advise that you work your way through this chapter systematically, carrying out the activities as you proceed.

4.2 ACADEMIC SKILLS

We could define academic skills as 'the skills that are assessed in university assessments'. The following are the key academic skills that will be tested in your assignments and examinations. The skills of critique, analysis and evaluation are often called the higher-level skills and these are tested more in years 2 and 3 of your degrees. However, it is worth concentrating on developing these skills as soon as you start to complete level 1 assignments.

KNOWLEDGE

There is no simple and agreed meaning to the word knowledge. Philosophy has debated the meaning for centuries. A working definition for the purposes of an assignment or examination will probably focus on the following aspects:

- the state of knowing something
- familiarity, awareness or understanding gained through experience or study
- specific information about something
- acquaintance with facts relating to a topic.

The probable types of knowledge that you will need to display are:

- facts
- theory, concepts, models, typologies
- research data
- approaches to problem-solving
- approaches to data-handling and representation
- benchmark and best practice approaches to standard institutional problems.

UNDERSTANDING

Rather like knowledge, understanding is a concept that is hard to tie down; most people can recognise it when they see it. But, what is it and how can you demonstrate it in your university assessments? Understanding might be considered to be the ability to think and act flexibly with what one knows. Clearly, this will require 'knowing' something, which is where the previous section comes in useful, but how can we demonstrate understanding?

Using our definition above, 'the ability to think and act flexibly with what one knows' would lead us to at least the following three ways of demonstrating understanding:

Offering explanations – People display understanding of things by offering explanations. This involves highlighting critical features of a theory or idea, such as explaining someone's enthusiasm for doing a task by offering the explanation of his or her desire for the reward that is offered by completing the task. This displays a rudimentary understanding of expectancy theory.

Displaying relational knowledge – People express understanding in explanations constructed of relational knowledge. This is a complex web of cause and effect explanation, whereas sparse explanation only involving one simple rule would suggest a sketchy understanding of an idea or theory. The example above would therefore need extension to display multiple motivations and theories.

Displaying a revisable and extensible explanation – People demonstrate understanding by revising and extending their explanations. Thus, explanations need to be both highly extensible and revisable in fundamental ways. If it were not, we would see limitations to the level of understanding.

ANALYSIS

What is analysis and how can I demonstrate the skill of analysis in my university work? This section will explore analysis, but it is connected to two other sections. First, it is almost impossible to demonstrate analysis without having an understanding of the relevant knowledge of the area you are analysing, so this section is closely connected to sections related to knowledge and understanding. Second, analysis on its own will not guarantee that your assignments and examinations will be awarded good grades; analysis needs to be connected to critique in order to create a skill and approach called critical analysis. However, it is easier to explain the two skills in separate sections, so this section will explore analysis and the following section will explore critique.

STUDENT COMMENT

My tutor says, 'Be more critical! More analysis needed!' That is what he always says about my assignments. But, I really don't know what he means.

I work really hard on my assignments and put in lots of work, but it is always the same comment. My grade is always around 55–60%. I want higher grades!

I don't know what to do now!

Definitions of analysis tend to focus on these types of approach:

- the study of the constituent parts and the interrelationship of the parts
- the breaking down and separation of the whole into constituent parts
- simplifying the whole into parts to display the logical structure
- an explanation of a process and the parts of that process.

If we explore these approaches in more detail and connect them more directly to business assignments, they may be more useful in guiding us towards greater levels of analysis.

The study of the constituent parts and the interrelationship of the parts, and the breaking down and separation of the whole into constituent parts

An assignment looking at reward management might reasonably need to investigate the constituent parts of reward management. In business analysis there is a need to use theory, ideas, models or typologies to carry out analysis. How can we look at the constituent parts of reward management using theory? Perhaps the simplest theory to demonstrate the approach would be to consider reward as being made up of **extrinsic rewards** and **intrinsic rewards** (Sansone and Harackiewicz 2000). Using this theory immediately separates reward into two parts and allows further analysis of those parts and the relationship between the parts. The analysis might then progress by looking in more detail at the nature of extrinsic rewards using the ideas of Mahaney and Lederer (2006) to analyse the practical use of extrinsic rewards in the success of information system projects and the relationship between intrinsic and extrinsic rewards.

Simplifying the whole into parts to display the logical structure

Reducing a thing, idea or concept to smaller and simpler parts will often be an effective form of analysis. Workplace attendance is a complicated organisational problem; it is possible to use a theoretical model to simplify the main phenomenon into parts that are easier to understand. Steers and Rhodes (1978) present such a model that separates institutional issues from cognitive personal issues; using this model would allow for a more effective analysis of absence management.

An explanation of a process and the parts of that process

Explaining a process and separating out the parts of that process is another slightly different form of analysis. In business and organisational studies 'change' is often the subject of assignments. Descriptive explanation of the change process will take the analysis only so far; introducing a model of the change process and analysing the change against the model will reveal more about the nature and extent of the change. Kotter (1996) proposes an eight-step change model for managing change in organisations; by comparing the subject of an assignment to the change model it is possible to analyse the changes. Closer inspection of the various parts of the change process will lead to further analysis.

 TUTOR COMMENT

Students still find the two skills of analysis and evaluation the most difficult to grasp, develop and then display.

They try to develop them as they proceed with their assignments, and this approach partially works. I think a better and more effective approach would be to do specific reading, and practise these skills, or attend one of the

university courses on critical thinking and evaluation.

It is these two skills and a student's ability to display them that predominantly determine the grade they will receive for their assignments.

The basic skills courses run for students never give enough attention to this important area.

CRITIQUE

Critique is the term given to the process of estimating the quality of something; strictly defined, it is the critical examination of something. In this chapter I have chosen to consider critique and evaluation as two separate sections. The critique element is the close examination of theory, research, writing, ideas and models; and evaluation is the judgement of the worth of those things. This is covered in a later section. In explaining these two skills it is helpful to keep them separate, and as you judge work it is worth considering the process as having these two separate parts. The review of the sources and evidence you use in your assignments and examinations will first involve critique – the close and critical examination of something – and then an evaluative judgement of the worth will be made.

Critique is a very important aspect of academic writing because your own claims and argument will be built on the sources that you use. The aim in using critique is to select the strong elements of sources and discard the weak elements.

What is the process of critique when used for theory or journal sources?

First, you will need to paraphrase the ideas contained in the work. Paraphrasing is a type of summary that extracts and presents the key elements of the writing. What is the key idea or focus of the writing? What component elements does the writing contain? Strictly, this is termed critical analysis. Next, set out the strengths and weaknesses of the writing – for this section use other writers' scholarly thoughts; these can be found in textbooks and in journal articles. Most writing that contains theory, research or ideas will be making a claim or a series of claims. How well are those claims supported by evidence? When a series of claims is being made, look for the evidence to support each separate claim; you are ultimately trying to assess the support for each claim. Unsupported claims should be exposed and disregarded. Also, consider if the argument is balanced. Does it present counterevidence or only the evidence that supports the argument? In the final section of the critique draw together the assessments and report the findings. Try to use a reporting style, such as, 'Ford argues that so and so is true, and provides some evidence of this, but there are some weakly supported statements, …'

CHECKLIST FOR CRITIQUE

- Paraphrase the theory, article or research.
- Draw out the main claim or claims.
- Consider the argument that builds towards the claims.
- Is a balanced argument or counterargument presented?
- Review the evidence for each of the claims.
- Bring the thoughts of other scholarly work to bear on the theory, article or research.
- Report the findings of your critique.

Chapter 10 looks at critical writing.

SYNTHESIS AND CREATIVITY

Synthesis can be regarded as the skill of bringing separate components together to form something new. In assignments and examinations one of the first and most frequently occurring syntheses is the bringing together of theories to form explanations about the subject of the assignment. Most 'new' ideas and solutions in business and management occur by combining existing ideas into new explanatory frameworks or ways of working. Branding as a concept, and as an idea, was developed by marketing academics and practitioners into a discipline we now call brand management; recently this concept has been applied to employers and we now have the developing area of employer brand management.

When selecting theory to explain your assessments it would be very rare if two independent researchers chose the same theoretical ideas to explain a phenomenon that was being studied. It is this diversity of theoretical approach that allows for new insights into well-studied areas. In business and management, theories are often drawn from social science disciplines, such as sociology and psychology. A well-studied area of business and management is the working experience of women managers, where narrative study has been combined with Jungian archetypes to investigate the role models guiding female managers (Olsson 2000). This presents a synthesis of theory to offer new insight into the experiences of women managers.

Synthesis is also commonly required in academic work where the combination of well-used ideas and approaches is brought together to offer new solutions. Synthesis can also occur using new combinations of tried and tested theory applied to new organisational contexts. Creativity is often linked with synthesis; indeed it might be argued that synthesis is a type of creativity, but for the purposes of assignments a working definition might be: 'the ability to bring into existence a new idea or insight'.

University assessments and workplace problems will provide endless opportunity for creativity, but the skill is most frequently displayed in final year assignments and projects. The insights from analysing data in your project will almost always present – bring into existence – new ways of looking at a problem. The recommendation sections of assignments and projects will be a place for creativity, but it is important that this creativity is grounded in the theory and research. Recommendations that appear from nowhere are open to criticism. However, strong creative ideas for dealing with your assessment problem will tend to achieve terrific grades.

EVALUATION

What is evaluation? How can I display evaluation skills in my university assessments? These are two of the essential questions that this section aims to answer.

Evaluation is the process of judging the worth of something. We make judgements all the time, every day. In the average day you will make judgements about all sorts of things: breakfast, football matches, handbags, lectures, people, articles, other people's work, our own work and lots more. If we make judgements (evaluate) all the time, then why is it so difficult to be evaluative in our academic work?

REFLECTIVE PERFORMING

MAKING JUDGEMENTS

Do you find it easy to make judgements about everyday things, such as driving behaviour, quality of dinner, someone's clothes, or a magazine article?

Assuming you answered yes or maybe to the above statement, reflect on how those judgements are made. What knowledge or experience do we use to make those judgements?

Could judging academic matters be as easy as making the judgements above?

In the majority of our everyday judgements we bring considerable experience to bear on the judgements we make. We have probably eaten hundreds of sandwiches in our life and we have formed a view on what makes a good sandwich. Judging the value of academic theory, research or methods is not quite so easy because we have much less experience of these things. One way to judge these academic things would be to compare them to a template or set of criteria. Mostly in these academic judgements no such template or set of criteria exists, so making evaluations will rely on more creative approaches.

One of the best approaches to evaluating theory and method is to allow other scholars to make the judgement. Using this method would require finding journal or textbook writing that critiques theory or method. There are normally some well-reported and well-developed critiques of most management theory, and this can be used to evaluate theory and journal sources in assignments. An example of academic criticism that can be used to evaluate the theory is shown below.

Academic theory can also be evaluated by how often and how successfully the theory has been used to explain research or to explain practical actions in organisations. By this method we will judge the most often used theory to be better than the less used theory. This approach can be problematic in that on some occasions inappropriate theory is used to explain action. If this inappropriate theory is used frequently we might assess it as good theory when in fact it is poor theory used frequently. This offers one further approach to evaluation in judging how well a theory can explain action; good theory tends to have more explanatory power than weak theory. This is often judged by the areas of action that cannot be explained by the chosen theory. If a theory explains most actions and events then it may be judged as useful; if it has very little explanatory power it can be judged as less useful.

EXAMPLE: EVALUATING THEORY

Herzberg's theory of motivation is often used to explain both motivation and reward management. But, just how effective is this theory in explaining motivation and reward?

Tietjen, M. and Myers, R. (1998) Motivation and job satisfaction. *Management Decision*. Vol 36, No 4. pp226–31.

This article outlines a number of major criticisms of Herzberg's theory of motivation by Locke (1976):

'Herzberg's view of man's nature implies a split between the psychological and biological processes of the human make-up. The two are of dual nature and function apart, not related to one another. On the contrary, Locke proposes that the mind and body are very closely related. It is through the mind that the human discovers the nature of his/her physical and psychological needs and how they may be satisfied. Locke suggests the proof that the basic need for survival, a biological need, is only reached through the use of the mind.

'With regard to Herzberg's correlation between hygienes, motivators, physical and psychological needs, it can be inferred that the first set are unidirectional, so too are physical and psychological needs. Locke notes there is no justification for this conclusion. Providing the example of the physical need, hunger, he writes that acts like eating can serve not only as aversions of hunger pangs, but also as pleasures for the body.

'The third criticism which pertains directly to the previous two, is simply the lack of a parallel relationship between the two groupings of factors and needs. Their relation is hazy and overlapping in several instances. A new company policy (hygiene) may have a significant effect on a worker's interest in the work itself or his/her success with it. The correlation lacks a clear line of distinction.'

In assessments it is important to evaluate the usefulness of the sources used to guide and support your argument. All theory will have strengths and weaknesses; these need to be explored and a final evaluative judgement made about each element of theory. Journal sources can be judged on a number of factors:

- How objective has the author been?
- What is the major claim of the article?
- How persuasive has the argument been?
- What evidence has been used to support the argument?
- What is the rank of the journal in which the article is published?
- Does the evidence presented support the major claim?

4.3 KEY SKILLS

INTEGRATED SKILLS

Universities communicate the skills and the performance of those skills using an assessment criteria grid. You may notice from the example that there are some required skills that do not have a criteria row in the assessment grids. One such skill is critique. This is a skill vital to successful assessments, is often not specified by a row descriptor, but can be found in some of the column descriptors. This is because critique is what is described as an integrated skill. This means critique is required in all parts of assessments. In the following sections, each of the major integrated skills will be considered and critique will be included in that discussion.

Another integrated skill is the ability to research widely and find appropriate sources. This skill will often not have a row descriptor, but may well feature in the column descriptors.

Logic is the skill of connecting ideas in ways that make sense to other people.

Argument is the skill of making a statement in a logical way and supporting those statements with evidence. Assessments that have weak arguments normally receive poor grades. Workplace reports that have weak arguments often do not progress to the implementation stage. Chapters 7, 10 and 11 develop ideas and approaches that will allow you to build strong, convincing arguments.

LEARNING DIARY ENTRY

I have just come back from the strangest seminar ever where the tutor asked us all what skills we thought we were good at and what skills we thought we were not good at. How should I know? How would I tell? Most of the rest of the class were fairly confused.

I got the message that the assignments should display skills and these would be marked.

But how would I know what skills I needed? The tutor did say we had been given a thing called an assessment criteria grid, but I don't remember that.

I have just had a look and indeed we were given a grid thing with a range of skills down the left-hand side. But I still have no idea what these things are! Still, it seems that these skills are really important so I had better do some work on them.

On the web I found lots of help with study skills. Not quite what I wanted in terms of the assignments but quite useful. I am going to have to find a way to develop these areas, so I think for the next five weeks I will concentrate on:

- Next week – knowledge and understanding
- Week 2 – analysis
- Week 3 – critique
- Week 4 – synthesis
- Week 5 – evaluation.

I will see how much I have progressed after this and maybe develop some other ideas to improve in this area. I suppose I could ask one of the second year students what they thought about all this.

Example of Level 3 outsourcing assessment criteria grid

Criteria	Weighting	70%	60–69%	50–59%	40–49%	Fail
Generic skill Independence in learning; critical and analytical rigour	10	Evidence of wide research using imaginative range of sources Critical understanding and degree of independence in thought	Evidence of wide research but more limited in range Some evidence of independence of thought Able to evaluate contrasting views	Evidence of research from prescribed texts and sources Limited evidence of independence of thought Able to present different viewpoints	Some familiarity with prescribed literature Little evidence of independence of thought May present different but not balanced views	Little reference to literature No apparent independence of thought Limited viewpoints explored
Knowledge and understanding	20	Thorough understanding of key concepts and underpinning theory through extensive and well-balanced research findings	Demonstrates a clear understanding of the development of outsourcing and key concepts underpinning through solid secondary research	Demonstrates some understanding of the way that outsourcing has developed and the underpinning issues for organisations	Demonstrates some understanding but limited view and underpinning of concepts weak	Little understanding demonstrated
Analysis	40	Excellent analysis of the advantages and disadvantages of outsourcing with ability to integrate a wide range of secondary data and company examples	A thorough insight into some of the advantages and disadvantages of outsourcing using a range of secondary data and company examples	Some analysis evident but tendency to describe with few company examples to support	Presents a partial view which is largely descriptive with limited company examples as evidence	No attempt to go beyond description of limited range of issues No reference to company examples to illustrate
Evaluation	20	Balanced and comprehensive approach to issues for consideration with excellent focus on HRM and high level of critical evaluation	Addresses some key implications for HRM with a solid level of critical evaluation	Considers some implications of outsourcing for HRM but limited evaluation	Limited consideration of key issues and not all related to HRM Minimal evaluation evident	Fails to address all parts of question set Incoherent and limited evaluation
Assignment parameters	10	Brief met fully Within word count Clearly written and presented Professional style, structure and referencing Excellent use of appendices to support the report	Within word count Meets brief fully Clearly written and presented Logical structure and good attempt to reference material Good use of appendices to support the report	Sometimes writing style and structure unclear Referencing sometimes incomplete Appendices generally used appropriately	Poor structure and presentation Problems with writing style Sources not fully referenced Overuse of appendices	Brief not fully met Far too long or too short Unclear structure and poor presentation Inappropriate referencing and use of appendices

STUDY SKILLS

Successful assessments that deliver terrific grades will need another set of skills that we call study skills. These skills are seldom assessed directly but they will make a big difference to the grade your work is awarded. They will be discussed and developed throughout this book in various chapters. If you develop your general study skills it will benefit all parts of your university and work life. The general study skills are:

- communicating
- planning and organising
- skills with IT, Word, Excel and the Internet
- time management and prioritising
- psychological coping strategies
- understanding and recording information
- self-evaluation and self-reflection
- working in teams and groups
- managing relationships
- using libraries and information sources
- relationship-building.

4.4 LIFE SKILLS

The World Health Organization defines life skills as 'abilities for adaptive and positive behaviour that enable individuals to deal effectively with the demands and challenges of life'. If we invent a new category of skills called 'work skills' they might be very similar to life skills. Work and life are so inextricably linked that where one ends and the other begins is often difficult to determine. This is especially so for managers, where the main work of managing is thinking and relationship management. You will have collected a lot of life skills from the experience you have already gained from life, school and work, but as with any skill, improvement comes from reflection, improvement and practice. Taking a conscious and reflective stance on the skills you currently have and the skills you need to be successful will help you to improve all aspects of your life.

Like many areas of this chapter I find myself saying there is no agreed list of life skills. The life skills you need depend on the life you lead. The following list represents my analysis of the required life skills for people studying at university or engaged in work.

SKILLS RELATED TO YOU FUNCTIONING IN THE WORLD — SELF SKILLS

- skills to develop self-awareness and self-knowledge that allow you to understand yourself and how you interact with the world

- skills for increasing your control of events around you
- self-esteem/confidence-building skills
- self-awareness skills, including awareness of your own strengths and weaknesses
- skills to set and achieve personal goals
- skills for managing feelings:
  - frustration and anger
  - dealing with anxiety
  - coping skills for the unexpected, loss and grief
- skills for managing personal and workplace stress
- skills for controlling your personal use of time
- skills for creating balance in your life.

DAILY FUNCTIONING SKILLS

- Be able to assess what is happening around you and make accurate and rational decisions relating to what you observe.
- Understand the basic principles of a healthy life: food, cleanliness, alcohol, drugs, physical exercise, sleep.
- Understand how your own actions lead to outcomes and being able to cope with the consequences.
- Be able to travel and navigate around the world with efficiency and safety.
- Be able to budget and manage money.
- Have empathy skills: the ability to listen and understand other people's needs and circumstances and express that understanding.
- Have the ability to make decisions about involvement in projects and activities and be able to refuse to be involved.

RELATIONSHIP SKILLS

- Have the ability to co-operate and be part of a team.
- Express respect for other people's contributions and styles of functioning.
- Assess your own ability and aptitude for contributing to groups and teams.
- Be able to network and build relationships.
- Be able to argue and persuade.
- Have advocacy skills to argue on behalf of others.
- Have personal and team motivation skills.
- Be reflective, thoughtful and informed.
- Be kind and compassionate but also positively challenging.

COMMUNICATION SKILLS

- Read accurately, reflectively and actively.
- Understand the basics of communicating with stories.
- Be able to listen actively and supportively.
- Have writing skills to construct sound and convincing arguments.
- Have speaking and presenting skills so that you are listened to and understood.
- Understand the basics of verbal and non-verbal communication.
- Be able to express feelings without blaming.
- Giving and receiving feedback.
- Convey assertiveness without arrogance.
- Be able to say NO!

REFLECTIVE PERFORMING

RELATIONSHIP QUIZ

Read each of the following statements and record if the statement:

Is very like me
Like me
Unlike me
Very unlike me

Remember there are no right and wrong answers and it is important your response represents your true feelings.

	Statement	Is very like me	Like me	Unlike me	Very unlike me	Score
1	I am in control of whether my relationships work out well or not					
2	I can accept other people's views without judging them					
3	I am a good listener					
4	To allow relationships to develop I am happy to reveal private things about me					
5	If I have an issue with someone or something I always get clear in my mind what I want to achieve before discussing it					
6	When I feel something is unfair I always try to discuss it with the other person					
7	In my close relationships I give as much as I receive					
8	I am aware of what I need from a relationship and I am prepared to say so					

9	If someone isn't listening to me I let them know I am unhappy about it.					
10	When I am working with others I feel I am their equal and my views are as valid as theirs					
11	In relationships I am not competitive but I am collaborative					
12	I am aware of what other people in a relationship need and want					
13	I am reflective about relationships and spend time thinking about how to make them work					
14	When I argue with people it is important to me that they feel the outcome is fair					
15	When planning what we do in relationships I like each person to feel they had an equal say					
16	Relationships where one person has more power than the other do not work					
17	I like to negotiate any changes in the relationship					
18	My relationship needs can only be meet by having a range of fulfilling relationships					
19	I find having one very 'full on' relationship is not effective					
20	I am empathetic to the needs of others in relationships					
21	I need to respect myself before I can respect other people					
22	I can't function in relationships where there is no mutual respect					
23	In close relationships I like to think of myself in there shoes					
24	When relationships go wrong I spend time and energy to put them right					
25	If my expectations of a relationship are unrealistically high it spoils the relationship					
	Total Score					

Feedback

Score 4 for every 'Is very like me' statement
Score 3 for every 'Like me' statement
Score 2 for every 'Unlike me' statement
Score 1 for every 'Very unlike me' statement

Add up your total score it is a percentage %

If you scored 25 – 50 % you are in the RED light zone and need to reflect on relationships and develop this area

If you scored 50 – 75% you are in the AMBER light zone and while aspects of your relationship skills are good there is scope for improvement.

If you scored 75% plus you are in the GREEN light zone and have good relationship skills but keep working on them so that your skills maintain their high standard.

PROBLEM-SOLVING SKILLS

- Recognise symptoms and the root causes of problems.
- Listen to and appreciate the problems of others.
- Understand how to use experience and/or theory to solve problems.
- Use math and scenario skills to solve problems and develop solutions.
- Be creative in the analysis and solution of problems.
- Recognise barriers to solutions and how to remove or navigate around them.
- Be proactive and confident about being able to solve problems.
- Be able to prioritise problems.
- Be able to create cost-effective solutions.
- Use planning to solve larger and phased problems.

CRITICAL THINKING SKILLS

- Have skills in researching and gathering information and ideas.
- Understand the role of theory and research.
- Have skills in breaking down an argument into its component parts.
- Be able to assess the evidence for claims made by others.
- Have skills in assessing the strength and logic of a proposal or argument.
- Be able to evaluate the future consequences of actions.
- Analyse influences and drivers of situations.
- Be able to reconcile competing claims on resources.
- Recognise flaws in approaches and arguments.

MANAGER COMMENT

I run a number of high-performance teams, 12 teams to be exact. From experience I have learned that if my team members do not have good life skills they are very little use in the pressurised setting of high-performance teams.

To this end I have invented a life skills training module that coaches each participant through the essential life skills. It is a two-day residential training unit that covers:

- discover yourself
- organising
- networking
- empathy and managing feelings
- understanding performance
- inspiration and creativity
- stress-coping strategies
- work–life balance
- being agile for change.

I treat this training module like a driving test; if my potential team members do not pass the module with 80+%, then I do not use them in high-performance teams. If they don't pass, they can try again after six months. It is interesting that of those that do not pass and try again, they all pass. I think sometimes they do not take the idea of life skills all that seriously, but I do!

4.5 GRADUATE SKILLS AND THE WORKPLACE

Graduate skills are generic and every graduate is expected to have them whether they studied zoology or business. A synthesis of what has been said by employers about the skills required by graduates reveals the following themes:

- getting up in the morning
- punctuality
- time management
- communication
- personal cleanliness and presentation
- writing skills
- soft skills in general (people skills)
- empathy
- teamworking
- listening skills
- personal planning and organising
- thinking
- presenting skills
- basic manners and consideration
- IT skills
- ethical behaviour
- negotiation skills
- basic finance skills.

The Association of Graduate Recruiters is an organisation that represents the views of graduate recruiting companies in the UK. They can therefore be expected to represent what employers are looking for in graduates. They regularly survey their member organisations, and the following is what employers regard as the most important graduate skills displayed at interview.

Motivation and enthusiasm – Employers want to select the best people but also those that have made positive decisions to work for the company. You need to be able to present a coherent logic about why you want to work for the organisation.

Teamworking – All graduate jobs, indeed all jobs, will require a certain amount of teamwork. These could be multi-disciplinary in nature or project teams. Employers look for evidence of successful teamworking.

Communication – Being able to communicate successfully in writing, on the phone, face to face and in presentations is a vital skill of business. Being able to influence others and to play the role of advocate is a vital and expected skill of graduates. Another area looked at by potential employers is evidence that you can negotiate effectively.

Flexibility and adaptability – The world of work is changing all the time, and employers want workers who are comfortable responding to change and are flexible enough to change direction quickly. You should be able to demonstrate that you can multi-task, and are adaptable to doing different things.

Being proactive and taking the initiative – Graduate recruiters expect those with degrees to be self-starters with planning and organising skills. They will also be looking for those that can take the initiative and get things done.

Personal development – Modern business is about being able to learn and develop from workplace experience. Recruiters will be interested in what you know but also in what you can do with what you know. Recruiters will favour those that can demonstrate a solid grounding in improvement through systematic learning. A well-developed learning log covering your time at university is good evidence of you being a reflective learner.

LEARNING DIARY

GRADUATE ASSESSMENT CENTRE

Short note for my diary – type: reflection on experience.

I went to my first graduate assessment centre today and the whole thing was a nightmare. It was in London at a company that makes textiles; they have the motto, 'make money and have fun'. That motto attracted me to them but I certainly didn't have fun.

I couldn't sleep so I was up all night. I had to go into London on the train and the trains were all late, so I only got to the centre with seconds to spare, I think I was actually late. When I got there I was flustered and actually shaking. Then I was always 'behind the game' all day, nothing went right and I was really upset and embarrassed by my performance. Nightmare!

I am not going to get this graduate place but I will do things very differently next time:

- Get a good night's sleep.
- Travel much, much earlier.
- De-stress before I start the centre.
- Practise some of the activities before I go.
- Learn more about the company before I go.

I might then stand a chance of enjoying it. I'll add some more structured development ideas to this later. I just wanted to write about my terrible day to get it out of my system.

WORKPLACE SURVIVAL SKILLS

In a study of 5,000 participants Talent Q discovered that employers thought new graduates lacked workplace survival skills. They also found that new graduates had unrealistically high expectations of their new jobs and employers.

When graduates were compared with the workforce as a whole, they fall down hardest in the following areas:

- resilience, for example, in handling criticism and setbacks
- confidence, in group situations and with senior managers

- communicating with colleagues, suppliers and customers
- the power to persuade and the ability to influence decisions
- taking things in their stride and being calm and relaxed.

REFLECTIVE PERFORMING

MY SKILLS

This chapter has looked at skills in a range of ways. On occasions you may have noticed some considerable overlap in the skills in each section. This activity is designed to synthesise and analyse the skills you will need for university and the workplace.

The first part of the exercise involves you reflecting on how the different skills might overlap. We have looked at skills under the following headings:

- academic skills
- key skills/study skills
- life skills
- graduate skills
- workplace survival skills.

Create a table with these views of skills at the top as column headings. Then list the skills in rows on the left. Where the skill is represented in a view, place an 'X'. Leave one extra column on the right. Include all the skills that you think are required, not just those listed. You will need to judge if a skill should be in a view and if so place an 'X' in that box.

The example below should get you started.

Skill/View	Academic Skills	Key Skills	Life Skills	Graduate Skills	Workplace Survival Skills	My Skill Level
Knowledge	X					
Critical analysis	X	X	X	X		
Evaluation	X		X	X		
Proactivity		X	X	X		
Organising		X	X	X		
Influencing						

Carry on to complete the table for all the skills mentioned here and any others that you think would be important in any given area. When the table is complete, carry on and complete the next section.

You will now have an extensive table of the skills you will need in various situations. The task in this section is to evaluate your current skill level for each skill. So, for instance, in the knowledge row you may feel that you know something about the academic knowledge related to business but not all that much, so you might give yourself a score of 4 out of 10. You may feel you are a very proactive person and give yourself a score of 8.5 for this skill. Carry on evaluating your skills until the table is complete. Print out the table and date it and add it to your learning diary or portfolio. You might feel you are very poor at influencing others and give yourself a score of 1.

What you have produced is a skills matrix for the general area of university and work. You could develop this further by:

- carrying out the evaluation every three months or so

- creating development plans to improve some of the skills where your evaluation is low.

4.6 STRESS AND HOW TO USE IT TO YOUR ADVANTAGE

It is important to realise that stress is a normal part of being alive. Stress can be good in that it can help to motivate you, help you to be more productive, and provide feelings of satisfaction when you have conquered a stressful situation. However, too much stress is harmful and you must be able to recognise the early symptoms and take remedial action. What is too much stress varies greatly between people, so one person's healthy stress level is another person's health hazard. Persistent high stress levels can lead to health problems such as heart disease, depression and leave you prone to infections. Prolonged stress will lead to inappropriate changes in behaviour and unhealthy behaviours such as withdrawing strategies, blaming, irritability, overeating or overuse of alcohol.

We could define stress as any situation that makes you uneasy, frustrated, angry or overly anxious. In practice we tend to call these feelings things such as being uptight, tense, having the jitters, panicky and hyped.

The first things you may notice about being stressed and anxious are some of the symptoms:

- twitching or trembling
- muscle tension, headaches
- sweating
- dry mouth, difficulty swallowing
- abdominal pain
- dizziness
- rapid or irregular heart rate
- rapid breathing
- diarrhoea or a frequent need to urinate
- tiredness
- irritability, including loss of temper
- sleeping difficulties and nightmares

- decreased concentration
- sexual problems.

If we look at the first symptom, most people will have experienced this at some point in their lives, for example, before examinations, interviews or important meetings. These symptoms will soon pass once you have started the exam, interview or meeting. This short-lived stress may be disconcerting but it probably prepares us for a good performance. If symptoms persist for more than a short time you will need to consider ways of reducing stress levels so that you are more comfortable and you avoid stress-related health problems.

REDUCING STRESS

The easiest way to reduce stress is to avoid it in the first place; this can be achieved by careful planning, organisation and prioritising. Expectations also create stress; this may be putting pressure on yourself or expectations from someone else. At university parental pressure often leads to unreasonably high expectations. Unreasonable workloads and expectations can also occur in the workplace. You will need to develop strategies to:

- set reasonable goals
- control your workload
- control your own expectations
- control the expectations of others.

The following are some of the most effective ways to reduce stress:

- exercise
- relaxation, including yoga
- sleep, both quantity and quality
- eating a balanced diet
- talking about the situations that are causing stress
- writing about the issues and events that are causing stress
- getting out and about – fresh air and a change of scenery will help to reduce stress
- avoiding isolation – social interaction will make you feel better and allow you to get a better perspective on the things stressing you.

STRESS AT WORK

Stress at work is different from stress at university. One definition of stress is being unable to control aspects of your life, and at work this will very much be the situation. You are employed and managed to carry out a set of tasks; this will restrict your ability to control all aspects of your working life.

The stress-inducing elements of work are likely to be different from university and may well include:

- high and excessively high workloads with challenging deadlines that will induce stress in even the most hardened and experienced employee
- insufficient work creates a different kind of stress – in that you fear losing your job
- dull, tedious and repetitive tasks that do not stretch you personally
- lack of control over your work activities and ways of working
- working alone with very little feedback and support
- coping with tasks that you are not trained to complete or feel you are unable to complete effectively
- relationship tensions with your manager or colleagues
- bullying, harassment and discrimination
- working in a blame culture
- management that is too weak or too strong
- working in environments that are constantly changing
- having multiple reporting lines to effectively more than one manager, where each sets priorities independent of the other
- fear of redundancy
- challenging physical environments – heat, cold, noise, fear, danger.

REDUCING STRESS AT WORK

There are many structural and practical ways to reduce stress in the workplace; the following may be useful:

- Set realistic work goals and agree these with all of your managers.
- Use effective time management techniques.
- Prioritise and delegate ruthlessly.
- Create effective support and assistance networks so when you are under pressure there is help available.
- Compartmentalise work, home and leisure.
- Create periods in the working day when you can unwind – such as going for a brisk walk at lunchtime or a mini-break away from the desk every hour or so.
- Create milestones and stick to them; this will ensure you can meet your deadlines.
- Be adaptable when things do not go to plan.
- Some people are motivated by the approaching deadline and feel no stress, but others suffer severe stress when deadlines approach. If you are in the latter category, set your own deadline at some earlier point.
- Use the 80% rule – most tasks are fine if they are 80% right; perfection creates stress.
- Don't procrastinate; delays create stress.
- Preparation and planning reduce stress.

- Don't overload yourself; learn to say 'no', but be tactful.
- Try to turn fear of stress into a more functional, stressful challenge; use self-talk to remember when you were successful in other stressful situations.
- Skilful reflective performance is the antidote to stress; practise things until you are skilful and in control.
- Take responsibility for your work; this places you in control.
- Look for the humour in work situations; laughter reduces stress.

JOKE ABOUT STRESS

A man's boss saw him sitting at his desk with his head in his hands. 'What's up with you?' he said. 'I am just so stressed out,' came the reply. His boss said, 'Get to the doctor's and let him give you something for it.' That evening the man saw the doctor, who prescribed something that he said would help. He took one that night and had a great night's sleep, waking up before the alarm clock. He had a leisurely breakfast and drove to work early. While sitting at his desk again and feeling very well, the man's boss came by. 'I went to the doctor's like you said and he gave me something that really worked – I feel great.' His boss said, 'That's all very well, but where were you yesterday?'

So we have seen that stress is part of life and there will be occasions when you will feel stressed. Careful planning and organising will go a long way to keeping stress at reasonable levels. You need to be able to recognise the symptoms of stress and be able to do something about it if you are stressed. In stressful situations try to calm down by breathing deeply and counting to ten or by holding one wrist and repeating 'calm, calm, calm…' while breathing deeply.

LOUISE AND SIMON

BECOMING REFLECTIVE PERFORMERS

Louise: 'You know I have this part-time job at a research company – Score Card Research.'

Simon: 'Yes. How's it going?'

L: 'Well, good! But, they keep asking me to do more work. I am working 23 hours a week and they want me to do another project that will take another seven hours a week. That will be 30 hours out of my week. I don't seem to have any "me" time.'

S: 'Wow! You can't be short of money.'

L: 'That's true, but I feel under pressure to say yes to this new project.'

S: 'All work and no play makes Louise a dull girl. Just say no!'

L: 'They have been really good to me and I feel I owe them something.'

S: 'This is work, not friendship!'

L: 'Yes, I know that. But when I really needed a job and I could not get one despite about 25 applications, they gave me one.'

S: 'It is easy – learn to say the "no" word.'

L: 'How exactly do I say no without them getting upset and either sacking me or not giving me any more work? I don't want them to see me as difficult.'

S: 'Think it out and get a grip! They are offering you more work; they must like what you do.'

L: 'I still can't see how I – ME – actually goes in and says I don't want to do the extra work.'

S: 'You're not normally this timid!'

L: 'Well, I am with work. I will need a reference from them one day, probably quite soon!'

S: 'This is not that difficult. Arrange a meeting with your boss and just explain the situation and all the things you need to do. Then they will see your position and there won't be a problem.'

L: 'I am not so sure.'

S: 'Set out all the work you currently do for them. Your boss may not realise just how much you are doing. Explain that you want to produce top-quality work and you don't like to let them down. Then explain all the work you have to do for uni. Finally, explain the things you do or want to do for leisure.'

L: 'Right, I will steel myself and do as you suggest.'

S: 'Wait – the final part is the most important part. At no point mention or even hint that you don't want to do the new project.'

L: 'I don't get that bit!'

S: 'Trust me! Under no circumstances mention, hint, suggest or say a word about not doing the new project.'

L: 'Are you sure this will work?'

S: 'Trust me! I know about this!'

Some days later, after Louise had met with her boss, she meets up with Simon for a coffee.

L: 'No, I'll pay for that, and get a nice cake as well!'

S: 'Thanks, that's really nice of you.'

L: 'You deserve it; you are some sort of genius.'

S: 'Am I!'

L: 'Yes. Your advice about how to handle my boss was absolutely amazing. I did as you said and discussed the various aspects of my life and said nothing about not doing the new project. After just a few minutes she said, "Oh yes, I can see you are a bit overloaded. Why don't we drop one of your other tasks and then you can have fun with the new job?" Effectively she said no for me.'

S: 'Great stuff then; all's well in the world.'

L: 'No! You haven't heard the best of it.'

S: 'There's more!'

L: 'Yes. She said that they hadn't reviewed my pay since I had started and as I was doing so well they would like to increase my pay rate.

S: 'Mega success. Perhaps I am a genius.'

L: 'In so many ways you are so dim, but I have to admit you certainly knew what to do in this situation. I will buy you a few drinks tonight.'

S: 'Good, I have just started drinking Champagne!'

MANAGING STRESS

Spencer & Smith is a large, private limited company in southern England. Its primary business is making furniture for organisations; its products include desks, cabinets, chairs, tables, lecterns and computer desks. Despite the downturn in the economy, it is doing quite well and has £24.6 million worth of work on its order book. At normal production rates that is 20 months of work. Spencer & Smith has 265 production staff, 85 office and functional support staff, 8 managers, 3 directors and a CEO. They pride themselves on being a lean and efficient company. The workforce is paid in the upper quartile of the average salaries for their industries, and the company paid a flat rate bonus to all staff last Christmas of £5,600. All the staff look forward to these bonuses and really need them to survive Christmas. The CEO says, 'They have earned the money for the company so they deserve a good Christmas bonus.'

Tom, Mary, Halimma, Rucira, Monica, Shaun, Robert, Donna and Sabba all work in the finance department and their manager is Ross. Ross is a no-nonsense manager who expects things to be done on time and exactly right. His favourite saying is: 'How difficult can it be? It is only money.' Ross prides himself on never having taken a day off in 26 years, and he often works at the weekend to meet deadlines. He is a little frustrated at the moment because on average one or two of his staff are sick at any point in time. He sometimes suspects that they are just malingering and lazy; after all, they only sit at computers all day. Ross has his own office but everyone else works in a large, single office.

Spencer & Smith has two problems at the moment. The credit crunch means that its invoices are being paid late and the level of debtors is rising quite quickly. No one is quite sure how quickly because the finance department is falling behind with the workload of chasing debtors and the year-end is due in three weeks' time. The year-end is always a nightmare for the finance staff because it occurs on 30 November and the accounts must be finalised and approved before the Christmas bonus can be paid. Just yesterday Halimma said to Robert, 'We are never going to get the accounts finished in time to pay the bonus – everyone will have a really terrible Christmas if we can't do it.' Halimma has a large family and they really rely on that Christmas bonus; it was really worrying her and depressing her.

The finance department is ten days away from the final accounts deadline but there is at least 3–4 weeks of work to do. When Ross asked the group to work over the coming weekend to make progress and meet the deadline, no one was very happy, but everyone except Halimma, Rucira and Sabba said they would. On Monday morning when these three got back to work the office looked like a bomb had hit it and everyone was bleary-eyed and very tired. Then Ross took a call from the bank explaining that they had exceeded their overdraft facility and that a number of Spencer & Smith's bills had remained unpaid. This created quite a panic and the next three days were spent chasing debtors to get out of the problem. As the next weekend approached, Ross again asked everyone to work at the weekend. This time everyone was not so willing and Robert said, 'If Halimma, Rucira and Sabba were not working again he wasn't either.' The others all joined in and said it was too much work and they needed a weekend off. Ross then went mad and made threats and was generally horrible and seemed to be going to punch Robert. Well, it calmed down and some of them worked the weekend, but not Robert or Halimma, Rucira and Sabba.

The following Monday it looked like they would not meet the final accounts deadline and the Christmas bonus would not be paid. Ross doubted if there was enough cash in the bank to pay the bonus anyway. Ross was holding a team meeting to discuss how to get out of the situation when a smartly dressed man came in and introduced himself as Mr Stone from the Health and Safety Executive. He asked Ross if they could go to his office, where he explained that he had received a serious complaint about workplace stress. He was going to carry out an assessment and, dependent on the outcome, the department and maybe the whole organisation would have to close until improvement measures had been taken. He would only say that the complaint had come from a member of the finance department, that they had provided evidence of working 72 hours last week and that they felt bullied into working these hours. He said this also contravened the Working Time Directive.

Spencer & Smith has no formal policies relating to workplace stress.

To think about...

- Detail all the elements that have created this crisis situation.

- Detail the actions that Spencer & Smith should take immediately.

- What should they do in the next 3–6 months?

- Research material available on the Internet to discover if there are any helpful websites relating to workplace stress.

- Acting as a consultant with the information you have gained, advise Spencer & Smith how to proceed.

SUMMARY

This chapter looked at a range of skill sets that will be needed for life at university and at work. They are known by different names depending on the context. You will have noticed some overlap and commonality between the skill sets.

- Academic skills:
  - knowledge
  - understanding
  - analysis
  - critique
  - synthesis and creativity
  - evaluation.

- Key skills:
  - Integrated skills do not appear on assessment criteria grids but are vital if you are to achieve high grades.
  - Study skills such as time management and researching skills are also a determinant of the grade you achieve for your work.

- Life skills are the ability to adapt and act with positive behaviours towards the challenges of everyday life. They can be categorised under the following headings:
  - self skills
  - daily functioning skills
  - relationship skills

- communication skills
- problem-solving skills
- critical thinking skills.

● Graduate skills are those that employers expect you to have when you leave university. A synthesis of these would give the following headings:
  - motivation and enthusiasm
  - teamworking
  - communication
  - flexibility and adaptability
  - being proactive and taking initiative
  - personal development.

● University and work are stressful places, so you will need to develop a strategy to reduce stress and use it to your advantage:
  - Set realistic work goals and agree these with all your managers.
  - Use effective time management techniques.
  - Prioritise and delegate ruthlessly.
  - Create effective support and assistance networks so that when you are under pressure there is help available.
  - Compartmentalise work, home and leisure.
  - Create periods in the working day when you can unwind – such as going for a brisk walk at lunchtime or a mini-break away from the desk every hour or so.
  - Create milestones and stick to them; this will ensure you can meet your deadlines.

EXPLORE FURTHER

FURTHER READING

Kotter, J. (1996) *Leading Change*. Boston, MA: Harvard Business School Press.

Mahaney, R.C. and Lederer, A.L. (2006) The effect of intrinsic and extrinsic rewards for developers in information systems project success. *Project Management Journal*. Vol 37, No 4. p42.

Moon, J.A. (2007) *Critical Thinking: An exploration of theory and practice*. London: Routledge.

Olsson, S. (2000) Acknowledging the female archetype: women managers' narratives of gender. *Women in Management Review*. Vol 15, Nos 5/6. p296.

Sansone, C. and Harackiewicz, J.M. (2000) *Intrinsic and Extrinsic Motivation: The search for optimal motivation and performance*. London: Academic Press.

Steers, R.M. and Rhodes, S.R. (1978) Major influences on employee attendance: a process model. *Journal of Applied Psychology*. Vol 63, No 4. pp391–407.

Tietjen, M. and Myers, R. (1998) Motivation and job satisfaction. *Management Decision*. Vol 36, No 4. pp226–31.

WEB LINKS

The Open University Skills for Study Website: http://www.open.ac.uk/skillsforstudy/

Talent Q: a talent management company: http://www.talentqgroup.com/default.aspx

Health and Safety Executive work-related stress site: http://www.hse.gov.uk/stress/

CHAPTER 5

Working in Teams

What skills will I develop in this chapter?

- group and team theory
- effective team behaviours
- high-performance teams
- the politics of teams
- why teams fail
- project teams
- leading teams

5.1 INTRODUCTION

In university life most of your actions and outcomes will be individual and your success will be individual. This contrasts with work, where most of your actions and outcomes will be achieved in groups or teams. Whether driven by culture or performance, most twenty-first-century organisations use teams and groups to achieve organisation goals. The skills involved with teamwork are taught in university but very seldom practised. If we follow one of our skill definitions relating to a well-practised set of actions, we may conclude that university does not prepare you for teamworking because there are relatively few opportunities for academic achievement in teams. Yet, to be successful at work you must display excellent team skills. Take a look at any job description and you will see a phrase such as 'must be able to contribute to team outcomes as an effective team member and also be able to lead teams'. Employers want staff who are skilled at working in teams and are able to lead teams. These are two very different skills.

This chapter considers some theories related to teams and group working. Team theory looks convincing when read from books or when tutors explain it. However, working in teams is essentially practical and every team operates in a specific context. Most of what you read about in this chapter will be displayed in the team television programme *I'm a Celebrity Get Me out of Here!* So, much of this chapter will address the practical skills of thriving and surviving in teams or groups. There will be some opportunities for group work at university and these can provide valuable experience of what you will find in the workplace.

5.2 GROUP AND TEAM THEORY

This section considers just two theories of how teams operate. It is not designed to be an extensive exploration of team theory; it is designed to be an introduction to team theory. If you are pursuing a business degree, you will study teams and groups extensively. I have chosen to look at two well-known and frequently used approaches to teams: Tuckman's theory of team development and Belbin's theory of team roles.

LEARNING DIARY

TEAM THEORY

I have been involved in three project teams at work and I could never see that the team was anything but chaotic. I knew all about Tuckman and Belbin, but none of it related to my experience of teams. Having recently joined another team right from the start with an experienced team leader, I can see that she is working the group through the early stages of Tuckman team development.

The really interesting part is that it does not seem like chaos; it all seems calm and straightforward. She is signposting where the team will go in development terms so that we all know what is happening.

I begin to wonder if she is the only team leader I have worked with that had any idea what she was doing. My previous experience meant that I was always less than happy to have to join a project team, but this experience really shows the 'buzz' you can get from a team that is working well.

Bruce Tuckman (1965) suggested a team development model that is still taught and used today. It is simple to understand and relates to both academic groups and the workplace. In its original form it had four stages (1–4) and was later adapted in several ways to add more stages. I will represent it in its five-stage form. As you read this account try to relate it to your experience of being in a group.

Stage 1 – Forming

Team members are introduced and get to know each other and begin to understand the reason for the team's existence.

Stage 2 – Storming

Storming, meaning stormy relationships, where differences in views and opinions have occurred and conflicts and arguments emerge.

Stage 3 – Norming

The group sets out the normal expectations and standards, agrees goals and how to achieve them.

Stage 4 – Performing

The team starts to achieve the outcomes needed to successfully complete the team's agreed goals.

A final phase (not in Tuckman's original theory):

Stage 5 – Mourning

This stage is about completing the project and dealing with the issues learned and the loss, sadness or relief of leaving the team.

How does this theory relate to your own experience of working in teams?

How does this relate to what happens in *I'm a Celebrity Get Me out of Here!*?

REFLECTIVE PERFORMING

TEAM DEVELOPMENT

Think of an example from your own experience when you joined a team at its beginning. Set out the stages you think the team went through. How do these stages relate to Tuckman's ideas?

If you are maintaining a learning log, set out your experiences of being in a team in chronological order over the time of your involvement with the team. Use two wide columns, recording your experience in the left-hand side and the Tuckman stage in the right-hand side. Reflect on whether all teams follow the Tuckman staged approach. If you think that your team experience was not as Tuckman predicted, why do you think this was so?

Learning from experience often needs deliberate and measured reflection. When you next join a team, keep a detailed record of your experience in your learning diary. Reflection both during and after the team experience will allow you to adapt your team behaviour and be a more effective team member or leader.

If you adopt this theory as a guide to action in teams, it would suggest certain behaviours for team members and facilitating actions for team leaders. Each stage is revisited in three sections: characteristics of the stage, team behaviours likely to occur and actions for leaders.

Stage 1 – Forming

Characteristics

During the forming stage team members will be getting to know each other. There are likely to be quiet uncommunicative phases until each member knows the team. Team members will be watching and listening to others and the leader. Members will offer guarded information about themselves.

Behaviours

- Members will present themselves.
- Try to understand and relate to the team goal.
- The team will try to define and explore the team goal.
- Try to set out steps to achieve the goal.
- Members will try to fit themselves into a role in the team.

Leader's actions

- Use 'ice breakers' to help the team to get to know each other.
- Set out a management vision for the team.
- Explain and make clear the dimensions and limitations within which the team must work: time, budget, and so on.
- Move the team on to the 'storming' stage at the correct time.

Stage 2 – Storming

Characteristics

Once a team has got to know each other you can expect there to be some stormy times as being polite and reserved gives way to real feelings and emotions. Control and personal influences on who is in control and what needs to be done must be argued out. Disagreements will occur and will need to be resolved. The storming stage is a very difficult stage and can cause the collapse of the whole team or some team members will leave if they are unhappy.

Behaviours

- Team members start to reveal their true selves, for better or worse.
- Team members start to be impatient and frustrated with the progress the team is making.
- Team members 'tread on each other's toes' and they defend their positions or leave.
- There will be general feelings of instability and mutiny.

Leader's actions

- Accept that the storming stage is vital to the team's success.
- Do not be put off or intimidated by the instability and aggression of this phase.
- Remind the group that this stage is a natural point in the development of the group.
- Manage the tensions and aggressions and turn them into positive actions.
- Surface and address the conflicts – the team cannot move on until this is done.
- Know the point to move the team on to the 'norming' stage.

Stage 3 – Norming

Characteristics

When the team has resolved the conflicts from the storming stage they will move on to agree the normal standards and expectations of being a group member. The focus of the team moves from conflict to performance. In the best teams genuine reflection takes place and the team performance is reviewed and improved until it is sufficient to complete the task.

Behaviours

- The rules of membership and performance that may have been overlooked in the conflict of the previous stage are now taken very seriously.
- There will be a move from ideas generation to planning and decision-making.
- There will be limited discussion and much more action.
- Subgroups, both formal and informal, may be formed to progress towards the final goal more quickly.
- There will be very little explicit conflict; there may, however, be some tacit (behind the scenes) conflict.

Leader's actions

- As leader you must keep the team focused on the task and its timely completion.
- Control the team and ensure they are following the agreed plans to completion.
- Control the amount of informal subgrouping that may occur.
- Watch out for and control tacit conflict (a spillover from the storming stage).
- Control and relieve stress and pressure; act as the team 'lubricant'.
- Inject some humour and fun.

Stage 4 – Performing

Characteristics

This is the achievement stage and is characterised by action and completion. The norming stage will have set milestones to complete the task; these will be achieved and performance evaluated. Successful teams will now be adaptable, performance-driven and task-centred. The team is likely to be proactive and not require motivation or management. The team will viciously support each other and will aggressively attack any outside person that criticises the team.

Behaviours

- Productive and output-driven, there will be very little unnecessary communication.

- The team will be cohesive and stick together.
- The team will be proactive and fast to respond to problems.
- The team will respond to criticism from within the team but be intolerant of criticism from outside of the team.

Leader's actions

- Watch out for teams running out of control and in the wrong or inappropriate directions.
- Reassert the output standards required and monitor team performance against the required standards.
- Devise praise methods and rewards as milestones are met.
- Relax and let the team perform without intervention from leadership; monitor and do not interfere – you will be treated as an outsider if you criticise.

Stage 5 – Mourning

Characteristics

The team reason for existing is gradually achieved and this can leave a vacuum that is hard to fill. Team members will gradually drift away and spend less time on this team's tasks. They may already have started to be involved in other teams.

Behaviours

- Elation at the success of achievement and then a sense of deflation as the challenge has disappeared
- A sense of loss as the tight, cohesive, social group is gradually disbanded
- Divided loyalties as team members move on to other teams
- Relief at being free of a dysfunctional team

Leader's actions

- Manage the finishing post so that the team finishes with a 'big bang'.
- Maintain the cohesive nature of the team until the end.
- Arrange reward, praise systems and a final 'wake' – actively mourn the end of the team.
- Manage and trap the organisational learning that the team has created.
- Arrange network structures after the death of the team.

In summary, there is an argument for recognising that teams work through progressive stages towards a conclusion. If this were accepted, then as a member or leader of a team it would seem effective to adjust behaviours towards the expectations of those progressive stages. Remember that most managers will have been taught this basic theory at some point, so your performance as a team member will be assessed against these expected behaviours.

For example, if you start introducing conflict in the performing stage, your behaviour will be viewed as dysfunctional. Or, if you insist on thinking about performance issues at the forming stage other team members will exclude or reject you. Remember that early in the team's life the participants can be changed; you have to be accepted to stay in the team.

This argument would lead us to the question of whether all teams must follow Tuckman's progressive stages. Clearly this would be too deterministic, but as you contribute to successful teams you will realise that teams do work through stages but they do not always follow the theory. Remember, some teams fail and do not achieve their goals. Teams are dynamic entities; they are driven by the people and personalities within them. You will experience wide variations of teamworking in the workplace; your aim should be to learn from each experience however weird, painful or enjoyable that experience may be. Learning logs and developmental diaries can be a very useful way of reflecting and making sense of your involvement with teams.

" MANAGER COMMENT

I have worked in hundreds of different teams since I joined this company 28 years ago. Not one of them was ever the same. The stages and the people always ensure that the experience is new and fresh. Some of them have left me crying. Some have left me shaking with anger. Others have left me feeling elated and fulfilled. When a new team joins together to achieve something you have no way of knowing if it will be successful or a living nightmare. But, I always learned something from every team. I would argue that I learned the most from the teams that went most

disastrously wrong. As long as you reflect and learn from the experience you will be a better person.

My advice to anyone new to work teams is to go to the first meeting and remember that you have two ears and only one mouth. Stay positive and remember to learn something from the experience.

One last point – avoid the politics if you can. We all enjoy doing things, creating things and achieving things. Very little is achieved related to team politics, spite and game-playing.

BELBIN'S TEAM ROLES

Belbin's original work in 1981 was entitled *Management Teams* and represented the culmination of a long research study of executive teams carrying out a business game at what is now Henley Management College. The key conclusion that now forms an essential part of most business and management courses is that effective teams have to cover nine key roles. If you put on your critical hat, you may be able to identify some problems with extending research from executive teams carrying out a business game to all effective teams. In general, be critical of all theory and don't allow the theory to be deterministic (that is, determine how you behave); theory is only useful as far as it helps you to understand what is happening and to improve performance by reflection.

In Figure 5.1 I have grouped these roles into the three large areas of doing, thinking and relationships.

Figure 5.1 Belbin's team roles

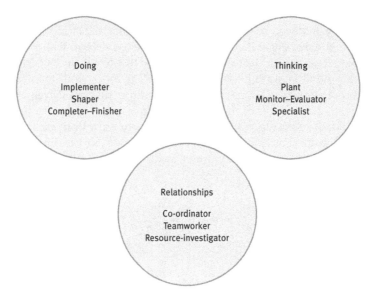

THE NINE KEY ROLES

Doing

Implementer – The implementer turns ideas into actions. Teams without an implementer tend to get very little done. Their concern with getting practical things done can lead them to be seen as inflexible and unimaginative. Their currency is what is achievable within the constraints.

Shaper – The shaper is the dynamic, proactive achiever of the group and provides the energy, drive and courage to overcome obstacles. This role may create conflict and difficulty with their drive and aggression.

Completer–Finisher – The completer–finisher is the detail person in the team. They spot flaws and gaps and keep everyone to schedule. They are slow and meticulous, which is essential, but this can be frustrating for other team members. They are the guardians of quality and the assurers of finishing on time.

Thinkers

Plant – The plant is the unorthodox, outcast team member that solves difficult and complex problems. They often communicate poorly and overlook important details. They can be creative, 'out of the box' thinkers.

Monitor–Evaluator – This role is the critical, strategic thinker of the group. They can dampen the spirits of the team by being overly critical, but the role is essential in accurately mapping the approach to the outcome and evaluating progress and outcomes. They may appear to lack drive.

Specialist – The specialist brings skills in short supply to the team and often contributes only on the narrow, technical front; but this is often essential to the success of the team. They often resist attempts to involve them in a wider role.

Relationships

Co-ordinator – The co-ordinator is the de facto leader of the group whose main work is to co-ordinate the effort of others. This role can become too controlling, and this can then be to the detriment of the team. The co-ordinator will enable all members of the team to contribute in a way that is appropriate to their role. This role will clarify goals, delegate work and promote decision-making.

Teamworker – This role is concerned with ensuring effective interpersonal relationships within the team. This role is the sensitive heart of the team and will console the slighted and damaged team member and suggest that the aggressive shaper 'cools it' a bit. This role, being concerned with relationships, can lead to conflict with the more task-orientated team members. This role creates team cohesion and generally eases conflict.

Resource-investigator – This role is a supreme networker, enabling them to collect resources and external know-how. This ability to network and gain resources and political support is essential to successful teams. In many ways this role is the PR person for the team. They can appear to do very little real work because networking is often an unseen art.

Having looked at the roles, now let's look at how this theory could be used and also consider some critical questions.

Does this mean that every team has to have nine people in it?

Team members can take on more than one role and some roles are not necessary in certain teams. Teams carrying out general activities often do not need any specialist knowledge.

Most university teams, other than sport, contain between three and six people and are organised for completing assignments or for study groups. Teams that contain between three and nine people tend to work most effectively. At work some teams will be larger than this, and if you are involved in one you may like to keep a reflective record of how the team performed. One clear message seems to arise from the analysis of Belbin's work, and that is that teams need a balance of roles. They particularity need a co-ordinator, who often is the chairperson or leader. Teams without a plant are often less successful than teams with a plant. Above all things, a team needs balance; this is one reason that I grouped the roles into *doing*, *thinking* and *relationships*. If your team has only three members, it would be wise to have people who mainly fill one of the roles of *doer*, *thinker* and *relationship-builder*.

The point at which Belbin's theory is most useful is at the team member selection stage. If you are able to influence the make-up of a team or are the designated leader, giving attention to the known attributes of team members can allow you to build a balanced team that is more likely to succeed.

When you join a new team, at the forming stage you may want to consider:

- the team roles that other members look likely to fill
- the team role or roles that you could fill.

There are tests available to predict your preferred Belbin role (see the 'Web Links' section at the end of the chapter). For most people there will be several roles that they feel comfortable fulfilling in team situations.

LOUISE AND SIMON

BECOMING REFLECTIVE PERFORMERS

Simon: 'Do you have to do that team assignment for HR?'

Louise: 'Yes. The whole year has to do it. All 420 of us.'

S: 'Wow. How many groups of four is that?'

L: 'Maths not your strong point then? 105!'

S: 'The tutors only use these group assignments to save them work in marking!'

L: 'No, I don't think so.'

S: 'Yes, that's what the second-year students think.'

L: 'But teamwork is the foundation of the workplace. They are giving us team assignments so that we can have some experience of working in teams where the outcome is important.'

S: 'Yes. I can't believe my grade will depend on the other members of the group.'

L: 'Well, since you get low grades that should help you out.'

S: 'Good idea! Get in a good group and I am guaranteed a 70% plus.'

L: 'How are you going to do that? You won't know which group you are going in until the tutorial.'

S: 'I thought I could pick the group I would be in.'

L: 'Don't be dim. No one would have you. You will be a liability!'

S: 'Well, thanks for the vote of confidence!'

L: 'That's okay.'

S: 'So how are the groups going to be picked?'

L: 'Well, I understand that there are always huge arguments about the groups, so the tutor now picks them like football ties.'

S: 'You're joking!'

L: 'No. Three tutorials are put together – that's 60 people – and then he uses a bag with 15 different coloured balls. He has a spreadsheet of names open on the screen and draws a ball for each person. Four balls of the same colour makes a team.'

S: 'So totally random then?'

L: 'Yes. That should stop a few of the arguments.'

S: 'What happens if you get someone who does no work and never attends the meetings?'

L: 'The groups have to keep a team diary that lists all the meetings and who attends and also the allocation of work and whether the person completed their work allocation.'

S: 'What gets done with that?'

L: 'When the work is submitted the group must indicate how the marks will be allocated. This assignment is out of 100, so a group of four has 400 marks to allocate; they would normally get 0.25 each, a quarter in old money.'

S: 'I am not sure I see how that is done!'

L: 'If everyone has contributed equally then the allocation is 0.25 each; then if the mark awarded is 70 x 4 = 280, they all get 0.25 of 280, making 70%. If there is a lazy non-contributor, then maybe they allocate the three hard workers as 0.28 each and the lazy one as 0.16. The 70% mark is then 70 x 4 = 280, the three contributors get 280 x 0.28 = 78.4% and the lazy person gets 0.16 x 280 = 44.8%.'

S: 'That is about as clear as mud!'

L: 'Don't worry. The tutor works it out; the group just has to indicate the effort put in and the allocation.'

S: 'So I am not going to get an easy ride!'

L: 'No. Work hard if you want a decent grade.'

S: 'That doesn't seem all that fair. I thought teams lived and died together.'

L: 'Well, they do in real life, but we can't have lazy people ruining the grades for the hardworking, intelligent ones.'

S: 'It still looks like it could cause a lot of trouble.'

L: 'I guess it can, but we'll see.'

5.3 EFFECTIVE TEAM BEHAVIOURS

Early research into teams identified three groups of behaviours that occur in teams:

MAINTENANCE-ORIENTED BEHAVIOURS

These are behaviours that build relationships and maintain the comfort of the team. The warm relationships that are built by this behaviour create a pleasurable environment in which to work. We could call these the friendly behaviours of politeness and respect.

SELF-ORIENTED BEHAVIOURS

Self-oriented behaviours interfere with the success of the team. They tend to distract and unsettle team members and require leadership time and attention to correct or ameliorate. The range of self-oriented behaviours is endless but might include:

- creating undermining subgroups
- poor attendance at meetings
- distracting other team members with non-task-related activities
- deliberate lateness of deliverables

- pursuing political points not related to the agreed goals
- undermining other team members – not being supportive or being deliberately aggressive and unsettling
- being constantly negative and critical
- withdrawing from the team by distancing and sullenness
- silence and non-contributing – sulking
- failure to move on from the storming phase by holding a grudge about not getting your own way in the forming or norming stages
- personal politicking.

STUDENT COMMENT

I hate doing assignments in teams! I can never see the point of them! They always seem to take three times as long and I never get as good a grade as when I do the work on my own.

I understand what the tutor says about teams being an essential part of business, but I still hate them. I wonder if there is a job 'out there' that doesn't need teamwork. I could just work away on my own with no one to bother me.

All these behaviours and many more have a two-fold effect in reducing the individual's contribution to the team and in distracting the leader or other team members from task-related activity.

TASK-ORIENTED BEHAVIOURS

Task-oriented behaviours are those that concentrate on important and agreed tasks that contribute to the successful completion of the team's objective. Task-oriented behaviour tends to be specific, planned and timely; we often call these deliverables. Teams that only concentrate on task-oriented behaviour tend to provide a rather dry, dull, antiseptic experience. When the team objectives are complete they disband without any lasting friendships or connections.

How can you contribute to a team in an effective manner?

- Recognise and be committed to the team's objectives – yes, I mean really committed.
- Understand your own role in the team – ask if you are unclear.
- Be sure to be involved and communicate with each team member.
- Listen carefully and actively in meetings.

- Contribute in proportion to the number of members in the team.
- Treat all team members with courtesy, care and respect.
- Try to understand the different approaches and motivations of other team members.
- Do not be personally judgemental – judge only tasks.
- Remember, teams live and die together – don't blame.

How can I judge if my team is effective?

Commitment – Effective team members see themselves belonging to the team. They are committed to group goals above and beyond their personal goals.

Trust – Effective team members have trust in each other to honour commitments, maintain confidences, support each other and generally behave predictably and consistently.

Purpose – The team understands how it fits into the overall business of the organisation. Team members know their roles, feel a sense of ownership and can see how they personally, and as a team, contribute and make a difference.

Task orientation – Effective teams invest most of their time in task-related activities. Other essential elements such as supporting, communicating and networking are carried out efficiently and quickly.

Communication – The team communicates effectively and frequently with each other. Effective internal communication allows the team to make balanced decisions, handle conflict constructively and provide each other with valuable feedback. The effective team communicates clearly with external stakeholders.

Involvement – Everyone has a role on the team and carries out that role. Team members support other team members in carrying out their roles. Despite differences in roles, perspectives and experience, team members feel a sense of partnership with each other. Contributions are respected and expected. True consensus is reached when appropriate.

Process skills – High-performing teams have a large number of process skills they can use when needed. Process skills include problem-solving tools, planning techniques, regular meetings, agendas and successful ways of dealing with problems, behavioural agreements and ways to improve and develop those processes within the team.

Continuous improvement – The team understands the importance of continuous improvement and has the tools, knowledge and time at their disposal to make continuous improvement really happen. All improvement efforts are done in support of the organisation's goals and objectives.

❝❝   MANAGER COMMENT

Since I became an experienced manager I will not work with teams I do not trust or those that do not trust me. Trust is everything. Most people do not have a very good feel for their own personal level of trust. When I first meet a new team I carry out this little icebreaker.

I sit the new team around a table and ask someone for a pound coin. I then just sit quietly while there is a bit of fidgeting in the chairs and a few looks to each other. Eventually someone offers a pound; I walk up behind them and ask them, 'What are your hopes and aspirations for being in this team?' I then take the pound and give it to someone else and ask them what are their hopes and aspirations for being in this team. When they have answered, I ask the group for a five-pound note. There then follows a little more fidgeting and watching each other and then out pops a five-pound note. The normal hopes and aspirations question is asked of the giver and then the note is given to a recipient and the question is asked again. I then ask for a ten-pound note and do the same thing.

Next I ask for a twenty-pound note; the pressure is now on the team members that have not given up any money and the stakes are getting higher. Then finally I ask for a fifty-pound note – sometimes I get this and sometimes I do not. If I don't get a note from the team I get one out of my wallet and give it to one of the team that has not spoken and then to one other person. Now everyone is a little worried as the money is spread around the room and some are quite large sums.

Then I ask for the money to be returned to the rightful owner and ask the team to reflect on:

- Did you volunteer some money, that is, take a risk? How did you feel?
- How did you feel if you offered up the twenty- or the fifty-pound note?
- Do you think the people who gave the twenty- or fifty-pound notes were foolish?
- Did you think you would get your money back?
- What does this tell us about trust and risk?

While this is going on I look closely at each person to see how comfortable and trusting they are feeling. I can usually tell the ones that will have trouble committing and trusting in a group. I then say that this is going to be a high-trust group and if anyone is uncomfortable with that they should feel free to leave the group right now or to see me afterwards. Strangely, very few people leave but I have made an important cultural point and I have already started to bind them into a trusting team.

5.4 LEADING TEAMS

Leading teams is not easy but it is a skill and, like any skill, can be learned with study and experience. Don't expect to be a skilled and competent leader straight away; it will take time and experience to develop this complex and dynamic skill. When you lead your first few teams, it is worth being honest about your experience to the members of the team – if teams know you are new to leading they will help and facilitate the leading process. There is a vast amount of theory and advice for those leading teams, but I would put forward the following as essential behaviours of leading:

Aims and objectives – Keep the aims and objectives of the team relevant, meaningful and visible. You may have to present the full range and extent of the purpose of the group in stages. It is your role to structure the aims and objectives so that they appear to be achievable. But, do this without deceit. If you need three stages of objectives, present the first stage and point out that there will be two other stages to follow. Make the aims and objectives visible with posters, headings, pictures and sounds.

Team roles – If you are able to choose the members of your team, give some thought to the balance of people required and the skills and attributes any member can bring to the team. Remember, balanced teams are successful teams. Once the team is formed, make clear the role(s) that each member is carrying out. Ensure that for each role the performance and output is clear, precise and achievable.

Leaders are members of the team – Leaders must be full working members of the team and will have a designated role as well as that of leader. The role of leader requires you to have some strategic perspective but also to do your share of the work. The leader's role is to bring some perspective and distance to the team and facilitate the team's success.

Commitment, confidence and trust – Team leaders need to be coaches, building commitment, confidence and trust in each team member. Analysing and developing skills appropriate to each team member is vital to the success of the team. Commitment, confidence and trust will allow team members to take the required risks and know that leader and team members alike will support them.

Facilitate success and take the blame – The leader's role is to create and engineer tasks and roles that allow all team members to be successful. When all team members are successful the team will be successful. Avoid creating a blame culture because this stifles involvement and risk-taking. When blame does occur the leader needs to take the blame on themselves. Success belongs to the team, blame belongs to the leader – it's tough, but that is the reality of leading. Remember, the leader needs to be the first person to tackle a difficult or dirty job – lead from the front, not from the back.

Pilot the ship – Finally and most importantly, the leader needs to 'pilot the ship' in the right direction. The leader is invariably the only person in a team that has the distance and perspective to see the right course to success. Monitor the direction and performance of a team continuously and make small changes to the course.

THE POLITICS OF TEAMS

Politics in teams is generally seen as a bad or dysfunctional thing. Politics could be defined as 'taking a particular view or position with the intention of personally gaining from that position'. But in every team there are political agendas, so it is as well to be aware of them but try to avoid being part of them.

Each person in a team and the people outside the team can be seen as behaving in one of the following roles:

- allies
- opponents
- adversaries
- bedfellows
- fence-sitters.

Allies are those people who align with the majority of team members. They are of like mind and fully associate with the team's objectives. They can be relied on to provide support for team members, defend the objectives of the team and work to their full potential.

Bedfellows are willing to align with members of the team but only because they feel they will benefit from the association. Their values and beliefs do not align with the majority of the team and they are willing to disguise their true feeling to be accepted as part of the team. At some later point they may choose to change allegiance to another team or group.

Fence-sitters remain neutral at all costs, reasoning that they can come off the fence at a later point; they often never do come off the fence because fence-sitting is a psychological stance or problem. They will contribute to teams but their support and allegiance to team goals is weak or non-existent. When a team is under attack from adversaries they will not support the team or the team's aims.

Opponents are open critics of the team's direction or aims. They will provoke more discussion and reflection about what the team should be doing. In the early stages of team development this is helpful, but once past the norming stage, opponents are a problem.

Adversaries are willing to expend effort to sabotage the work of the team. Adversaries often disguise their role by appearing to be an ally or bedfellow.

Aim to make your team a politics-free zone, but be aware that it will probably not be free of politics. Opponents can be turned into strong allies if adequate amounts of time are given over to discussing the aims and objectives at the forming and norming stages. Bedfellows can be allies if the motivation and rewards are strongly aligned with what they want. Fence-sitters are a psychological problem and you can do very little about this allegiance. They can be useful in teams but try to avoid doing anything that gets them off the fence on the wrong side.

Adversaries are a very different matter. Try to be alert for allies or bedfellows who are actually adversaries. The crunch question is, where do you keep your adversaries? As the saying goes, 'keep your friends close and your adversaries even closer.' Challenge adversaries about their negative and subversive behaviour, but again, as an old saying goes, 'if you cannot change the person, change the person.' The other approach is to banish adversaries as far away as possible.

WHY TEAMS FAIL

If you keep a learning log of your experiences in teams you will soon develop your own list of why teams fail. In many ways if you attend to all the areas that this chapter has looked at, your team should be a success. So the following very personal list is probably best seen as the flip side of not attending to all the things discussed above:

- inappropriately formed teams or teams that have a poor balance in the roles that are taken
- teams that have arrested development – they are stuck in the forming or norming stages
- teams that lack trust and commitment
- teams that lack a clear focus on the aims and objectives
- teams that plan poorly and have no clear and organised path to completion and success
- teams that lack essential skills
- teams that are overly political
- teams with weak or overly controlling leaders.

LEARNING DIARY

MY FAILURE OR THE TEAM'S?

Tuesday – I have just been asked to leave a project team I was working on! This has really upset me as I thought I was really contributing and helping the team to get along. When the team leader asked me to pop into the office I just thought it was a routine request to do another aspect of the job. When they said, 'I know you are trying really hard but I am going to have to ask you to leave the team.' I was so shocked I forgot to ask why.

Wednesday – I have fretted about being 'chucked off the team' all day. I have got practically no work done today. I really feel angry and sad in equal measure. I must pluck up the courage to ask what was so wrong with my performance.

Friday – I finally got to speak to the team leader about being removed from the team!

I have to say I am relieved and happy in equal measure. How can I be happy about being removed from a team I was working so hard on helping? Well, when I spoke to the team leader she said it was nothing personal but that the project was running over budget and she had to remove three of the team to keep the costs down. It seems that my time is recharged to her project, which I hadn't realised before. She said that my end-of-team report, which is made on each person, would be very good.

I think there is a moral here in that I need to stay emotionally detached and always ask for an explanation. It seems easy to think that you are asked to leave a team because of something you have done, when often it is unrelated to your performance.

5.5 TYPES OF TEAMS

We could argue that there are basically two types of teams: teams that recommend things and teams that do things. At university or in the early stages of your career, you are likely to mostly encounter teams that do things.

TEAMS THAT DO THINGS

The majority of teams you will be involved with at university or in your early working life will be teams that do things, such as:

- make products
- carry out research
- complete an assignment
- design a marketing campaign
- deliver a service
- teach
- make a presentation
- run an event or a series of events
- sports team.

The unique element of teams that do things is that they will have performance outputs that have to be met. The tasks they carry out are often large and complex. The team element may be a representation of the whole workforce. They are also characterised by not having a finite life; teams that do things tend to go on indefinitely and this adds another dimension to their functioning. In teams that exist continuously, the entry and exit of team members will be important. How new team members are welcomed and how old team members are celebrated will impact on how effectively the team operates. Note that Tuckman's model does not cope well with teams that exist continuously.

TEAMS THAT RECOMMEND THINGS

There are a whole range of teams that recommend things; these include groups or teams that:

- audit other things, such as accounts or health and safety
- assess quality and recommend improvements
- develop and recommend strategy
- investigate problems and underperforming areas
- carry out analysis and recommend actions, such as evaluating new products against market leaders
- represent others, such as unions
- make decisions about courses of action or spending, such as research council committees that decide how funds should be allocated to projects.

There are several unique issues with teams that recommend things. They are often severely time-constrained and must deliver recommendations by a set date. They often have to work out their own 'terms of reference' and the scope of the activity they are being asked to do. Finally, if their recommendation(s) is to be implemented, they must present a well-argued and finely balanced argument with practical actions.

TYPES OF TEAMS

You will find all kinds of teams into today's modern society; some exist for specific times and others operate continuously. You will commonly encounter some of these types of teams:

- cross-functional – a grouping of people representing the functions of an organisation to fulfil a project
- committee – a temporary or permanent group of people assembled to make decisions
- taskforce – a temporary team assembled to investigate a specific issue or problem
- problem-solving – a temporary team assembled to solve a specific problem
- product design – a temporary team assembled to design a new product or service
- work group – a permanent group of workers led by a manager
- work team (also called self-directed work team or self-managed work team) – an ongoing group of workers who share a common mission and collectively manage their own affairs within predetermined boundaries
- quality circle – a group of workers from the same functional area responsible for quality and quality improvement
- research – team that produces research and other related outputs; members are not necessarily from the same organisation
- virtual – teams where members are separated by distance and who meet virtually facilitated by technology
- high performance – a specialised team arrangement (explored more fully below).

HIGH-PERFORMANCE TEAMS

High-performance teams are a special class of team that is often used in 'change' situations. They often carry out the most difficult tasks in change programmes or re-engineering programmes. The participants will all be experienced high-performers. They solve the more difficult problems and are often involved in the 'culture change' programmes typical of major change. The key point is to achieve dramatic results quickly. They are like an elite force and are normally self-directed from within. Even though the participants will often know each other, they will try to use an accelerated team development approach with 'forming', 'norming' and 'storming' all being done in just one short meeting. High-performance teams will expected to learn and develop quickly. As the project proceeds they will often have specific techniques to 'trap' and use learning. The high-performance team will often be the central hub of a change programme, with one or more members acting as group leaders for other teams involved in the change programme. High-performance teams normally report at director or board level.

CASE STUDY

THE DYSFUNCTIONAL TEAM

Tom, Kirsten, Marilyn, Priya, Veronique, Sasha, Katrina and Russell are all at the first meeting of a new cross-functional team that is developing the production of a new piece of exercise equipment, the 'Isometcross'. The Isometcross is a revolutionary invention of the company's owner, Art Hermes, and it is the team's job to get this into production as soon as possible. Art believes this could be the finest and most profitable product Hermes Industries has ever produced. This puts added pressure on the group because they are clearly bringing Art's 'baby' into existence.

The Isometcross is a piece of professional gym equipment that increases the pressure of any part of the body working the equipment in response to the pressure applied. Art describes this as a super-isometric process. The arms, head, legs, feet, hands and hips can all be worked. As you apply muscle pressure to the arms of the equipment, they push back at the same rate as your muscles exert pressure. This means there is very little joint movement but a lot of muscle training. The prototype has received rave reviews. Art wants to exploit the equipment before competitors can create anything similar – advice was that it would be uneconomic to patent any part of the equipment, so speed is of the essence.

The team consists of:

Russell – an experienced engineer and leader of project teams, he will lead the group. He is slow and meticulous and always takes his time to create top-quality engineering. He has chosen all the other people in the team.

Sasha – is the accountant for the group and is concerned that the production and research and development costs are very high already.

Veronique – is the PR and advertising person and thinks the equipment looks great, although she does not take any exercise herself – she hates it. She believes that sales are directly proportional to the amount spent on the advertising campaign. She is also keen to change jobs and work in television; all this engineering is a bit beneath her. She thinks a big TV campaign might help her get a job in television.

Tom – is the production engineer and does not like Russell, as some old argument or slight has made them bitter enemies. He does not want to be on this team and intends to do very little to help; he cannot say this obviously. He thinks Russell may only have him on the team to punish and humiliate him.

Kirsten – is the HR specialist. She is warm and enthusiastic and is really looking forward to working in her first team. She is a bit of a dreamer and has real trouble doing anything to a time scale.

Priya – is the production manager and responsible for the day-to-day production of the Isometcross. She thinks the product is great. There have been some issues with the technical side of producing the prototype equipment, with constant machine breakdowns of the new equipment that produces the Isometcross. Priya told them it was madness to use a Korean supplier and that if things went wrong, fixing it would be a nightmare. No one listened to her then and she is sulking and miserable at the moment.

Marilyn – is the distribution and packaging manager and will be responsible for delivering the equipment. She is efficient and very task-focused; she has to be because she is probably doing the work of three people.

Katrina – is looking after the administration of the sales and goods-in for the product. She is young and not sure how anything works and has only worked for Hermes Industries for two weeks. She is very scared about attending her first meeting.

The meeting is scheduled to start at 8:00am sharp. It is now 8:20 and only Russell, Marilyn, Tom and Priya are present. Russell doesn't see much point in starting, so they all sit around and wait. At 8:46 Katrina turns up flustered and explains her bus was late. Sasha arrives at 8:52, sits down and says nothing. It is 9:15 before everyone is at the meeting. By this stage Marilyn, Priya and Tom are pretty angry about waiting 75 minutes to start the meeting. Russell introduces everyone and gets straight down to business. He issues a Gantt chart showing all the steps needed to meet a first delivery deadline in 16 weeks and who is responsible for doing them. He then stresses how important this project is and asks if anyone has any questions. Marilyn notices that no tasks are allocated to Russell but she doesn't say anything. Priya then says, 'We will never make that deadline. The production kit is always breaking down!' Russell tells her to treat this as a priority and impresses on her the need to meet the deadline. Priya goes to reply and at that point Russell puts his

finger to his lips and says, 'No arguments.' Tom then says he is unhappy with how the meeting is being chaired, 'We should have started hours ago! This is a shambles!' He gets up and walks out. Marilyn then follows him saying she has important work to do and can spare no more time. Russell finishes the meeting at that point.

Russell tries to hold a productive meeting on three more occasions but either he cannot get everyone there or, when he does, no one will co-operate. At one of these meetings Sasha points out to Russell that there are no 'proper' costings for the Isometcross. Katrina has not been present at any of the meetings after being late for the first one. Kirsten has been to every meeting but has not said one word. Priya constantly goes on about the equipment breakdowns. Tom 'chips in' occasionally but only to undermine Russell and cause trouble. Veronique has been busy and produced the storyboard and costings for a big TV campaign that will cost Hermes £2.4 million.

To think about…

- What are the issues in this case that mean this team seems so dysfunctional?
- How would you advise Russell to have gone about creating this team?
- What stage is this team at in relation to Tuckman's team development theory?
- What can be done now to get this team and the production of the Isometcross back on track?
- Categorise the members of this team by their political approach.

SUMMARY

Many actions at university and work will be carried out in teams. Team skills are highly valued at work and may be required when you encounter team-based assignments at university.

- Tuckman suggests that teams progress through various stages:
  - forming
  - storming

- norming
- performing
- mourning.

- Belbin proposes that effective teams contain a mix of nine roles:
  - Doing: Implementer, Shaper, Completer–Finisher
  - Thinkers: Plant, Monitor–Evaluator, Specialist
  - Relationships: Co-ordinator, Teamworker, Resource-investigator.

- Effective team behaviours fall into the following groups:
  - maintenance-oriented behaviours
  - self-oriented behaviours
  - task-oriented behaviours.

- When leading teams, pay attention to the following aspects:
  - aims and objectives
  - team roles
  - being a member of the team as well as leading
  - build commitment, confidence and trust
  - facilitate success for the team, take the blame for failure
  - remember you are the ship's pilot.

- Be aware of team politics but avoid being part of them.

- Be aware of why teams fail.

- There are various types of team found in business and university:
  - teams that do things
  - teams that recommend things
  - high-performance teams.

EXPLORE FURTHER

FURTHER READING

Belbin, M. (2004) *Management Teams: Why they succeed or fail*. Oxford: Elsevier Butterworth-Heinemann.

Heller, R. (1998) *Managing Teams*. London: Penguin Books.

Jelphs, K., Dickinson, H. and Markiewicz, L. (2008) *Working in Teams*. Bristol: Policy Press.

Levi, D. (2007) *Group Dynamics for Teams*. London: Sage.

Tuckman, B. (1965) Developmental sequences in small groups. *Psychological Bulletin*. No 63. pp384–99.

WEB LINKS

Get Set: the Belbin team role predictor for young persons: http://www.belbin.com/rte.asp?id=40

CHAPTER 6

Effective Reading Skills

What skills will I develop in this chapter?

- developing different styles of reading
- effective use of the traffic light system
- improving your reading speed and comprehension
- critical reading skills
- effective use of the SQ3RW method
- keeping track of your reading

6.1 INTRODUCTION

University life requires you to read a lot of material. Developing effective approaches to reading, understanding, reflecting and using this material is a vital part of success at university and later in the workplace.

This chapter aims to develop a range of skills that will make you a more effective learner. These range from reading faster and more effectively to the efficient recording of what you have read. As effective reading is such a vital skill, I would advise you to read the chapter slowly and carefully, carrying out each of the reflective activities.

After you have incorporated some or all of the ideas in this chapter into your university or work life, you may want to reread the chapter after about two or three months to see if further improvements could be made to the way you read.

6.2 TYPES OF READING

We read for a number of different reasons – it is important to identify the different types of reading that you will do at university and at work.

Reading for detailed understanding of the content – This is vital for learning because it provides the basic understanding of the key concepts of a subject. It is likely to be the type of reading you do in textbooks and in journals. In business you will also have to adopt this approach for reports and important documents.

Exploratory reading – This is the technique used when you are exploring a book or article to see if it contains any useful material. The most common method of exploratory reading is **skimming**. In **skimming**, only the first line of every paragraph is read, or the first line of each section. Once you have found an appropriate section, the reading method changes to **detailed reading**. To be an effective reader it is vital that you are able to switch quickly between **skimming** and **detailed reading**.

Another type of exploratory reading is **scanning**. The focus of scanning tends to be whole chapters or whole articles. Once again, you will need to be able to effectively switch from **scanning** to **detailed reading**.

Critical reading – This is a detailed and intensive reading of the text, often more than once, with the aim of uncovering and challenging the assumptions and argument.

One of the roles of reading at university is to develop a good understanding of the concepts and ideas involved in a subject. This initial understanding of the main concepts will mostly come from standard textbooks. An effective strategy may be to investigate the concept in three different textbooks. Effective reading involves keeping notes from your reading (covered in section 6.3 below). It would be normal to **skim** the text until the right section is found and then to switch to **detailed reading**. Finally, the highlighted areas will be reread using the **critical reading** approach to expose and critique the underlying assumptions of the theory, concept, research or model. Once the main concepts have been explored and are well understood, your reading will move on to find more detailed aspects of the subject.

After reading the main chapters relating to a subject area in two or three textbooks, an effective strategy would be to move on to look at journal sources. Normally most of the journals you will need can be obtained by searching the Athens© databases. Athens is a standard set of databases to which most university libraries subscribe, and access is often through whatever e-learning platform is being used by your university. Blackboard© is a common platform for e-learning. See Figure 6.1 below. Once logged into Athens it is possible to search the databases using key words.

LEARNING DIARY

A READING MOUNTAIN TO SCALE

I had a really depressing day today. We have a few really large readings to prepare for a Monday seminar and I spent all day on it. I was up at 9, wow – too early – and worked in the library until 7, but I didn't even finish one reading. They are so difficult to understand, and so boring. I can't face another day tomorrow, so I reckon I'll miss the seminar on Monday (that's not good but I am going to be embarrassed if I haven't done the reading and everyone else has).

I'm beginning to think there must be something wrong with me – slow reader,

I guess. I'm a bit scared to mention it to anyone. They will think I am such a nerd. This can't go on; reading this much stuff is just impossible, if I can't make it I'll leave.

I really have no idea what to do about this. Maybe, see the skills tutor?

I was going to go out tonight but I can't face it – early to bed! How can reading ruin my life, career and everything?

Figure 6.1 Database search using ProQuest

From the activity above you will now have about 4–8 journal articles focused on your subject area. But, this is still a lot of reading, perhaps 15,000–30,000 words. You will need to employ different reading styles to effectively evaluate the material. If you are selecting material in preparation for an examination or assignment, not all of the articles will be directly useful, and you may find the following approach useful.

REFLECTIVE PERFORMING

SEARCHING PROQUEST

Choose from one of the broad areas below:

- branding
- outsourcing
- economic demand
- strategic choice
- motivation.

Use the web to log on to Athens© and then enter the database ProQuest.

Use the broad area you have chosen as the search term, for example 'branding'.

Then click on the search button.

Well done! You have carried out your first database search.

But, there were a few problems:

- Your search found over 10,000 documents.
- Many of the articles were not focused on what you were looking for.
- Some documents were not from journals.

To make searching a more useful exercise, a number of adaptations are necessary. You can select these adaptations on the search page:

- Limit the results to scholarly journals.
- Limit the date range.
- Limit to full-text journals.
- Use more than one word in the search line, for example 'retail branding'.

This will focus the search to about 10–15 journals. You would then select the most appropriate 4–8 journals to investigate further.

As you become familiar with the use of the search engine, you will be able to search more effectively. Practice makes perfect!

THE TRAFFIC LIGHT SYSTEM

(You will need to print the journal articles for this exercise and have three coloured highlighters – this is not very cheap or environmentally friendly, but it does make the technique easier to understand.)

Let's imagine you are selecting articles that could be useful for an examination.

Step 1

Fully and carefully read the abstract to each article. Use a highlighter to mark the article with a bar along the top with one of three colours:

- red – of no direct use

- yellow – may be relevant but not that important
- green – directly useful.

Step 2

Skim-read all the articles marked with a green highlighter. Use the green highlighter to indicate the most relevant paragraphs in the article. You can also use small sticky notes to indicate the useful areas.

Step 3

Read in detail the paragraphs that you have highlighted in green. Make brief notes relating to the ideas, concepts, theory or data in these sections.

Step 4

Now, reread the highlighted areas of the articles, focusing on the author's assumptions, argument, evidence base and logic. Make notes of the assumptions behind the writing, the evidence used and also note any weaknesses in the argument and the logic. There is more detailed guidance in Chapter 10 on being critical when reading and writing.

LEARNING DIARY

THE TRAFFIC LIGHT SYSTEM

I tried out the traffic light system and thought it worked really well. But it cost a fortune in printing and is so unfriendly to the environment. In three years at uni I would have had to cut down about ten trees just for my printing.

So I have adapted the technique to do it all online. I read the abstract for each article in the search and then 'mark' any that look suitable. It is just a little tick box at the side of the article. Then when I have marked all that are useful – that can be about 20–30 articles – I send them to my email account.

These are the ones I would have marked with green highlighter.

Once in my email I can read them using skimming. Any part of the article that is really useful I cut and paste into a Word document with the citation – which is the author's name, etc. The really useful items I will paraphrase in another Word document.

Now I have a fairly effective way of reading and reviewing journal articles, and I don't destroy the environment or my budget in the process.

Journal sources can be useful in providing a number of important elements in your university work. Many articles provide critique of standard business theory in an academic area. Reading and **paraphrasing** this critique of theory will allow you to incorporate it into your own writing. This will develop the critical aspects of your work, and well-referenced journal-driven critique is valuable in achieving a high grade. Journal articles can also provide valuable **empirical** data that can be used to support your argument, or it can be used to challenge your argument (counterargument). Using counterargument is a reflective technique that is covered in a later chapter. By using evidence that both supports and questions your argument you can provide an important balance to your work. Journal sources can also provide new, more up-to-date theory. Academic writing is focused on trying to develop theory to explain a phenomenon or reality and may well provide a new perspective on existing subjects. All new theory appears in journals before it will appear in a textbook. Journals are the focus of theory development and the lead time to publish is usually shorter for journals than for textbooks. Leading-edge theory is therefore more likely to be found in journal sources.

EXAMPLE

Alison was investigating the use of outsourcing in human resource management.

She searched using the terms 'outsourcing' and 'HR' in the ProQuest database and found seven journals, which she printed out.

She read the abstracts for each article and, using a highlighter, she marked three of the articles with red, two with yellow and two with green.

Alison highlighted the following articles in green:

Pollitt, D., Gelman, L. and Dell, D. (2004) Outsourcing HR: The contrasting experiences of Amex and DuPont. *Human Resource Management International Digest*. Vol 12, No 6. pp8–10.

Stroh, L.K. and Treehuboff, D. (2003) Outsourcing HR Functions: When – and when not – to go outside. *Journal of Leadership & Organizational Studies*. Vol 10, No 1. p19.

She highlighted the following section of the first article:

Of 125 companies surveyed for HR Outsourcing Trends, a research report by The Conference Board and sponsored by Accenture HR Services, two-thirds currently outsource a major HR function and most of these are seeking to expand what they do. Rarely has any company stopped outsourcing a function once having started. The research reveals that fewer than 1 percent of outsourced HR functions have been brought back in-house.

She reread the main sections of the article again using a **critical reading** approach and made the following notes:

- The research was sponsored. Does this question the **objectivity** of the survey?

- The statement, 'Rarely has any company stopped outsourcing a function once having started,' seems rather vague, and is not supported by evidence.

- The two claims that two-thirds currently outsource and that 'most' are seeking to expand do not appear to be supported by evidence.
- The research was based on a sample size of 125.

She also noted that despite some critical worries, this would be useful data for her assignment.

6.3 READING FASTER AND MORE EFFECTIVELY

We have looked in the previous section at how to develop an effective strategy for reading that adopts a deliberate change of pace at certain stages. Most people are real 'snails' when it comes to reading the words on a page. You can make yourself a more effective reader by changing a few things and speeding up your reading.

You are reading this section now and you are probably vocalising each word as you read. You may be reading out loud or just reading in the mind. This is not necessary and slows down your reading; it does not allow you to remember more of what you have read.

Avoid vocalising, or the silent version of 'subvocalising', by using a pointer, a finger, pen tip or knitting needle. But, don't point to each word as this will just slow you down even more; the pointer is moved down the centre of the page. (We will come back to this in a moment.)

The other area to work on in speeding up your reading is to read in larger chunks. Most people will read two or three words at one look, called a **fixation**. You need to train your eyes to see sentences or larger blocks of words.

Try this

Run a pointer down the middle of the page in a steady but reasonably fast movement so that a page takes 15–20 seconds to read. Allow your eyes to look only once left and once right of the pointer for each line. You may notice that you are not subvocalising. It is the pointer and the speed that stops the vocalising as your brain is working much harder to input the information. You will need to practise this technique before you can achieve full and complete comprehension.

How your eyes track the page is also important. I have suggested above that you go down the page but this isn't the only or the most effective way. Try letting your eyes hop about the page looking at blocks of words or zigzag down the page.

The above techniques will improve your reading speed if you practise at these much faster rates for four or five short sessions a week for about five or six weeks. As you get faster, increase the pace of your reading more and more, and with practice you can read at over 500 words a minute and easily up to 1,000 words a minute. You will be surprised how much you can remember at these higher speeds.

Do you need to read every word?

The short answer is no! You would be surprised how the detailed meaning contained in writing can be discovered without reading every word.

What are the main ideas in the following passage (originally 114 words)?

Tutorials are different ____ ____ _____ ___ _____ _____. ____ ___ _____ students _____ _____ ____ _ tutor to try and understand material ____ ____ _____ _____ ____ __ _____ unit of study. Tutorials take many different forms ___ ___ __ _____ ____ ____ ___ _____ __ smaller groups, student-centred ___ _____ high levels of student interaction.

Student participation is the key __ ___ _____ __ _____. Facilitating interactivity __ ____ _____ ____ __ ___ tutors' greatest challenge. Students ___ asked __ review ___ consolidate ___ knowledge ____ gained in lectures _____ __ talking about __ ____ _____ _____. ____ ___ _____ responding to questions, informal discussion, _____ in subgroups __ _____ ____ presentations. [55 words]

You may have found the main ideas were:

- Tutorials are different from other university classes.
- There is student and tutor interaction.
- Tutorials are concerned with understanding material.
- It is a student-centred class.
- Students contribute to the class.
- Student participation is a key ingredient.
- Activities tend to be reviewing, presenting and talking in groups or subgroups.

Hopefully this passage of writing illustrates that you can get the full meaning of most writing by reading only half the words. In some types of writing you may only need to read 10% of the words. This does not increase your reading speed by ten times, but it will probably increase reading speed by five times. Use this technique with caution; it is not suitable for all types of reading. When you are using detailed critical reading, you will need to read every word.

The full text of the passage is:

Tutorials are different from both lectures and practical classes. They are where students come together with a tutor to try and understand material they have experienced somewhere else in their unit of study. Tutorials take many different forms but you can imagine that they are generally in smaller groups, student-centred and involve high levels of student interaction.

Student participation is the key to the success of tutorials. Facilitating interactivity in this environment will be the tutors' greatest challenge. Students are asked to review and consolidate the knowledge they gained in lectures usually by talking about it with other students. This may involve responding to questions, informal discussion, working in subgroups or making oral presentations.

SQ3R is a very popular reading method

SQ3R is short for: Survey, Question, Read, Recall and Review.

You may have experienced the problem of having read a piece of writing and then immediately afterwards you cannot remember any of it. It may be that you can remember something but not very much. The SQ3R method is designed to improve the effectiveness of your reading. You will need to do a lot of reading at university, so it pays to do it as efficiently as you can.

Survey

Survey the article, document or book to establish its purpose and to get the main ideas.

Concentrate on:

- titles
- pictures
- introduction and conclusion
- bold or italicised print
- questions
- first and last sentences in paragraphs
- contents page
- illustrations
- section headings
- summary sections.

Question

Form three or four questions related to the reading and keep these in view as you read. Focus in on aspects of the reading that will help to answer these questions. But also form questions about the text as you read. Start making notes on a single sheet of A4 paper, and have the questions in one half of the paper and the answers in the other half.

Another technique is to build a mind map as your read. Place the questions that relate to the reading in the middle and then let your notes radiate outwards from the questions. Use as much colour, underlining and small images as you can.

Also add questions that arise from the reading. Many of these are covered by the critical questions in a later section. Write down the thoughts that arise as you read the work. Such as:

- Why did they use this method?

- What message is this document trying to convey?
- Does the sample seems to be too small?
- Is this a balanced argument?
- Is this all the theory there is on the topic?
- What is the unexplained assumption here?
- Does that conclusion come from the evidence?
- How would I apply this in my assignment?

Read

Read the detailed areas that will address the questions you have set out. You will need to reread some sections to make sense of them. As you read make notes about the main points. You could set out the logical steps in the author's argument and highlight any illogical jumps. You could note the main findings and then list the evidence that supports these main findings. There are many ways to make notes about a topic or piece of writing. Do not copy any areas of the text because this is a waste of time. Information in the text needs 'processing' if you are to make any sense of it and remember it. Information needs to pass through your brain for it to have any meaning at a later stage.

Recall

After you have read, answered and made notes of your questions, it is helpful to recite the questions and your answers – an aural summary. This reinforces what you have learned and may provoke further thought about the issues.

Review

Using your notes, mentally go over the material immediately. Then go over the material again within 24 hours of reading it. One further review about a week later will firmly embed the ideas in your brain. If you are reading work-based documents such as reports, you may have to shorten this timescale, so that you immediately review, then in 30 minutes and then in two hours.

 TUTOR COMMENT

In my experience students never get to grips with the amount of reading required at university. There are course notes, textbooks, research for assignments and projects, supporting papers, tutorial readings. Without a clear strategy and good reading habits, they will never get through the reading they need to do.

The best grades are only attainable by those that read widely and can turn that reading into critical and evaluative assignments and examinations.

My favoured approach is to push active learning, speed-reading and SQ3R.

A modification to the SQ3R method, to create the SQ3RW method

I cannot emphasise enough the need to write while you read. Note-making is an essential part of effective reading. It keeps you active, thinking and creating. It provides the method to recall the ideas at a later stage. The form you choose to store the writing will need some thought. Pen and paper is useful, but perhaps using Word, OneNote or bibliography software may be more effective.

Whichever form of recording you use, try to:

- record the source of your notes exactly (author, title, date, publisher and page numbers – a reference)
- record the date on which you wrote them
- revise the record so that it is clear and precise
- keep the notes to one page
- use a logical and memorable layout for the page (a mind map will work well)
- use colour, diagrams, capitals and underlining to format the text and create an interesting layout.

Recording information will be more efficient if you work out a set of useful abbreviations for commonly occurring words. There are some standard abbreviations that you can use, such as:

e.g. – for example
i.e. – that is
c.f. – compare, remember in this context
N.B. – note well, important
= – equals, is the same as
≠ – does not equal, is different from
< – is less than
> – is greater than
… – therefore

The content of your notes will vary but try to systematically record:

- the author's main ideas and any important details
- the logical structure of the argument (use a mind map where possible)
- any important references and links to other writing
- paraphrase, do not copy – use your own words
- use Word in outline format to create the bare bones of the content and argument
- add sections under these headings if you think it is important
- be brief; aim for a reduction factor of over 50, so that your writing is less than $1/50^{th}$ of the original.

Once you have produced several one-page summaries of sources, create a top-level document listing all the notes pages and the main theme of the page (these are short notes on notes), rather in the form of an extended contents list.

A clock index may work well. This will allow for easy navigation of the writing and provide a top-level revision sheet. You can store your notes as pen and paper sheets in a loose-leaf file, OneNote sheets in an electronic file or as Word documents.

Efficient studying and successful assignments rely on having an effective reading and note-making strategy. Develop a personal approach to this area early in your studies.

Ten ways to read more effectively

1 Have your eyes tested; many people turn out to need some form of optical assistance.

2 Make sure you don't subvocalise words or say things aloud as you read.

3 Try to read in chunks so that your eyes stop only two or three times in a line of print instead of at every word. With practice you can read whole sentences in one look.

4 Read from a wide range of sources.

5 Extend your vocabulary by making a note of words you read but you are not sure of their meaning. After reading look up these 'new' words in a dictionary and keep and review the word list regularly.

6 Keep a separate list of technical words related to your subject area – we often call this a glossary.

7 Force your reading speed higher by allowing only a certain amount of time to read passages, gradually reducing the amount of time allowed. Aim to be able to read a 4,000-word article in 15 minutes. This would include making notes of the key points.

8 Use the traffic light system to choose the appropriate reading speed.

9 Don't expect every text to be fully understood at the first time of reading. You may have to go through it several times. Several rapid readings will probably give you a clearer understanding than a single detailed reading.

10 Consciously practise reading and writing and spend time reviewing your performance.

> ## ❝❝ MANAGER COMMENT
>
> We are a large company and managers, even junior ones, are expected to read a lot of reports. We are heavily research-driven and managers are expected to incorporate the research into the product range. I am often amazed that the graduates we employ really flounder when they see the amount of reading they must do. I had always assumed they would be really good at this aspect of the managing job. Now that I know they are often very poor at doing this, I plan training for all the new graduates.
>
> First thing I send them off to do is speed-reading training. When they first come to us they are often real 'snails'. Once they have done the speed-reading course they can all handle reading at well above 1,000 words a minute. I then send them off on a critical reading programme we run that helps them evaluate the quality of the research reports they receive.

6.4 READING THE RIGHT THINGS THE RIGHT WAY

TEXTBOOKS

Large and more difficult to navigate, textbooks are structured as chapters, sections and paragraphs. You will mostly only need a small part at any particular time, so navigate to the section you need using:

- index
- contents
- section headings
- diagrams and illustrations.

Textbooks should be the first place you go when researching a new subject area. They will provide a clear, structured overview of the topic area quickly. One textbook source will not be sufficient to provide the background reading that you need. At the start your aim should be to review three textbooks relating to any new subject area or assignment. You will quickly be able to navigate to the correct chapter using either the contents list or the index. At this stage read and note the ideas and approaches for the whole chapter, not just the sections that appear to relate to your specific use. This will provide a general grounding in the subject area. Textbooks rarely contain the detailed sources, ideas and information you need for assignments, but they do provide a number of ideas and links to other sources.

JOURNAL ARTICLES

Journal articles are normally either reporting the findings of a research study or critically debating a theory, approach or concept. You need to identify which type you are looking at early in the reading process. The structure of these two types is quite rigid.

Journal articles usually have a structure that is determined by the particular journal in which they appear and by the type of research being reported. This makes extracting information from them sometimes easier than from less rigid textbooks. The reporting of empirical research will mostly follow the format of abstract, introduction, methods, results, discussion and conclusion.

Journal articles that are critically debating ideas and concepts will often follow the format: abstract, introduction, history of an idea and summary of the current thinking, main section dealing with the critique of the ideas or concepts, summary and ideas for further research or critique.

Abstracts should provide a complete overview of what the article is about, what it did, how it did it, what it found and what the results mean. The abstract should be the first section that you read. You will then be able to 'weigh up' if the article will be useful.

In research articles introductions usually provide a brief review of previous research, a rationale or reason for the research and an outline of exactly what it is that the research is aiming to do. Method sections describe and evaluate the methods used in the research. Results sections do what their title suggests – they report the findings of the research – but be alert that they will only report what the authors think are the most important findings. Be critical and ask yourself what other findings there might have been that would challenge the claims of the article. After the findings section will be a discussion of the findings where the authors will give their interpretation of what the results actually mean in terms of the subject and the original research question or hypothesis.

Concluding sections will present a summary of the research or critique. They will also set out the implications of the research and make recommendations about further research or policy and practice.

The main message in this chapter is to develop efficient reading and recording approaches. But, it is also important to read critically. The next section looks at a range of questions that will help you to read critically.

Critical reading

In the main do not form a view about the value of an article until you have done the following:

- have understood the main message
- evaluated the evidence supporting that message
- evaluated the writer's perspective.

Displaying to your tutors that you have read sources critically is vital to achieving good grades. Do not accept any writing or arguments as sound without evaluating this for yourself. Show how you have reviewed and evaluated the source(s) in your writing. This is best done by a combination of subtle evaluative statements in your writing, reflective accounts of your thinking and critique and the use of source tables, with a summary and evaluation of the source.

Examples of a subtle evaluative statement include:

Despite the rather small sample size, Farrindon's (2008) data is useful in extending our understanding of...

Havelock's (2009) analysis, despite the omission of Hall's (2006) work, provides a good summary of the research related to...

While there are flaws in the logic, the Brasenose (2004) argument for freeconomics is still the best account...

Reflective accounts set out your thinking on the source and its limitations. You would incorporate your thinking from some of the critical questions below into a paraphrased account of the strengths and weaknesses of the source document. This works well when there are only a few sources. Where there are more than four or five sources, it may be better to summarise using a table with two columns. The first contains the main claims of the source document and the second contains your view of the limitations of the source.

BECOMING REFLECTIVE PERFORMERS

Simon: 'Louise! What are you going to do your project on in the final year?'

Louise: 'I have done some work on this, but why are you asking now? Year 3 is months away.'

S: 'The project methods lecturer came into our lecture today and told us all about what to expect next year. She said it was going to be a really busy year and that there is only just enough time to complete a project by the Easter submission date. She suggested we start thinking about the topic and doing some preliminary work over the summer.'

L: 'Oh great! I was looking forward to taking it easy over the summer, making some money and relaxing with some novels.'

S: 'I am sure you will still be able to do that. Are you coming down to my place in Cornwall over the summer? You had a great time surfing last year.'

L: 'Am I invited?'

S: 'Yes, sure thing. We could even do some work on our topics. You can't surf all day!'

L: 'I was thinking more of lying on the beach all day. That is a brilliant little bay below your house.'

S: 'Great! When are you going to come? For August again like last year?'

L: 'If you don't mind, then yes please.'

S: 'How are we going to prepare for the project?'

L: 'It's months away. Let's worry about that later!'

S: 'No! You taught me to be organised, so let's get organised. How will we do it?'

L: 'You went to the project introduction lecture. What did the lecturer say you should do?'

S: 'Oh yea! She said to work out what we wanted to do and get some of the background reading done.'

L: 'So what area is your project going to be in?'

S: 'Well, I need it to be in marketing so I can push the job prospects along a bit.'

L: 'So you are thinking of doing a survey on something marketing-related?'

S: 'Yes, not sure what but something like that.'

L: 'Do wake up – you can't be organised with "something like that". Organisation is precision. What exactly are you thinking of?'

S: 'Yes, yes, you're right. Be precise!'

L: 'Well then?'

S: 'No, nothing is coming. How will I figure it out?'

L: 'Are you familiar with the university survey software? SNAP, isn't it?'

S: 'No! I don't know that at all.'

L: 'Well, that is the first thing for your to-do list. There is an online tutorial.'

S: 'Is there? You don't normally know anything about computers.'

L: 'I am ahead of you on this one. I did a survey in the last holiday for my employer and I had to use SNAP, so I know it really well.'

S: 'Surprise, surprise. What are you going to do your project on?'

L: 'I have already decided.'

S: 'Really!'

L: 'Yes, I came across this article when I was researching an assignment. It's about the Jungian archetypes that women managers use. It did qualitative interviews with 26 women managers. I am going to do a very similar study with 12 women managers in the company my dad works for.'

S: 'Wow – that is what you call organised.'

L: 'It's better than that. I already know who is going to supervise me and we have discussed the project and she has pointed me to the main literature. I have read some of it but I'll do the rest over the summer.'

S: 'As usual – super organised.'

L: 'It's just the way I am. I'll need some more surfing lessons in the summer. Also, have you got a sun lounger?'

REPORTS

One of the main business communications forms is the report. There are many different types of report; some are one page and others are many hundreds of pages. There is a shift in business towards the one-page report, the argument being that if you cannot communicate the important elements of what you want to say in one page then the message is not clear enough. Clearly the implication is that shorter communication is more effective communication.

Reports take a standard form:

- **title, author, date**
- **executive summary** – an overview of subject, findings and recommendations
- **table of contents** – a list of numbered sections in the report and their page numbers
- **introduction** – terms of reference, outline of report's structure
- **main body** – numbered headings and subheadings that convey the message in the argument
- **conclusion** – states the major outcomes and recommendations
- **reference list** – list of reference material consulted during the writing of the report
- **appendix** – additional material that supports your argument but is not essential to its explanation.

Reports should be easy to read and understand because of this formal, rigid and effective structure. The executive summary provides an efficient window into the report, allowing you to judge its relevance to your needs. You will need to read reports in the same critical manner as any other document, and you may judge the effectiveness of a report by assessing it against the following questions:

- Are the purpose and aims clear?
- Are readers' needs taken into account?
- Are the main points included?
- Are the points supported by evidence?

- Is all the information relevant to the purpose?
- Is the order logical?
- Are the headings and numbering clear?
- Is the information presented clearly?
- Do figures add up?
- Is there a good use of graphics?
- Is the language clear and easy to understand?
- Is the style formal?
- Is the tone suited to the purpose?
- Are there any unnecessary words or phrases?
- Are the conclusions and recommendations clearly linked to the purpose and based on findings?

LEARNING DIARY

MY FIRST REPORT

At work I am the project manager for a small electronics firm. I had to produce my first report the other day. It related to a small problem with a new integrated circuit-testing machine. I took a lot of time over the report and wrote it in my most clear, logical and argued way. It was a terrific piece of work and would have got an A grade at university.

When I presented it to a meeting the reaction was a bit muted. It was about five pages of well-argued logic and came up with a useful conclusion. It wasn't discussed much and the meeting soon moved on to the next item on the agenda. I was a bit disappointed. All my hard work and it was not read and nothing was done.

The next day my manager asked me to call in and have a chat. He was very kind but also pointed out that I had created a very good assignment – but not a business report. I was so embarrassed. It was made worse when he asked me if I knew what a report looked like. I have to say I did not really have a clue. Again, he was very kind and showed me a couple of reports about other things that various people had produced. The difference between these and my offering were very stark. Each of them was just one page in length. One paragraph of executive summary, one paragraph was setting out the main issues and evidence, one paragraph of conclusion and one paragraph of actions to be taken.

I think I learned the difference between university and work that day. Reports are there to create action.

6.5 KEEPING TRACK OF YOUR READING

At university you are going to read large volumes of books, journal articles, reports and web-based material. It is a good idea to develop a system for keeping track of this reading. This can be incorporated into another tracking system if you have one, such as a OneNote file or spreadsheet.

BIBLIOGRAPHIC DATA

Bibliographic data starts to accumulate at university from the very first moment. Realising this and planning a method to trap, record, access and display this data is essential or a very large and difficult-to-solve problem will become apparent later in your studies. This problem, if not addressed, often arises at the later stages of larger university work, such as dissertations or projects. This is very often when the average student is already very busy with the tasks of analysing data and writing up the research for a project or dissertation. Early planning will remove this problem. There are several approaches that can be adopted, and your chosen approach will often depend on how much money you can spend, or how familiar you are with spreadsheets and databases. I will work through the options from the simplest and cheapest to the most expensive and complicated.

Your awarding university will indicate which form of referencing you should use; it is very important that you conform to this requirement. In business awards this is commonly Harvard referencing.

USING A WORD DOCUMENT

Many assignments, projects or dissertations are written each year and the bibliography data is stored as an alphabetical list in a Word document. You add new references manually into the correct alphabetical space as the work proceeds. Any small errors or entries in the wrong place are manually corrected. This approach is simple, cheap and easy to understand. However, it is not very flexible, is time-consuming and only contains the basic reference data. Word 2007 contains features that allow for the development of a bibliography (see Chapter 14). As you write you add citations (references) in the text; this is linked to a source and the bibliography is automatically produced as and when you require it. In this version you are able to choose your reference system and change it dynamically. It is also easy to find a source you have previously used with the 'find source' command. Using this built-in system in Word will provide a quick and useful reference and bibliography list. While it may be suitable to keep track of the references in an assignment, it is not as functional and helpful for storing data about your general university reading.

USING EXCEL OR A SPREADSHEET

Spreadsheets are simple to use and do not require extra or up-to-date software; they also allow you to be creative in how you store your bibliographic data. The basic arrangement for storing bibliographic data in Excel is to create columns of data that you feel will be important in your studies. A typical set of column headings might be:

- reference number – this helps with searching and linking
- reference, in the standard style (sometimes this can be author, title, and so on, in column fields)
- brief summary

- keyword 1
- keyword 2
- keyword 3
- evaluation – a short evaluation of the worth of the source
- link to other reference 1 – links to other references in the list
- link to other reference 2 – links to other references in the list
- link to other reference 3 – links to other references in the list.

REFLECTIVE PERFORMING

BUILDING AN EXCEL BIBLIOGRAPHY

This activity will take about 30–40 minutes. Building effective bibliographies in Excel is easy and can provide enhanced functionality compared with a Word document.

Open a new Excel spreadsheet. Add the column headings below:

- Column A: reference number – this helps with searching and linking, for example 1, 2, 3 and so on
- Column B: author surname and initials, for example Horn, R.
- Column C: book or journal title, for example Motivation at Work
- Column D: place of publication, for example London
- Column E: publisher, for example Sage
- Column F: journal name (if journal source), for example People Management
- Column G: edition number, or journal volume number and page number, for example Vol 12, pp234–432
- Column H: brief summary, for example 'This article is about … It argues that … It uses this evidence…' (extend this to about 5–8 sentences)
- Column I: keyword 1, for example 'motivation'
- Column J: keyword 2, for example 'pay'
- Column K: keyword 3, for example 'cognitive dissonance'
- Column L: evaluation – a short evaluation of the worth of the source
- Column M: link to other reference 1 – links to other references in the list, for example 122
- Column N: link to other reference 2 – links to other references in the list
- Column O: link to other reference 3 – links to other references in the list

Add the detail in the column cells for about 10–12 sources. (If you search for documents on the Athens databases related to your research, you will be able to cut and paste the reference detail and the abstract into the newly created spreadsheet.)

Spend some time thinking about the possible links between the references – enter the cross-reference numbers.

To sort the list alphabetically:

- 'Ctrl a' – this highlights all the cells (Ctrl is the Control key, positioned in the bottom left and right of a standard keyboard).
- Click 'data' on the top 'tools' bar.
- Click 'sort'.
- On this panel click 'my list has header row' from the drop-down menu, 'reference' button, 'ascending', then choose Column B.
- Then 'ok'.

Your reference list and all associated data is now in alphabetical order – of course the reference numbers will now not be in order.

Open Word and use Mail Merge to import:

- author name
- year of publication
- title
- place of publication
- publisher.

This is how you create a bibliography using Excel. If you amend the bibliography data in the Excel spreadsheet you will need to cut and paste a new bibliography after having deleted the original one in the Word document.

This is a great technique for storing details about your general reading. As you will find it is a little awkward in terms of creating the bibliographic list. You can use the reference and bibliography tools in Word to create specific bibliographic data. If you create all the notes in Word documents, you can use the facilities in Word to create a master reference list for all your bibliography material (see Chapter 14).

Using this arrangement allows for a number of useful additions to a standard bibliography. The brief summary gives a brief overview of the article, book or other source. Keywords allow you to search for those keywords at a later date. The evaluation cell allows for a brief or more detailed evaluation of the source; this can link to the next feature. Links to other references are very useful for grouping ideas and references. For example, if the current source has a number of standard critical journal sources relating to it, these can be linked in the columns behind the evaluation. If two or three theories are normally linked, then these can be specified.

USING A DATABASE

If you are familiar with databases and their use, the same sorts of data can be stored in a database. The functionality is further improved and it is very likely that one database will serve all your needs for storing bibliographic data for years to come. Dealing with the creation of this database is beyond the scope of this book, but see the Web Links at the end of this chapter. Microsoft Access© has a sample database for a book collection; this can be easily adapted to create a bibliography database. You can then create the bibliography for documents by using Word's mail merge tool (see Chapter 14).

SPECIALIST BIBLIOGRAPHY SOFTWARE

Specialist software to manage references, citations and bibliographies is available and has a tremendously useful range of functions. It stores the information in very usable forms, but can also 'collect' reference data from various sources. Most importantly the reference data can be imported from Athens and other database search engines, and if you have existing bibliographic data in Word or Excel these can be imported. One publisher owns three of the most familiar software packages: Endnote, Reference Manager and Procite. These all cost in excess of £100, but student versions are cheaper. Bibliographix has a very simple version that is free and a full-function version for about £75; Refworks and Biblioscape are about £100. There are free versions of bibliographic software available. Check out:

- WIKINDX is a free bibliographic and quotations/notes management and article authoring system.
- Bibliography Writer, by Impact Software LLC, is a free bibliography-writing program that makes it quick and easy to source work.
- EasyBib is a web-based reference manager.

Whatever method you choose to manage this aspect of your studies, it makes sense to start recording this data as early as possible.

CASE STUDY

DEVELOPING A READING STRATEGY

The aim of this exercise is to illustrate just how effectively you can read once you have a well-thought-out and developed reading strategy. A warning: this exercise may at first glance look impossible to achieve. But, have faith and carry out the instructions as effectively as you can.

The following is a list of articles that you will find on the Athens database. You will then read and paraphrase each article. The maximum time for this task is two hours. In two hours you will have read and paraphrased 20,000 words. This sounds impossible, doesn't it? Clearly you will need to use all the ideas already covered in this chapter if you are going to find, read and make notes on 20,000 words in two hours. You will effectively be reading at between

about 300 and 500 words per minute. This is not at the speed-reading level that we normally think of as over 500 words per minute. It is an effective, quick-paced reading strategy. The journal names are highlighted in bold.

First, find the following articles on the Athens database. If you are having trouble finding these exact articles, you can substitute them for articles of a similar length. (The references are not in Harvard format.)

A good business strategy need not be difficult: How Simply Strategy can improve your business. Peter Nieuwenhuizen, Richard Koch. **Strategic Direction**. 2007. Vol 23, No 3. p3.

New generation organizations: Motivating employees through creative working practices. **Strategic Direction**. Nov/Dec 2006. Vol 22, No 11. p22.

Education for life? Quantifying the factors behind students' choice of HE. **Human Resource Management International Digest**. 2007. Vol 15, No 3. pp30–2.

The impact of a threatening e-mail reprimand on the recipient's blood pressure. Howard Taylor, George Fieldman, Saadi Lahlou. **Journal of Managerial Psychology**. 2005. Vol 20, No 1/2. pp43–50.

Sink or Skim: Textbook reading behaviors of introductory accounting students. Barbara J Phillips, Fred Phillips. **Issues in Accounting Education**. Feb 2007. Vol 22, No 1. pp21–44.

Approach – I would suggest that you use the following approach:

- Read the abstract completely.

- Read the conclusion completely.

- Skim-read the whole document, marking any sections that seem to contain important results (mark these with a highlighter) (mark sparingly – only the important outcomes),

- Return to the highlighted sections and make notes on the key outcomes of the article.

You must work quickly but also thoroughly, so skim-read fast but read the important sections more slowly, make brief notes about the key outcomes.

It is quite possible that you will complete this task well inside the allotted time. If you do, make a note of how long the task took to complete.

If you have carried out this exercise in a tutorial or group setting, it would be useful to recite the notes you have made to the group. This follows the SQ3RW approach, and you may find some interesting aspects of effective reading are revealed.

SUMMARY

- Read efficiently by using different types of reading:
  - skimming
  - detailed reading
  - critical reading
  - speed-reading.

- Use the traffic light system to select and read books and journals.

- Read faster to be more effective.

- Use the adapted SQ3RW method:
  - survey
  - question
  - read
  - recall
  - review
  - write.

- Read different sources in different ways:
  - textbooks
  - journal articles
  - reports
  - critical articles.

- Devise a system for keeping track of your reading:
  - pen and paper notes
  - Word documents
  - OneNote file
  - spreadsheet
  - database.

- Use a standard form of recording bibliographic data:
  - bibliographic software
  - Word 2007.

EXPLORE FURTHER

FURTHER READING

Fairbairn, G. and Fairbairn, S. (2001) *Reading at University: A guide for students.* Milton Keynes: Open University Press.

McMillan, K. and Weyers, J. (2007b) *The Smarter Student: Study skills and strategies for success at university.* Harlow: Pearson Education Limited.

WEB LINKS

Try this easy to use free speed reader trainer: http://www.spreeder.com/

CIPD website address: http://www.cipd.co.uk/

Speed reading website from Mindtools: http://www.mindtools.com/speedrd.html

Speed reading test: http://www.readingsoft.com/

CHAPTER 7

Developing Good Writing Skills

What skills will I develop in this chapter?

- how to develop good writing habits
- how to plan what you will write – macro writing
- how to write and express yourself clearly – micro writing
- how to develop good ideas and be creative
- how to write effective paragraphs
- how to develop clear, effective arguments
- how to reference and avoid plagiarism

7.1 INTRODUCTION

Investing time at the beginning of your university studies developing good writing skills will reward you with excellent grades for assignments and examinations. These skills can then be used to good effect when you join the world of work. Employers will be looking for managers who can express themselves clearly, precisely and effectively. Developing the skills to create strong and compelling arguments will ensure good university grades and later will mark you out as an effective manager. This chapter aims to develop the basic building blocks of writing and arguing.

This chapter also addresses the detailed issue of referencing, explaining the Harvard style. This style is used extensively in business and management degree awards. If you are to avoid accusations of plagiarism you will need to be aware of referencing and develop a consistent style of acknowledging the work of other writers.

Developing good writing skills takes time and effort, so my advice for using this chapter would be to read it thoroughly and carry out the reflective performing activities. But also to return to the chapter every few months and review how your writing reflects the ideas contained in this chapter.

7.2 DEVELOP GOOD WRITING HABITS

If you look in books and on the Internet you will find myriad helpful hints for writers. Strangely, they hardly every say the same things. What follows is my advice on the actual writing process required for university and work.

UNDERSTAND THAT WRITING IS JUST LIKE ANY OTHER SKILL

Writing is not a magical skill. It is a skill with a standard set of approaches and procedures that can be learned and learned relatively quickly. If you took up a new sport when you came to university, you would not expect to become very good without some practice. So it is the same with writing; it can be learned but it takes some time and practice. Most universities have excellent study skills support units that will help you develop your writing skills. Many universities have e-learning and web-based support for writing skills. Many students never get around to involving themselves with developing their writing skills. This is a real shame because underdeveloped writing skills put you at a disadvantage at university and in the workplace.

DEVELOP A WRITING HABIT

Writing is a skill and skills need to be practised. The best practice for writing is to write. Early in your university studies there will be very few opportunities for writing large pieces of work. But, you should get into the writing habit early. You can create opportunities for writing by reviewing, paraphrasing and critiquing some of the important theory in your subject area. These skills will then be useful when you write the more critical assignments in levels 2 and 3. In my view, in the early part of your university studies you should set aside at least four to six hours a week to develop your writing skills. The development nature of this writing will be further enhanced if you can record the process in your learning diary and arrange for someone to give you feedback on your writing.

USE FEEDBACK TO IMPROVE YOUR WRITING

We are often very poor judges of our own writing. To enhance our skills in writing we need to overcome our fear of showing our writing to others. This is where a small study group can be really useful. Get feedback on your writing from your study group. You will also get valuable feedback from the skills unit of your university. The added benefit of using the skills unit is that they will diagnose any weaknesses and point you to development resources to improve that part of your writing. Your tutors may also be willing to assist in helping with writing skills.

UNDERSTAND THAT WRITING TAKES TIME

Writing takes time so you need to plan and organise carefully to ensure you have enough time to carry out the writing and the reviewing process. Failing to set aside a sufficient amount of time to carry out the writing will lead to rushed work and poor results. Typically, you will need about six to eight hours to complete (think, write and review) 1,000 words of academic writing. This assumes that you have done the background planning and research. See the section below about macro and micro writing.

READ, THINK, DESIGN, WRITE AND REREAD EVERY DAY

Writing, thinking, planning, reading and rereading needs to become a daily habit when you are completing university work. Unless you have carried out the reading of background material and thinking about that material, you will not have anything to write. When I say thinking, I mean understanding, critiquing, analysing, synthesising and evaluating. Once you have written a passage of work you will need to reread it to make sure it is correct, makes sense and has clarity of thought and a strong argument. Try to set aside time every day for these tasks.

DEVELOP 'STICKABILITY'

You may not have come across the term 'stickability': it means the ability to concentrate on a task over various periods of time, especially when the task seems to be getting increasingly difficult to complete. Stickability is a frame of mind. Successful people are often quite stubborn and will not be beaten by anything. This can make them difficult to live with sometimes but stickability is necessary at university and in the workplace. Some people are naturally stubborn and stick at things. If you are not, you may want to think about developing your stickability. Stickability first comes from having goals you believe in and want to achieve – completing excellent university work should be one of those goals. Then plan and organise your time and allocate space to writing; if you plan to spend two hours writing, do only this. Do not be distracted – stick at it. Gradually you can increase the scheduled writing periods until a four-hour session is possible. Set session goals, such as 'I will complete 400 words in this writing session,' and do not stop until this goal is achieved. Finally, don't allow distractions when you are writing: no stopping for drinks or a bit of net surfing, texting, a phone call or snacks.

THINK AND PLAN AND MAKE NOTES BEFORE YOU WRITE

A later section in this chapter will introduce and explore the notion of macro and micro writing. Essentially macro writing is the planning that is done before you start to write. In a highly structured approach you would plan each chapter, section and paragraph before you start to write. This ensures that when you do write the process is less daunting, in that you simply extend the planned paragraph into a complete paragraph. You will need to develop and personalise your planning style, but it is essential that you do plan, think about and make notes before you start writing.

GET IT 'WRITE' FIRST TIME

Following on from the idea of careful and extensive planning is the notion of writing structured, well-planned, well-argued and evidenced paragraphs. This structured approach means that you are likely to write a paragraph that is 'write' first time. If you type first and think after you are likely to need to make extensive and time-consuming revisions. The quickest and most effective way to write is to think, plan, structure and organise and only then 'write'. Your work will probably then be 'write' first time. There will always be a need to revise and correct small parts of what you have written.

UNDERSTAND THE NECESSITY TO REVISE YOUR WRITING

An idea forms in your head and is then transferred to type. While the idea may be well thought through and well evidenced, the writing process will always need review and improvement. You need to plan a strategy for reviewing and revising your work. One effective strategy has been outlined in these good writing ideas. The first phase of writing is always clear and detailed planning. Once the words are typed, review each sentence in the paragraph before you go on, then review the whole paragraph. When you have read it several times and made corrections to the English usage, clarity of idea and form of words, then move on to write the next paragraph. Leave the writing for at least a week and then review whole sections and make revisions and adaptations. If you are able to enlist the help of someone else – friends, family, study group – let them read it and comment.

I feel sure if you are able to follow some of these approaches you will find the writing process enjoyable and you will produce clear, precise and correct writing.

LEARNING DIARY

I AM BRIGHT BUT NOT THAT SKILFUL

I know I am bright as I can do really well at examinations without really trying. I pick things up quickly and I can remember them. But, I don't seem to be able to get really good grades for my coursework. It is a bit of a mystery! I understand the question and know what has to be written but I cannot seem to get a decent score. I have been getting low 60s for my assignments. My friends think it is hilarious and say I must have upset the tutors – they know I am clever and bright.

It was my mum that started me thinking a bit about what could be wrong! She asked how long I spent on writing and reviewing my work before I give it in. I had to admit that I generally write my assignments a few days before the deadline, give them a quick review and then submit them.

I tend to get comments back from the tutors like: 'Good ideas, just underdeveloped.' 'You need a stronger argument!' 'Develop your writing style a bit more.'

When you put these two things together, I think maybe it is not what I know or the quantity of the ideas that is letting me down; it might be the quality of my writing. I think I might get some help from the uni skills unit and see if they can help.

7.3 UNDERSTANDING THE MACRO APPROACH TO ACADEMIC WRITING

The 'macro micro' idea of writing is not difficult to grasp, but it is often difficult to remember to accurately switch between the two modes of writing. Macro writing is a form of planning and organising at the macro levels. Notice I use the term macro 'levels', because planning and organising can be carried out at several levels. Micro writing involves close attention to the content and structure of sentences and paragraphs and will be dealt with later in the chapter. Most writers will switch between these modes in a personalised manner. My argument is that a more focused and strategic approach to macro and micro writing will improve the quality of your writing.

GENERATING IDEAS AND BEING CREATIVE

Good assignments, examination answers and work solutions come from generating good ideas. The following sections look at a number of ways to generate ideas.

To generate ideas you will need to develop the ability to think creatively. Creative thinking might be thought of as the ability to generate something new. In your assessments there will be endless opportunities to create and use new ideas. This is a vital part of the assessment process but one that is often forgotten or ignored, leading to rather dull and one-dimensional writing. Creative thinking can be done in a variety of ways and some of these will be considered in the coming sections. The ideas for assignments and the workplace do not need to be brilliant, astonishing ideas. What is needed are good, sound ideas for solving problems, creating new theory, using an existing idea in a new way or adapting an existing theory to explain things better.

BRAINSTORMING IN GROUPS

This is a technique that can be used in seminars for case study enquiry but can also be used by a group of friends or a study group to generate ideas for assignments. As a warm-up technique, use brainstorming to generate ideas for a fun activity such as themes for a party. This will get the creative juices flowing and create the right atmosphere.

Then move on to the main topic by establishing the exact focus of the session, for example 'solutions to a poor motivation problem'. If you can use one of the university seminar rooms or group study rooms you will have a whiteboard and some paper flipcharts to record the ideas. One person is nominated to record the ideas, and the rest of the group think and then suggest ideas that are recorded on the board or flipcharts. These sessions can quickly degenerate into chaos and recriminations, so follow these rules:

- postpone and withhold your judgement of the ideas
- be positive – every idea is useful
- encourage wild and exaggerated ideas
- no critical comments are allowed
- quantity counts at this stage – not quality
- encourage contributions from everyone

- if you have an idea, even if it seems silly, record it
- recognise that one person's idea will spark off a creative thought in someone else
- build on the ideas put forward by others
- every person and every idea has equal worth.

The role of each person is to:

- suggest ideas that will work as solutions
- suggest ideas that will stimulate solutions in others
- record every idea that comes to you
- remain uncritical of any idea.

Brainstorming sessions will have a natural flow to them, with periods of frantic ideas generation and then periods of reflection and then more ideas, followed by periods of refining the ideas by combination, extension or transformation. Sessions can last from a few minutes to a few hours. A typical session for a workplace problem will probably last around 40–50 minutes. Make sure that there is at least one break in proceedings for coffee or a drink; when the group returns you will find they can generate more ideas and refine further the existing ideas.

There are variations of this technique you can use:

Anonymous ideas-generation using Post-It® notes – Ideas are written out and posted on the walls under headings. This frees the creative process from personal criticism because no one is aware of who suggested which idea. A version of this can be done on the computer using a discussion board in the e-learning suite.

Blind brainstorming requires each person to write out ten or so ideas at the beginning of the session and then post these on the walls (Post-It® notes are best). The first person puts their ideas up on the walls with a quick commentary, then the next person puts their ideas on the wall. If the second person's idea is similar or the same as one that exists, then they put their note with the other idea. The process continues until everyone has posted his or her notes. What you will have at that point is a consensus brainstorm. Common ideas will have several notes from different people. Remember, the most common idea is not always the best idea.

You can use any of the techniques suggested with a **graded brainstorming** session, where each idea is given a rating between 1 and 10 by the author of the idea. This works against one of the basic premises of the technique, but you will find it changes the dynamic in strange and creative ways. A slight variation of this technique is to have each person rate the ideas 1, 2, 3 and so on.

Once the ideas have been generated and maybe graded, they will need to be recorded in a form that can be distributed. The most common way that this is done is by one person transcribing the ideas into a Word document and sending it to all the participants. If you used a discussion board then the ideas will already be recorded.

BRAINSTORMING ON YOUR OWN

This is not as effective as a group session but is still better than no brainstorming at all. Start by writing down the problem or assignment question. Use Post-It® notes and write one idea on each note until you have no more ideas. Silly and apparently ridiculous ideas are just as good as more sensible ideas, so do not restrict the creative process. Then post up the notes on a wall or board. Follow this with a period of reflection and development, where you may generate some more ideas or develop ones that already exist. Finally, organise the ideas into groups that make some sort of sense and record the most promising ones in a Word or OneNote document.

NEGATIVE BRAINSTORMING

Remember that the idea of brainstorming is to create new ideas, solutions and ways of looking at things. So this idea may sound really ridiculous, but try it out before you reject it. It can be a group or individual activity. Start by selecting and defining a topic or problem as with brainstorming. It is important to frame the topic in a positive way, such as 'How can we reduce absenteeism?' Organise into groups and nominate someone to record the ideas or use the Post-It® note technique. Now reverse the topic so that it becomes 'How can we make people take more days' absence?' I told you it was a crazy technique.

Now let's try to answer that question. How could we make people not come to work?

Some ideas might be to:

- not pay them
- make their lives at work a misery
- give them boring and repetitive work to do
- insult and disrespect them
- and so on...

Human nature often means it is easier to come up with the negatives than the positives. As before, record the ideas and don't judge them. Also try to create weird and unusual ideas – the crazier the better.

Then take each of the ideas and reverse them, so that we have:

- pay them well
- make their lives at work interesting and enjoyable
- give them varied and engaging tasks to do
- ensure that they are respected and valued
- and so on...

NEGATIVE BRAINSTORMING

I am an assistant section manager at my local retail store. Once a week we have brainstorming meetings for 45 minutes where we try to come up with solutions to store-related problems. This week we had an outside trainer come to facilitate the sessions and she introduced us to negative brainstorming. The topic was store cleanliness.

I made a bit of a fool of myself as I had loads of negative ideas about cleanliness, loads and loads, and nobody else had very much to offer. At one stage I thought my store manager would sack me on the spot. But, the trainer was encouraging me and I kept on responding.

Once the trainer encouraged the group to reverse the negative ideas into positives, the group began to see the value of the approach. It ended up as one of the best sessions we have had. Afterwards my manager said, 'Well done. You really contributed to that and made it work.'

ASSUMING A NEW PERSPECTIVE

This is a technique to generate new ideas that might otherwise be overlooked. It is very easy to get stuck in thinking about a problem from just one perspective. This can be a group activity, or one person can take on several roles. Each member of the group is asked to think about the problem from a different role, or you must take on all the roles if you are working alone. Ideas will be recorded on flipcharts or Post-It® notes.

If we investigate the problem of absenteeism again, each person in the group would be asked to take on one of the roles:

- a worker's sick dog
- a worker's poorly mother
- section manager with deadlines to meet
- a married person with children who are ill
- someone with children in a holiday period
- a worker with a hangover
- someone who wants to watch the Olympics, cricket or Wimbledon rather than come to work
- someone who travels a long way to work
- a customer whose order is late
- the colleague of a worker who is off work ill.

In each role you are asked how this person might solve the problem. You can also use brainstorming to generate ideas for the roles.

The techniques above should help you to generate useful ideas for solving assignment and workplace problems. But it is also important to keep in mind the creative thinking processes – the following section looks at creative thinking.

It is my belief that business is dead without ideas. The best ideas come from the workforce, and it is important to encourage and reward ideas. To this end we have two schemes running, both of which have rewards attached.

First, there is a structured meeting where the team leader throws out a problem and the team contributes ideas. Each team member writes their idea on a Post-It® note and sticks it on the wall. After this every team member gives the idea a rating from 1 to 10. At the end of the session the team leader creates an ideas log that is shared with the team and sent to the line manager. The team member with the highest-rated ideas gets a £20 voucher. The organisation has 36 teams in total so this scheme costs £720 per week. Our business analysts have calculated that in the past year this scheme has generated savings or revenue for the company of £2.2 million.

We also have a more conventional drop-box for ideas. The analysts calculate that this system has generated £1.5 million of savings or revenue. The top 10 ideas, as rated by senior management, get an array of gifts. Top prize last year was a Caribbean holiday worth £3,000.

CREATIVE THINKING

Everyone can be a creative thinker; it is a state of mind and a set of skills. The following sections should help you to be more creative. Being creative is about spotting ideas and possibilities. It is also a process, and it is these processes that we will investigate.

Creative evolution uses an existing idea to develop a better one. Small refinements in solutions and theory can generate useful new ideas. Solutions to existing organisational problems can often be refined and improved and used in your assignments or at work. When carrying out your project or dissertation, research methods is a useful area to consider creative evolution. Published research methods were designed for a different context from your own research but don't be afraid to engage in creative improvement of a method so that it works better with your context and research questions.

Creative synthesis – Synthesis has already been discussed, and you will be aware that it is the combining of things to create a new thing. This can be very useful in developing theory, methods, data analysis and practical solutions. Try bringing ideas from other areas and applying them in business.

Creative revolution throws away old ideas and asks 'what about the impossible?' When you are looking for a creative revolution you do not need to think about what has been used before; you just need to think if something will work. If your assignment is concerned with solving a problem, finding a creative revolution would require you to ask many 'what if' questions: 'What if we… Or, what if we…' In this way you will try out lots of improbable ideas or solutions until you have a 'eureka' moment. This would be the equivalent of 'brainstorming' ideas.

Creative reapplication involves looking at something old in a new way. Clear your expectations of how old ideas can be applied and opportunities 'open up'.

Try to look at your assignment tasks in new ways and look for new solutions based on existing solutions. Reapplication in coursework and assignments works well with theory, evidence and solutions.

Creative solutions and breakthroughs occur when we stop trying to implement a solution and start trying to find a solution.

> ## ❝❝ STUDENT COMMENT
>
> I think I am a diligent student who works hard and does his best. I do quite well in assignments and examinations that require critique and elevation. But if I have to come up with ideas in class or for an assignment or examination, I just cannot do it. My brain just does not seem able to generate new things.
>
> Having read Edward De Bono's *How to Have Creative Ideas*, I feel able to contribute in the creative direction. The book has loads of exercises to get you thinking and creating. It has made such a difference to how I go about assignments and examinations.

CLUSTERING

Once you have generated a lot of ideas it may be difficult to know what to do with them. Clustering is a technique that puts ideas together into groups. It requires you to do a fair amount of critical thinking to establish why one idea should be put with another. There are several ways to cluster ideas, such as:

- logical clustering – ideas that have the same logical base go together
- forced clustering – ideas that are opposites are forced together
- comparative clustering – ideas at the two ends of a contrast continuum are put together
- outcome clustering – ideas with similar outcomes are put together.

Clustering is a creative process. At the initial stage you will just be 'trying out the clusters' to see how they look, what they suggest. But, eventually you will need to cluster ideas together to create headings or paragraphs to answer the assignment question. At this stage you can add these headings and paragraph ideas to an outline Word document.

7.4 PLANNING WHAT YOU WILL WRITE

Once you have carried out research, background reading and generated some ideas, you will need to plan what you will write. This is an important iterative (that is, goes through planning cycles) process if your work is to achieve a good grade. Planning your macro writing can be done in various ways:

Mind maps, where each section and each subpoint is in the shape, with paragraph ideas leading off these. Numbering the shapes and ideas carries out the ordering of these sections and ideas.

Pen and paper is used to set out headings, subheadings and paragraph headings. Numbering and renumbering the headings and sections creates the ordering of ideas.

MIND MAPPING

Try out the following process for mind mapping.

Stage one

Place a large, memorable title in the middle of a sheet of paper. This will probably be the title of the assignment, but you may need a subtitle.

Let's try: 'My TV advert – Saving the planet'.

Stage two

Now add some main branches to represent the main points you want to make in the advert. Make sure the branches go well away from the title so you have lots of room for ideas. Use different colours and vary the types of boxes and lines that you use.

Stage three

Add branches off the existing branches to give the detail for each of the points you have made. Again, vary the colours, styles and shapes.

Stage four

Create any links that seem to be useful between one idea or point and another.

Did you know? In the newer versions of Word you can create mind maps. You can add images, words, audio and video – it is a great tool. But, essentially mind maps are a simple pen and paper tool for thinking and planning.

Using Word in outline mode allows for structured headings, subheadings and several levels below this. It has the advantage that it will create the structure in Word that you will later use to write your assignment. Ordering the paragraphs is done by adjusting the position in the list, and reordering and reorganising is easy. You may find that using Word in outline view is the most effective way to create assignments and work documents. The following sections guide you though how Word operates in outline view.

Once the headings or main ideas are organised, try to write one full sentence about the content of each paragraph. This will indicate if the paragraph has any real substance; if you find you are unable to write one full sentence, this heading or paragraph point is not substantial – remove it. The first sentence should contain the main claim of the paragraph. This one sentence will allow you to return and continue from that one sentence. This macro writing is often called outlining.

Each point you make in outline mode will become a paragraph. At the first attempt you will have generated many ideas for each section, and how you select and order those ideas will be very important to the quality of argument you create. It is important to reorder those ideas into a logical structure. Logical structures will take several attempts before you are sure you have the most effective structure. A question arises about what is a logical structure in the context of your document.

Figure 7.1 Mind map – 'Saving the planet'

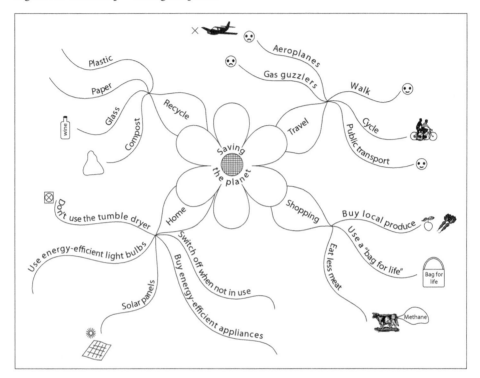

To use outline mode in Word you will need to change views in the view menu to 'outline'. Then you will see a toolbar with arrows for promoting and demoting headings.

1 Once your file is opened, click the **View** tab and select **Outline**.

2 Add the headings that you created from clustering, at the top level – level 1.

3 Add the sections under the headings and demote them one rank – level 2.

4 Add the paragraph points and demote them one rank – level 3.

5 Write the full paragraph for each of the points you want to make at level 4.

6 While you carry out this process you must have the purpose of your writing in mind. Coursework and assignments are often most effectively structured by 'mirroring' the assignment brief, so that the main headings answer each part of the assignment and the headings below these set out your argument.

SEQUENCING

At some point in the macro writing process you will need to change the sequence of the points you are making. You can click and drag sections into different orders and sequences. You can also promote and demote points. Each section can be collapsed and opened so that you can clearly see the section you are working on.

Figure 7.2 Word in outline view

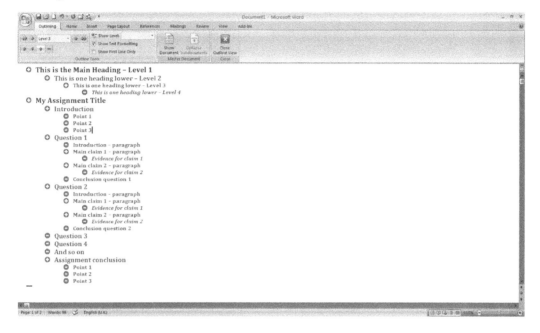

PRUNING

Once you have created a sequence of ideas that answer the assignment, you may judge that there are sections that do not belong in the assignment or you may form this view at the reviewing stage. In outline view you can click on the plus or minus sign and then hit the delete key. Remember that when you delete a heading, you delete everything under that heading. So take care! A more secure technique is to have a section at the end marked as deleted items, and instead of deleting an item or headings, cut and paste it into the deleted area. It is amazing how often the section you thought was rubbish and not needed turns out to be vital after you have deleted it.

ORDERING

Ordering the ideas in the whole document and considering how the sections flow will improve the readability and credibility of your writing. The macro-level task of ordering is very important and this task needs to be completed from several 'logical' positions. Each position should be evaluated in relation to how readable, credible and plausible it is. As the detail of any section is written, it may be necessary to reconsider the ordering of the points being made. This ordering occurs at many levels in the writing. We looked earlier at ordering theories in a literature review section. Each section relating to each theory will also need to be ordered into paragraphs, and each paragraph will have a set of ordered points.

REFLECTIVE PERFORMING

ORDERING IDEAS

Let's imagine that you have a literature review section that has five significant theories. You have already decided that you will arrange the section as separate theories. But, you cannot decide in which order to present them. Reflect on this problem!

The essence of this problem is, 'What would be a logical way to organise these five theories?' Some thoughts on the ways you might organise them include:

- historically – the earliest theory first
- complexity – most easily understood first leading to the most complex
- instrumentality – the most frequently used theory in literature first
- evaluation – moving from the least useful to the most useful.

REFLECTIVE PERFORMING

ORDERING WITHIN AN ACADEMIC THEORY SECTION

Following on from 'Reflective performing: ordering ideas', you are now ordering the ideas for each theory. You have the following points that you want to make but you are not sure of the order in which to write them:

- critique of the theory, three main critical elements
- evaluation of the theory
- five research studies that have used the theory as the main research guidance
- description of the theory
- advantages of the use of the theory to understand business research
- limitations of the theory in understanding business research
- practical uses of the theory in management
- description of a related theory developed from the first theory.

Using just these points, 'play' with the order and establish which is the most effective order in which to make these points.

From these two reflective performing exercises you may be able to see the importance of ordering and reordering.

SELECTION

Once you have created a range of ideas, solutions and approaches you will need to refine them. An important aspect of macro writing action is selection. As you plan and organise the chapters, sections and paragraphs of your writing, you will have more ideas, points, theories, opinions and evidence than can be included within the word limit. In the first macro planning stage do not be selective; you should include all the ideas you generate. In the second macro planning stage you should carry out two tasks:

1 Select the points or statements you will make and the evidence you will use to support those points.

2 Then order the points you have selected in a logical manner.

LOUISE AND SIMON

BECOMING REFLECTIVE PERFORMERS

Simon: 'Louise! I think my brain just fell out on the paper!'

Louise: 'What!'

S: 'I have been trying to plan that large change assignment using a pen and a piece of paper. A mind map, but as I say it looks like my brain fell out on the paper.'

L: 'Well, if it did it would only make a small splash!'

S: 'Oh very funny! Take a look at the mind map.'

L: 'Yes. That looks like your kind of planning. You seem to have lots of ideas. Why are you having trouble? Just refine them into an argument that answers the questions.'

S: 'Well! I seem to have too many ideas. I just can't see how I can organise them into an answer.'

L: 'I could let you in on my personal secret for thinking.'

S: 'Louise, you're holding back on me. Why haven't you told me this before? What is it?'

L: 'I use a thing I called stair logic.'

S: 'I can get upstairs on my own. I've been able to do that for years now!'

L: 'Well, if you don't want to know I'll keep my greatest secret to myself.'

S: 'No. No. Do tell. I really need some help with this.'

L: 'Stair logic is a diagrammatic way for me to think. I have these blank sheets with stairs drawn on them. I put what I am trying to get to at the top. Let's say, from your assignment, "How important is organisational structure in organisational change?" That goes on the top step.'

S: 'Yes, what do you do then?'

L: 'Now this is really clever, if I say so myself. The left-hand side are the positive steps to support the argument. The right-hand side is the argument against it, the counterargument.'

S: 'I am a bit lost now. Can you draw it?'

L: 'Yes look –

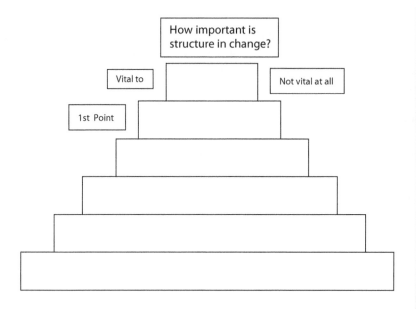

S: 'Yes, I've got it. Arguing for up the left and arguing against up the right.'

L: 'Yes, you have got it now.'

S: 'So using this I have to build my argument step by step?'

L: 'Yes, and the diagram helps to ensure that there are no illogical steps.'

S: 'What do I do with it once I have made all the steps?'

L: 'Then I convert this to a Word document, with each step being a paragraph. Easy!'

S: 'Well, I'll try it and let you know.'

L: 'Do you want another really good idea on the thinking stuff?'

S: 'Yes, go on, shoot.'

L: 'Get de Bono's *Six Thinking Hats* out of the library and read through that. It only takes a couple of hours and it really changes the way you think.'

S: 'I'll do that. Now, isn't it your turn to clean the kitchen?'

IDEAS ARE ONE THING BUT YOU ALSO NEED THEORY, CRITIQUE AND EVIDENCE

So far this chapter has not differentiated between ideas and other content in your documents. However, most of your writing will not contain only ideas. The layout and approach you use in your writing will be partially affected by your use of theory, critical statements and evidence. A later chapter will look at how to construct arguments using these elements, but here it is worth thinking about how to use these elements to build strong and effective arguments.

Theory is most often used in university writing for two reasons. First, it is used to analyse the context of an assessment question. So if your assignment asks you to explain what is happening in a given context, you might use theory of these contexts to understand the actions. When you are asked to analyse and explain the actions of an organisation undergoing change, it can often be confusing. Let's imagine you have been asked to analyse and evaluate change in the British Post Office (Royal Mail) between 2000 and 2009. You could bring many different types of theory into play to explain what happened. These might include:

- economic theory, looking at supply, demand and competition
- industrial relations theory, looking at changes to the employment relationship
- political theory, looking at which groups were powerful and which groups have become powerful
- marketing theory to investigate how the Royal Mail has developed its brand.

Second, this same theory can be used to generate solutions to problems and as a structure for recommendations.

Critique and a critical stance are required in all your writing. If you introduce theory into your writing, always introduce critique of that theory. Ideally, you will need to follow the following format when you use any theory:

- Introduce more than one theory; in 2,000–3,000-word assignments or examinations try to introduce three theories.
- Critique the three theories. Set out what is good and what is weak.
- Make a judgement (evaluation) about which theory would be most useful in the context of your assignment or examination.
- Use the chosen theory to explain actions and structure solutions and recommendations.

In terms of macro writing, each theory you introduce will be a paragraph, and the general structure of this paragraph might be:

1 Describe the theory (description – textbooks and journals).
2 Explain what is strong about this theory (critique – journal sources).
3 Explain what is weak about this theory (critique – journal sources).
4 Explain where and how this theory has been used in the past (judgement – from journal sources).
5 Make a judgement about the usefulness of the theory (evaluation).

Evidence in the form of journal sources will be used to support any argument you make. The normal form for statement paragraphs might be:

1 statement about some aspect of the assessment question
2 evidence to support the statement (other writers' ideas or research evidence)
3 more evidence to support your point (two or three pieces of supporting evidence)
4 counterevidence that does not support your point (balanced arguments are strong arguments)
5 summary statement.

EXAMPLE: STRUCTURING A MARKETING ASSIGNMENT

What follows is an example of how you might structure a marketing assignment.

Executive summary

Introduction – Briefly outline purpose, scope (what you're going to cover) and any background needed to understand the assignment.

Part 1   Macro forces – what are they, how does each one affect your topic area? Name them all; don't leave any out. As you examine each one, add in more detail for the most important ones. Include positive and negative impacts, actual or possible effects (short-term, long-term). Sum up – indicating which are the major 'drivers'.

Part 2   Marketing mix – define.
Choose two companies, discuss differences.

- company 1: how positioned in the market, primary target markets; marketing mix (4/7Ps)

- company 2: how positioned in the market, primary target markets; marketing mix (4/7Ps)

- comparison

- sum up the major points of comparison between the two companies

- Where are they similar, where different?

Conclusion – summarise what you have found and your final position. If needed, add solutions and recommendations.

LEARNING DIARY

LEARNING DIARY ENTRY

I had a note about my writing style from one of my tutors today. It just said 'chaotic'! What does that mean, I wonder? I may have to go and see him again.

It could be to do with how I write my assignments. I normally think about it for a while, do some background reading and then just start writing the main sections. These will get quite large, so after a while I will reduce them a bit and then add a section at the beginning to introduce the assignment. I don't know that this is the best way to do it. But it is the only way I know how to do it. It was the way I did it at school and it worked okay.

I wonder if I will have to go back to basics and rethink how I write. The way I am doing it does have a few drawbacks:

- It takes ages to write.

- I have to spend ages reading it and removing bits.

- I am always over the word count; the last assignment target was 2,500 words and mine was nearly 5,000 words – that has to be a waste of time!

- My grades are nearly always in the 50s.

- Sometimes I miss bits of the assignment out because I just forget to do them.

- I have got so many assignments to do I am getting behind – a better method might be faster.

However:

- I can't really spend any time at the moment adjusting my style.

- It's how I have always done it so my grades may go down if I change my approach.

- Danger – I might change my approach and then start failing stuff.

- It is going to take ages to change how I write.

But:

- This cannot go on because of the time it is taking.

I will go and see my tutor and go to the skills unit and see if either of those can help.

Then I will set myself some development goals and SMART objectives.

7.5 EFFECTIVE MICRO WRITING

SENTENCES

When you start to construct the main writing in any of your macro planned paragraphs, the first layer of building blocks will be sentences. Most people write in sentences quite naturally without really knowing what makes a sentence. More importantly it is possible to write in non-sentences. And while readers can often understand a non-sentence, your writing will have more clarity and 'punch' if you use sentences. Simple sentence structures are often more effective than longer sentences in academic writing. So the building block for your work will be short sentences. That leads us to ask, 'what is a sentence?'

It turns out that this is not an easy question to answer. I will try to answer it with a list of the contents of a sentence and a few practical exercises. Sentences should have the following:

- a capital letter at the start

- a full stop at the end

- a subject – what the sentence is about (short sentences have one subject)

- a verb – a word that tells us what is happening to the subject.

In this form it looks like we will have very little trouble writing in sentences. But, there are many variations of this basic structure and requirements. Such as:

- Sentences can be long or short (try to write in short sentences, but you are likely to need long ones as well).

- Sentences can be simple or complex (try to write in simple sentences, but you will need complex ones as well).

- Sentences can be broken into smaller parts with commas, semi-colons and dashes.

Our main aim is to ensure that any collection of words we write is a clear sentence that conveys meaning. The word checker you use may sometimes 'wiggly' underline a collection of words in green, and when you right-click into this section it will say 'fragment'; unhelpfully it will often say 'no suggestions'.

Green wiggly underlines indicate that your sentence is not grammatically correct. Do not submit work that has red or green wiggly underlines. Words underlined in red are deemed by the spell-checker to be spelled wrong, but watch out because most spell-checkers will not recognise some of the more specific words related to business. Also, check that your spelling and grammar checker is set to UK English – it is surprising how different US English is.

Let's try a few sentences and decide if they are in fact sentences.

1　Did the tutor tell you? [This is a question, but is it a sentence?]
　　Answer – Yes. Can you explain why?

2　What a noise they were making.
　　Answer – Yes.

3　A long curve with a short tail.
　　Answer – No. But why? It has no verb; nothing is happening.

So short sentences should be fine; however, it is difficult to express academic issues with short sentences alone. The problem may then become one of overly long and complex sentences, such as: 'Buying small competitors can be an effective and quick way for a developing organisation to grow its locally based brand; however it is not the only way.'

This would be improved if the one sentence were split into two short sentences.

REFLECTIVE PERFORMING

USING SHORT SENTENCES

Your paragraph plan shows that you want to express the following points:

Female students spent £56 per year more than male students on books each year. Male students were 22% more likely to buy only the book recommended for a module. Female students used their module textbooks for an average of five hours per week and male students used their module text for only two hours per week. There were roughly equal number of female and male students in the book-buying survey. All the analysis outputs from the study relating to male and female trends were significant. It appears that female students spend more on books and use those books they buy more often and for longer periods. In both male and female students, older students tended to spend more on books. If students were employed, they spent more money on books each year. The average spent by employed and not employed was £248 for non-employed and £327 for employed. Female student employment rate was 67%; the male employment rate was 76%.

● Task one – use these paragraph points and express in your own words the points in five sentences.

● Task two – use these paragraph points to express in your own words the points in ten sentences.

● Task three – reflect on:

　– the difficulty of tasks one and two

　– the clarity of expression in tasks one and two.

Issues of clarity and using short, clear statements are connected to sentence punctuation. The following sections look at some of those issues.

THE COMMA

The comma can be used in several ways to improve the clarity and accuracy of your sentences:

- to separate items in a series, such as 'oranges, lemons, and so on'
- after an introductory clause: 'If this data is valid, the two respondents...'
- after a long introductory phrase: 'During the conduct of this research, ...'
- after an introductory phrase with 'to' and a verb: 'To win, ...'
- after a when, where, why, how clause: 'After you complete the assignment, ...'
- to separate a non-essential phrase, clause or interpreter word: 'Peter, the researcher, arranged all the interviews.'
- between co-ordinate adjectives: 'We met a happy, proactive focus group.'
- to form a compound sentence: 'Peter read the transcript, but Susie listened to the audio recording.'

THE SEMICOLON

Most commonly, semicolons link two closely related, complete sentences, eliminating the need for a comma and co-ordinating conjunction (and, but, or, for, so, yet) to join them. You must choose either to use a semicolon or to use the comma and the co-ordinating conjunction. A comma by itself constitutes a comma splice error or sentence run-on error – avoid these (see the section below). A semicolon with a co-ordinating conjunction is not grammatically correct:

'I read more than other students; I enjoy books.'

Semicolons can also be used together with transitional phrases or conjunctive adverbs in order to emphasise a pause and the nature of the relationship between two independent clauses:

- words such as: consequently, finally, however, indeed, instead, similarly, specifically, therefore
- phrases such as: as a result, even so, for example, in conclusion, on the other hand, in other words.

'Peter did a lot of studying; however, it seemed like he studied the wrong things.'

THE COLON

A common use of colons is to introduce a list of items.
'The following are important reasons to write in short sentences:
    clarity
    simplicity of writing
    and so on...'

If each item in the list is a complete sentence, then each will start with a capital letter and end with a full stop. If the list contains fragments of sentences, then each item starts with a lower-case letter and there is no full stop at the end of each item, but there is a full stop at the end of the list.

Colons can also introduce a more specific or particular statement that amplifies or clarifies the preceding one. The words that follow the colon may be a complete clause or simply a word or phrase. For example, 'I wish it was easier to write sound academic sentences, but such is the nature of good writing: you have to learn as you go along. There is always a lot of rewriting to do. Remember: no one reads your first draft.'

Colons are also used in academic writing to introduce quotations, especially long ones.

RUN-ON SENTENCES

Run-on sentences represent a particular grammatical error that you should try to avoid. When two (or more) independent statements or complete sentences are joined with a comma it is called a run-on error, that is, your sentence has run on when it should have stopped, or should have been punctuated with a semicolon, or have a connecting word. So that, 'I read more than other students, I really enjoy books,' should take the form of:

- I read more than other students. I really enjoy books.
- I read more than other students; I really enjoy books.
- I read more than other students because I really enjoy books.

Avoiding run-on sentences will make your work clearer and more readable. It is also the correct grammatical form. In some instances and some styles of writing the run-on sentence is acceptable, but in academic work it should be avoided.

7.6 UNDERSTANDING THE STRUCTURE OF PARAGRAPHS

A paragraph tends to develop a single idea, statement, finding or line of argument. A series of paragraphs will form a section or a chapter. Try to adopt some of the following ideas related to paragraph use:

- Vary the lengths of paragraphs to maintain the reader's interest.
- Try to avoid very short, one-sentence paragraphs.
- Avoid long paragraphs; there should be a minimum of four or five per page of single-spaced text. Any longer than this and the reader will get lost and you will lose their attention.
- Paragraphs need to have a natural 'flow':
  - first sentence – introduces the paragraph
  - main points
  - last but one sentence summarises the paragraph

- final sentence links to the next paragraph or to the overall theme of the section or chapter.
- Use link words and phrases such as although, in contrast, however, but in this finding, and so on.
- Vary your use of common words to avoid monotony. Try to aim to never use the same word twice in any one sentence, and no more than 3–5 times in any one paragraph.

STATEMENT, ANALYSIS AND FINDINGS PARAGRAPHS

In assignments and projects many paragraphs will be introducing and evidencing statements, analyses and findings. These paragraphs will need a particular structure, as set out below:

- paragraph statement (introduction)
- the main claim or statement of the paragraph
- **first** evidence to support the claim or statement
- warrant – how the evidence supports the claim or statement
- qualification of the evidence (exceptions and anomalies)
- **second evidence source**
- **third evidence source**, and maybe up to five or six sources of evidence
- summary sentence
- link sentence to a new paragraph.

You will also need to use various sources of evidence to create a convincing argument.

LINKING AND SIGNPOSTING

To improve the clarity of your writing it is important to provide links and signposts. Sentences, paragraphs and sections can all be linked. Aim to provide extensive links between sentences and paragraphs and, to a lesser extent, sections.

Paragraph links are often provided in the first or last line of a paragraph. The last line of a paragraph can link forward.

Forward links (my explanation in brackets)

- However, this was not the only issue related to gender. (there is another coming up in the next paragraph)
- Some issues remain to be resolved in this data. (explored in the next paragraph)
- This evidence brings back some striking points that as yet we have not discussed. (but soon will be)
- However, although these points make a compelling argument in favour, there are counterpoints that need to be explored. (counterargument in the next paragraph)

REARWARD LINKS

- Although we have seen the evidence of a gender-based pattern of behaviour, there is evidence and data that does not support this position. (it is in this paragraph)
- While most of the data relates to quantitative measures, we also investigated some qualitative elements. (these will be coming up in this paragraph)
- There are weaknesses in the argument above that will need further exploration. (that will happen in this paragraph)

Another way to link paragraphs is to use key words, phrases or closely related words. The link is created by the continuity of the words and phrases. These links add clarity to your argument and allow the argument to flow onwards in your writing.

SIGNPOSTING

'Signposts' are a mark of good writing and help the reader to understand the argument more easily. They also provide a sense of where the reader is in the text. The signpost is created with words and phrases, such as:

- for example
- however
- similarly
- some problems with
- in contrast
- this programme
- despite this counterevidence
- this suggests
- however, in future research
- in the following section
- the next chapter will look at
- in the last chapter we looked at
- while this was covered here, that will be covered there
- a recent study reported
- the seminal work in this area was.

In each phrase there is a link to something already mentioned or something that will be mentioned in the future. Signposts can look backwards as well as forwards. Signposts can work at various levels, from sentences and paragraphs to sections.

7.7 ARGUMENTATIVE ERRORS AND HOW TO AVOID THEM

The ultimate goal of your assignments and examinations is to present an original piece of writing and convince the markers that your ideas and statements are valid and convincing by setting out a logical and coherent argument. As you construct each paragraph, try to think about the logic and the evidence you are presenting. The following sections present some of the most common errors that appear in academic writing.

THE VALIDITY AND OPENNESS OF ASSUMPTIONS

Assumptions are statements or ideas that you have accepted without demonstrating they are true. If you want to argue that people are motivated mostly by money (a common misconception), then you will need to explain the assumptions in this statement and prove that this is the case. You may believe that this is so but it is not sufficient for you to believe it. If you state it you must present the assumptions and prove it. Most of the statements you make in an assignment are what we might call 'contestable'. You may argue a point one way; I may argue it the other. Without an explicit setting-out of the assumptions and the provision of evidence to support the statement, the critical reader will assume this is an assumption and disregard it. Clearly, if all your statements were unsupported and not explicit, then your whole assignment could easily be disregarded and awarded a low grade.

LOGICAL ERRORS

If you do not explore the assumptions in statements, research and theory, you are likely to accept assumptions as facts. When reading others' works, expect the assumptions to be made explicit and the statements to be supported by evidence. If you find writing that does not do this, then be critical of the writing and point out the unsupported assumptions (critique). Once you have accepted an unsupported assumption, there is a danger of creating illogical arguments and unsupported conclusions. These are often called a *non sequitur*, meaning 'it does not follow'. Arguments need to be built in a stepwise fashion. Think of an argument as a house: place the foundation building blocks in first and then build more complex arguments on the foundation ideas. The logical blocks in the argument should build up to the concluding point so that the critical reader cannot find a *non sequitur* in the argument.

AVOID PREJUDICE AND STEREOTYPES

Prejudices and stereotypes exist everywhere, but you must resist repeating them in your academic writing. One technique for avoiding prejudice is to create a reflexive account of your beliefs and assumptions about any important area in your assignment or project. These can range from believing that all qualitative research is just chatting to personal beliefs about men being less able than women. You need to explore your own beliefs and make them explicit to both you and the readers of your work.

UNSUPPORTED ASSERTIONS

Asserting something to be true when you do not provide support for that assertion is an argumentative error. Using an unsupported assertion means that the reader has no way of knowing or judging if it is true because you have offered nothing in support of the statement. The reader or marker will probably disregard the point. Arguments with unsupported statements are weak arguments; strong arguments have support for all the main points. If you adopt the paragraph style suggested earlier you will be much less likely to make unsupported assertions.

The same problem occurs when you suppress evidence or provide incomplete evidence. These positions are more difficult because they require you to make a judgement. If you were to state, 'business is driven by profit', you have to make a judgement about whether this point is universally recognised as being true. If it would be accepted as universally true, you can assert it and it requires no evidence in support. I think you can see the problem! Not every assertion needs supporting evidence, but be careful! Every part of your main argument that might be contested will need supporting evidence. Failure to do this will weaken your argument.

The suppressing of evidence occurs when you know there is evidence that is counter to your argument but you choose not to include it. Most contested positions will need evidence in support and evidence that contradicts. This is what is termed a balanced argument. Balanced evidence is to be expected, so if you use a one-sided argument it is very likely to be viewed as a weak argument. Strong arguments are always balanced arguments.

❝ TUTOR COMMENT

We don't explicitly teach our students about argumentative errors. They just have to learn by trial and error. I think this is a really ineffective way for us to do this. I have developed a tripod of extra sessions that work on this problem. The sessions cover:

1 What are argumentative errors and why should I avoid them?

2 Spotting argumentative errors in published writings.

3 How to avoid making argumentative errors in my own writing.

The students who attend these sessions produce work that is markedly free of the common argumentative errors normally seen in the majority of undergraduate work.

7.8 REFERENCING

There are several styles of referencing. The most commonly used in business and management is Harvard and I will present only this style. The Web Links at the end of the chapter provide access to the other referencing styles. Unless your university department requires a specific style, use the Harvard referencing system. What follows is by no means exhaustive – and some areas are contested. But if you follow this guide, you will encounter few problems when you submit your work.

All of your ideas will have been based on someone else's ideas or research, so it is vital you acknowledge these ideas. Where you are using quotes you are acknowledging the use of the actual words. If you fail to correctly acknowledge ideas and quotes, you will have committed the academic offence of plagiarism. There are severe penalties for plagiarism.

There are good academic and practical reasons for getting organised in terms of references and acknowledging the work of others. The credibility of your writing is grounded on the sources you use. Being organised to accurately record and use references was covered in an earlier chapter – take another look at that section before you read on. As you read, take notes of the detail of the theory or research and record the reference to the work.

A **book reference** will require:

- the author's or editor's name (or names)
- the year the book was published
- the title of the book
- the edition (but not the first edition)
- the city the book was published in
- the name of the publisher.

A **journal reference** will require:

- the author's name or names
- the year in which the journal was published
- the title of the article
- the title of the journal
- the volume and issue number
- the page number.

An **electronic source** requires:

- the date you accessed the source
- the electronic address or email
- the type of electronic resource.

A **direct quote** requires all of the above and:

- the page number of the quote.

WORKING PATTERN WITH REFERENCES

If you are following one of the ideas in Chapter 3 for maintaining a reference list, then refer to that section for the detail of how to maintain the references. It is not uncommon to just use a Word file as a file of references. In this system you add the reference material in the correct alphabetical position as you read and use a book, journal or website. Reference lists using Harvard are often termed bibliographies. A bibliography is a list of references and a list of works you consulted generally. Unless your university indicates a different arrangement, use a list of references and works you consulted called a bibliography and place the full list at the end of your assignment, but before any appendices.

YOU MUST ALWAYS REFERENCE:

- Any ideas that you use to develop your argument or research method – this will require extensive referencing in some parts of the work. The main sections of assignments often contain 10–15 references.

- Direct quotations – where you copy another author's material word for word. A direct quotation must have quote marks placed at the beginning and end of the word-for-word section. Traditionally, double quote marks have been used ("), but it is now acceptable, and in some ways preferable, to use single quote marks (').

- Try to avoid using direct quotations; they will often waste words and cannot replace your own argument. But sometimes it is difficult to avoid the direct quotation because the author's words may precisely describe the point you are trying to make or provide evidence of the point you have made. When you use direct quotations, you must reproduce the author's words exactly, including all spelling, capitalisation and punctuation errors. If you recognise an error. place the word (sic) after the error; it indicates you are aware of the error.

- Paraphrasing – is when you take an author's ideas and put them into your own words. This is a common and effective approach in assignments. Be sure to indicate the original author of the idea by correctly referencing the source.

CORRECTLY USING REFERENCES IN THE BODY OF YOUR WORK

Using the Harvard system requires the author(s) name(s) and the year of publication.

Let's imagine that Weick has a book on sense-making in organisations. We could summarise and reference his book with a phrase such as, 'Weick (2005) suggests there are eight distinct ways of making sense in an organisation.' The full reference would then appear in the bibliography.

An **idea or paraphrase** from a book or journal article with one author would look like this:

- Horn (2009) suggests that we view time using the Sweet Jar Analogy. (This is where the name forms part of the sentence.)

- There have been suggestions that time should be viewed as analogies to other things (Horn 2009).

The same rules apply when there are two authors:

- Horn and Farmer (2009) suggest that we view time using the Sweet Jar Analogy.
- There have been suggestions that time should be viewed as analogies to other things (Horn and Farmer 2009).

When the number of authors goes beyond two, it is best to use the form '(Horn et al)', or 'Horn et al (2009) suggest'. 'Et al' means 'and others'.

A **direct quote** will take the same form as above but also include a page number – for example (Horn 2009: 64–5) – the author's words will be within single quotes or double quotes.

A **corporate source** will look like this:

- The HSE (2008) argues that accidents are in decline…
- Accident research (HSE 2008) suggests that accidents are in decline…

You will encounter situations where authors have written more than one publication in one year; you distinguish between these by placing a lower case 'a' behind the first date and a lower case 'b' behind the second and so on. In the above example we might have Horn (2009a) and Horn (2009b).

When the author you want to quote is **quoting from another work** you would reference this as:

- Horn and Farmer (in Smith 2006) argue that…

But try if you can to use the original text for reading, quoting and paraphrasing. Using second-hand ideas often leads to distortion of the original idea.

You will sometimes wish to quote from **anonymous books**. The normal convention is to replace the author with the name of the book:

- The cognitive elements of understanding people's action in organisations will always require extensive research (*How to make sense of work* 2007). (Remember a quotation will require a page number.)

Newspaper articles are treated in the same manner as other sources. It is more common for newspaper articles to have no stated author, so we would adapt the technique above:

- *The Times* suggests that illogical and inexplicable behaviour at work is commonplace (No sense at work 2009). (This uses the article name and then the date.)

You will find quite commonly that you need to quote **more than one source**, and this is dealt with using punctuation. For example:

- The idea of making sense in organisations is not new and there has been extensive and diverse research carried out on this issue (Weick 2004; O'Connell 1998; Freeman 2006).

Lecture or other taught material would be referenced thus:

- 'No one can make sense of an organisation without reflecting on their own cognitive processes' (Horn 2009: 18). (The number after the colon represents the slide number in a PowerPoint presentation.)

However, quoting from lecture notes is normally a very weak approach to using source material. You will normally be able to access the source material that the lecturer used, so read that and use the argument firsthand.

If the author is unknown then use the technique we have already established of using the title or institutional source:

- 'No one can make sense of an organisation without reflecting on their own cognitive processes' (Chilterns University, School of Business, 2009: 18).

Electronic sources are referenced using the author and the date as usual. However, it will sometimes be the case that the author is anonymous and there is no date. Webpages often present in this fashion so we revert to the title of the piece or the organisation and 'n.d.' for no date, for example (*Sensemaking: A collaborative inquiry*, n.d.).

BIBLIOGRAPHY

Every reference you use in the main body of your work must have an entry in the bibliography – most markers check that this is so. It is also the convention to list sources that you have used in a more general fashion. I won't call this background reading, but there will be a set of resources that do not directly feature in the argument but that do influence the general location and thrust of your work.

When creating a bibliography, the sources should be listed alphabetically by author's surname, should be left-justified and a bullet point or number should never precede the references. Where the author is anonymous or unknown for any one source, insert that source in the alphabetical list using the title of the source instead of the author's name. All sources should be listed in one list; there should not be a separate lists for books, journal articles, electronic and newspaper sources. In the printed document ensure the bibliography starts on a new page. Store the Word file for the bibliography in a separate Word document.

For some awards and some universities you may be asked to produce an annotated bibliography. This is a bibliography list with an added section that summarises and evaluates the source. This style of bibliography is sometimes used at the proposal stage of projects.

The following section covers the main documents you may want to add to a bibliography.

Book with one author
Hampson, S. (2002) *The Construction of Personality*. London: Routledge.
[Author, Initial. Date. *Title (italicised)*. Place of publication: Publisher]

Book with two authors

Gentner, D. and Stevens, A. (2006) *Mental Models.* Mahwak, NJ: Erlbaum.

Book with three or more authors

Terborg, J., Richardson, P. and Pritchard, R. (2008) *Person–Situation Effects in the Prediction of Performance: An investigation of ability, self-esteem, and reward contingencies.* London: Sage.

Book – second or later edition

Fransella, F. and Dalton, P. (2009) *Personal Construct Counselling in Action.* 3rd edition. London: Sage.

Book by same author in the same year

Weick, K. (2005a) *Sensemaking in Organisations.* London: Sage.
Weick, K. (2005b) *Establishing Organisational Trust.* London: Sage.

Edited book (different authors write separate chapters)

Garnham, A. (ed.) (2009) *Thinking and Reasoning.* Oxford: Blackwell.

Chapter from an edited book

Watkins, J. (2009) 'Methodological Individualism and Social Tendencies' in Garnham, A. (ed.) (2009) *Thinking and Reasoning.* Oxford: Blackwell.

Books with an anonymous or unknown author

My Best Encyclopaedia. (2003) London: Sage.

Journal article

Hill, Y. (2007) Metaphors and Mental Models: Sensemaking and sensegiving in innovative and entrepreneurial activities. *Journal of Management.* Vol 46, No 6. pp1057–74.
[Author, Initial. (Date) Title. *Journal Name* (italicised). volume, issue. page.]

Journal article from CD-ROM or database

Hill, Y. (2007) Metaphors and Mental Models: Sensemaking and Sensegiving in Innovative and Entrepreneurial Activities. *Journal of Business [online].* Vol 46, No 6. pp1057–74. Available at: http//www.sage.direct/0670-2398(06)01210-6 [accessed 2 February 2009].

[Online] refers to the type of media where the source is located. If it is a CD-ROM source, you would put 'CD-ROM' in the square brackets instead of 'online'. As with a normal journal example, the volume number, issue number and page numbers are listed. At the end of this example, note that the name of the database has been listed, along with the identification/access number of the article and an access date (in square brackets).

Teaching materials

Farmer, P. (2009) *Unit 5: Employee Reward.* Chilterns University: Business School.

Unknown author

Chilterns University (2009) Unit 5: Employee Reward. Business School: Author. (Note: 'Author' at the end means that the publisher is the same as the author.)

Government publications

Department for Education and Employment (DfEE). (2009) *Skills for Life: The national strategy for improving adult literacy and numeracy skills.* Nottingham: DfEE Publications.

Conference papers

Heron, Z. (2008) *Impressions of the Other Reality: A co-operative inquiry into altered states of consciousness.* Social Realities – Conference Proceedings, Chilterns University Conference, High Wycombe, pp245–56.

Newspaper articles

Fanning, A. (2009) I can't make sense of work. *Sunday Mail.* 1 January, p12.

Unknown author

I can't make sense of work. *Sunday Mail* (1 January 2009), p12.

CASE STUDY

FOR ASSIGNMENTS

Yin has done quite a bit of reading and thinks that she knows the subject area quite well; she has many pages of notes about the main sources of her assignment. She is not quite sure about how to organise the ideas into a meaningful structure.

Task

Without worrying about the actual content, prepare a structure for Yin's literature review. You will need to provide:

- section headings

- paragraph headings

- paragraph points

- word targets for each section.

CASE STUDY

FOR PROJECTS

Tonna has progressed her project to the point of having gathered and analysed the data. She is not too sure how to proceed to write the findings section.

Task

Without worrying about the actual content, prepare a structure of Tonna's findings chapter. You will need to provide:

- section headings
- paragraph headings
- paragraph points
- word targets for each section.

SUMMARY

Develop your writing skills early in your university life and they will pay off handsomely in the grades you are awarded for assignments and examinations. Your approach to writing will need to be structured by systematic techniques.

- Develop good writing habits:
  - Understand that writing is just like any other skill.
  - Develop a writing habit.
  - Use feedback to improve your writing.
  - Understand that writing takes time.
  - Read, think, design, write and reread every day.
  - Develop 'stickability'.
  - Think and plan and make notes before you write.
  - Get it 'write' first time.
  - Understand the necessity to revise your writing.

- Learn and become skilful in the macro–micro form of writing.

- Use creative techniques for developing ideas:
  - brainstorming
  - negative brainstorming
  - assuming new perspectives
  - creative thinking
  - clustering.

- Plan writing before you begin the detailed micro writing:
  - pen and paper
  - mind maps
  - use Word in outline mode
  - sequencing
  - pruning
  - ordering
  - selection.

- Support your ideas with theory, critique and evidence.
- Focus on the detail of micro writing:
  - sentences
  - punctuation
  - avoid run-on sentences
  - avoid argumentative errors.
- Understand the structure of paragraphs and linking and signposting.
- Check your university regulations to decide on the style of referencing you will use. If no specific method is stated, use Harvard referencing.

EXPLORE FURTHER

FURTHER READING

De Bono, E. (2000) *Six Thinking Hats*. London: Penguin Books Ltd.

Neville, C. (2007) *The Complete Guide to Referencing and Avoiding Plagiarism*. Milton Keynes: Open University Press.

Rawlinson, G. (1986) *Creative Thinking and Brainstorming*. Aldershot: Gower Publishing Ltd.

Seely, J. (2005) *Oxford Guide to Effective Writing and Speaking*. Oxford: Oxford University Press.

Sinclair, C. (2007) *Grammar: A friendly approach*. Milton Keynes: Open University Press.

Venolia, J. (2001) *Rewrite Right! Your guide to perfectly polished prose*. Berkeley, CA: Ten Speed Press.

WEB LINKS

General referencing guide to different styles: http://www.bma.org.uk/ap.nsf/content/LIBReferenceStyles

The student room, a social site covering all things academic: http://www.thestudentroom.co.uk/

A site dealing with university writing: http://www.llas.ac.uk/materialsbank/mb063/eap/01/assignments_academic_writing.htm

The Open University Learning Space: http://www.open.ac.uk/openlearn/home.php

CHAPTER 8

Presentation Communication

What skills will I develop in this chapter?

- improving your understanding of the nature of presentations
- learn how to structure presentations
- delivering with confidence
- reflecting on your performance
- using PowerPoint
- adding multimedia elements to presentations

8.1 INTRODUCTION

Presentations are a vital business skill. From the informal chat to the large formal presentation, if you have a weakness in communicating it will limit your promotion prospects. Managing has often been described as the 'art of getting things done through other people'. Presentations communicate what needs to be done and how. At university you will be set assignments that require you to present your ideas. The sooner you get to grips with presentations the sooner you will start enjoying them and become an effective communicator.

Your presentation skills will develop over time and there is no substitute for experience. The best way to use this chapter is to work through it and carry out the reflective exercises. Once you have developed the basic skills to present in a confident and effective manner, further improvements will only happen through reflective experience. This means that as you deliver presentations you need to honestly reflect on how well things went. A learning diary will significantly assist you in this process. Record your own experiences but also record notes and ideas when watching others present.

Presenting is a skill that does not develop smoothly. You may initially make good progress and then possibly seem to slip back. Don't worry about this; it is quite normal. You will need to display 'stickability' and keep working away at improving your presentations.

8.2 THE NATURE OF PRESENTATIONS

Presenting to groups is one of the most important skills a manager can develop. The essence of management is to achieve things through other people. Managers are not judged by how hard *they* work. They are judged by how effectively *their* teams work. Managing is about communicating, and one of the key tools of communicating is the presentation. It is your presentation skills that will probably clinch your next job interview. Most forms of employment selection for managerial jobs use some form of presentation. Your universities will probably have a number of assessments based on presentations – they know it is a key skill of business. Finally, when you have secured your new job the teams you manage will judge you on your presentation skills. I hope I have convinced you that there are so many occasions that require you to present that you cannot leave this skill to chance. Spending time developing presenting skills at university will reward you later in your career.

Most people feel uncomfortable when they are asked to present. Many people are very nervous and scared of presenting – standing in front of people and talking is a scary business. The only way to calm the nerves and learn to love presenting is to practise, develop and succeed. Nothing will improve your confidence in presenting as much as carrying out successful presentations. The ability to learn from the presenting experience will be enhanced by using reflective practice and recording your experiences in a learning diary. When you present it is easy to feel that the presentation is all about you and the clear transmission of your message. To some extent it is – but not a very great extent.

The single most important observation related to presenting is that it is not the transmission of the message that is important – it is the reception of the message. Now this presents a problem, because when you are preparing a presentation you are tending to focus on your performance. For your message to appeal to an audience it must 'speak' to them and connect with them. You will need to know your audience to be able to appeal to them. Early preparation for a presentation should involve thinking about the nature and needs of your audience. For example, if you are presenting to a group of managers you can assume a certain level of knowledge about management. You would therefore not need to explain basic concepts but could concentrate on the important and clear message that you want to deliver. Another example is if you are presenting your organisation's products to a group of customers you will need to find out exactly the products that most interest them. This can be difficult. A standard technique of smaller presentations is to ask them at the beginning of the presentation. You will then be able to adjust the examples and the focus of the presentation to cover their interests. This approach has the added advantage of involving them in the presentation – so that you are talking *to them* and not *at them*.

Presentations can also have benefits for the presenter. First, it is a showcase to display your abilities. As a student your presentations will be assessed and a grade will be awarded. Your tutors have an intimate understanding of the pressures and difficulties of presenting, so you can expect an empathetic response from them. They will also be able to provide useful feedback on how to improve. At work your abilities will be showcased in a different way. Here you are on show for your team and your senior management. The team will gain confidence from your clear and decisive leadership whereas senior colleagues should be impressed with your communication skills.

Second, presentations give you access to the feelings, ideas and thoughts of groups. Try to plan presentations so that you leave knowing more about your audience than when you started. If you are presenting to customers, this can be vital to the success of any contracts that may follow. As you speak and answer questions there are many clues and guidance about what the audience thinks and wants.

Finally, presentations are also an opportunity to change minds. If you are planning a presentation to change the minds of the audience, you will need to know what they currently think and have a clear idea of how you will convince them to change their view.

As you become more experienced and successful you will realise that presentations are the chance to have fun and enjoy yourself.

8.3 STRUCTURING PRESENTATIONS

Choosing the correct structure for your presentation is vital to its success. All presentations need structure but the structure needs to support the message and not get in the way of the message. Presentations without structure will end up as a confusing mess that do not convey the message you wanted to deliver. The following sections look at some of the common ways to structure presentations.

SEQUENTIAL STRUCTURE

This is a simple and effective structure and can be regarded as the default way to organise your presentation. It consists of a set of linked statements, and possibly evidence, that lead to a conclusion. It works best when each of the statements and evidence is separated into distinct parts. When you start the presentation you lay out the sequential steps, and at various points you summarise and remind the audience of where they are in the sequence, finally leading to your conclusion. If the steps and the evidence convince the audience they will accept the conclusion. This is a suitable structure for presentations that have a clear goal and message and are designed to convince the audience of something.

Deconstructing structure

In the deconstructing structure the main topic is broken down into smaller parts to aid understanding. The level of deconstructing can be adjusted from relatively simple deconstruction into a few parts or topics to major deconstruction into basic building blocks. This is a useful structure when the presentation is aimed at exploration and understanding of a problem or issue. Each section should be related back to the whole so the audience is not lost: a diagrammatic representation of the overall structure is a useful way to do this.

QUESTION STRUCTURE

This structure is often used in management meetings where a previous decision is being explained and explored. It is also a format that is useful when seeking approval for a plan of action. The structure is variable but often follows this format:

- Introduce and describe the decision or problem.
- Explore the possible solutions or actions.
- Explain how the decision was made, or the reasoning for the proposal.
- Analyse the pros and cons of the decision or the proposal.
- Justify the decision or seek the approval.
- Invite questions and debate.
- Summarise the debate and any adjustments that will be made to the decision or the proposal.

PYRAMID STRUCTURE

This structure introduces the conclusion or main point of the presentation at the beginning. In practical terms it starts with a 'bang'; other structures build up to the 'bang.' After the main 'bang' the subsequent sections develop certain themes that the main point introduced. Further sections may explore these themes in more detail. There are three main advantages to this arrangement. First, the audience is immediately interested and engaged by the main point of the presentation. Second, the audience becomes convinced by the argument as they become familiar with the main point of the presentation. Finally, it is easy to adjust the length of the presentation as the main points are delivered at the beginning.

CLASSROOM STRUCTURE

Classroom structure follows a simple beginning–middle–end format, so called because it follows the structure of a classroom-taught session. The presentation should follow this layout:

1 Get the audience's attention.
2 Introduce the topic, theme or idea – often stating 'the aim of this session is to...'.
3 Establish what the audience knows about the topic area.
4 Deliver your material, but take into account point 3.
5 Summarise what has been said and how well you have met your aim.
6 Question and answer session.

A SHORT NOTE ON THE CONTENT OF PRESENTATIONS

Very little has been said about the content of presentations up to this point. This chapter is about the delivery of the presentation, so very little will be said about content. However, what you say is as vital to a successful presentation as how you say it. Developing the content and the argument of the presentation is a complicated affair and other chapters will look in detail at how to do this. If you are preparing the content of a presentation, you may want to look at the following chapters:

- Chapter 7 – Developing Good Writing Skills
- Chapter 9 – Business Calculations
- Chapter 10 – Critical Reading and Writing Skills
- Chapter 11 – Analysis and Evaluation Skills
- Chapter 13 – Thinking and Memory Skills

8.4 THE PRESENTATION DELIVERY

There is no easy way past the problem of presenting anxiety other than confronting it head on. When you first stand up at the front of a class or meeting, no matter how confident you are, your body will let you know that presenting is stressful. Many people, even experienced presenters, will find that the following happens:

- You start sweating.
- Your hands shake.
- Your knees are a bit wobbly.
- You cannot seem to think clearly.
- You suddenly become all 'fingers and thumbs'.
- Your heart will beat rapidly, or indeed miss a few beats.
- Your mouth will become dry.
- Your voice will become a bit quivery.
- You may develop a dry, tickly cough.

Luckily all these symptoms of stress will gradually subside as you progress through your talk or presentation. There is a great feeling of achievement and satisfaction when you have successfully completed your presentation – and survived. You can also take some simple precautions to avoid the worst of these symptoms. The simple act of having some water to hand will deal with the cough and dry mouth problem. Staying calm before the presentation and breathing deeply and slowly will also help. Above all, as you become more experienced and successful, these symptoms will be more easily controlled. Don't let these 'stress' issues put you off presenting; you will soon master them and then start to enjoy the presenting process and find that you can have fun.

You might ask way this happens. Our bodies have what is called a 'fight or flight' mechanism. This is an ancient response to ensure our survival. When our ancestors came face to face with a velociraptor they had to fight or flight – either way they needed a big hit of adrenaline and noradrenalin. When you get up to speak your body does the same thing, but pumps way too many of these stimulants into your system. All the responses above are related to that ancient mechanism.

Once you have got over this initial stress response you can settle into your presentation. Presenting software will be considered later in the chapter. For now, we will look at some of the presenting skills you will need to get your 'message' to the audience.

SPEAKING

Speaking is a key part of your delivery. When you are nervous you will tend to speak much faster. You will need to deliberately counteract this by slowing down and trying to add pauses into your speaking. When you are presenting to larger groups without microphone assistance, you must project your voice. Projection is really about sensing the space your voice occupies and adjusting it to fill more of the space available. It is certainly not about shouting. Try this: hold your hand out in front of you, palm to your face and at eye level. Gently hum for about five seconds and then project that hum towards your hand. Now change the hum to an extended word such as 'helloooo'. Practise this a few times and then look for an object a little further away – maybe a picture in the room – and push the voice towards that picture. Remember, no shouting; hum, then form a word. Again, practise this a few times and then in your presentation practice sessions lift your voice and speak normally but slightly louder and project it to the back of the room. This technique should allow you to be heard in a reasonably large room without microphone assistance. When using microphone assistance check the levels of sound before you start your presentation and remember to use conversational speaking volume.

Variation of tone is another aspect of your voice that will need conscious control. We call a flat, single-tone speech 'monotone'; it is very boring and will send your audience off to sleep very quickly. If you were speaking conversationally your tone would change with the emotion of the subject. Exciting elements cause the voice tone to rise. Important parts cause the voice to lower. Try to actively maintain the tone of the voice depending on what you are saying. Another closely related voice issue is pace of speaking. Pace should be varied throughout your presentation in relation to the topic and the emotion. Plan the tone and pace of your voice just as you do with the content. Think of your presentation as being like a piece of music; one-tone and one-pace music would be very boring.

Silence … is a vital part of speaking. When you are nervous you will tend to try to fill every space. Avoid this by planning pauses into your presentation. In practice we do this by our notes, saying 'count 1, 2, 3'; this forces the pause. Use silence before an important point and after it. This warns your audience that a big point is coming – and to pay attention. But it also allows them time to reflect on the point after you have made it. Use silence to wait for the audience if you have delivered a punch line to a joke or had a response of clapping; wait and wait until the audience has settled again – performers call it 'milking the applause'. Finally, use silence when you have asked a question. There is a tendency to ask a question and then provide the answer – avoid this. Ask and then wait.

EYE CONTACT

Eye contact works in two ways. Your audience will make contact with your eyes and will judge your honesty, openness and confidence from what they see. You may have been to presentations where the speaker only looks at the floor or their notes. How does this make you feel about their honesty and confidence? In smaller settings your audience will be able to see much more of your eyes and will judge a number of things by the eye contact they make. They will judge your friendliness, honesty and intimacy from your eyes.

Eye contact also works in the other direction. If your audience thinks you are not watching them, they will probably not listen to you. You will gain so much information about how your message is being received if you look at the audience. You will see if they are bored, asleep, angry, disinterested, believing, disbelieving, sceptical and much more. You will need a systematic way for making eye contact with the audience. In small groups this can be done one to one and you should aim to make eye contact with each person every minute or so. In larger groups you will not be able to make individual eye contact, so you would create imaginary zones in the room – about six to eight zones – and look into those zones every minute or so and hold the look for about five to six seconds.

LEARNING DIARY

BEING PREPARED

I went to a graduate assessment interview last week and everything electrical was against me. In the presentation I had printed out full-colour handouts, three to a page, for the interviewers. They were very impressed with this. Half way through, the laptop died on me. Luckily I was able to talk my way through the handout I had given them. I think they were really impressed that I was able to keep going. In fact, I wasn't sure if the presentation was better once the PowerPoint had died. I did more talking to them and looking at them.

So, mental note to always take a handout for the audience or interviewers. I guess I should also take a back-up set of overhead transparencies.

Facial expression is closely related to eye contact. Your facial expression will have an effect on the audience. If you look listless and ill at ease, they will reflect this.

If you look angry, the audience will have a split emotion – some being angry and some being scared. Try to compensate for your nerves and the distance from you to the audience. Be natural, be yourself.

APPEARANCE

In business there is an assumption that you will dress smartly. The normal business attire for men and women is a business suit and a collar and tie for men. If this is not your normal attire it can seem restrictive, so when you practise do it as a dress rehearsal.

YOUR HANDS

You will need to work out what to do with your hands. Fiddling with things does not work, so avoid pens, keys and remote controls. A natural use of hands would be to place them at your sides when standing and in your lap when sitting. You can make better use of your hands by moving them expressively.

Think of using your hands in three levels:

- high, above the shoulder, for spiritual or uplifting things
- low, below the waist, for disputable or discouraging things
- middle, between waist and shoulder, for normal things.

In middle gestures open your arms for welcoming. Turn your palms upwards for supplication, openness or support. Bring one arm and hand down in the middle to divide things. Hands drawn apart show division. Use a fist for aggression or success. Point a finger for singling out or to turn the attention of the audience onto the audience. If you are thinking of introducing gestures into your presentation, try them out on a selected audience first or video them and review the effect they have.

STARTING YOUR PRESENTATION

The success of your presentation will depend on how well it starts. It is very difficult to recover a presentation once it goes wrong – so plan the beginning carefully. There are five main elements to getting your presentation off to a good start:

1 **Get the audience's attention**. Time the moment of the start of your talk; let everyone get seated and ready, then try to grab the audience's attention. An attention-grabbing activity at the start may work well – this is likely to be visual or noisy. Alternatively, use background music and moving images – when this stops your audience will know it is time to start.

2 **Establish your aims and objectives immediately**. The audience will want to know what you are intending to do and how. Set out how long the talk will last and what things will be done – this is a sort of time plan for the session.

3 **Create rapport**. You must win the audience over in the first minute. One standard method is to introduce yourself and give a very brief history of your background. You will build a strong rapport if you engage the audience early on by asking them brief questions about what they hope to get out of the session. This works well in smaller groups.

4 **Promise them something interesting**. Audiences have a short and fickle attention span so you need to interest them and keep them interested. If your first few minutes are boring, slow or promise nothing, you will likely lose them for the whole presentation.

5 **Tune into their visual side early in the presentation**. Visual stimuli are important to maintain the interest of your audience – especially for visual learners. Ensure there is at least an even balance between text, talk and visual stimuli in the early part of your presentation.

LOUISE AND SIMON

BECOMING REFLECTIVE PERFORMERS

Louise: 'How's that presentation assignment going? Only a week left!'

Simon: 'Yes, I am ready to go.'

L: 'Are you nervous about the presenting?'

S: 'I can't say that I am. Are you?'

L: 'I am petrified! Every time I think of doing it I feel physically sick!'

S: 'Oh come on, it is not that bad. You're only talking to a group of 30 students. They will probably all be asleep anyway.'

L: 'Strangely, it is the silence that worries me. Me all on my own at the front.'

S: 'Well! You could do some practising until you feel better about it.'

L: 'I can do the practising in front of the mirror without feeling nervous. I have practised it over and over again. It's when I come to do the real thing that I fall apart.'

S: 'There is an obvious point here!'

L; 'What's that?'

S: 'Do it in front of a group.'

L: 'Will that help?'

S: 'Experience is the only way you are going to feel comfortable with presenting.'

L: 'I hate it so much that I would sooner take my chances on the day.'

S: 'That's illogical madness. If you are going to be rubbish it's best to get it out of the way in front of friends where it doesn't matter.'

L; 'No, I don't think I can face that.'

S: 'You mean you would sooner let it defeat you and get a rubbish mark than do something about it?'

L: 'You've got a point there about the mark. The last assignment with a presentation I got 82% for the content and 30% for the presentation. I just dried up into a knotted heap. It was really embarrassing.'

S: 'Well, as you normally say, "face up to your fears".'

L: 'I can't say I want to do that but I sort of know you are right.'

S: 'Start small time and then move up. Let's book a study room and our little study group can review your technique and then try to help out.'

A day or so later and with some apprehension Louise gives her presentation to the group. After the presentation four people including Simon give her feedback on how the presentation went.

This is what she got:

- There were three simple spelling errors in the text.
- The presentation lasted 7 minutes and 22 seconds – it should have been 15 minutes.
- Five suggestions that she could involve the audience more and look at them more frequently.
- All four told her to stop looking at the cue cards or her feet and look at them.
- There were three areas where it seemed difficult to understand what she was saying – one said she mumbled; the others just thought it was not clear.
- Two people suggested that she needed a bit more visual interest.
- Three people thought they had got lost in places.

- One (very brave person) thought her voice was a bit weak and monotone.
- Two people thought she looked a bit 'shifty' on a couple of occasions.
- Three people said the content was 'spot on' but the message wasn't coming over that clearly.

After the first go at presenting Louise did the talk eight more times. She would have tried it again but the group begged her to stop – 'we've been at this for hours; please stop'.

In discussion after the session every member of the group thought that they had learned something that would help them improve their performance in the presentation.

Louise took all these points on board and changed a lot of things in her presentation. When she eventually delivered it for real she was particularly proud to finish the presentation 15 seconds inside the time allowance.

Result: Louise was awarded the highest grade in the class: 77%.

8.5 BEING REFLECTIVE ABOUT YOUR PRESENTATIONS

Once your presentation is over and you have had time to collect your thoughts, try to evaluate your presentation performance. You can do this alone but it is more effective with the help of friends or tutors. Think about reflecting on your performance by considering the Kolb learning cycle from Chapter 3. The process was:

- having an experience – the presentation
- reflecting on that experience
- learning from the experience
- changing and planning something different.

KOLB AND MY PRESENTATION

Well, I have just completed my first presentation and I thought I would use Kolb to reflect on how it could have been improved.

The experience – it was an assessed presentation on reward management for a level 1 module. I gave the talk for 15 minutes in a large room with about 25 students in the audience. I was very scared and nervous at the start. My hand was actually shaking and I had a real fight to actually look at the audience. They were fine but it was so quiet you could hear a pin drop – very scary.

Reflecting on my performance – I was well organised with PowerPoint and handouts and I had my notes on little cue cards. But, being nervous meant that I went off at a hare's pace, really fast, and I just delivered what I had to say. I hardly stopped to take in breath. At this speed I didn't do anything other than look at my little cards, speak and move on the PowerPoint slides. I only looked up at the end – they were all still there but still quiet. From what my tutor said I delivered what I thought was a 15-minute presentation – that is how long it took when I did a trial run – in six minutes. I can see there is a pace issue here. I was like a horse let out of the stable; I just galloped off. I think this is not really a good way to present but nerves and lack of confidence got the better of me. My cards were the same as the PowerPoint slides so I was reading the slides – this seemed a bit boring.

Learning from the experience – clearly I have got to get the timing sorted out. There is also the issue of reading my cards all the time. I know I should look at the audience but that seems impossible when I need the cards to remember. I think also that my speaking pace was way too fast and a little high pitched. I think there were a lot of other things wrong but I might concentrate on these points for now.

Change – I have a few clear ideas about how to change it for next time. I have to slow down and look at the audience. When I practise I am going to do it in front of a group of friends and work on going more slowly and looking at them. That means I must not use the cue cards. I am going to have to know what I am going to say and not need prompting from the cards. I will also use the slides as the basis for what I will say and not just repeat what is on the cards. I am really going to try to talk to the audience and engage them and not just talk at them. I think I may keep a watch in view while I present so that I can keep to time. When practising I am going to make sure that I change the tone and the pace of my voice.

ASSESSED PRESENTATIONS

When your presentation is assessed it is likely that the tutor will use an assessor's checklist to mark your performance. A good strategy is to ensure that what you say and how you say it conforms to the expectations of the assessor. Ask if you can see the checklist before the presentation.

Normally an assessor's checklist is likely to cover the following:

PERSONAL PRESENTATION

- Was the presenter dressed appropriately for the audience and the presentation?
- Use of hands – too much/too little?

- Facial expression – smiling? confident? open?
- Eye contact with audience – amount? frequency? quality?
- Posture – standing still, moving around, standing up straight or slouching?
- Position in relation to audience – blocking screen?
- Mannerisms – any irritating movements or facial expressions?
- Voice – too quiet or too loud? clear or muffled?
- Pacing – too fast or too slow? too one-paced?
- Voice tone – varied or monotone?

CONTENT

- Did it use an appropriate and effective structure?
- Did it have an introduction and conclusion?
- Was the content appropriate and well prepared?
- Timing – finish on time? too long? too short?
- Was there a good balance of talk, text and visuals?
- Was the talk too simple or too complex?
- Was it interesting?
- Did it engage the audience with its content?
- Were notes or cue cards used? Were these just read out or used as support?
- Were questions invited?
- How well were the questions handled?
- Did the content engage with the audience?

VISUAL AIDS

- What delivery system was used? Was it effective and appropriate to the audience?
- How did the delivery system engage with visual, aural learners in the audience?
- If multimedia was used, was it effective?
- Were access and disability issues considered?

8.6 USING PRESENTATION SOFTWARE

PowerPoint™ is the most frequently used presentation software and this section will exclusively address the use of PowerPoint. There are other presentation software packages but the points made here can easily be transferred to other software. This section will assume that you have thought through, been critical and evaluated the content that you intend to use in the presentation.

FIVE PARTS OF POWERPOINT

It is possible that you may not, at this stage, even realise there are five parts to the PowerPoint presentation software. You as an audience member may well have only see one part – the slides.

Slides – are the basic building block of a presentation and can contain text, pictures, graphs, tables or anything that can be visually represented.

Slide master – allows you to set all the background elements that will appear on every slide. This may typically be your name, the organisation you work for, graphic elements, the title of the slide show and images.

Notes page – is a useful device for storing speaker notes or prompts so you can print out useful cue cards. Notes pages can also contain important extra information that can be printed and distributed to the audience.

Handouts – allow you to print a smaller version of your slides for the audience to use. You can vary the formatting to include space for taking notes.

Outline view – allows you to see your presentation as an outline. This is the fastest and most efficient way to create and organise a presentation. The functionality comes from being able to see all the content easily and make adjustments to the structure and flow quickly. You can also print handouts in outline form.

Once you have the main content organised you can apply a slide design that will set colours, layouts, fonts and patterns for the whole presentation. You can set the slide design by clicking **Format** and **Slide design**.

Choose your preferred design and then hit the **Apply** button.

Slide transitions and animations can be added to your presentation once the content is complete and the design has been applied. But, be careful with these two techniques because audiences can soon find slides flying in and moving off quite irritating. Transitions and animations will add little of value to your presentations and sometimes *less* is *more* and, importantly, easier to follow and understand.

CLARITY AND ACCESS ISSUES

Remember, the primary reason to make a presentation is to communicate; your audience will need to be able to see your presentation for you to communicate. The audience will be varying distances away from the screen and the presentation may be given in rooms with different light levels. Some of the audience may not have excellent vision or hearing. To ensure your presentation can be seen by everyone, follow these basic rules:

- Use a sans serif font such as Arial.
- Use a minimum font size of 24 pt.
- Use no more than six bullet points on each slide.

- Avoid capitalisation or punctuation.
- Use plain backgrounds.
- Do not vary the background from slide to slide.
- Avoid transitions and animations.
- Check sound levels before the presentation.
- Ask the audience if they can see and hear clearly.
- Use visual elements to create variation and visual interest.
- Use dark backgrounds with light text, such as dark blue background with white text.

REHEARSING AND CONTROLLING YOUR PRESENTATION

Once you have created your presentation use a teaching room to practise and rehearse. If possible use the actual room where you will be presenting. The quickest and easiest way to start the presentation is to press the F5 button.

Controlling the presentation

Main controls:

- Use any key to move forward – the space bar or enter key works well or N (for next).
- Use backspace to return to an earlier slide or P (for previous).

Other useful controls:

- Go to slide <number>: <number>+ENTER.
- Display a black screen, or return to the slide show from a black screen: B.
- Display a white screen, or return to the slide show from a white screen: W.
- Stop or restart an automatic slide show: S.
- End a slide show: ESC.
- Return to the first slide: both mouse buttons for 2 seconds.

To fine-tune the length and timing of your presentation you can 'rehearse' the timings. Use the following commands: **Slide show** (top menu), **Rehearse timings**. The slide show will run with a timing window open that allows you to see the time on this slide and the total time of the slide show. You can then deliver your speech part and be given a clear indication of how long each slide and the whole presentation will take.

When you have finished you will be asked if you want to save these timings – click 'yes'. Then you will be asked if you want to review the timings in slide sorter – again click 'yes'. You will now be able to see the amount of time you spend on each slide. It is then an easy matter to adjust the content and organisation of slides until you have the perfect timing for the whole show.

TUTOR COMMENT

There is no substitute for repeated rehearsals. You can do it in front of a mirror, or to an empty theatre, or a room of people. Perfect presentations require practice of everything – every little gesture. In my experience students never do enough practice to feel really comfortable when it comes to the 'big' day. It is only when you practise and practise that you get used to the sight and sound of yourself. One important element is to accentuate your gestures and vocal projection so that you get used to the sound and sight of yourself in presenting mode.

MANAGER COMMENT

I know most mangers find presenting to be a difficult skill to master. Most of them do not like doing it and will avoid it if they can. I have an aversion technique that I use with the younger managers. We have quarterly, large, set-piece conferences where managers are expected to present. The presentations will be about all sorts of things: budgets, products, marketing, HR strategy, anything the organisation does. These can be a bit overwhelming because the average audience will be hundreds and sometimes thousands. There are always plenty of senior managers at these so the pressure is high. I wouldn't say a poor presentation will ruin a career, but it is not far off that.

A manager will know they have to present about a month in advance. I expect them to prepare early and well – my reputation is on the line with theirs. Exactly one week before the presentation I arrange a meeting with each person presenting at the upcoming conference. I don't warn them what it is about.

We meet in my office and then I take them to the large conference arena, about 500 seats. I fill this with every member of staff who is at work that day – a three-line whip. They are expected to give their presentation with about five minutes' notice. Sometimes they have the presentation material with them and sometimes they do not. Either way they give their presentations in the best way they can. Every member of that audience fills in a card and leaves it as they walk out – on average about 80–120 returned cards.

It is a brutal baptism of fire but it does at least two things. It gives them feedback on what they are proposing to say. Importantly, it motivates them to use the last week before the presentation to adapt, polish and improve. As I think about it, it also does one other important thing: it shows the general staff that managers have to muck in and do not have as an easy life as they may have thought – very good for general staff morale. It certainly shows which managers can survive on their wits.

CHECKLIST FOR USING POWERPOINT

- Use the slide master to create a consistent and simple design template. Vary the content of each slide but keep the background and colours consistent.

- Limit the amount of information on one slide. Only include essential information. Try to create a slide that balances text, visuals and clear space.

- Use images sparingly and ensure they are good quality and are clear when projected onto a screen.

- Limit the number of slides in your presentation to a maximum of one per minute.
- Ensure you know how to control the presentation – forward, backward, return to a specific slide and blank screen.
- Rehearse the presentation and use timings to fine-tune this.
- Do not read from your slides and face the audience at all times.
- Ensure that your version of PowerPoint and your memory stick are compatible with the presentation software/hardware. Carry a back-up on CD.
- Ensure your presentation can be seen and heard from the back of the room.
- Have a back-up plan if the presentation software or hardware fails. A simple set of overhead transparencies is the normal back-up.

8.7 USING MULTIMEDIA

Once you become competent in giving presentations you may want to add multimedia elements to your presentations. But remember, the multimedia will add very little to a poorly structured, badly organised or poor content presentation. Multimedia is no substitute for well-thought-out and presented messages. Workplace presentations are far more likely to use multimedia elements. In commercial presentations it is important to make an impact and differentiate your proposition from the opposition.

The cheapest and easiest multimedia add-in is to use a sequence of high-quality pictures. This will make an immediate visual impact. You can set the images to move on automatically in PowerPoint. The next element might be to add sound to the picture sequence.

To add sound to slides:

1 In slide view, display the slide you want to add music or sound to.

2 On the 'Insert' menu, point to 'Movies and Sounds'.

3 To insert a sound – browse to the folder that contains the sound or music and then double-click (you can also use sounds from the clip gallery).

A sound icon then appears on the slide. When presenting, the icon needs to be clicked to start the sound. This can be set to play automatically by using **Slide show**, **Custom animation**, **Play settings**. Be careful when using commercially produced music in your presentations; most of this will be copyrighted and should not be used without the correct payment to the copyright owner. There are copyright-free websites with music that is outside of copyright (see the Web Links section at the end of the chapter). If the sound file is large you will need to link to it rather than have it in the presentation. Use the PowerPoint help file to find out about linked files.

Finally, you can add video to your PowerPoint presentations. You have to consider how these will be produced. Many computers have video-making software and digital video cameras are now relatively cheap. YouTube can be a useful source of video excerpts – but be careful, many of these contravene the copyright rules by using illegal 'digital grabs' from commercial sources. These are inserted into PowerPoint in the same way as sound files and large files will have the same linking issues. When you present PowerPoint files that are linked to sound or video sources, remember to have the linked file on the same media source or it will not run.

Table 8.1 Supported media formats in PowerPoint

File type	Explanation	Attributes
MIDI	Musical Instrument Digital Interface	Sound
WAV	Microsoft Windows audio format	Sound
MPEG	Motion Picture Experts Group	Standard video format with a constant frame per second rate
AVI	Microsoft Windows video format	Video format with a constant frame per second rate
GIF	Graphical Interface Format	256-colour picture that supports animation

CASE STUDY

THE BIG PITCH

Moibhi Industries provide fitting out and operational services for sports centres. Chiltern University has built a state-of-the-art £32.2 million sports centre and has invited tenders for the fit-out and operation for the next five years. This represents a contract worth £8.8 million. If Moibhi can win this contract it would represent 12% of the annual turnover.

The tender process involves a presentation to a board of directors. This presentation is to showcase what Moibhi can do for Chiltern University. There is no title given – that is up to Moibhi. The presentation will last for 30 minutes and there will then be another 30 minutes for questions. Moibhi really want to win this contract and have set aside a budget of £60,000 for the presentation. There will be a project group managing the process and the delivery of the presentation consisting of:

- Business Director
- Marketing Director
- Sales Manager
- Creative Manager
- Operations Manager
- Advertising and Creative Executive
- Presentation specialist from HR.

The group reports to the CEO of Moibhi Industries. The presentation is six months away.

To think about...

- Set out the preparation steps that this group needs to take.
- How well do they need to know the client in this situation?
- How can Moibhi create a feeling of confidence in the supplier?
- What will be the focus of the presentation – a 'sort of' agreed presentation contents list?
- What multimedia elements should the group consider?
- What non-media elements should the group consider?
- What other areas should the group consider?

SUMMARY

- Dress smartly – don't let your appearance distract from what you are saying.

- Posture – try to appear confident by ensuring you stand upright and relatively still.

- Greeting – greet the audience with a smile and say hello; they will smile and say hello back to you.

- Notes – don't look at your notes; you should know what you are going to say. Look at your audience.

- Speaking – speak clearly and slowly: being nervous will tend to make you speak faster and in a higher pitch than normal; ensure you change the tone and speed of your speech to avoid monotony.

- Silence – use silence to emphasise a point; before a key point slow down and allow a moment of silence; confident speakers use silence to get attention.

- Timing – keep within the allotted time for your talk.

- Eye contact – try to make eye contact with every member of your audience every few minutes.

- Involve the audience – try to involve your audience by asking them questions or seeking their opinion.

- Reading your slides – if you are using PowerPoint do not just read your slides because this soon becomes boring and predictable. You need to use your slide content as a structure or illustration for other points that you want to make.

- Humour – humour is a good way to engage an audience and keep their attention. Appropriate anecdotes work well as does picture humour, but try to avoid a string of jokes.

- Pacing – use a wrist watch to keep each section of your talk to time; failing to do this will mean that you have to miss sections at the end. Rehearse the timings using PowerPoint.

- Practise – 'practice makes perfect', so make sure that you know the content of your presentation and can deliver it in a precise timescale. Test out presentations beforehand on a selected audience before the big presentation.

- Reflecting – after the presentation, spend time reflecting on the good and the bad so that you can improve. Keep a record of your experiences in a learning diary.

EXPLORE FURTHER

FURTHER READING

Forsyth, P. (2006) *How to Craft Successful Business Presentations and Effective Public Speaking*. Slough: Foulsham.

Hindle, T. (1998) *Making Presentations*. London: Penguin Books Ltd.

Levin, P. (2006) *Perfect Presentations!* Milton Keynes: Open University Press.

Zelazny, G. (2008) *Say it with Presentations: How to design and deliver successful business presentations*. Maidenhead: McGraw-Hill Education – Europe.

WEB LINKS

Microsoft site dealing with all things PowerPoint 2007: http://www.microsoft.com/office/2007-rlt/en-GB/Default.aspx?s=whatsnew&id=powerpoint&WT.mc_id=ad&WT.srch=1

Royalty-free music site: http://www.mediamusicnow.co.uk/

YouTube: http://uk.youtube.com/

CHAPTER 9

Business Calculations

What skills will I develop in this chapter?

- understanding the nature of business calculations
- simple business calculations involving adding, subtracting, multiplying and dividing
- using positive and negative numbers
- accounting for things
- more complex business calculations
- using basic business data
- using trends, distributions and charts to represent data
- working with business money

9.1 INTRODUCTION

Business requires calculations. There is a whole range of important areas of business that require simple calculations. The good news is that these are easy to understand and with the use of a spreadsheet are easy to calculate and display. If in the past you have not enjoyed this area of business, I urge you to read this chapter. This chapter will help you to overcome any fears you have of this area and allow you to develop a very useful range of skills that will make your student and business life easier.

This chapter looks at calculations only in a business context. This will make everything easier to understand and very relevant to your studies and your early business career. The aim of this chapter is to focus on understanding what can be done with calculations. The calculations will all be dealt with by computer software – so don't worry about being able to 'do' these. Instead focus on understanding the ideas and making use of them to solve business problems.

9.2 THE NATURE OF BUSINESS CALCULATIONS

Before we consider the nature of business calculations, let's spend some time thinking about you. Carry out the activity set out in the learning diary entry below.

MY MATHS FEARS

Other than those people involved in mathematics professionally, everyone has some fears and uncertainty relating to maths or, as I prefer to call it, business calculations. So it is a good idea to get those fears out in the open so that we can crush them. The following is a set of reflective questions that only you will ever see the answers to – so be honest and reveal the things that worry you about maths. Try to write several paragraphs in response to each of these questions:

1   Finish this sentence: 'When I hear the word maths I feel...'

2   One thing about maths that I can do well.

3   If I could do one thing in maths better, it would be...

4   The thing I am worst at in maths is...

5   The main thing that frustrates me about maths is...

6   Describe to someone else why maths is so important to business...

7   If maths was one of the types of things below, what would it be?

- type of food
- animal
- sport
- colour.

Finally, think about your favourite food, animal, sport and colour and imagine changing maths to each of your favourite things and at the same time change the word you use for maths to business calculations.

You will already be aware that keeping a learning diary is a useful and developmental tool for changing your attitude and approach to learning. Try for the first year of your course to reflect at least once a week about business calculations and your abilities, fears, successes and failures.

The key element of business calculations is their applied nature. In short, calculations do something useful. The next few sections will look at the types of things that calculations can do.

MAKING JUDGEMENTS

Managers and businesses make judgements all the time, every hour of every day of every week of every month of every year. Simple calculations allow those judgements to be made in a reliable and consistent manner. Let's illustrate this point:

*Peter is the manager of a small team of 15 staff carrying out a service function. Naturally his staff are sometimes ill and off work. Peter's organisation is very old fashioned and does not keep a record of illness. Peter keeps a tally of how many days everyone has off on a simple sheet of paper. This currently shows that his staff were absent between 0 and 22 days in the year. When someone is ill he simply **adds** one more day to his or her total. A couple of his staff came to see him to point out that when he thought they were ill they had actually been unable to come to work because the train* *service had been stopped due to snow. Peter accepted this point and **subtracts** the two days when the trains were not running. One member of staff points out that a more equitable way to record illness is to not only record the days off but also to record the number of spells of illness (a version of this idea is called the Bradford Factor). Peter agrees and records illness as days ill **multiplied** by the number of spells of illness. For example, Kashia has 12 days ill but this was all in one go when she was in hospital; Kashia's illness score is therefore 12 × 1 = 12. Gaynor, on the other hand, had only six days ill but this was three spells of illness of two days; her illness score is therefore 6 × 3 = 18. Later on Peter's manager asks him what the average number of illness days are that his staff take in a year. Peter uses the total Illness Score and **divides** by the number of working days in a year (240). So Gaynor's average is 18 divided by 240 = 0.075.*

You can see that simple calculations can provide a lot of information. Using just these four calculations:

- adding: 12+14+16+23
- subtracting: 12–2
- multiplying: 6 × 3
- dividing: 18 ÷ 240

You might say that we have not used these numbers to make many judgements – and you would be correct. This illustrates a really important point about calculations: you need to accumulate numbers (data) and make calculations before you can make judgements.

Let's carry on with our illustration.

Peter's manager explains that the organisation is going through difficult times and Peter must make four of his staff redundant – today. His manager explains that the organisation has agreed with the representative union that the criteria for redundancy will be number of days' sickness in the last year as calculated by the Illness Factor. This saddens Peter, but he can quickly decide who must be made redundant.

SUMMARY

Business can accumulate a lot of data and make consistent decisions by using just the four basic calculations – *adding*, *subtracting*, *multiplying* and *dividing*.

To use calculations to make judgements you must have the numbers (data) and the calculations before you need to make the judgement.

You can keep these simple calculations on paper, but it is more functional and easier to communicate if you keep calculations in a spreadsheet – there is more practical help for this in Chapter 15.

ILLNESS

Take on Peter's role as manager and help him with his illness reports. He has 15 staff and their yearly illness days per episode of illness is shown below:

Paul	2, 2
Priya	1, 1, 1, 1
Yin	1
Yang	0
David	1, 1, 1, 3, 2, 1
Gaynor	2, 2, 2
Kashia	12
Recura	0
Sam	7, 3, 1
Petra	2, 3
Anna	22
Thomas	6, 7, 12
Trevor	8, 5
Derrick	1, 9, 1
Jill	2, 2, 1, 1

Derrick and Sam have agreed with Peter that two of the days that are recorded as illness are actually days when the trains were not running, so these need to be removed.

Peter needs to calculate an Illness Score for each person. The Illness Score is calculated by multiplying the total number of days by the number of times ill; for example, Paul is ill for four days in two bouts of illness, so his illness score is 4 x 2 = 8.

Peter's manager wants to know the average illness (this is slightly more tricky than it looks – is it the number of days absent or the Illness Score, or the average days and the average illness episodes?).

Finally, Peter's manager wants to know the names of the four people who must be made redundant under the criteria of the highest Illness Score.

Research how to calculate the Bradford Factor. If this calculation were used, would different people be made redundant?

(Note in practice it is very unlikely that redundancy would be decided on illness record alone – the activity is for illustration of a business calculation.)

There are a few more things you will need to know about these basic calculations.

The positive '+' and negative '–' **signs** must be taken into account when making calculations.

Adding and **subtracting** do not cause too many problems. But, sometimes you can end up with a negative number.

For example, if someone puts in a claim for £342 expenses and by error is paid £442, the calculation to work out the repayment would be 342 – 442 = –100.

The signs have a different effect when used in **multiplication**. Multiplication can be thought of as a form of shortened addition. So that 4×3 becomes $3 + 3 + 3 + 3 = 12$.

$(+4) \times (+3)$ is a shortened form of $(+3) + (+3) + (+3) + (+3) = +12$.

(Note: we do not normally show positive signs in calculations.)

Now let's think about $3 \times (-4)$ is a short form of $(-4) + (-4) + (-4) = -12$.

(Note: multiplying a positive number by a negative number always creates a negative number.)

The same applies in reverse.

$(-3) \times (4)$ is $-(4) - (4) - (4) = -12$.

(Note: multiplying a negative number by a positive number always creates a negative number.)

That just leaves us to look at multiplying two negative numbers:

$(-3) \times (-4)$ is $- (-4) - (-4) - (-4) = +12$

(Note: taking away a negative number like $-(-4)$ is the same as adding 4.)

RULES OF MULTIPLYING

(+) x (+) = positive number +
(−) x (+) = negative number −
(+) x (−) = negative number −
(−) x (−) = positive number +

Dividing numbers follows the same logic:

- positive number ÷ positive number = positive number
- positive number ÷ negative number = negative number
- negative number ÷ positive number = negative number
- negative number ÷ negative number = positive number

I am sure you can see the pattern in these sequences; they can be summarised by the statement 'same sign positive, different signs negative'.

9.3 ACCOUNTING FOR THINGS

Business has to account for things so will need procedures and calculations to achieve this accounting function (the term here is used in the sense of keeping an account of things). Typically business accounts for:

- money and finance
- stock and goods

- pay and pensions
- staff and hours worked
- costs and overheads
- assets and equipment
- documents and data
- income and sales
- debts and creditors
- customers
- products and brands
- knowledge
- problem-solving
- reporting
- making decisions
- understanding the past
- predicting the future.

Let's illustrate the accounting ideas and calculations with an example. Ambreen has just started work with Zobra Ltd, a small but expanding company supplying modern lights and light fittings. Their company motto is 'live each day'. Ambreen studied business at university and has been employed to carry out inventory control or, as it used to be called, stock control. Ambreen is not impressed when on her first day she discovers that there is no real system of stock control. She asks Mr Zobra if he intends getting any stock control software, but he says the company cannot afford it at the moment; they have to spend all their money on getting new stock to supply their expansion.

Ambreen's first task is to stock-take what is in the stores. It takes quite some time to stock-take the 1,620 different items. The following is an example of the information she has recorded:

Part No.	Description	Stock as at 1 Jan. 2010	Cost price £	Sale price £
3456789	Bern ceiling fitting	420	56.42	95.56
3567811	LED track 4	108	26.55	35.22
3694547	Dublin fitting	120	45.66	126.58
3559948	1-watt patio light	3	12.66	15.98
3988547	Monaco 2-arm LED	260	42.56	61.75
3225641	Bressica uplight	80	18.99	21.99
3747422	Lisbon ceiling fitting	170	22.50	54.36

Just as she is finishing her 'stock take' Jonno comes in to take out 12 1-watt patio lights. 'Damn,' he says. 'There are only three of these and I need 12. Can you order some ASAP?' he asks Ambreen. 'How many do you want?' 'I need nine more,' says Jonno. Ambreen asks, 'How many do we use of these each week?' Jonno replies that they use about 100 a week in the summer and none in the winter. Ambreen then decides she needs to see Mr Zobra and discuss a few things. When they meet she asks him the following:

1 How much of the stock is broken or damaged on site? (about one-quarter of all stock, he replies)

2 By how much do you want the sales price to be above the cost price? (100%, he replies)

3 How much stock do you want to hold of each item? ('enough to last one week' is the reply)

4 How much money do you have tied up in stock at the moment? ('don't know' is the reply)

5 What is the cost of holding stock? ('this is 18% of the cost price' is the reply)

Ambreen needs to make a few simple calculations to implement these answers. Let's tackle the first one.

First, one-quarter (¼) of the stock is damaged on site and therefore she will need to allow for this loss. Fractions are actually ratios represented like the one above as one number / (divided) by another number. We call the top number the **numerator** and the bottom number the **denominator**. In business calculations the top number is normally smaller than the bottom number, and when this is the case it is called a '**proper fraction**'. Proper fractions are always less than one, and in business are used to indicate the proportion of something, in our case breakage and loss.

We can think about this ¼ in several ways. First, let's think about it as a cake cut into four parts – that's easy to see when it is ¼, but much more difficult when it is 1/7. So we can think of fractions visually, but only large proper fractions. We can also think of it as a calculation when it is 1 / divided by 4 = 0.25. So, ¼ and 0.25 are the same. Now this turns out to be useful for Ambreen as she needs to calculate how much extra stock is needed to allow for losses.

She knows that ¼ or 0.25 **decimal** is lost or broken while on site. So she needs to do two things. First, when she can see that 100 light units will be needed in the next week, she must order more than 100 to account for the losses that occur on site.

She can calculate this in two ways:

- 100 lights, of which ¼ will be broken before fitting. What is ¼ of 100? This is easy so you may be able to see the answer straight away, but let's look at how she could calculate it: ¼ × 100 is (1 × 100) / 4 = 25, so she must order 25 extra; that makes 125 lights.

- Alternatively she could calculate this by using the 0.25: 0.25 × 100 (easy on a calculator) = 25 extra; so again she orders 125 lights.

You will note that there is slightly less calculator button-punching to do with the second calculation. And if you were using a spreadsheet to do the calculation, as Ambreen would have to do in real life, it is easier to enter 0.25 × 100.

REFLECTIVE PERFORMING

HELPING AMBREEN

Ambreen still has a few calculations to carry out:

1 The selling prices must be calculated as 100% of the cost price.

Use the techniques already developed to calculate the selling price of each of the stock items.

2 Zobra Ltd wants to hold enough stock for one week. Calculate the weekly stock order for each product. The table below shows the amount of each product used in 2009. You can assume even usage throughout the year.

Zobra Ltd used the following amounts of each product in 2009:

Part No.	Description	Amount used 2009
3456789	Bern ceiling fitting	600
3567811	LED track 4	2,500
3694547	Dublin fitting	480
3559948	1-watt patio light	1,250
3988547	Monaco 2-arm LED	4,000
3225641	Bressica uplight	7,500
3747422	Lisbon ceiling fitting	3,500

Calculate the amount of each product Ambreen should order each week.

3 How much money does Zobra Ltd have tied up in stock on 1 January 2010?

Part No.	Description	Stock as at 1 Jan. 2010	Cost price £	Sale price £
3456789	Bern ceiling fitting	420	56.42	95.56
3567811	LED track 4	108	26.55	35.22
3694547	Dublin fitting	120	45.66	126.58
3559948	1-watt patio light	3	12.66	15.98
3988547	Monaco 2-arm LED	260	42.56	61.75
3225641	Bressica uplight	80	18.99	21.99
3747422	Lisbon ceiling fitting	170	22.50	54.36

4 What is the cost of holding stock? This should be calculated as 18% of the cost price.

There is one further and easier way to do this calculation, and that is to recognise that the number must be increased by ¼, 0.25, or 25%.

We haven't looked at % as yet. **Percentages** are merely fractions of wholes, in this case 25/100.

The simplest calculation would be to use $100 \times 25\% = 25$.

Or easier still $100 + 25\% = 125$, the number of lights that Ambreen needs to order.

When entering this into a spreadsheet we would use $100 \times$ (* in a spreadsheet formula) $1.25 = 125$.

SECTION SUMMARY

This section has introduced a few more calculation ideas:

- **fractions** that represent proportions of things
- **decimal** representation of fractions
- **percentages** to represent proportions.

9.4 MORE-COMPLEX BUSINESS CALCULATIONS

So far in this chapter we have used a range of basic calculations, but sometimes it will be necessary to make more-complex calculations. Being able to interpret and use simple formulas is a vital skill of business. Let's stay with Ambreen's stock issues and illustrate the use of formulas. One important aspect of business performance is the control of stock levels so that there is always stock available for sale but not too much is held at any one time. In Zobra Ltd, the cost of holding stock is regarded as 18% of the cost price. If on average you hold £1 million of stock, this will have cost you £180,000 per year.

Business calculations of this kind are normally represented by a formula. The stock turnover formula is:

$$\text{stock turnover} = \frac{\text{cost (£) of the goods sold}}{\text{average value (£) of stock held}}$$

Your role is to ensure that you use the correct numbers in the calculation and then to interpret the results – work out what it means.

Let's say that in total Zobra Ltd sold goods in the year that cost £1,000 (a low number to keep the calculation simple). They also held stock on average throughout the year that was valued at £400.

We use these numbers in the calculation, exchanging them for the general terms, and come up with the following:

$$\text{stock turnover} = \frac{£1,000}{£400} = 2.5$$

Now we need to ask, 'What does this mean?' An answer of 2.5 means that on average the stock is sold and replenished 2.5 times in the year. Is this a good figure? That really does depend on the business, so to answer this question you would need to compare this performance with other similar businesses. In Zobra's case this is actually a fairly poor performance. In a small retail sector you might expect an average performance to be 5 or 6 and a good performance to be 10 or above.

Most businesses would hold this type of data for each product they sell. This would then allow decisions to be made on which products are selling well and the effectiveness of the stock control. These calculations would be handled by a spreadsheet, so don't worry about how to make the calculation.

FORMULAS AND CALCULATIONS IN SPREADSHEETS

Spreadsheets have a wide range of formulas for use in business calculations. These are easily accessed:

- Click into a cell where you want to enter the formula.
- Enter a = sign in the formula bar.
- Start to type Aver...
- From the drop-down box choose 'AVERAGE'.
- Complete the formula.
- Finish: by clicking the green tick symbol.

Figure 9.1 Excel spreadsheet view

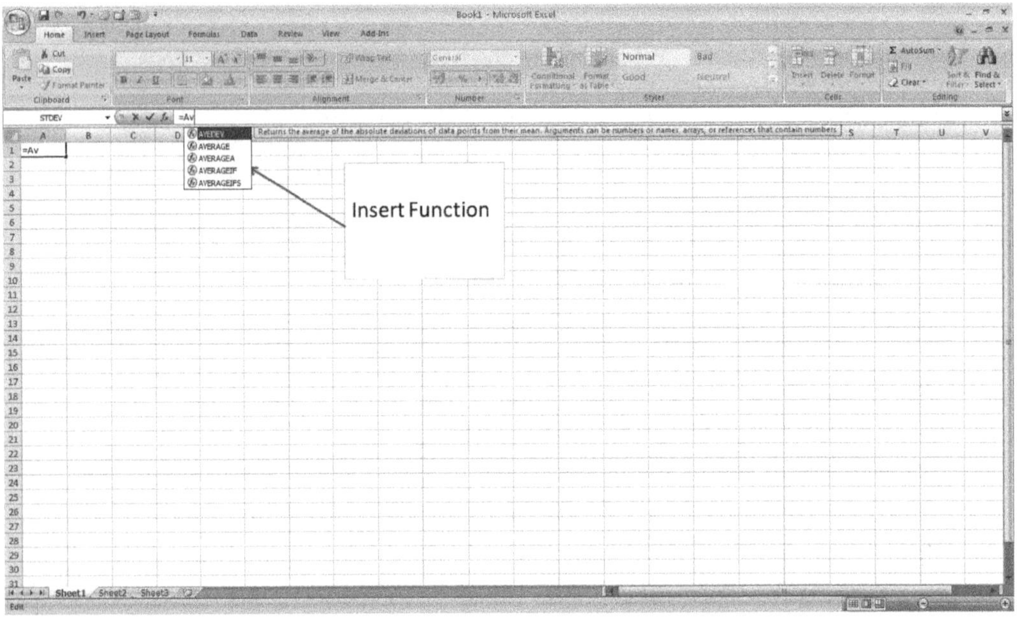

9.5 BASIC BUSINESS DATA

The business report is a standard form of organisational communication. It consists of a narrative (written) section explaining something, often a problem or a plan of action, and evidence to support the narrative section. The supporting section is often numerical. You will therefore need to be familiar with using simple numerical measures. The following section looks at the sort of measures you may need to use in a business report or an undergraduate project.

THE AVERAGE (MEAN)

This is more correctly called the *mean*. It is the first statistic that you generate from any set of data and it describes the centre of your data. The mean is calculated by adding all the values in your data and dividing by the total number of values. So if we have the values for staff illness in a year of 12, 18, 6, 5, 8, 1 and 2, we add them together (52) and divide by the number of values (7). This gives us **7.43**. So we can say that on average these seven staff have taken 7½ days' illness in a year.

When I made the calculation of the average above I did something to the result before I wrote it down. The actual average is 7.428571428571. The 12 numbers after the decimal point do not tell me very much (you may also have noted that the numbers repeat themselves 428571). Indeed, I can learn all that I need about the average with the first two numbers after the decimal point. So in the example above I have reduced the numbers to the right of the decimal point from 12 to 2. We call this action *rounding*. It removes some of the unnecessary detail. In rounding a number we have to look one number to the right of where we want to stop to round the number as accurately as possible.

In the example above I rounded the number 7.428571428571 to 7.43. To do this as accurately as possible I looked at the next digit to the right of the place at which I was interested in stopping. 7.42, but the digit to the right is an 8, so to accurately represent this I increased the 7.42 to 7.43. The general rule for this is if the number is 7.424 or smaller I round down to 7.42; if the number is 7.425 or above I round up to 7.43. Knowing how many decimal places to represent is not a simple or easy thing to decide, but with experience you will get a feel for what is needed.

The *mean* is a simple statistic, easy to calculate but also very useful for describing your data and is essential for calculating other statistics.

Excel uses the following function to calculate the mean:

- AVERAGE(A1:A5)

where the data is held in cells A1 to A5.

THE MEDIAN

The *median* literally means a line dividing something down the middle. In statistics that is the middle value of a set of values. If we reorder the numbers we used above into a rank order, lowest to highest, we will easily see the middle value:

1, 2, 5, **6**, 8, 12, 18

The median of this set of values is 6. Notice that this is different from the average of 7.43.

The median is easy to find in a set of data with an odd number of values.

Where the range of values is even, the median will fall between two values. If I add one value to the range of values, you will see the problem:

1, 2, 5, 6, 8, 12, 18, 20

What is the median value?

It falls halfway between 6 and 8, so the median of this range of values is 7.

With the extra value in the range, the mean is now 9.00.

The median is just as acceptable as the mean for describing the centre of your data. You would use the median if you wanted to know the typical number of illness days in a data set. You would use the mean if you wanted to know the average.

If we add one more value to this set of data, we can see one advantage of using the median.

Let's add 42 to the illness days, representing a member of staff who had a serious illness and was off work for over eight weeks.

Now we have:

1, 2, 5, 6, 8, 12, 18, 20, 42

The mean is 12.66.

The median is 8.

The effect of what we might call an 'outlying', 'extreme' or 'unusual' value is to move the mean up by 3.66. The median has moved up by 1. The mean value of a set of data is very sensitive to outlying data.

THE MODE

The *mode* is the most frequently occurring value in a data set. The mode is mostly used with nominal data (data that represents names of things) so that if one of your questions was 'my favourite colour is...', then a descriptive statistic of the centre of the data might be the mode, which might have been 'purple'. With categories and opinion scales, the mode is the only expression of the centre of the data that will mean anything.

This section has introduced a way of looking at the middle of data. To offer a more complete picture of data you will need to show how spread out the data is.

THE RANGE

The *range* expresses the lowest and the highest value of a data. Using our example above, the original range of values was:

1, 2, 5, **6**, 8, 12, 18

The range is indicated by 1–18. The range is often forgotten as a way of expressing the spread of data, but it does convey useful information.

THE INTER-QUARTILE RANGE

Don't be put off by this rather grand and confusing name; it merely means separating the data into quarters. The statistic is normally calculated for ranked data (values in a list in ranked order, that is, smallest to largest). The main number that is returned is the inter-quartile range. Don't worry about the name; it means the middle two quarters – in other words, the middle half of your data ignoring the upper and lower quarters.

Figure 9.2 Table showing inter-quartile range

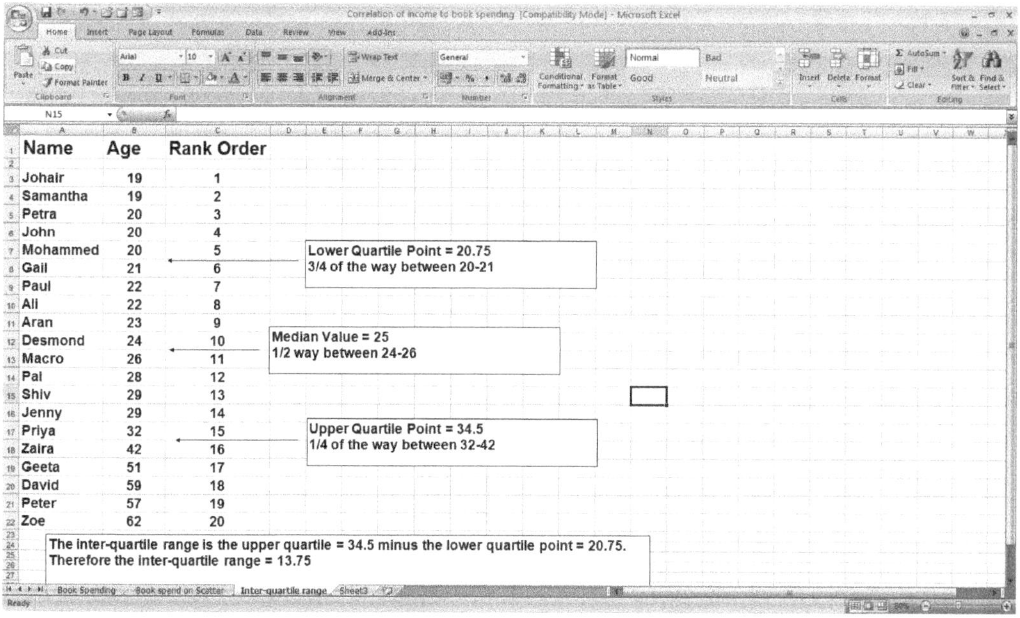

Name	Age	Rank Order
Johair	19	1
Samantha	19	2
Petra	20	3
John	20	4
Mohammed	20	5
Gail	21	6
Paul	22	7
Ali	22	8
Aran	23	9
Desmond	24	10
Macro	26	11
Pal	28	12
Shiv	29	13
Jenny	29	14
Priya	32	15
Zaira	42	16
Geeta	51	17
David	59	18
Peter	57	19
Zoe	62	20

Lower Quartile Point = 20.75
3/4 of the way between 20-21

Median Value = 25
1/2 way between 24-26

Upper Quartile Point = 34.5
1/4 of the way between 32-42

The inter-quartile range is the upper quartile = 34.5 minus the lower quartile point = 20.75.
Therefore the inter-quartile range = 13.75

We have already seen the problem of 'outlying' or 'extreme values'; using the inter-quartile range overcomes the effect of these extreme values by excluding them.

In Excel this can be calculated using the quartile function:

- **QUARTILE(A3:A12,1)**

The first numbers inside the brackets are the values in the range of cells A3 to A12. The number at the end should correspond to whichever quartile you want.

Remember to put the data in rank order (smallest to largest) – this is easy in Excel using the sort command.

1 = first quartile (25th percentile)

2 = median value (50th percentile)

3 = third quartile (75th percentile)

To calculate the inter-quartile range you would subtract the (in Excel's terms) the third quartile from the first quartile, or the upper quartile from the lower quartile.

You may also note that the median can be calculated using this function.

THE STANDARD DEVIATION

The *standard deviation* expresses data spread in a slightly different and more useful manner. Each value in your data is compared to the mean value for all of the data. So for the range of values, 18, 21, 23, 32, 36, 45 and 68, the mean is 34.71. The standard deviation calculates how far each value is away from the mean:

- 18 is –16.71 from the mean
- 68 is 33.29 away from the mean
- and so on.

To avoid negative numbers being generated, the difference is squared (multiplied by itself), so that we now have:

- 18 is –16.71 from the mean: $-16.71 \times -16.71 = 279.22$
- 68 is 33.29 away from the mean: $33.29 \times 33.29 = 1,108.24$
- and so on.

(notice those two '–' signs changing the result to positive)

Then the amount of each squared deviation from the mean is added together, and then averaged; finally the square root of the number is calculated and this is the standard deviation.

Excel has a standard function to calculate standard deviations:

=STDEV(A3:A9) – where the data is held in the cells A3 to A9.

In business the standard deviation and the mean are useful in understanding if the data has a *normal distribution*. A 'normal' distribution is one where the data displays a 'bell shaped' frequency curve. The *empirical rule* states that 68% of the data will lie within one standard deviation either side of the mean, and 95.4% of the data will lie within two standard deviations either side of the mean, and that 99.7% of the data will lie within three standard deviations either side of the mean.

Figure 9.5 on page 220 shows the time taken, in weeks, for 20 students to secure their first graduate job. Examine the data and consider what these values mean and how we might predict things from the data. It is possible to say that the

Figure 9.3 Standard deviation calculation

	Value	Mean	Difference between mean and value	Square of the difference	Square of the difference
Table of values and the Standard Deviation calculation					
Value 1	18	34.71	-16.71	279.37	279.37
Value 2	21	34.71	-13.71	188.08	188.08
Value 3	23	34.71	-11.71	137.22	137.22
Value 4	32	34.71	-2.71	7.37	7.37
Value 5	36	34.71	1.29	1.65	1.65
Value 6	45	34.71	10.29	105.80	105.80
Value 7	68	34.71	33.29	1107.94	1107.94
Average	34.71				
Sum of the differences				1827.43	1827.43
Average of the differences				261.06	304.57
Squareroot of the differences				16.16	17.45
Excel calculation of Standard Deviation of the Sample					17.45
Excel calculation of the Standard Deviation of the Population			16.16		

Average based on Sum/n-1

Figure 9.4 Standard distribution curve

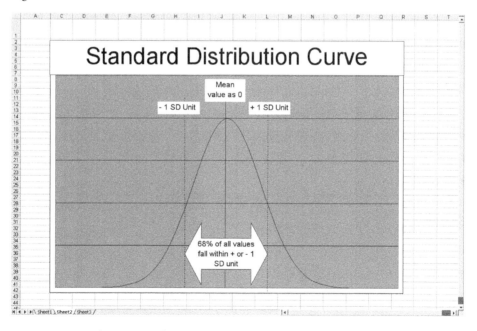

mean time to achieve a graduate job is 17¼ weeks. Using the empirical rule it is possible to say that 68% of the students would secure a graduate job in plus or minus one standard deviation either side of the mean. This would give us two-thirds of the students getting a graduate job within the period 13–22 weeks; 96% of the students (plus or minus two standard deviations) would get a job in the range 8–26 weeks. In practical terms it might be an effective idea to provide extra support and advice to students who are taking longer than 26 weeks to find a graduate job. You might also be able to predict that this extra support would be needed by only 2.3% of students.

Figure 9.5 Table showing standard deviation and mean

Table of the time taken by students to be employed in a graduate job after completion of a degree course

Student ID	Time to find a graduate job Weeks	
206145	12	
205448	13	
205896	14	
206254	14	
205689	14	
206321	15	
205887	15	
206451	15	
205778	15	
205899	16	
205874	16	
205881	16	
206522	17	
207811	17	← **Mean**
207544	18	
205495	19	
205892	21	
206102	23	
205621	26	
205863	28	
Std Dev	4.26	
Mean	17.2	

REFLECTIVE PERFORMING

HELPING GRADUATES FIND A JOB

Reflect on why the extra support would be required only by 2.3% of the students. You might have expected the support to be provided to 4.6% of the students – those lying outside the two standard deviation range of the empirical rule.

9.6 TRENDS, DISTRIBUTIONS AND CHARTS

Raw data is stored in software in rows and columns. In any data more than a few rows and columns, it will be impossible to see any trends in the data. To see the trends better in data you will need to represent parts of the data in tables or graphs. Once the data is entered into software, don't be afraid to generate tables and graphs using a wide range of types – it will throw up 'interesting' connections of ideas. We might call this 'playing' with data, and it is really important that time is spent just 'playing' with outputs from tables and graphs. Once you generate a table or graph, ask several questions about what you see:

- Does this look like a true reflection of the data?
- Is this clear and understandable?
- What is this telling me about the data?
- Can I adapt this to generate a clearer message?
- Is this going to be useful in my report?

Does this look like a true reflection of the data? It is very easy with the powerful software used for analysis to generate either rubbish or representations that are wrong.

Is this clear and understandable? Problems occur when you have a lot of categories with small numbers in them and when tables and charts are trying to display too much data. Give some thought to the type of display that is best for displaying the data. Summary charts tend to be pie charts and bar charts; detailed charts tend to be line and scatter graphs.

What is this telling me about the data? When you have a clear and accurate chart, ask what it tells you about the data. Is it indicating one clear message?

Figure 9.6 Excel data table and frequency distribution table

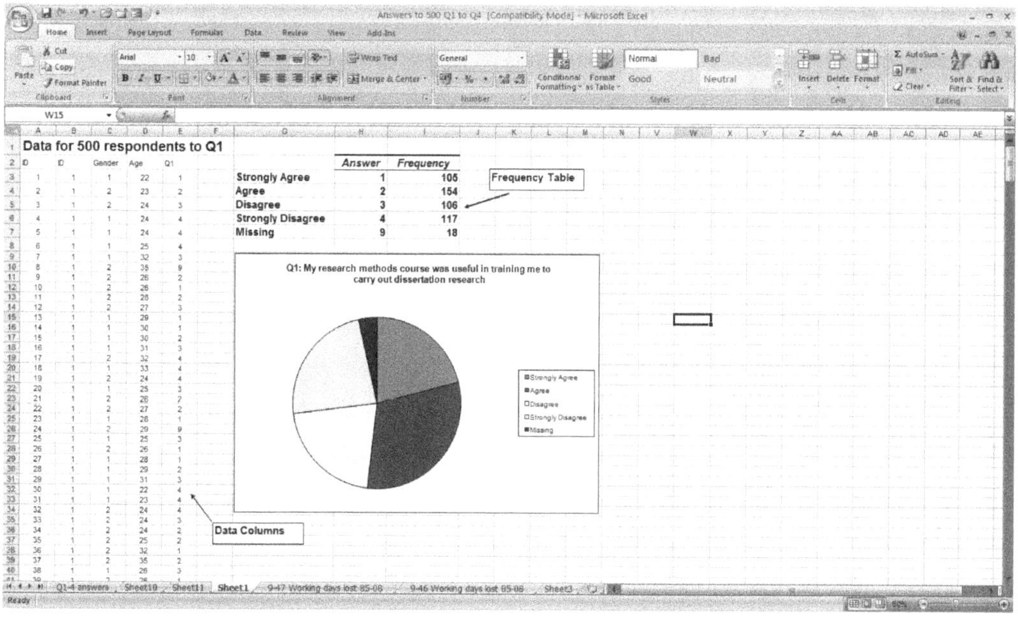

FREQUENCY TABLES

Frequency tables and frequency distributions summarise data – in statistical language, this means the number of cases or elements in each category. Frequency tables are an important source of data for the subsequent analysis using more powerful inferential statistics.

Let's imagine we have developed a questionnaire asking questions about a course of study. The first question asks if you enjoyed your business economics module; 500 responses were provided to the questionnaire. It would now be necessary to summarise the answer to this question in a way that sends a clear message. Figure 9.6 above shows part of the data table of 500 responses and the frequency distribution table. It also shows a 'pie chart' of the frequency distribution table.

CHART TYPES

Column charts

A column chart displays a series of vertical bars that are grouped by category. Column charts are useful for showing data changes over a period of time, such as quarters, and for illustrating comparisons among items. The plain column chart is closely related to the bar chart, which displays series as sets of horizontal bars (see Figure 9.7).

Figure 9.7 Example column chart

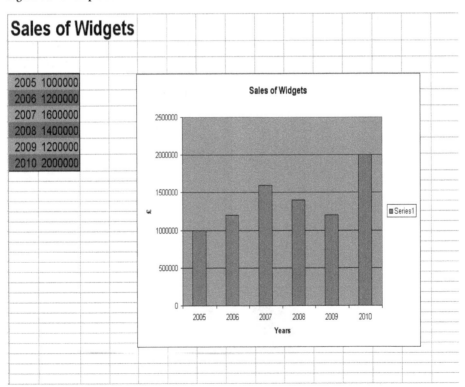

Line graphs

Line graphs are a series of data points connected by a line. More than one series can be used if a comparison is required. They are most useful for displaying data over fixed time periods, such as months in a year (see Figure 9.8).

Figure 9.8 Example line graph

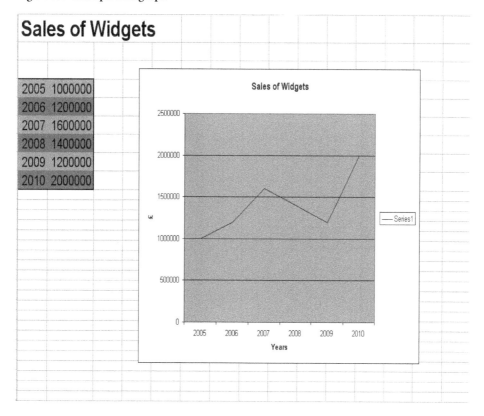

Pie charts

Pie or doughnut charts display data groups as a separate slice on the chart. Pie charts are popular in reports because of their visual impact. However, pie charts are a very simplified chart type that may not best represent complex data. Only use pie charts when you have six or fewer data groups; beyond this they become confusing and unclear (see Figure 9.9).

Figure 9.9 Example pie chart

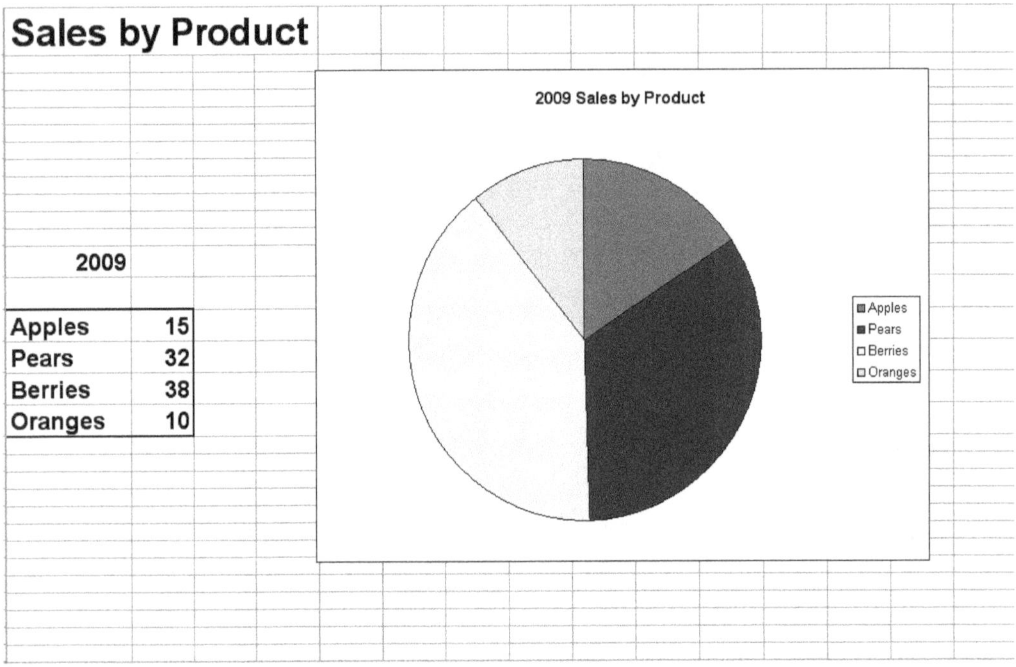
Sales by Product
2009
Apples 15
Pears 32
Berries 38
Oranges 10
2009 Sales by Product
Apples
Pears
Berries
Oranges

XY scatter charts

An XY scatter chart displays the relationship between two variables. Figure 9.10 represents data from 16 students. The X axis (horizontal, or across the page) represents the average number of hours they study each week. The Y axis (vertical) represents the average grade they have achieved in all taught modules. XY scatter charts display the relationship between these two variables. The first student represented bottom left averages only four hours of study per week and the average grade for this student is 20%. Whereas the student represented farthest right of the chart averages 42 hours of study and achieves an average grade of 58%. If the relationship between hours spent studying and the grade awarded were linear then the data points would be in one straight line from the bottom left to the top right. In this chart the data points are spread around, indicating that there is a relatively weak relationship between the number of hours a student studies and the average grade they achieve.

Trends

Business data is often collected over a period of time. Some examples might be absence rates, product failure rates, call-out times, delivery times. Trend data is normally presented in line graphs using the variable measure along the vertical or Y axis and the time along the horizontal or X axis.

The format of these charts makes a large visual difference, as can be seen by the same data shown in two formats. Figure 9.11 is formatted to show a rather effective drop in working days lost to absence. Figure 9.12 shows a more natural representation of the data.

Figure 9.10 Example XY scatter chart

Hours study per week	Ave module grades
9	35
21	52
42	58
35	74
36	85
38	64
37	71
22	62
21	57
19	41
14	39
4	20
15	51
17	81
20	48
30	69

Figure 9.11 Example line graph, version 1

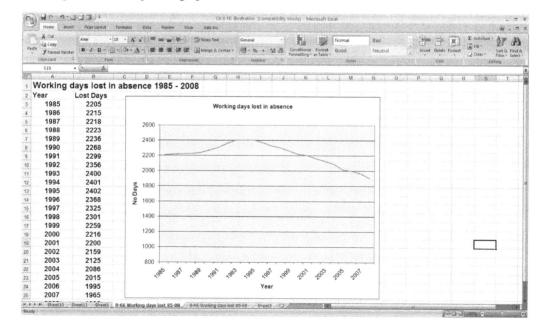

Figure 9.12 Example line graph, version 2

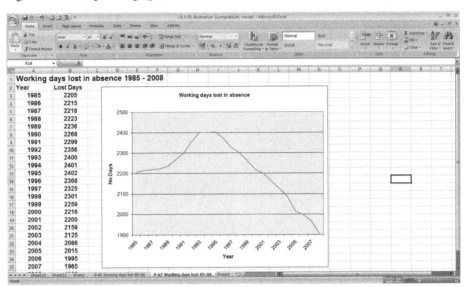

When creating charts of all kinds you need to think about the scales used and the formatting of the object to display accurate, clear messages.

9.7 WORKING WITH BUSINESS MONEY

As a manager you will have control of a budget. Budgetary control is an area of managing that is often not well understood or liked. By developing skills in this area you will be able to keep control of the monetary element of your teams or department. A budget is a guideline estimate of the monetary elements under your control. Nearly all departments will have a **cost budget** that sets out the estimated and agreed spending for that department. Some departments will also have a **revenue budget**, which is the estimate of how much money or revenue the department will earn.

Budgets are agreed annually with your line manager, and you will be expected to operate your team or department **within budget**. Some other concepts related to budgets now need to be investigated.

Actuals – These are the sums of money that have been paid out of your budget to date. These sums will represent things such as goods bought, services bought, staff salaries and all other costs. It is normal to get monthly printouts of your budget, so you will see entries entitled 'total actual to date', 'total expenditure' and 'total payments'. These all mean the same thing. It is also normal to have a total budget set out in **budget lines** or **spending lines**; the agreed total budget is divided into parts such as:

- staff costs
- stationery

- computing
- transport
- training
- casual or part-time staff
- and so on.

The budget is agreed in total and agreed for each budget line. Your job as manager is to remain within budget as a whole and within budget for each agreed spending line.

Commitments – The monthly actuals report will list all the spending that has occurred, that is, goods or services you have ordered and paid for. Commitments are items that you have agreed to pay but that have not as yet been paid. For example, you may have agreed to buy three new office computers; the order has been sent but the goods have not as yet arrived; when they do arrive the invoice for payment will not arrive for 28 days. If the computers cost £1,500 you need to be aware that the actuals report will be understating computer spending by £1,500. To obtain a true picture of your computer budget, you need to add the commitments to the actual total.

A typical budget report might look like this:

Department A – as at 30 June 2009

Agreed budget	Actual	Commitments	Available	Totals	Variance
£365,000	£210,000	£65,000	£90,000	£365,000	£000

You will notice that the last column is entitled 'variance'. Variance is the difference between the budgeted figure and the actual figure. This is a key aspect of financial management. Positive cost variances occur when you are over budget; you have spent more than was planned. Negative cost variance occurs when you are under budget; you have spent less than was planned. In order to allow variance to guide the actions of budget-holders, budget spend will normally be allocated proportionately to monthly budgets. So, if you have a staff budget of £240,000, it will be allocated at £20,000 per month. So, if you are overspending on staff costs this will be apparent in the monthly report. Perhaps in April 2009 your monthly staff budget was £20,000 and your actual monthly spend was £25,000; this would show as a monthly cost variance of +£5,000. If this level of spending continued you would be well over budget by the end of the year. Getting a clear budgetary picture each month allows you to change things so that you can stay within your budget.

Maintaining an adequate flow of cash into and out of a business is vital. You will also come across **cash budgets** that help businesses manage this important area.

WHY DOES BUSINESS USE BUDGETING?

1 It allows management to control the business. Managers can make decisions based on variances. For example, when variance analysis shows that the business is moving away from its predicted path, it can:

- when costs are too high – remove waste and inefficiency or negotiate cheaper alternatives

- when sales are too low – increase efforts in sales and promotion

- when production is too low – investigate the production process to remove inefficiency or bottlenecks.

2 Budgets allow for forward planning and the setting of targets to achieve the organisation's objectives. Differing targets can be set for different parts of the organisation.

3 Budgets provide a measure for performance. Many organisations will use key performance indicators and variance analysis to ensure areas are performing correctly. Key performance indicators are comparative measures and may compare departments, different businesses or different sectors. For example, Business A may have a stock cost of 9% and Business B may have a stock cost of 16% (selling the same range of items).

4 Budgets can be motivating when they set challenging targets. Departments and sections can aim at clear goals.

LOUISE AND SIMON

BECOMING REFLECTIVE PERFORMERS

Simon: 'How's it going, Louise?'

Louise: 'Well I have a new part-time job in Tesburys grocery store.'

S: 'Stacking shelves?'

L: 'No! Assistant manager of frozen goods.'

S: 'Well done! I bet you're really happy then?'

L: 'Well, yes and no.'

S: 'What's the problem?'

L: 'My manager is off sick and the other assistant is on holiday so I have had to report on the monthly budget.'

S: 'So what is the problem? You're a maths swot, aren't you?'

L: 'Well, I don't understand the terms and I cannot make head or tail of the budget report. What is an "outturn"?'

S: 'You mean "out turn". It is the actual amount of anything in the period. So your sales out turn is the amount of produce you sold. I guess each product is listed separately?'

L: 'I only know budgeting from the theory and we always called that an "actual".'

S: 'Sorted. Let's go and have a drink.'

L: 'Well, at least that is easy!' Now, what is a "UPOU"?'

S: 'Is that a small South American rodent?'

L: 'Do try to be helpful. I am really worried about this.'

S: 'Well, I don't know! Do you have a column in the report called variance?'

L: 'No, I cannot see one of those.'

S: 'Well, my guess is that UPOU is the variance column. Maybe something like "unplanned over under".'

L: 'Why do they have to make this so difficult?'

S: 'I suppose the columns aren't big enough for variance as a heading.'

L: 'Well, that is all right then. Trouble is that I have some quite large numbers in the UPOU column. I mean really big! Minced beef is showing a UPOU of £23,000. Does that mean I am in trouble – I wonder?'

S: 'What sign does it have in the column?'

L: 'It's a plus sign. So I am over budget by £23,000 on one product.'

S: 'No, that is a sales variance. Your department has sold £23,000 more than expected. That makes you a star not a sinner.'

L: 'I have to go to a meeting next week to discuss this. What do I say?'

S: 'Look in the total UPOU column. What does it say?'

L: 'It is showing +£107,000.'

S: 'That is just brilliant, I think? Go to the meeting, smile and say very little. You should be okay. Buy me a drink if it is all okay.'

…

S: 'How was that budget meeting?'

L: 'I'll get you a pint!'

S: 'Well, how did it go?'

L: 'Brilliant. I said practically nothing and the department got congratulated.'

S: 'So you didn't need to worry then!'

CASE STUDY

WHAT DO STUDENTS THINK ABOUT MATHS?

This case study involves a small research project that will help you build skills for carrying out projects and dissertations. It will be easier to complete if you use Excel to store the data produced.

Farrah is the Student Union President and she has been told that many students at Chiltern University do not like maths and find it very difficult to study. This concerns her, as she knows that maths skills are highly prized in the workplace. She holds a meeting to discuss this and, after a lot of debate, it is decided that a small research project is needed to discover if this view is a widely held view. She asked one of the level 2 business tutors if they would allow a group of students to carry out the project. The tutor agreed but asked for more details about what needed to be done.

Tasks:

Stage 1 – Questionnaire design

Prepare a short questionnaire. You will need to discover a number of biographic factors:

- age
- gender
- course of study
- subject area
- level of study
- any other biographic details that you think might explain the student's views on maths.

In terms of their view of maths, the following may be worthy of investigation:

- Have they completed a previous qualification in maths, for example GCSE maths?

- Do they see any use for maths in business?

- How do they rate their maths ability?

- Do they like maths? Why?

- What do they dislike about maths?

- Any other questions you think would be appropriate in discovering their views.

Try out the questionnaire as a **pilot** on about 10–12 students. You may need to adjust the questions after this pilot. Make sure it takes no longer than six minutes to complete.

Stage 2 – Gathering data

Administer your questionnaire to the required 50 students.

You will have to decide if you will fill in the questionnaire or leave it to the students to fill in.

Note down any difficulties that arose.

Stage 3 – Data entry

Enter the data in Excel; one row for each student. The columns will contain the question answers. See Chapter 15 for more detail about how to do this.

Stage 4 – Data output

a Devise graphical ways to display the data for each question.

b Explore ways to illustrate the views of students depending on:

- age

- gender

- level of qualification.

SUMMARY

The actions and judgements of business can all be improved if they are based on simple business calculations. The actual calculation will normally be performed by a spreadsheet or database; your role is to understand what can be done with calculations.

- Many simple decisions and judgements can be made using basic maths:
  - adding
  - subtracting
  - multiplying
  - dividing.

- When you perform multiplication and division you need to be aware of the signs of the numbers:
  - $(+) \times (+) =$ positive number +
  - $(-) \times (+) =$ negative number –
  - $(+) \times (-) =$ negative number –
  - $(-) \times (-) =$ positive number +

- Simple maths can be used to 'account' for various aspects of business.

- Business mostly makes use of proper fractions, such as ¼; this can also be represented as:
  - decimals, where ¼ is 0.25
  - or as percentages, where ¼ is 25%.

- More complex calculations can be made by using simple formulas.

- Business data can be analysed using some simple standard techniques:
  - the average
  - the median
  - the mode
  - the range
  - the inter-quartile range
  - the standard deviation.

- Trends in data over time can be represented by using different charts:
  - column or bar charts
  - line graphs
  - pie charts
  - XY scatter charts.

- Business money – mostly costs, cash and revenue – is controlled using budgets. Budgets need to account for:
  - actuals
  - commitments
  - variance.

EXPLORE FURTHER

FURTHER READING

Amir, A. and Sounderpandian, J. (2004) *Business Statistics*. London: McGraw-Hill Education – Europe.

Bradley, T. (2008) *Essential Mathematics for Economics and Business*. 3rd edition. Chichester: John Wiley and Sons Ltd.

Wood, F. (2008) *Business Accounting*. 11th edition. Harlow: Financial Times Prentice Hall.

WEB LINKS

BBC Skillswise site – Numbers: http://www.bbc.co.uk/skillswise/numbers/wholenumbers/

Google video page showing how to use Excel: http://video.google.co.uk/videosearch?hl=en&q=excel+calculations&um=1&ie=UTF-8&sa=X&oi=video_result_group&resnum=4&ct=title#

CHAPTER 10

Critical Reading and Writing Skills

What skills will I develop in this chapter?

- how to read critically
- how to recognise and assess assertions
- how to understand and assess arguments
- how to assess evidence sources and how to use evidence effectively in your own writing
- how to develop critical reading strategies
- how to write a 'critique'
- how to construct sound arguments in your own writing
- how to review and evaluate your argument
- how to use critical thinking at work

10.1 INTRODUCTION

The skill of critical thinking will mark out your work, both at university and work, as of the highest order. At university, sound critical writing will achieve excellent grades. At work, critical thinking and judgements will mark you out for promotion. Critical thinking skills are what employers are looking for. This chapter considers critical thinking in a progressive and practical way. Being critical is a skill and a frame of mind.

The chapter progresses through critical reading (assessing the work of others), critical writing (assessing your own work) and finally the nature of being critical at work. It is best to read it entirely in sequence, but also to return at times to refresh your critical skills.

10.2 CRITICAL READING

In Chapter 6 we considered an adapted reading method known as SQ3RW; if you cannot remember this or missed that section, you might like to read it before you read this chapter. The essence of SQ3RW is to survey, question, read, recall, review and write. Critical reading involves focusing on the questioning area of this approach. Some of the questions suggested in that chapter were:

- Why did they use this method?
- What message is this document trying to convey?
- Why was the sample so small?
- Is this a balanced argument?
- Is this all the theory there is on the topic?
- What is the unexplained assumption here?
- Does that conclusion come from the evidence?
- How would I apply this in my assignment?

These questions are all designed to make you think critically about what has been written. But a better understanding of critical thinking can be developed if we investigate the component parts of critical thinking.

REFLECTIVE PERFORMING

WHAT ARE THE ASSERTIONS?

Take a look at this short excerpt from an article in the *New York Times*, September 2003, by John Schwartz, entitled 'The Level of Discourse Continues to Slide.'

'Is there anything so deadening to the soul as a PowerPoint presentation?

'Critics have complained about the computerised slide shows, produced with the ubiquitous software from Microsoft, since the technology was first introduced 10 years ago. Last week, *The New Yorker* magazine included a cartoon showing a job interview in hell: "I need someone well versed in the art of torture," the interviewer says. "Do you know PowerPoint?"

'Once upon a time, a party host could send dread through the room by saying, "Let me show you the slides from our trip!" Now, that dread has spread to every corner of the culture, with schoolchildren using the program to write book reports, and corporate managers blinking mindlessly at PowerPoint charts and bullet lists projected onto giant screens as a disembodied voice reads

every
word
on
every
slide.

'When the bullets are flying, no one is safe.

'But there is a new crescendo of criticism that goes beyond the objection to PowerPoint's tendency to turn any information into a dull recitation of lookalike factoids. Based on nearly a decade of experience with the software and its effects, detractors argue that PowerPoint-muffled messages have real consequences, perhaps even of life or death.

'Before the fatal end of the shuttle Columbia's mission last January, with the craft still orbiting the earth, NASA engineers used a PowerPoint presentation to describe their investigation into whether a piece of foam that struck the shuttle's wing during launching had caused serious damage. Edward Tufte, a Yale University professor and influential expert on the presentation of visual information, published a critique of that presentation on the World Wide Web last March. A key slide, he said, was "a PowerPoint festival of bureaucratic hyper-rationalism."

'Among other problems, Mr. Tufte said, a crucial piece of information – that the chunk of foam was hundreds of times larger than anything that had ever been tested – was relegated to the last point on the slide, squeezed into insignificance on a frame that suggested damage to the wing was minor.'

Reflect on...

What is the main assertion that Schwartz is making?

What other assertions are made?

ASSERTIONS

Critical reading requires you to understand and recognise assertions. An assertion is a 'declaration that something is so'. If I say that taking regular exercise will improve your cardiovascular endurance, I have made an assertion. If I say that taking regular exercise will improve your examination scores, I have made an assertion. If I say that students with a larger income will spend more on books, I have made an assertion. When you read books and journals, you need to understand and recognise that they are all making multiple assertions.

The first key point in critical thinking is to recognise the assertion. Arguments are made up of multiple assertions. By focusing on or 'surfacing' the assertions, we are taking the first steps in critical reading. However, in normal writing there are multiple assertions and the assertion is not always clear. To read critically you will need to uncover the assertions and the argument. Incidentally, this skill will also help you to write clearer arguments that get better grades.

It will help you to focus on what is being asserted if you can provide some structure to the analysis. In Figure 10.1 below you will see what I call 'The Assertion Spider'. This is a template you can use with any writing to 'tease' out the assertions and place them on either side of the argument. Supporting assertions are on the left and counter-assertions are on the right. Any argument is likely to have support and counterevidence, so if all the assertions are on one side of the spider there may be a problem with the balance of the argument. Use the spider by writing on the horizontal hairs of the spider's legs as you encounter an assertion. As you read you may get a sense of things being asserted by association rather than directly. You should write these on the back legs of the spider. Write the obvious assertions on the front legs of the spider.

Figure 10.1 The assertion spider

Figure 10.1 The assertion spider

The spider assertion template

Supporting assertions   Counter assertions

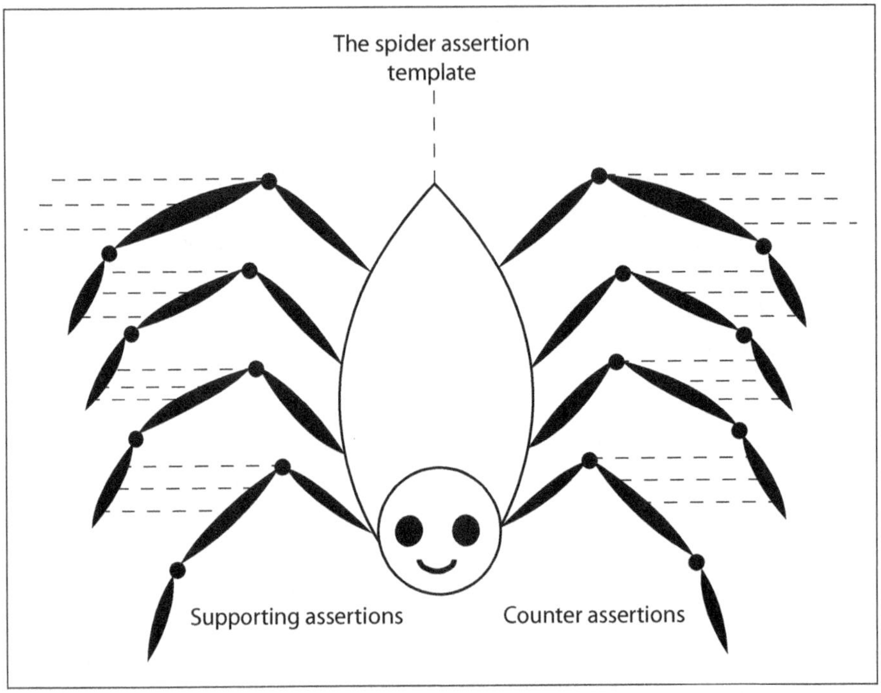

Let's test out the assertion spider by using it to analyse some writing:

I am the Managing Director of Best Fitness Ltd, which runs 12 fitness centres in the south of the UK. On any one day I will have up to 36 of my staff off sick. The total workforce is 322. This is unacceptable and just shouldn't happen. I think the only fair way to cope with this is to not pay them when they are off sick. After all, how does this square with the staff that always turn up for work? If I had my way I would sack anyone who took more than a couple of days off each year. All my staff are fit and young; there can be no excuses. It is only the old and unfit staff that are ever 'really' ill. A lot of young people are lazy and lack a work ethic. I wish there was a way of spotting them at interview, then I could save myself so much trouble. There is evidence in People Management *to show that many workers just can't be bothered to come to work.*

It is not as if I don't pay them well. They are all on a bit more than the minimum wage. Even the worst and laziest, the ones with degrees, get paid the minimum wage. I have had a consultant check up on all the staff with more than a few days' absence and he says a lot of them are malingers although he found that some of them do seem to be ill. I think they are just the good actors. Anyway, the law is no help with these lazy souls, so what can I do about it?

Now a lot is being asserted here, so read the extract again and note down any assertion – a 'declaration that something is so'. You may find there are clues to assertions that are not made directly. Put these on the back legs of the spider.

ARGUMENTS

So far I have described arguments as a collection of assertions. Arguments are more than this in at least two ways. First, arguments are presented in standard forms. The most common is the premise–conclusion format. The conclusion is supported by the premises; if the premises are true and strong then the conclusion can be accepted.

Figure 10.2 The temple of argument

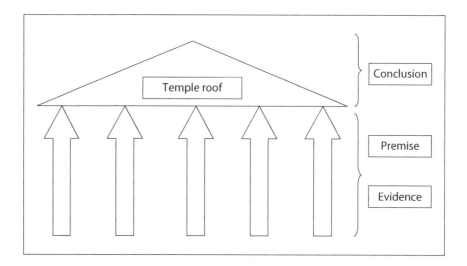

Classic Greek temples have a roof that is held up by strong columns. If the argument were the roof, then strong reasons and evidence would hold up strong arguments. The reasons and the evidence are the premises – the columns. Your role in being critical is to check the strength of the premises (columns) and pull down those that are not strong. In critically looking at arguments we would check and evaluate the logic, applicability and support for any premise. In practice the columns holding up the temple roof will be supported by premises that themselves need support. For clarity I will avoid too much complexity at this stage.

Second, we often analyse the 'tightness' or 'coherence' of an argument. This does not just ask if there are columns supporting the temple roof but how the columns are placed. If the premises and the evidence are loose, the argument is not well supported and you will notice a metaphorical 'lean'.

Figure 10.3 The temple of argument with poor support

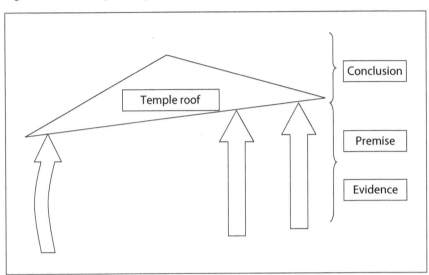

Let's illustrate this with an example:

Argument 1 – Astrology argues that the position of the stars, sun and planets at the time of your birth affects your destiny. There are many, many more astrologers than there are astronomers. While it is popular and written about every day in the newspapers, astrology is not a science.

Argument 2 – A distinguishing characteristic of science is that it makes testable predictions. Astrologers make predictions but they are so vague that they cannot be tested and verified. Using this measure, astronomy is a science and astrology is not a science.

If we look at those two arguments, the first one has three sentences that are loosely connected. It also makes no clear claim. The second argument has a clear claim, 'Astrology is not a science,' and it supports that claim with two premises: astrology may look like science but it is not, and to be science it must generate testable predictions.

THE STRUCTURE OF ARGUMENT

If we move on and set out the argument in linear form it may reinforce the points already made. This is the premise–conclusion form of argument.

We will follow some of the argument of the Managing Director of Best Fitness Ltd:

- Premise 1 – Young people are never ill.
- Premise 2 – Young people lack a work ethic.
- Premise 3 – Young people are only motivated by being paid.
- Conclusion – Don't pay any person who is off work with sickness.

Now in this case we can see that there is a lot wrong with the premises and the argument. I set it out as an illustration of the normal form. If we were evaluating this argument we would expect there to be support for each of the premises and that the supported premises then lead logically to the conclusion.

So the form of argument becomes:

Premise 1 – Young people are never ill.
> Evidence 1a – survey (2009)
> Evidence 1b – research study that investigated absence in the young where many participants said that they often took days off sick for no real reason
> Evidence 1c – etc

Premise 2 – Young people lack a work ethic.
> Evidence 2a –
> Evidence 2b –
> Evidence 2c –

Premise 3 – Young people are only motivated by being paid.
> Evidence 3a –
> Evidence 3b –
> Evidence 3c –

Conclusion – Don't pay any person who is off work with sickness.

EVIDENCE

Critically assessing arguments requires you to consider the nature, weight, presence and applicability of evidence. In the premise–conclusion form above I have suggested that each premise will have several forms of evidence. In practice this will not be so. If writers had to fully justify every premise, they would be caught in an infinite regression cycle where each form of evidence must be supported by more evidence. Now this makes assessing the argument a little more difficult because you must judge which premises need no evidence and which need a lot. As a rough guide, you should expect more evidence when a premise is:

- central to the argument
- disputable – not commonly accepted
- surprising, out of the ordinary or counterintuitive.

You will also need to consider the source of the evidence. In academic writing very little weight should be given to personal statements. So avoid them in your own writing and give no weight to them in other people's writing. Source material for academic arguments can come from:

- textbooks – reliable but not specific, not up to date and, importantly, not peer-reviewed
- journal sources – reliable, peer-reviewed and generally evidenced-based

- research sources – specific and reliable but still assess the worth of the claims
- Internet sources – less specific, less reliable, often contain unsupported assertions that should not be used
- personal accounts – these can be useful but this will be heavily dependent upon the context.

❝ TUTOR COMMENT

The way academic peer review works in business and management is that an academic writes an article and submits it to a journal for review. The editor reads it over and finds between three and seven other academics to review it.

These academics then read and comment on (critically assess) the content, method, literature and findings of the article and report back to the editor. In this way any errors, omissions, lack of evidence, illogical parts or unjustified statements are revealed. The author of the article then has a chance to amend any areas that are seen as weak or wrong. The article is then submitted again. If the reported errors have been removed, the article is published. In practice this review/ revise cycle nearly always goes though several cycles.

Once the editor and the reviewers are confident the article is sound, it is published. This means that journal articles are a far more robust source of evidence than any other source. When you read them they will have been criticised, developed and are likely to be reliable. No other source has this level of rigour. In academic writing we expect the main sources of evidence to be from journals.

I sometimes wish we could do the same thing with student assignments. Most seem to be very underdeveloped.

In critically assessing sources and evidence you will need to ask questions. You will build a body of experience about which questions to ask in which circumstances, but start off with questions such as these:

- Who is saying this?
- What authority and experience does the author have?
- Is this peer-reviewed?
- Is the evidence from a reliable source?
- How plausible is this evidence?
- Is there evidence on both sides of the argument?
- Is the evidence couched in emotive language or objective language?
- Does this evidence apply in this exact context?
- Is this evidence commonly used to support the type of argument it is applied to?
- Am I judging this evidence in a manner that other scholars would support?
- Am I applying undue scepticism to this evidence?

CRITICAL READING STRATEGIES

We have now looked at the component parts of critical reading. You will need to develop a way, a process if you like, of reading critically. Later in the chapter we look at writing a critique of existing writing, but for now I will suggest a few ways to tackle the practical task of reading critically.

Making notes (annotating) is a fundamental task when critically reading. Refrain from writing on or marking any book or journal you do not own. Use a separate piece of paper to record your thoughts. Critical reading is a personal thing, and there is nothing worse than opening a textbook to find someone has written his or her critical thoughts in the margins. The text can be annotated in many different ways:

- underlining key words, phrases or sentences
- marking the premises, evidence and conclusions
- making notes in the margin
- using coloured highlighters
- drawing a schematic of an idea or approach
- using arrows to connect ideas or contradictory passages
- you may find that you make notes on more than one occasion each time you read a piece of writing
- writing contextual points, for example 'this wouldn't work in this situation…'

Previewing – Don't just dive into the full critical approach. Spend some time learning how the text is structured and what the main claims will be. Use a 'skimming and diving' technique so that you read fast and then focus on interesting parts. These will often be the introduction and the conclusion. Try to get an understanding of the stance of the writer.

Contextualising – Think about how this writing will fit into a cultural, historical or organisational setting. All writing is grounded in context. Identify the writer's context. But, also place the writing in other contexts. Importantly think about the writing from your own personal or organisational context. All writing is first read through the lens of your own eye – your personal context. Recognise this and reflect on how it affects your reading of the text. Deliberately place writing in different contexts. If something is written from a manufacturing context, then consider it in a service sector context and ask how well it would work. Business is global so it is always worth asking how something would work in a different part of the world.

Questioning – There are two types of question that you can ask of a text. First, there are questions that help you understand the writing. Questions might include: How did that work like that? What happens when this is like that? Then there are questions that explore the ideas, premises, evidence and conclusions. Questions might include: How old was that study? How many people said this? What effect did that method have on the results? Would that study in manufacturing apply just as well in this setting? Is that conclusion driven directly from the three premises? Is there enough evidence to support that premise? Is there a missing or hidden premise here?

Some of the questions will have ready answers. Some of the answers will support the argument and some will undermine the argument. Some questions will not be able to be answered but may still be very important. Experienced writers will know the standard approaches to critiquing a subject and will express and assess their claims in the light of those known criticisms. If you find yourself asking, 'Why didn't they address this from that perspective?' it can turn out to be a serious omission from the argument. Questions around what has been forgotten or omitted are just as important as questions about what is present.

Personal reflection – Reading critically will challenge your personal belief system. Reading will impact on the things you believe in. As an illustration, have you ever found yourself saying, 'no, that just isn't so'? At that point something you have read is challenging your beliefs. When you read critically mark up sections of the text when you feel they are 'at odds' with what you believe. You can then return to these and ask yourself why this does not accord with your view of the world. If you do not 'surface' your own feelings and beliefs, they can act as an unconscious filter affecting your critique without you being aware of it.

OUTLINING, PARAPHRASING AND SUMMARISING

Active learning is a crucial part of effective critical reading. One way to be actively critical is to outline, paraphrase or summarise the ideas expressed in any writing. These three approaches are different and focus on different aspects of the writing.

Paraphrasing is the least critical of these three processes. Paraphrasing involves putting all or part of a piece of writing into your own words. A paraphrased passage is usually shorter than the original. The purpose of the paraphrasing determines how much shorter the passage is than the original. When paraphrasing for understanding and recall, you might aim to have writing that is one-hundredth of the size of the original. If paraphrasing to understand and reuse the ideas in your own work, then there may be no reduction in the length of the writing. To paraphrase accurately you need to understand the source material and then write it in your own words. Paraphrasing is essentially a restatement of the original ideas in your own words and adapted to your own context.

Outlining can be a more critical process. It involves restating the main ideas to form the 'backbone' of the argument. Outlining should make clear the structure and logic of the writing. In outlining the subsidiary ideas, evidence and argument are stripped away to reveal the core of the argument. Once revealed, this core should make the argument clearer and easier to understand. It is a critical and evaluative process. The critical element involves making decisions about which parts of the writing to represent in the outline. The evaluative element requires you to make judgements about the structure that remains. When you have outlined a piece of writing you should have a clear and evaluated idea of its strengths and weaknesses. Many writers use an outline before they begin writing. When you outline you are essentially trying to recreate the author's original outline.

REFLECTIVE PERFORMING

DISCOVER THE OUTLINE

This activity is designed to give you practice at discovering the original outline that a writer may have used. As a minimum it requires two people to complete it. It is suitable for a small tutorial group.

Stage 1

In preparing for a future assignment produce an outline of the writing. Refine this until it is an accurate map of the required writing, that is, do not start to write the assignment until the outline is an accurate template for what you will write. Carry out the outlining in Word and save the outline before completing the work – this creates the outline template that will be needed later.

Stage 2

Carry on and complete the assignment and submit it in the normal manner.

Stage 3 – Tutorial

Bring two documents to the tutorial: the complete assignment as submitted and the outline.

Instructions:

Each member of the group is given an assignment completed by someone else. They are asked to outline the main argument of the writing. The emphasis is to create an outline as close to the writer's original as possible.

Stage 4 – Comparative

Compare the outline you have produced with the outline now supplied by the author of the assignment.

To think about…

- How close to the author's outline was the one you produced?
- If there are differences, how do you think these occurred?
- Reflect on how this activity could assist you in creating the outline of your next assignment.

Summarising is the most critical process of the three. It involves creating a shorter synopsis of the writing using your own words and containing critical elements. The summary normally starts with a brief outline, then proceeds to a creative synthesis of those ideas. Essentially the ideas are recreated in your own words and to your own structure. The new writing will include critical comments about the ideas and the structure of the original writing.

EVALUATING

Evaluating returns us to the notion of assertion. All writing contains assertion that we want to accept as true. But critical evaluation requires that we do not accept anything at face value. All contestable assertions need to be investigated critically and assessed for the contribution they make to the argument. For the argument to be accepted the support (evidence) must be appropriate and sufficient. The parts of the evidence must also be consistent and compatible. Finally, the evidence needs to display a reflective balance, that is, display an understanding of the arguments that might be ranged against it.

LEARNING DIARY

HOW DID I NOT KNOW THAT?

This entry finds me depressed and fed up. I have just been to a skills tutorial for argument.

For the first time ever someone has set out how an argument, a premise–conclusion argument, should be structured. I have completed 18 assignments at university and I never knew this or, if I knew it, I never understood it.

What is so ridiculous is that once it has been pointed out to you it is like a

secret password to understand how most academic writing is structured. I'd never seen it before. That is so much wasted effort on my part. I have been struggling to understand how to put assignments together and create 'a strong argument', as my tutor calls it.

The more I write, the more livid I get. Why don't the tutors point this out at the beginning instead of when I am in my last year? Grrr.

10.3 WRITING A 'CRITIQUE'

Writing a 'critique' is a task that requires you to critically evaluate some form of text, object or other creation. It can be set as a university assignment or you can use it as a developmental activity. Remember that the skill of being critical requires practice to develop. In year one of undergraduate degrees very little critical work is required. You can develop your critical skills by writing critiques of texts and journal articles even at this early stage. The critique requires the two highest levels of academic skill. These are being critical and evaluative. You will also need to be able to synthesise ideas from other authors and texts to use as comparative material in the critique.

Deciding the merit of an article or text should be based on criteria. Criteria set out the general rubric by which you measure and evaluate. You will need to create and reflect upon your own criteria for critiquing academic writing. To get you started there is a table of criteria and a list of possible questions below. Do not accept these uncritically. Discard those that do not seem to work and develop your own criteria in the light of your critiquing experience. A good way to do this is to have a separate section in a leaning diary that addresses solely the issue of critiquing books and journals. Set aside time to develop these important skills.

Table 10.1 Critical review questions

Significance and contribution to the writing	• What is the writer's aim? • To what extent has this aim been achieved? • What does this writing add to the body of knowledge? (This could be in terms of theory, data and/or practical application.) • How does this writing relate to other writing in the same subject area? • Does the writer acknowledge the work of other scholars? • What is missing or skimmed over? • Does the missing material challenge the claims of the writer?
Methodology or approach	• What is the general approach that was used for the research? (for example, quantitative or qualitative, inductive/deductive, comparative, case study, personal reflection…) • How objective/subjective is the approach? • Is the approach consistent with the theory around the subject matter? • Are the results valid and reliable? • What analytical framework is used to discuss the results?
Argument and use of evidence	• Is there a clear problem statement, aim statement or hypothesis? • What claims are being made? • Is the argument clear and consistent? • Does the argument have a metaphorical lean? • What kinds of evidence are presented in support of the argument? • Are the premises and evidence sufficient to hold up the conclusion? • Is this appropriate to the subject? • How valid and reliable is the evidence? • How effective is the evidence in supporting the argument? • What conclusions are drawn? • Are these conclusions justified on the evidence presented?
Writing style and text structure	• Is the writing style appropriate to the intended audience? • Is the writing coherent and convincing? • Does the writing adopt a balanced and reflective style? • Is the writing organised and structured in a manner that allows for easy comprehension? • Is the writing appropriately referenced and grounded in theory?

You will need to approach the reading in a systematic manner. My suggestion is to initially follow the actions below:

• Skim-read the writing, paying particular attention to the introduction and the conclusion. If anything interesting catches your eye, slow down and read that section. This is the **skimming and diving** technique. Make brief notes about the main aim of the writing and the structure.

- Read the whole writing carefully and slowly. Highlight any words or areas that you do not understand.

- Look up the words you do not know and reread the sections that you did not understand.

- Reread the entire article, making notes about the structure, the aim, contextual points, critical thoughts and any questions that arise.

- Finally, map the main argument out in pictorial form or as a linear argument. Express this in the standard premise–conclusion format.

Do not accept my suggestion as the only way to do this task. Active learning requires you to reflect on how learning actions work for you and in your context. You should quickly develop a more effective and personal way of critiquing academic writing. You may need different approaches for different sources.

WRITING THE CRITIQUE

Critical reviews typically vary between one and four pages. Try to keep within these guideline lengths, but to start with you might create longer reviews. Once you are experienced you could aim to produce only one-page critical reviews. The structure will normally be the same regardless of length.

Introduction – This should consist of one paragraph for a journal article and maybe two or three paragraphs for a book. Start with a short one- or two-sentence biography of the author: who they are, where they work, what other important work they have written, any affiliation with organisations. Set out the aim and purpose of the writing. Set out how the writing is structured. Summarise briefly the main argument. Explain the evidence base that is used. Give a brief evaluation of the writing. This can be positive or negative but will normally be a balance of the two.

Argument map – This is a summary of the main argument. The premise–conclusion format is a common one in academic writing, so the argument map will set out the premises, the evidence and the conclusion. This section is mainly description so that the argument and conclusion is clear to readers of your critique.

The critique – The critique should start by discussing any notable features of the writing. Then follow this with a reasoned and evidenced discussion of the strengths and weaknesses of the writing. Remember to base the discussion on a set of criteria suitable for the type of writing you are critiquing. Good critique will bring in the writing of other scholars for comparison, critique and evaluation. Be sure to correctly reference these sources.

You can sequence the critique in several different ways. You will develop a preferred style, but to begin with try these approaches:

- Journalistic style – have the most important points first and then the less important later.

- If your critique is mostly positive, present the negative aspects first and finish with the positive aspects.

- If your critique is mostly negative, have the positive aspects first and the negative last.

- Sequence the criterion points one chapter at a time with detailed discussion of the positive and negative aspects of each point.

- In brief reviews have one paragraph of positive points and one paragraph of negative points, or vice versa, followed by a concluding paragraph.

Conclusion – The conclusion should be short and punchy. It should briefly restate the aim of the writing. Then represent the thrust of your argument on the merits and weaknesses of the work. This should be followed by a restatement of your evaluation of the writing. You might then suggest areas that need improvement or further research. How well has the writer achieved what they set out as the aim of the writing? Finally, present recommendations if this is appropriate to the form of writing.

References and appendices – Include a section of references at the end. Append any important data or material at the end as an appendix.

10.4 SEVEN HEAVENLY ACTIONS IN CREATING A SOUND ARGUMENT THAT WILL STAND UP TO CRITIQUE

The skills you develop in critiquing writing can also be put to good use in improving your own writing. If you can create sound and persuasive arguments, you will achieve heavenly grades at university and succeed in the workplace. I set out below a prescriptive set of heavenly actions to create convincing arguments. In many ways they are the embodiment of the critical points made in the early part of this chapter. But note, they are prescriptive and you should beware and critique prescriptive statements. I would expect you to critique and evaluate these points. If they do not help you to write convincing arguments, reject them or adapt them.

HEAVENLY ACTION 1

A good argument makes a **clear and precise overall claim**. Set your main claim out early. Working out what your main claim is can sometimes be tricky. If it is not absolutely clear to you – the author – it will not be clear to the reader. Make sure you are making one main claim. Don't confuse your reader by making multiple claims. If you need to make multiple claims, separate them into sections.

HEAVENLY ACTION 2

A good argument is supported by **strong premises and evidence**. Once you have a clear and precise argument, you need to convince the reader that it is correct. Think about how a reader would challenge your argument. 'Why should I believe that?' 'How does the author know that?' 'Is that true?' How do I know that is true?' Challenge your argument from many other positions; this will alert you to the types of evidence you will need to convince the reader. If you have trouble with this action you may be claiming something without the evidence to support it. If there is no evidence, don't claim it. Claims without evidence are unsupported assertions – readers will reject them. If your argument relies on a chain of premises and conclusions – 'a sequential argument' – one failed claim and the argument fails.

HEAVENLY ACTION 3

A good argument **explicitly addresses points of disagreement**. All readers will have doubts about any argument. The best way to deal with these doubts is to raise them yourself. This creates an expected balance. No argument is ever completely one-sided. There are many elegant ways to introduce these concerns:

- 'While the majority argue that this is so, there is a vocal minority that argues differently.'
- 'There is a large body of evidence suggesting this is so, but we must also consider the evidence that challenges this position.'
- Avoid building a 'straw man'. This is where you present a weak counterargument that is easy to blow down.

It takes some practice before you can honestly present a balanced argument. Make sure there are always some points in your argument that present the possible objections.

HEAVENLY ACTION 4

A good argument contains **no factual errors**. Check and check again the factual and interpretative elements of your argument. Nothing brings down an argument quicker than some element that is clearly wrong. A variation on this is to present a fact that is 'economical with the truth'. This means that all the facts must be presented, not just the ones that suit your argument. Half-truths and partial truths are easily spotted and can ruin the convincing argument you are attempting to make. Using research findings is a particularly difficult area. If you only select the research outcomes that support your position and ignore the outcomes that work against your argument, the reader – upon checking – will feel you have cheated. If there is a lot of counterevidence, you may have to revise your argument. Your argument must be supported by the evidence; too much contrary evidence and your argument fails.

HEAVENLY ACTION 5

A good argument uses a **wide range of evidence**. You will also need to use the correct kind of evidence to support your argument. If you are arguing that the majority of people believe this or that, you will need evidence that is derived from a large group of people. Try to bring the widest range of evidence to support your argument. Having five types of the same evidence does not make it five times more convincing. Three types of different evidence would be more convincing. It is surprisingly easy to use the exact same evidence source more than once when it is presented slightly differently in several sources. If you cannot find a wide range of evidence to support your argument, maybe your argument is not that strong. Don't try to support the unsupportable.

HEAVENLY ACTION 6

A good argument is, like a good shrub, a well-pruned argument. What this means is that you must have **one clear central argument**. This is quite a difficult one to get to grips with early in your academic experience. As you build your argument there is a tendency for it to blossom in size and scope. Like a shrub, it just goes on growing. Each strand of your argument seems to need further and further argument to get it to make sense. Heavenly action 6 is then in conflict with heavenly action 2 in that you are trying to build strong, well-evidenced arguments and these tend to be large and well-branched.

There are several strategies to develop a well-pruned argument. First, structure paragraphs (see Chapter 7) so that there is only one point being argued. Second, make sure that the paragraphs flow in a natural way. Finally, expect to have to remove chunks and sections that do not precisely support your argument – 'pruning'.

HEAVENLY ACTION 7

A good argument is a **visible argument**. The reader should never be asking, 'What is being argued here?' That should always be crystal clear in the reader's mind. When reviewing your work, check that each sentence is clearly, precisely and visibly adding to the argument. Set out the argument at the beginning in the introduction and reinforce the argument by restating it at the end. In the main sections recap and remind the reader of the argument and where you are in expressing that argument.

If you ask someone else to read your work and they cannot easily see your argument, it is time to rewrite it. This often occurs for at least two reasons. First, when we start arguing we are not really sure of what we are trying to argue. If this is a problem, rethink and rewrite in summary form the argument as we did earlier in the chapter. Second, as we set out the argument our thinking about it develops and changes. There is no shortcut here; you just have to rewrite things. Each iteration will improve the argument and the clarity of that argument. This is a perfectly normal process and is to be expected.

In summary, these are my seven heavenly actions for arguing. I hope they get you started and help you to write good arguments. Don't rely on them for too long. Active learners will develop and improve how they write arguments.

10.5 USING EVIDENCE IN WRITING

You will probably have already got the idea that the evidence that is used to support an argument is a crucial element that we must subject to critical thinking. As we saw from the temple figure above, if the premises and evidence are not strong enough the temple roof will fall. This section looks at types of evidence and how to use evidence to support arguments.

THE EVIDENCE DOES NOT SPEAK FOR ITSELF

When you present evidence in support of your assertion, premise or argument (claims), you must also state how the evidence is relevant to your claim. This normally takes a standard form in academic writing. It is part of the premise–conclusion form of argument. Let's extend what we already know to reveal the standard form in which evidence should be used.

The general format for supporting all claims is set out below.

1 a claim

2 evidence that supports your claim

3 a warrant – that is, a general principle, assumption or premise that explains why you think your evidence is relevant to your claim

4 a qualification that makes your claim and evidence more precise, and explains anomalies.

Here is a light-hearted example to show the technique:

1 Claim: There must have been a party in the halls of residence last night.

2 Evidence: There are balloons and streamers everywhere.

3 Warrant: Party debris normally indicates that a party has taken place.

4 Qualification: There are occasions when people have dumped their rubbish in the halls of residence.

You are unlikely to need to make claims about parties in your academic writing, unless you are researching the effects of parties on student performance. But the example shows the format that should be adopted in your academic writing. The variation required from the example is that you will need to provide multiple sources of evidence so that the form becomes:

Claim 1

- Evidence (a), warrant (a), qualification (a)
- Evidence (b), warrant (b), qualification (b)
- Evidence (c), warrant (c), qualification (c)…
- and so on, until you have fully supported the claim.

In critically evaluating claims and statements you will be concerned with the strength of the evidence, the logic of the warrant and the openness of the qualification.

Claim 2 would follow the same format.

It is worth noting that when set out as an explanation, this looks very contrived. In real arguments this structure needs to be present but it will be written in flowing sentences and paragraphs.

What counts as evidence is heavily dependent on the context in which you use it. The following sections explore a range of evidence sources that might be used in academic writing related to assignments, examinations and dissertations.

Course notes and handouts as a form of evidence for assignments, examinations or dissertations are very weak. Your tutors will have developed lecture notes and handouts from academic sources and offered them in class in a form suitable for teaching. These sources are almost always not suitable for supporting arguments in assignments, examinations or dissertations. If you want to use an idea or a source from course materials, return to the original source and critically evaluate its usefulness before using it in any writing.

Primary and secondary research data is a valuable source of evidence to support arguments. Primary research is research that is used in its original form. Primary research data is the collected data used in the study where the data was collected. Secondary data is data that was collected in one study and is subsequently used in another study. The important difference in these two sources is the context in which the data is collected and used. Using primary research, you are guaranteed that the context is appropriate and suitable. Studies that use secondary data will have adapted the context and this adaptation needs to be critically assessed.

We covered the usefulness of evidence from **books and journals** in section 10.2. There are also a lot of other print-based sources that can be used as evidence. The personal accounts in diaries, memos, emails and notes can be used to support arguments about personal experiences, such as discrimination, bullying, politics and change. Newspapers can be a valuable source of evidence for contemporary or historical events. Fiction and biographies offer evidence of a personal experience.

Direct observation by watching, listening or being involved in an activity can be a form of evidence suitable for supporting arguments about personal experience. Observation can also supply numerical data. If you want to argue that there are too many motorists who talk on their mobile phones when driving, a compelling form of evidence is to observe and count this behaviour. Alternatively, you could use a study that has already carried out such research. This returns us to the notion of context. If you want to argue that there are too many motorists who talk on their mobiles phones and endanger the lives of students who walk to Buckinghamshire New University, then your evidence must be collected in and around the environs of Buckinghamshire New University. If your argument has a more general context, then a research study from some other part of the UK would be acceptable evidence.

Interviews can provide valuable qualitative evidence. Interviewing a cohort of people will provide general evidence of a view, experience or opinion.

Interviewing an expert will provide valuable specific evidence. **Surveys** will provide numerical evidence of opinions, beliefs, desires or wants.

Experiments will provide scientific evidence about material or personal behaviour. Some subject areas have a stronger tradition in this regard. Evidence that specific sports training has any effect would be gathered by experimental means. Experiments often take the form of a control group (where no treatment is applied) and the research group (where a treatment is applied). The difference in some measurable factor represents the effect of the treatment.

Personal experience can be used as a powerful and emotionally charged form of evidence. But note that earlier I indicated that personal experience was unsuitable as a form of evidence. Personal experience on its own is never likely to be regarded as sufficient support for most arguments. As an extra piece of evidence that has great personal appeal to the reader, it can be useful. But do be very careful with using this type of evidence in academic arguments.

Quotations can be a useful way to support your argument. The authority of the writer or speaker is of the utmost importance in judging if a quotation adds support to your argument. If the quotation is from your auntie, it is not likely to carry much weight. If the quotation is from the leading scholar in a subject area, then it will carry a lot of weight. You will need to be particularly careful about the stated warrant for any quotation evidence. Remember, the evidence does not speak for itself. You will need to explain how any quotation you use relates to your argument and how it supports that argument. When quotations just appear in writing with no warrant, we call them 'plop quotations', meaning that they are just plopped into the argument. Think of a drop of water plopping into the ocean. It has no visible effect.

HOW CAN YOU BE SURE THAT YOUR ARGUMENT IS CONVINCING?

You have followed the ideas in this chapter and developed your argument and supported it with evidence, but how can you review how effective it is? Here are a couple of techniques to help you decide.

Map the argument in summary terms, setting a short statement about each claim, the evidence, the warrant and the qualification. If you use a Word document for this in 'outline' mode, you can quickly and easily see the structure and flow of your argument. In this form it will also easily reveal where your argument is poorly supported by evidence. You can also add this argument map as an appendix to your assignment. This will demonstrate to your tutor that you have seriously considered how your argument is constructed and supported (see Figure 10.4).

Use the traffic light analysis system to reveal the balance of elements in your writing. You will need five coloured highlighters and a printout of your writing. Read through your writing and mark each sentence with the following colours:

Figure 10.4 Word in outline mode for argument review

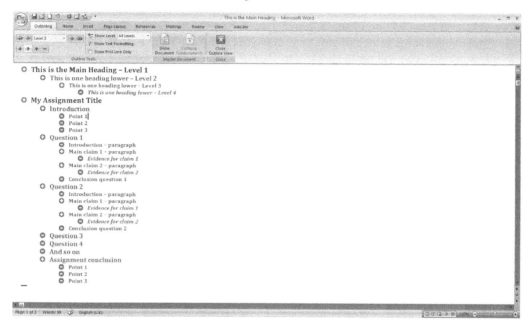

- claims – assertions where you 'say something is so' (pink)

- premises – statements that support the claims (blue)

- evidence – facts, quotations, reports, books, journals, and so on (green)

- warrants – your statement of how the evidence applies to the claim, premise or argument (orange)

- qualifications – reflective statements about the weakness or anomalies in applying this warrant (yellow)

- conclusions – your summary and evaluation of how effective your argument has been (pink).

Now, what sort of balance might you expect to see once you have highlighted your work? This is my personal view and it is based on academic student writing at Level 3 of an undergraduate degree:

- 10% – pink (claims and conclusions)

- 15% – blue (premises)

- 35% – green (evidence)

- 10% – orange (warrants)

- 10% – yellow (qualifications)

- 20% – not highlighted.

In the early stages of your skill development in writing critically, you may find that there is a larger proportion that is unhighlighted. Top-quality academic work will have every sentence contributing to the argument. Unhighlighted areas are not contributing to the argument. You will always need a certain amount of connecting and linking sentences, but try to keep these to a minimum so that your argument will be clearer and will 'punch' harder. By punch I mean it will be more convincing, more difficult to refute. Once you have reviewed your work in this manner you will probably want to change some areas by adding evidence and removing sentences that do not push the argument onwards.

Remember that this is my personal view of what writing will look like. Don't accept this uncritically. Writing and being critical are skills areas that should have a dedicated section in your learning diary. Your view on the proportions of the elements in your writing should change over time. Use the learning diary to make your thinking and reflection on these important areas explicit. The diary entries will provide a useful historical map of your development.

REFLECTIVE PERFORMING

CRITIQUING YOUR CLASSMATES' WRITING

This is a reflective exercise that works most effectively on work that is about to be submitted. Complete the assignment work a few days earlier than the deadline and arrange a study group meeting of about five or six people. The exercise takes about two hours to complete. You will need to bring as many copies of your work as there are members of the group. Your tutor may also set up a similar exercise for a seminar class. You will need to bring a set of coloured highlighters and a pen and pencil.

Each member of the group is given a copy of the other assignments, so that in a group of six each person will have five assignments to read. Your role is to highlight the following elements in the work you are reading:

- pink for claims, assertions and conclusions
- blue for premises
- green for evidence
- orange for warrants
- yellow for qualifications.

As you read the work underline any spelling or grammatical errors. When the logic of the argument appears to go wrong, not follow in sequence – a *non sequitur* – place a ring around the argument in pencil. You can also add helpful comments in the margin about how convincing you found the argument and how it might be improved.

The work is then returned to the author.

The author can then reflect on the analysis of the study group, particularly:

- any small errors
- any missing or underdeveloped parts of the logical structure
- the balance of the argument
- how convincing the argument appeared
- how the argument might be improved.

One final technique is to advocate your argument to an audience. You would do this by reading your writing to a small tutorial or study group. Then you invite them to interrogate you about it. This can seem a bit scary at first, but you will soon become comfortable with doing this. Having to justify your argument verbally will allow you to spot any weaknesses or poorly evidenced parts. It will also 'surface' something that until this point we have said very little about. Logical errors in your argument occur when there is not a smooth flow of ideas, one to another. These are often called a *non sequitur*, meaning 'it does not follow'. Arguments need to be built in a stepwise fashion. Think of an argument like the temple discussed earlier in the chapter; place the foundation building stones for the columns in first and then build more complex arguments on this foundation. Finally, your argument should stand as the roof of the temple – well supported and well balanced. Once this advocacy is complete you may want to adjust the flow and logic and the evidence you have used.

LEARNING DIARY

REFLECTING ON MY ARGUMENT

1 March 2009

I don't know whether to laugh or cry! I think I will do both.

My tutor encouraged me to go to a reflective feedback seminar for my soon-to-be-submitted assignment. There were four of us there and we all read and commented on each other's assignments – submission is four days' time.

Well! Mine came back covered in coloured highlighter, writing and pencil. I just looked at it and thought they have ruined my hard work. Hardly any comment was positive; they were all comments and notes about what was wrong and what I could do to improve it. I have to say I hated everyone at that seminar. I was so upset. These things are so hurtful.

I have thrown them all in the bin – unread mostly.

4 March 2009

I just thought I would add another note to the earlier points.

I am still really upset! I have just submitted my assignment. But I did get those assignment comments out of the bin after I had thrown them away. I don't know why I reread them but as I did and once my initial anger had calmed down I realised that some of the things they wrote, while still hurtful, were actually useful and would improve my work.

Well, in the end I had read all the comments and notes and made about 100 changes to my assignment. That seemed to improve it a fair bit.

25 March 2009

My assignment grade came back and it was the best grade I have ever got – 12% higher than any other. I guess all that pain and anguish was worth it.

I must try not to be so sensitive to the criticism in future.

10.6 CRITICAL THINKING AT WORK

The critical thinking skills you develop at university will also serve you well at work. But the critical thinking skills you need at work are slightly different from those you use at university. I'll restate my definition of critical thinking as a starting point.

Critical thinking at work is the skilful, reflective and responsible thinking required as you consider a problem, strategy or solution. It consciously and explicitly considers the competing needs of different groups and forms a solution that is visibly equitable. The judgements are made openly and against a set of critical, public criteria. Critical thinking at work is reflective, accepts feedback and is self-correcting.

This definition is based on a number of important elements:

- Skilful requires that you have experience and practical aptitude for thinking with a critical mind. It is also reflective in that it requires an element of self-awareness and estimation of abilities.

- It is open and responsible in that the critical elements are available for all to see. It creates judgements that are equitable to all parties.

- Criteria-based judgements are those that compare the circumstance to the criteria. The judgement is then visibly made using those criteria alone.

- Critical thinking must accept feedback and correct actions in line with that feedback. Reflective thought must lead to self-correcting actions based on the elements above. It must also critique its own actions in being critical.

This is only a short section that relates the academic critical thinking process with the more action-oriented process required at work. In academic critical thinking the object of critique tends to be writing. In the workplace the object of critique is action, process and judgement. The same basic critical processes are required where the claims, premises for action, evidence, warrant and conclusion are subject to critical thought and scrutiny. The case study that follows investigates these work-based critical processes in more detail.

LOUISE AND SIMON

BECOMING REFLECTIVE PERFORMERS

Louise: 'Have you ever appointed anyone at work?'

Simon: 'No, I am not important enough!'

L: 'Well, I am a bit bothered at the moment as I have appointed three people to my team in the last six weeks and they are all turning out to be less than I expected. I dismissed one this week at the probation point.'

S: 'Oh I see! How did you make the appointments and carry out the interviews?'

L: 'We did all the normal things like have a job description and a person specification.'

S: 'Did a panel of people or just you make the appointment?'

L: 'It was a panel but I had the biggest say in who we appointed.'

S: 'So what sort of problems did you have with them?'

L: 'One was consistently late and I don't think ever did a bit of work. I inducted them well and helped them to settle in and then started to assign them work but it never really got done. I invariably had to do it myself or reassign it to someone else.'

S: 'What other problems?'

L: 'The other two are sort of okay but need way too much supervision and don't have the skills they said they had at interview!'

S: 'You mean they lied at interview. Told you they had experience of things and then you found out they didn't.'

L: 'Yes, that is exactly what seems to have happened.'

S: 'Doesn't everyone lie on application forms and at interviews?'

L: 'Well, I didn't, so I didn't expect anyone else to lie.'

S: 'Come on, you must have exaggerated what you could do; if you didn't you would never get a job.'

L: 'Well, I suppose I must have. But, then when it came to it I could do the job once I had got it. These three appointments can't do the job and look like they never will be able to.'

S: 'So what you are really saying is that you're rubbish at choosing people to work for you.'

L: 'Well! Is that what I am saying? Am I just a lousy chooser of staff?'

S: 'Well, it looks that way.'

L: 'Well, you may be right. Not that I am going to necessarily follow your advice, but how would you go about choosing someone for a job?'

S: 'For one thing I am not going to believe what they put on the application form. Haven't you seen *The Apprentice*? They apply for that with outlandish statements like "I am the best marketer in Europe".'

L: 'So if I cannot rely on the application form how can I evaluate and choose people?'

S: 'If you think about it, it is a classic critical judgement and evaluation problem. So set out criteria and judge them against the criteria.'

L: 'I thought the person specification did that.'

S: 'That depends what you put in the person specification.'

L: 'Perhaps I should put "good liar required".'

S: 'Maybe that is a skill you require but think about what a skill is and you might stand a chance of appointing people who can do the job.'

L: 'What do you mean?'

S: 'Well, if you want someone who can analyse research, then add that as a required skill. Then ask them if they have any experience and interrogate what they say to ensure they have actually done some analysis of research.'

L: 'I still don't see that that would help. The last lot all told me they could do that.'

S: 'Wait for my *coup de grâce*. Then at interview give them some data and ask them to analyse it. That will soon sort out those who can from those who say they can.'

L: 'Now that is a good point!'

Some weeks later after Louise has appointed two more staff. . .

L: 'I will buy that drink for you!'

S: 'Well – thanks. Is it my birthday?'

L: 'Do you remember that advice you gave me about appointing staff a week or so back? Well, it was inspired.'

S: 'I guess I am just a practical person and a good judge of character.'

L: 'I held interviews with six potential staff and all of them said they could carry out analysis of research findings. When I sat them down to a test of doing just that, only one girl could actually do it. She was quiet and had not stood out at the interview stage but was brilliant with doing the analysis. So I appointed her and she turns out to be brilliant – the best employee I have ever had.'

S: 'Let that be a lesson to you! You don't appoint people to talk; you appoint them to do something. Except maybe lecturers, where you do appoint them to talk.'

L: 'I wonder if they ask lecturers to lecture when they get appointed?'

S: 'Probably not!'

THE DOMESTIC ROBOT

Zeeborg Corporation plc makes domestic robots that clean and tidy the house when the owners are absent. Until 18 months ago the Zeeborg robot would tidy up while you were in the house. A series of unfortunate accidents meant that nine people died and 72 people were injured when the robots mistakenly tried to clean up people they thought were trash. The adaptation to solve this problem was to only allow the robot to operate when the house was empty. Pets can still be a problem as the robot operates with pets in the house.

Glenys is the operations manager for the production and distribution plant. At this moment she is in a senior management meeting. A number of urgent problems are on the agenda. The order book, since the adaptation of the Zeeborg robot, has mushroomed and now order fulfilment is 21.2 months. Everyone in the world wants the Zeeborg. These are unacceptably long delivery times according to the managing director. He wants to know what Glenys is going to do about it. Glenys suggests that they add another shift and increase the maintenance on the production equipment. This is an expensive solution but she believes it will be best in the long term. The accountant suggests that there isn't enough profit in the 'Borg' to produce it that way. He reminds them that they have a huge compensation payout for the deaths and injuries. He suggests that they move to compulsory weekend working until the order fulfilment is reduced to 12 weeks. A heated debate follows and the managing director eventually decides that the compulsory weekend working is the solution. Especially, he says, as this can come into operation next weekend and costs practically nothing. Glenys isn't happy but she could not argue past the compensation payment problems causing a severe cash flow drought. She thought afterwards the accountant never said how much that would cost and she thought some of it was covered by insurance.

The next issue concerned the unionised workforce, which were looking for an 8% pay rise and a reduction in working hours to 30 hours per week. This outraged every senior manager, but there were few proposals about what to do about it. The marketing director, in an outburst, said, 'All those working-class union blokes were out to screw the company for all they could get. We should sack them all!' Glenys intervened at this point and said she thought this was not so and that they all grafted really hard and many did unpaid overtime – no one seemed to listen to her. This 'banter' went on for some time but no real progress was made, so the point was held over until the next meeting.

The final point discussed was the delivery problems that had occurred. Transport was working flat out to deliver the 'Borg' but they were falling behind. Setting up each Borg at every house was proving to be a time-consuming process. Production was slow and delivery was even slower. This time the solution was more worker-friendly, and it was agreed that the delivery team would have an extra shift – one shift working 6am until 3pm and the next shift taking over the vehicles and delivering from 3pm until midnight.

After that the meeting finished and the directors went back to 'make something happen'.

One month later...

- Order fulfilment has increased to 28.4 months.

- The union had taken five days of strike action in pursuit of their pay claim and more were planned.

- Transport delivery had slowed to only half what it was the previous month as over half the trucks were off the road broken down.

- Zeeborg was facing compensation claims for 207 pets that had been killed.

To think about...

Carry out some library or Internet research on the following critical thinking issues:

- the fallacy of composition
- projection errors
- unintended consequences.

How do these three critical thinking issues relate to the scenario at Zeeborg?

SUMMARY

By way of summary I have set out below some of the attributes of critical thinkers. The list is not exhaustive and represents my personal views.

CRITICAL THINKERS:

- ask the right questions
- recognise assertions
- understand the basic arguing format of claim, premise, evidence, warrant, qualification and conclusion
- assess the strength, applicability and relevance of evidence
- are able to admit when they don't know or understand something
- are curious and inquisitive
- clearly define criteria before making judgements
- are willing to self-assess their abilities and develop their weak areas
- think flexibly and overcome bias
- are organised and systematic
- can follow logical argument and challenge the *non sequitur*
- are willing to be open about their opinions and beliefs
- are able to balance judgements and come to a decision.

EXPLORE FURTHER

FURTHER READING

Bowell, T. and Kemp, G. (2005) *Critical Thinking: A concise guide*. London: Taylor & Francis Ltd.

*An introduc*tion to thinking clearly and rationally for oneself, which equips students with the skills to tell a good argument from a bad one.

Fisher, A. (2001) *Critical Thinking: An introduction*. Cambridge: Cambridge University Press.

This book shows students how they can develop a range of creative and critical thinking skills that are transferable to other subjects and contexts.

Moon, J. (2007) *Critical Thinking: An exploration of theory and practice*. London: Routledge.

Critical Thinking is an exploration of and exposition on the elusive concept of critical thinking that is central to the operation of advanced stages of education and professional development.

WEB LINKS

A link to the Critical Thinking Community: http://www.criticalthinking.org/

Link to a site for creating argument maps: http://projects.kmi.open.ac.uk/osc/compendium/amap/

A link to the Foundation for Critical Thinking: http://www.wdil.org/resources/the-foundation-for-critical-thinking

CHAPTER 11

Analysis and Evaluation Skills

What skills will I develop in this chapter?

- how to understand and use the higher-level skills
- understand Bloom's taxonomy
- analysis and how to use it in writing
- analysis of argument
- how to use the 'premise–conclusion' form of writing and how to evaluate its use in other people's arguments
- how to consistently evaluate
- how to improve using the improvement cycle
- using criteria to assess theory
- how to evaluate your own writing

11.1 INTRODUCTION

The skills of analysis and evaluation are described as higher-level skills. If you are able to display higher-level skills in your academic work it will achieve an excellent grade. The term higher-level skill comes from Bloom's taxonomy, which categorises intellectual behaviour. After looking at Bloom's taxonomy, the chapter then moves on to look at the construction and evaluation of argument. The focus is on one form of argument: the premise–conclusion form. Data analysis is a specific form of analysis that is used extensively in projects and dissertations and in the workplace. Finally the chapter considers the skill of evaluation and how to evaluate theory and your own writing.

Like many of the chapters in this book, it is developmental. Therefore the most effective way to use the chapter is to read it sequentially and carry out the reflective practitioner tasks. The higher-level skills will take some time and effort to develop so you may need to revisit this chapter as your degree course progresses. Try to use a section in your learning diary that addresses assessing and developing the higher-level skills.

11.2 WHAT ARE THE HIGHER-LEVEL SKILLS?

We have already taken a look at analysis in Chapter 4, but it is worth recapping the points made there because in this chapter I want to build on those basic ideas. This chapter explores analysis in more depth and considers different types of analysis. Analysis on its own will not guarantee that your assignments and examinations will be awarded good grades; analysis needs to be connected to critique in order to create a skill and approach called critical analysis. However, it is easier to explain the two skills separately, so Chapter 10 considered critical thinking and this chapter will explore analysis and evaluation. The group of skills that will really send your assessment grades into the first-class area are known as 'higher-level skills'. These are the skills of critique, analysis, synthesis and evaluation. In the 1950s Benjamin Bloom, an educational psychologist, worked with a group of colleagues and developed a classification of levels in intellectual behaviour – known as Bloom's taxonomy (see Figure 11.1 below). In this figure you will notice that the higher-level skills are built on the lower three levels that were covered earlier.

Figure 11.1 Bloom's taxonomy

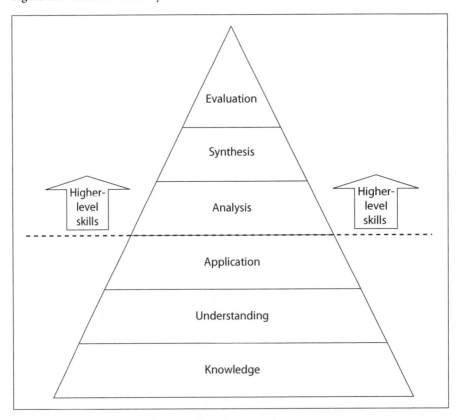

Your actions and outputs at university and work can be classified into the levels of Bloom's intellectual behaviour. Being able to focus on and produce assignments and examinations that display the higher-level skills will ensure your work receives consistently high marks. An explanation of the levels might be:

- **Knowledge** – involves being able to represent facts and information in your work.

- **Comprehension** – requires you to demonstrate that you have knowledge and that you understand the meanings and implications of that knowledge.

- **Application** – builds on knowledge and comprehension and requires you to apply that knowledge to achieve something.

- **Analysis** – requires you to study the relationship between parts or break down ideas or data into constituent parts.

- **Synthesis** – is the skill of connecting ideas or things to create new things or ideas.

- **Evaluation** – is the skill of judging, appraising and valuing.

 TUTOR COMMENT

The higher-level skills are quite difficult to acquire and then use in university work. In my experience students always acquire them before they leave university, but often it is too late in their studies to provide any benefit. This always seems a real shame because, like riding a bike, once they have 'got it', they thrive and produce really good work.

This will normally benefit them in the project or dissertation, but if they acquired them earlier all their work that counts towards the degree classification would be higher. Most universities award first-class degrees to only a small percentage of the students. Last year in business we awarded just 6% of the year. But if the higher-level skills can be acquired much earlier, say starting in level 1, then that percentage could go up to 20%.

I try to do work in the first year that prepares them for performing the higher-level skills, but at that stage they often don't 'get it'.

11.3 ANALYSIS

The process of analysis tends to focus on:

- the study of the constituent parts and the interrelationship of the parts
- the breaking down and separation of the whole into constituent parts
- simplifying the whole into parts to display the logical structure
- an explanation of a process and the parts of that process.

If we explore these approaches in more detail and connect them more directly to business assignments, they may be more useful in guiding you towards greater levels of analysis.

THE STUDY OF THE CONSTITUENT PARTS AND THE INTERRELATIONSHIP OF THE PARTS AND THE BREAKING DOWN AND SEPARATION OF THE WHOLE INTO CONSTITUENT PARTS

Focusing on a problem at work, you might reasonably need to investigate the constituent parts of the problem. In business analysis there is a need to use theory, ideas, models or typologies to carry out analysis. Let's assume we have a problem with reward management. What are the constituent parts of reward management as depicted in management theory? Perhaps the simplest theory to demonstrate the approach would be to consider reward as being made up of **extrinsic rewards** and **intrinsic rewards** (Sansone and Harackiewicz 2000). Using this theory immediately separates reward into two parts and allows further analysis of those parts and the relationship between the parts. The analysis might then progress by looking in more detail at the nature of extrinsic rewards using Mahaney and Lederer's ideas (2006) to analyse the practical use of extrinsic rewards in the success of information system projects and the relationship between intrinsic and extrinsic rewards.

In this form of analysis problems are broken down, using theory, into simpler-to-understand parts that are easier to research and solve. This breaking down can carry on until any problem is reduced to the primary constituent parts. In practice it is not always necessary to analyse problems until the very tiniest parts are 'spread out' in analysis. Often the breaking down or deconstruction of practical work-based problems is carried out one layer at a time until it is possible to solve the problem. In our example of reward management, if an acceptable and workable solution is found after the problem is expressed in the first layer of analysis – intrinsic and extrinsic – then no further analysis will be required.

Academic analysis for assignments and examinations is likely to require complete analysis until it is broken down to the constituent parts. This is especially useful when the analysis is carried out in preparation for research. It is considerably easier to research one small and tightly defined area of a problem or a theory.

SIMPLIFYING THE WHOLE INTO PARTS TO DISPLAY THE LOGICAL STRUCTURE

Reducing a thing, idea or concept to smaller and simpler parts will often be an effective form of analysis. Workplace attendance is a complicated organisational problem. It is possible to use a theoretical model to simplify the main phenomenon into parts that are easier to understand. Steers and Rhodes (1978) present such a model that separates institutional issues from cognitive personal issues; using this model would allow for a more effective analysis of absence management. Analysis to display the logical structure is often carried out using several competing theories. This not only allows the simplifying of concepts or ideas, but also the viewing of the concepts or ideas from a different theoretical standpoint. This pluralism of views allows for comparative analysis to be carried out.

REFLECTIVE PERFORMING

PLURALISTIC ANALYSIS OF WORKPLACE ATTENDANCE

(This activity is designed to last 60 minutes.)

This reflective activity is based on Internet and/or library research. It has already been suggested that workplace attendance can be analysed using Steers and Rhodes's (1978) theory. If your academic analysis required you to present a pluralistic analysis of workplace attendance, what other theories would you use? When using more than one theory, the analysis becomes more complicated and you must find an effective way to report this pluralistic approach.

To think about...

What other theories can be used to analyse workplace attendance?

Choose two theories and consider how you could represent the two analyses in one document or report.

Prepare the outline (300–500 words) of that document or report.

AN EXPLANATION OF A PROCESS AND THE PARTS OF THAT PROCESS

Explaining a process and separating out the parts of that process is another slightly different form of analysis. In business and organisational studies 'change' is often the subject of practical action, assignments and examinations. Descriptive explanation of the change process will take the analysis so far. Introducing a model of the change process and analysing the change in comparison with the model will reveal more about the nature and extent of the change. Kotter (1996) proposes an eight-step change model for managing change in organisations. Comparing the subject of an assignment or workplace change (the change that actually happened) to the change model, it is possible to analyse the changes. Closer inspection of the various parts of the change process will lead to further analysis.

Processes drive business. This assertion makes this form of analysis particularly important when analysing the actions and processes of business. Processes are so important to business that a whole raft of techniques are based on this form of analysis. If you open any periodical or newspaper that has a recruitment section, you will find a multitude of jobs for what are called 'business analysts'. Business analysts carry out specific and important functions in organising, diagnosing and changing work processes. There are a multitude of acronyms and names for these processes. Here are just a few:

- TQM – total quality management
- BPR – business process reengineering
- BPM – business process management

- BPI – business process improvement
- Six Sigma
- Kaizen
- lean manufacturing
- systems thinking.

This reinforces the point made earlier that analysis needs a frame of analysis. A frame of analysis in business is often based on theory. So to carry out analysis in the sense created above, it must be driven by theory. You will most likely find the theory you need for analysis in books and journals.

11.4 HOW DO I ANALYSE ARGUMENT?

We have already looked at argument in the previous chapter, so how would you analyse an argument? When marking your work, your tutors will be analysing your argument. At work your colleagues and superiors will be analysing your practical actions as argument. In essence, the critical analysis of argument means considering the claims of assignments, theorists, governments, managers, people, writers and so on. Critical analysis asks how the arguments are structured, what they are based on and how far one context can be applied to another. To analyse argument we must split it up into the component parts. From the previous chapter we know that the component parts should be:

- the claim
- the premises that hold up the claim
- the evidence that supports the premise
- the warrant about how the evidence relates to the premise
- the qualification of the warrant
- the conclusion.

The claim

Is the claim clear and precise? If there is more than one claim, separate them out so that each is clear for analysis. One erroneous way to get an unsupported claim to be accepted is to connect it to another supported claim. Look out for this false claim that is closely related to a true format in your own writing and in the writing and actions of others.

The premise

Does the premise always hold true in every situation? If an element in a premise, or the whole premise, is untrue, then the argument does not hold up. We will need in terms of our critique to explain the nature of weak or false arguments, such as: 'the argument is false because this premise is false'; 'the argument, while generally sound, has two weak premises'; 'the argument requires more evidence to support three of the premises'; 'the argument is weak because it presents little or no counterevidence'. You will develop your own way of expressing these things but you must find a way to express balance. The crude analysis of argument would suggest that if one tiny element of the premise is weak, the argument is false. In real arguments analysis cannot be like this. All arguments have flaws. You will need to develop sophisticated analysis that can detect and express both the strengths and weaknesses in an argument and come to a summary evaluation.

The evidence

Most premises will need several forms of supporting evidence. The first question to ask is if any evidence has been presented to support this premise. You might be surprised how often you are 'asked' to accept a premise where no evidence is presented. This might be acceptable for those premises that are not contentious, but in academic writing you would expect evidence in support of all claims and premises. Once evidence is presented you will need to establish if it is sufficient to support any claim or premise. Evidence should come from varied sources and be of a type that is appropriate to the argument being made.

The warrant

In the section above you were asked to evaluate the presence and quantity of the evidence supplied. In evaluating the warrant, does the writer or speaker expressly, clearly and precisely explain how this form of evidence supports the claim or premise? Once again, you would be surprised how often you will be asked to accept the evidence to support a premise without ever being told how that evidence applies to that specific premise. Remember – the evidence does not speak for itself.

Here is a simple but short example:

- Claim – Cars are polluting and destroying the environment; cars should be banned.
- Premise – Cars burn hydrocarbons and these give off carbon dioxide.
- Evidence – Cars released 4.3 gigatonnes of carbon in 2008 (Rummel 2009).
- Warrant – Car-released carbon destroys the ozone layer and causes the earth to warm up, destroying the environment.

I am sure you can see flaws in this short argument! I will look at just one. Cars that run on hydrogen do not release carbon dioxide so do not destroy the environment. The premise is false in this situation. Crude analysis would then go on to say that the premise is false in certain situations, so the argument is false. Now as a responsible and sophisticated analyst, you do not want to express your analysis as: 'the premise is false so the claim is false; cars do not pollute the environment'.

Let's look at the whole argumentative structure before we condemn this claim as false. If after the warrant the writer had carried on and made a qualification of the warrant, the argument would be analysed differently.

The qualification

Qualification – there are some types of cars that pollute less and some that do not pollute at all. Electric cars only pollute the environment with carbon dioxide from the generation of power and green sources of power produce a lot less pollution. Hydrogen propulsion using solar energy to produce the hydrogen creates a zero pollution running car. However, the production process of cars would still release carbon into the atmosphere.

You may now see the vital importance of using qualifications in your own arguments. Once the argument expresses the possible false contexts, it does not falsify the argument. It does weaken it in one way, but it could be argued that it also strengthens the argument. Self-reflective and honest arguments should be evaluated as stronger arguments.

Dealing with chain premises

In many 'real' arguments one premise leads stepwise to another premise. We often call this a chain premise. They are dependent on each other. In our temple analogy, from the previous chapter, two premises create one column to hold up the temple roof. If one premise is false the column crumbles. If one premise is not correctly connected to the other the column crumbles. When assessing chain premises you must consider the two, or more, premises separately then how they are connected and finally how they operate together.

Dealing with context

In many arguments evidence is presented from one context and it is argued that it also applies in another context. This contextual shift will need careful analysis and evaluation to ensure the contextual shift is acceptable. To analyse these contextual claims you would need to investigate the conditions under which one piece of evidence works and compare this to the new conditions where the argument claims it will also work. Some of the conditions you might want to investigate include:

The types of things or people involved in one form of evidence – Are the things or people in the new context similar? For example, an argument may use adult research as support for an argument and argue that this would also apply to children.

Time – Evidence from research in the 1960s may not apply in 2009. Even evidence from 2005 may not apply in 2009. In fast-moving subject areas, evidence becomes old and unusable much faster than evidence from unchanging areas. One area to investigate with all evidence claims is when the research was carried out.

Authority – What authority does the evidence have? If the evidence is derived from one lone master's dissertation, it does not have the same authority as evidence derived from the leading expert in a field of study.

Size – Arguing that one example of something can apply to all is a weak form of evidence. Using evidence from a study of 1,000 participants is stronger evidence.

These points are all weighing the strength of the evidence in the context in which it is used. Clearly as the evaluator of an argument, you can either fully reject the evidence or, on a continuum, evaluate all the way to fully accepting the evidence. Your reasoning for your evaluation should be explicit. In making your evaluation explicit you will probably need to use evidence and argument. Systematic analysis of argument will involve you crafting and evaluating your own counterargument. You will need to use all the substantive parts of the premise–conclusion format.

Linkage of claim–premise–conclusion

These three points in the argument must be explicitly and logically linked for the conclusion to be accepted. Any breaks in this argument chain will lead to the evaluation that the argument is false or weak. A common problem encountered in student work at university is that the conclusion is not fully and logically connected to the previously espoused argument. In the worst cases the conclusions are not connected in any way to the claims and premises. The normal expectation is that the writer or speaker makes this linkage explicit in the argument. A sound way to make this point clearly is to present the structure of the argument in the introduction, main body and in the conclusion in this shortened and stylised form:

Introduction – I intend to argue that Claim A is supported by premises (a1), (a2) and (a3). Claim B is supported by (b1), (b2), (b3) etc. Then Claim A connects to Claim B in this way and to Claim C in this way. When you connect these three claims together they support my conclusion of Z.

Main section – This section closely argues the points in a logical manner.

Conclusion – I have argued that Claim A is supported by premises (a1), (a2) and (a3). Claim B is supported by premises (b1), (b2), (b3). Then Claim A connects to Claim B in this way and to Claim C is this way. When you connect these three claims together they support my conclusion of Z.

Now this is a very contrived structure but it does make the claim–premise–conclusion very clear. I would advise that you start arguing in this very contrived manner and then develop a more subtle and skilful approach. In analysing arguments, expect this linkage to be present, explicit and logical; if it is not, then evaluate the argument as not clear or precise.

11.5 WHAT IS DATA ANALYSIS?

We have already explored the four approaches to analysis. These were:

a the study of the constituent parts and the interrelationship of the parts

b breaking down and separation of the whole into constituent parts c simplifying the whole into parts to display the logical structure

d an explanation of a process and the parts of that process.

When you work with data you are predominantly approaching analysis in modes (b) and (c). These modes – when used with research data – take the whole of the data and draw from it a restricted amount of data to simplify it and represent some aspect of the research. In many circumstances research data will be large and will be held in electronic form. This data is effectively concealed from the observer without some form of mode (b)/(c) analysis.

REFLECTIVE PERFORMING

DATA ANALYSIS

Take a look at the figure below, which represents a screenshot of a spreadsheet with 500 responses to four questions of a questionnaire. The figure shows the first 14 records and then at the bottom (the screen is split) 11 records. While you can see only about 25 records from 500, what do you think you could say about the response to Question 1?

Figure 11.2 Answers to questions 1–4 (25 records)

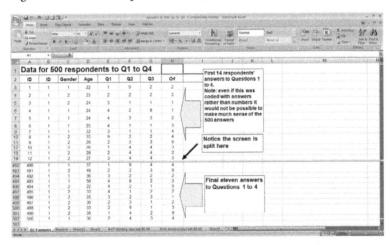

I imagine you cannot make much sense of what you are seeing. This data needs analysis in a mode (b)/(c) sense before anything clear can emerge. In this case, using some of the standard tools of numeracy will complete our analysis.

Now what can you say about the answers given by 500 respondents to Question 1?

To think about...

● From the data you can see in the second figure, develop three simple points.

● Consider how you can use other simple numerical approaches to analyse data.

● Carry out Internet research to discover what is meant by inferential statistics.

Figure 11.3 Answers to questions 1–4 (all records)

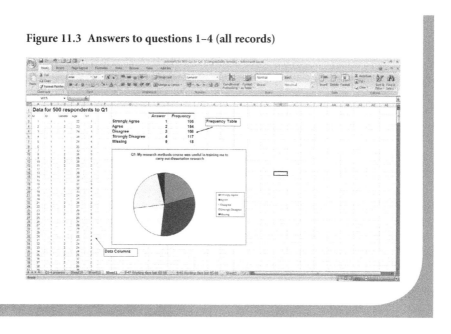

Chapters 9 and 15 provide more detail on the commonly used techniques to analyse data.

11.6 EVALUATION

How do we know if something is good? Do you know a good cake from a poor cake? I would guess that you do. How do you know a good essay from a poor essay? This becomes a bit trickier. How do you know a good theory from a poor theory? This is a step or two more difficult. Moving to the work context, how do you know a good work process from a poor work process? Finally, how do you know a good work output from a poor work output? I accept that I have laboured this point, but many many things require evaluation. Developing the skill of evaluation is not easy; it takes time and practice. However, being able to skilfully evaluate is an essential part of university life and a performance-centred skill at work. You will remember that in Bloom's taxonomy it is the highest of the higher-level skills.

You will also remember the Kolb learning cycle from Chapter 2. The improvement cycle is a similar cyclic idea. You could use it to improve your assessment grades; business uses this idea to improve business processes.

Let's relate the improvement cycle to an assignment you have submitted:

- You **plan** by setting out the ideas that you want to express.
- You **act** by writing and submitting the assignment.

- Your tutor marks your work and you **evaluate** the outcome of the assignment, for better or worse.
- You **change** something before planning the next assignment.

Figure 11.4 The improvement cycle

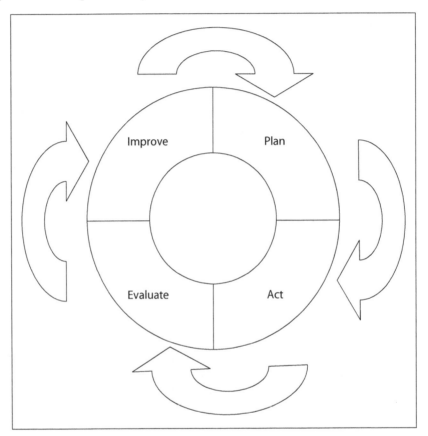

You may, like me, think this notion looks intuitively correct. This looks like it should work! Yet, how do we explain the practical evidence, which will occur for some students, that they changed things, submitted the next assignment and yet got the same score? It is called the improvement cycle, not the 'stay the same cycle' or, worse, 'the getting worse cycle'. I have used this example to highlight one of the problems with ideas, practice or theory. They don't always work. Let's investigate why the improvement cycle might not work.

We can return to our example above. You planned, acted, evaluated and changed. The two areas where you would find the greatest difficulty are the evaluating and the changing. They are the dynamic change elements in this cycle. If you evaluate that your tutor was an idiot and wouldn't know good work if it bit him, you would have changed very little or possibly changed your tutor. If you then submit your next piece of work and receive a lower grade from a different tutor, you would logically assume that the next tutor was a bigger idiot than the first.

What has gone wrong in our example?

The error has occurred at the evaluation stage. How could you evaluate this? How many ways are there to evaluate this? What sort of bias might enter the evaluation phase? There is no distinct answer to these questions. If anything is evaluated without a framework of criteria, it becomes a personal evaluation. There is nothing wrong with a personal evaluation of a cake. But do you want your assignment to be personally evaluated? Probably not! Universities produce assessment criteria so your assignments are **compared** to the criteria and evaluated against the criteria. Incidentally, assessment criteria are based on Bloom's taxonomy, wherein the highest-level skills attain the highest grades. So we have established that one method of evaluation is **comparison**. The comparator is often a set of criteria, but it does not have to be – more of that a little later.

REFLECTIVE PERFORMING

CRITERIA TO ASSESS THEORY

Before you look in detail at my personal view of the criteria that should be used to assess theory, carry out this exercise either alone or in a small group. It is experiential in that its aim is to allow you to experience the process of creating evaluation criteria.

Start with a blank sheet of paper and a theory you want to assess. If you cannot easily come up with a theory, use one of the following:

- Kirkpatrick's theory of training evaluation
- SWOT analysis theory
- profit maximisation
- Ansoff's marketing matrix.

In your group, brainstorm the types of criteria that might be used to work out if the theory is good theory or bad theory. Warning! This is not easy. If you find it difficult to start, try creating criteria for more everyday activities or things. How do you assess a cake, coffee, handbag or a football match? Once you have focused on an object and built a set of criteria, test them out by giving the object and the criteria list to another person or group and asking them to evaluate the object.

To think about...

Is their evaluation of the object the same as yours?

Now back to that blank sheet of paper! Is there anything that you have learned from developing the criteria to assess the everyday object that can be transferred to evaluating the theory? Effectively you will be producing a list of things to think about and observe.

When you have produced a list, compare it to the list of another group or person.

One area of university life where you can attain excellent grades for your assessments is to make sure that you evaluate those ideas on which you base your argument. Assignments and examinations should be based on theoretical ideas. So, back to our original question: How do we know a good theory from a poor theory? One way is to assess or evaluate a theory against a set of agreed criteria. Does such a set of criteria exist? Sadly not! What follows are my personal criteria for evaluating theory. These might be accepted by many academics but I have no evidence for making that claim. As with so much in the higher-level skills area, you should use it to get started but work hard to reject it in favour of better criteria from research or your own criteria related to your own subject area.

Before we investigate the detailed aspects of theory it is worth noting the purpose of theory. In essence theory is used to understand something. Theory in business and management is derived, mostly, from research. So you might expect theory to be focused on business issues such as change, people behaviour, the business in its economic environment, financing, performance, and so on. If theory can simplify and explain business issues, it might be regarded as useful. Theories tend to be either useful or not useful; useful theory is used a lot to explain things. Less useful theory is not used or discussed to any great extent. New theory is likely to arise when business areas are investigated by using research methods and acquiring data. The researcher will then attempt to explain the data using either existing theory or by generating new theory.

You will need to evaluate theory before you use it in your assessments, projects or dissertations. You could think of this as a recruitment event for theory. You interview (assess), let's say, six theories and choose the best one to use to explain your assignment, examination or project. In practical writing terms you may informally assess six theories that could be useful and then create a shortlist of three that you write about in your assessment. Revealing your evaluation of the three theories and your argument will determine which is the most useful. This open argument to select the most useful theory displays your evaluative skills and will allow your work to achieve high grades. Good theory helps to guide and focus attention, identify variables and make clear the relationships between them.

CRITERIA FOR ASSESSING THEORY

Scope – Theories will vary in the range of things that they try to explain, understand or analyse. The range of a theory is called its scope. Micro theories address small, distinct elements of business and management. Macro theories address wider, whole-business and whole-industry elements. Theories should indicate clearly what they intend to account for and what is excluded. Does the theory do this? Do the propositions covered match with the declared scope of the theory? Do the theoretical outputs extend outside the declared scope? The theoretical scope of a theory is how generally it can be applied. General theories that can be applied widely are assessed as being better than very narrow theories.

Operationality – Good business theory can be applied in practice. This means it is defined in terms that can be used and measured in practice. Many interesting ideas and theories are untestable because they cannot be reduced to operational level. An operational definition is needed to research the theory and to use the theory in practice. Does the theory express operational elements in this manner? Does the theory express clear and precise variables and the relationship between them?

Structure – Useful theory expresses relationships between elements, constructs and concepts; it does not deal with these things in isolation. The essence of good theory is that it makes clear the relationships between elements, constructs and concepts. This would allow the theory to be used for analysis. Good theory is built on existing knowledge and concepts. Theory that is not grounded is often described as 'theory in a vacuum'. Good theory is grounded in existing knowledge. Theory is often hierarchical, with one idea building on another. Good theory makes use of clearly defined and supported layers. Is the structure appropriate to the subject being explained? Does the theory rely on restating its assumptions to make progress? We call this 'tautological'.

Empirical – Good theory has empirical support. This requires that there is evidence in the form of data that supports and explains the theory. Research will support theory or present elements of weaknesses. Evaluate theory by weighing the supporting evidence. Does the research evidence suggest that the theory works well in the context for which it was designed? Does follow-up research support the claims of the earlier research? Remember the idea of the temple roof held up by columns of evidence from the last chapter. What is the nature of the empirical evidence? If it is quantitative, is this correctly grounded in statistics? If the evidence is qualitative, how was this analysed and presented? How was the empirical data sampled? Is that sample appropriate?

Is the evidence reliable? Did other studies find the same or similar data? Is the evidence valid? Does it measure what it claims to be measuring? Does the evidence lead to the claimed conclusions in a logical fashion?

Generates curiosity – Good theory generates interest and curiosity. We call this its 'heuristic' value. Good theory presents models and ideas that stimulate people to 'try it out', use it, question it, attack it and adapt it. Effectively good theory is interesting theory that stimulates more work on the phenomena or subject of the theory. In practical terms this point always links to the operability of the theory. If it cannot be applied and extended in practice, it is not good theory. If other researchers cannot continue researching and extending the theory, it is not good theory.

Balance and precision – Good theory has balance and openness. Any theory has to compete against other theories; they are judged by comparison. Good theory needs to express itself in terms that recognise other competing theories. Theory that does not recognise the competing claims of other theories may be regarded as assertive dogma – this would be regarded as weak. Claims made for theory need to express evaluative balance. This is easy to spot when theories claim to be the only and the most effective theory. But, as with all judgement, you will have to assess and evaluate how much balance should be expressed and how much is expressed.

A good theory must have precisely defined elements, relationships, constructs and prepositions. Be on the lookout for vague parts of theory. Vague areas often indicate weakness in a theory. Precise expression will allow the argument and detail of the theory to be challenged and falsified.

Simplicity – Good theory is simple but viable theory. This is often called 'parsimony' and it means that theory should present the simplest theory that explains the phenomena. When you use theory to analyse some part of business, it should give you a moment of revelation when you say, 'oh yes, I see that fits the situation!' Remember, theories are meant to explain things and simplify them. You must judge if the theory adds any clarity and understanding. Good theory will do this – poor theory often seems more complex than the thing it explains. Any assumptions or 'leaps of faith' should be appropriate to the context. This is an important point in that new theory is often proposing a partial explanation. It is like a bridge with a few bits missing. To make theoretical progress you have to leap across the gaps in the hope that progress is made and the gaps can be filled in later.

Usability – This is the ability of the theory to explain and account for events with increasing accuracy. This is often called 'instrumentality', meaning how much the theory contributes to knowing and understanding. We can judge this by how often a theory is used to explain things. You will already have noticed that some theories in business keep cropping up over and over again regardless of the subject area. On a usability scale we would judge these theories to be better than theories that are used less frequently.

We have explored in detail the criteria you might use to assess any theory you rely on in your academic work. This is because while at university you are likely to need to develop your academic evaluation skills. There are many other areas of business where judgements are required.

Work projects are normally evaluated against a set of agreed performance criteria. These will often have a financial element. This appears to reduce evaluation to a numerical exercise. If one of the project criteria was to deliver the project at a cost of £32 million and the final cost was £48 million, then the target performance was missed by 50%. Projects are also commonly assessed against a delivery date, so once again performance is easy to quantify. Where some difficulty may arise is with project outcomes that are not so easy to quantify. There is a tendency with business projects to only assess against measurable outcomes. However, this often undervalues important social outcomes in projects. For example, if a project were set up to improve young entrepreneurs' confidence, how could this outcome be measured? It may be many years later that any measurable output could be assessed. Gradually business is developing these 'soft' outcome measures using research-inspired instruments to assess socially valuable outcomes.

You may not have experienced action research; it is a form of research where the stakeholders or the participants carry out the research. In developing 'soft' outcomes, one model of action is to engage the participants in creating and developing an appropriate set of criteria. These are often expressed in qualitative terms. This makes them more difficult to use than quantitative criteria but it does provide a method to assess important social outcomes.

REFLECTIVE PERFORMING

ASSESSING 'SOFT' OUTCOMES

Assessing 'soft' outcomes is new enough to mean that there are no well-developed ways of doing it. The essence of soft outcomes is to ask who will benefit from any actions or approaches. Using a mind map is a good way to do this. Use brainstorming techniques to build the first elements in the mind map – all those affected by this action. For each of the affected groups, brainstorm how they will be affected. This will be mostly benefits, but note that you should think about any adverse effects as well. Then finally investigate what soft measures could be used to assess these changes or outcomes. The appropriateness of soft measures, and therefore the usefulness, will be improved by the involvement of the groups affected.

The process in detail

- Look closely at the aims of the project or action. Quantify those elements that can be quantified.

- Consider using an action research approach to uncover the qualitative benefits that may come from the project or action. Define as precisely as possible what these benefits will be.

- Build a criteria sheet to assess the benefits – effectively a list of signs and indications of how anyone would know that some benefit had taken place.

- Refine these criteria so that they measure what was intended – validity – and also that they can accurately repeat the measurement time after time – reliability.

- Test the criteria in 'real' circumstances (as a pilot test); adapt and improve the measures.

- Develop a systematic way of 'trapping' the information required. Qualitative methods work well, such as diaries, video records, audio records, observation reports.

- Allow the criteria and the 'trapping' instrument to develop over time. However, ensure this development is explicitly recorded in a reflective account.

Points to consider

The methods used to 'trap' the information must be appropriate to the group using the method. If you are trying to 'trap' information on young children, highly literary techniques would be inappropriate – you would perhaps use observation. If you were 'trapping' information from a more elderly group, you might avoid highly technical methods like video diaries.

Whatever method is chosen, you will need to provide clear and detailed guidance about how to use them. If participants all do slightly different things, it will be difficult to compare outcomes at a later stage.

Examples of soft outcome indicators

- Personal outcomes – confidence, self-esteem, empathy and behaviour.

- Distanced travelled – involves an initial assessment of where people are to act as a baseline. Then the journey is documented before a final assessment of what has been achieved. This indicator is a longitudinal assessment of progress and achievement.

- Technical outcomes – the ability to manipulate systems and equipment, such as the skills of the filmmaker.

- Key skills – understanding, appreciation, organisation, working well with others and IT skills.

Figure 11.5.1 The Audit Commission's Guide to Evaluating Projects

Appendix – Guide to evaluating projects

1. The difference between outcomes and outputs

Projects need to measure both outputs and outcomes as part of an evaluation. Outputs are collected as part of the regular monitoring data used by the project to keep a check on progress. They focus on quantifying what the project has done, and the throughput of the project.

Examples of outputs are:
- number of referrals;
- number of attendees;
- number of sessions delivered; and
- cost of each session.

Outputs give an *indication* of whether the project is on track to be able to deliver its outcomes.

Outcomes show the difference the project has made to its local community, or the changes that happen as a result of young people attending the project. These are the impacts the project had.

Examples of outcomes are:
- residents are less worried about anti-social behaviour;
- young people re-engage with mainstream education; and
- young people gain qualifications in football coaching.

It is important to monitor whether there are any differences in the type of outcomes achieved for different groups of attendees. For example, do boys do better than girls, or do younger age groups achieve more than older age groups? Collecting monitoring data about the profile of attendees ensures that you are able to see whether any such differences exist, and then take action to improve things.

2. Intermediate and long-term outcomes

Some outcomes, for example stopping entrenched patterns of offending or years of educational under-achievement, happen over the medium to long term (three to five years). Projects can still measure progress in the shorter term by focusing on intermediate outcomes. These are the milestones on the way to achieving the long-term outcomes (Table 1). Intermediate outcomes give you an indication of whether the longer-term outcomes are likely to be achieved.

Figure 11.5.2 The Audit Commission's Guide to Evaluating Projects

Table 1 – Long-term and intermediate outcomes

Long-term aim	Intermediate outcome measures	Long-term outcome
To reduce levels of anti-social behaviour by young people in the area	• Number of young people involved in positive activities. • Number of successful interventions in response to ASB hotspots. • Project workers report young people behaving more pro-socially.	• Reductions in level of anti-social behaviour by young people • Reduced proportion of residents who feel anti-social behaviour is a problem in their area • Increased participation by young people in other community activities.
To increase the proportion of school leavers entering education, employment or training	• Proportion of young people accessing careers advice • Self-assessed change in young peoples aspirations for the future.	• Reduced number of NEETs

3. Using hard and soft outcomes

Outcomes can be quantitative (hard outcomes), or qualitative (soft outcomes). Using both types of outcomes will give you a better overview of whether the project is working. Qualitative data can help you to understand the reasons a project is working, so you can build on good practice. It can also help you to improve by pointing to weaknesses.

Examples of quantitative (hard outcomes) include:
- complaints to the police about anti-social behaviour;
- truancy rates; and
- educational attainment levels.

Qualitative (soft outcomes) include:
- user feedback;
- self-assessed changes in confidence levels; and
- feedback from schools about changes in behaviour.

4. Examples of outcomes and how to measure them

As well as measuring quantitative and qualitative outcomes, you may also want to include outcomes that measure different aspects of progress (Table 2). This will give a more reliable assessment of the project than relying on just one source of data. For example, levels of anti-social behaviour may not be reducing, but measuring other outcomes reveals that young people identify that they find some of the sessions at the project boring and attendance is sporadic.

Figure 11.5.3 The Audit Commission's Guide to Evaluating Projects

Table 2 – Examples of outcome measures and ways of measuring them

Type of outcome	Example	Ways of measuring
Attitudes	• Attitudes towards offending • Attitudes towards drinking or taking drugs	• Self-assessed by young people • Assessed by staff • Quizzes or questionnaires
Self-confidence	• Level of self-esteem and self-confidence • Taking part in new opportunities • Meeting new people	• Self-report by young people • Assessed by staff or other partners
Behaviour	• Engagement in anti-social behaviour • Engagement in positive activities • Volunteering • School attendance levels	• Police data • Survey of residents' perceptions • Self-report by young people • Project records • Records from other partners
Skills/ability	• Gaining football coaching qualification • Producing a music CD	• Self-report by young people • Assessed by project staff • Project records
Knowledge	• Increased awareness of the effects of alcohol on the body	• Self-assessed by young people • Assessed by staff • Quizzes or questionnaires
Costs	• Cost of the project • Cost benefit ratio for the project	• Project records • Comparison with other data
Change in social circumstances	• Entering training or employment • Re-entering mainstream education • Levels of educational attainment	• Projects records • Self-report by young people • Records from other partners
Feedback from users	• User views on the project, self-reported changes	• Interviews, focus groups, questionnaires
Feedback from staff	• Staff views on changes in young people • Staff views on the effectiveness of the project	• Interviews, focus groups, questionnaires • Project records
Feedback from other stakeholders	• Changes in young people from parents/carers, schools, other partners • Changes in local area from residents, local businesses, other partners	• Interviews, focus groups, questionnaires • Records from other partners

11.7 HOW DO I EVALUATE MY OWN WRITING?

This section is effectively a long checklist of questions that you should ask about your own writing. It equally applies to assignments, examinations and workplace writing. Your tutors will assess your work in a similar manner.

1 Does your writing answer the question completely and fully? Have you covered all the parts that were required? Have you gone off-track a bit and forgotten some parts or spent too much time on other parts?

2 Does your writing have a clear introduction that briefly sets out the argument for each part of the question set? Does it also have a clear and logically derived conclusion that returns to the argument and assesses how well you have answered the question set?

3 Does your writing contain all the elements specified in the assessment criteria in the appropriate proportions?

4 Is your writing structured in the same way as the assignment or examination question? Beyond this, does it follow the normal convention of introduction, main argument, conclusion? Does the structure allow your argument to 'flow'?

5 Does your writing make sense? Give it to someone else to read and ask him or her to tell you what it is about. If they cannot answer this, you will need to revise your writing until it does make sense.

6 Is the sequence of your writing the most effective it can be? If you followed the ideas and approaches in Chapter 7, you will have planned the sequence of paragraphs, but it is still worth reviewing if this can be improved.

7 Is your writing balanced? Does it balance both sides of an argument? Strong and effective writing displays reflection and acknowledges counterargument.

8 Is your argument supported by evidence? Academic writing needs extensive supporting evidence.

9 Are your ideas and sources correctly referenced? There should be a bibliography of sources at the end of the work.

10 Does your writing display critical evaluation of the sources you use?

11 Is the writing correctly formatted?

LOUISE AND SIMON

BECOMING REFLECTIVE PERFORMERS

Louise: 'How's that assignment going? Only a week left.'

Simon: 'Yes, loads of time, I have a plan of what I am going to write and loads of stuff to put in it.'

L: 'Yes, I forget you like to leave it late'

S: 'What do you mean late? I still have a week; that's tons of time.'

[Reluctantly, knowing it might cause a row]

L: 'I have told you before, top grades come from work that is reviewed and refined, not some stuff you threw together the night before submission.'

S: 'It's the way I like to do it.'

L: 'Yes, forget it; you'll never learn.'

S: 'No, no, little miss smarty pants, tell me what you do then.'

L: 'I started that assignment by planning it six weeks ago, then did the research, and wrote it two weeks ago, now I will just review it and I'll get my normal 70+. Remind me, what was the grade for that last piece of yours, 48% was it?'

S: 'No you little stinker, it was a 58%, so there.'

L: '58%! Wow, big grade.' [sarcastically]

S: 'You are so, so annoying.'

L: 'Ha ha!'

S: 'Anyway, you are missing a trick by not getting someone else to review it. You could bring it to the study group, then six of us could review it and sort out the techo gibberish you write.'

L: 'Yes, I am going to let B graders review my good stuff. C graders where you are concerned.'

S: 'Looking at your stuff will help us all to improve. You like to help and it is not a "zero sum game".'

L: 'Well, you're right there. I could let you all "paw" over it.'

A day or so later and with some apprehension, Louise lets the study group look at her latest piece of work. After about 90 minutes the five people, including Simon, give her a single sheet of paper with their analysis written on it. She wasn't expecting very much, after all she was helping them.

This is what she got:

- 12 simple spelling errors
- seven comments about not being evaluative enough
- 15 small grammatical errors
- five suggestions where she could link and signpost better
- three areas where it seemed difficult to understand what she was saying
- eight paragraphs where there seemed to be errors in how the paragraph flowed
- six paragraphs where people thought the evidence was insufficient to support the statement made
- three suggestions where the flow of the argument could be improved
- two wrong references, and three missing from the bibliography
- one small section of evaluation that she had missed entirely
- a note about the total amount of evaluation not matching the assessment criteria, it was supposed to be 25% and the reader thought it was probably less than 10%
- 16 highlighted sentences that seemed to add nothing, or very little to the argument, and suggestions that they are removed
- one person pointed out that the work was 230 words over the word count [by removing the above section she was 23 words under the word count]

In discussion after the session every member of the group thought that they had learned something that would help them improve their grade.

Result: Louise was awarded the highest grade in the class – 87%.

ANALYSIS AND EVALUATION OF STUDENT WRITING

The following is an excerpt from a student assignment. Using whatever approach you have developed for reading, critiquing, analysing and evaluating writing, read and assess this submitted work. There are some suggested areas to investigate at the end of the excerpt.

This case study is developmental and designed to last for about two hours. It is designed to be a detailed analysis and evaluation. When you have completed analysing the case study, you may wish to make reflective notes in your learning diary related to the activity.

This case study is also ideal for group analysis in a seminar group or study group after the initial reading and analysis phase.

Career Models and Theories that Support Career in Today's Labour Market

As aforementioned it could be deemed that 'traditional career' could be dead due to 'widespread internal changes in organisations which wreck havoc on traditional career' (Kenneth et al 1996), thus Driver's (1982) model of career paths supports this argument highlighting the change of linear careers to transitory careers as below:

Linear careers are based on traditional career with careers being based on steady paths and according to Kenneth et al (1996) 'under traditional career you could reasonably expect to join a company, work your way up the ladder and hit top management but not anymore' as careers are moving to a more transitory state, which Driver (1982) identifies due to the result of 'downsizing and restructuring of companies in the 1980s and 1990s' (Kenneth et al 1996). In today's labour market jobs are not deemed for life and 'very few can be totally

confident that their job is safe' and Driver's (1982) career path model under transitory state links to the concept that traditional career is dead as transitory spiral career paths are based on continuous change and multiple jobs/careers.

However Driver's model was developed in the 1980s when organisations began to delayer and remove job security, but do organisations today need to retain staff and attract talent therefore maybe organisations need to offer a more linear career path to retain staff? According to Kenneth et al (1996) 'organisations now need to offer some degree of commitment and stability.' Driver's (1982) model is also not very descriptive in terms of the shift from linear to transitory and is this model based on a specific industry where managerial careers were based on linear structures 'some 20 or 30 years ago, embarking on a managerial career was a safe and secure option' (Kenneth et al 1996) therefore is Driver's (1982) model based on one specific career path that being management?

Another model that supports career in today's labour market is Super's (1957, 1980) career stage model. The model shows an individual's progress over their working life and links to the concept that traditional career is dead as Stage 2 and 3 would require an individual to take on new roles and learn new skills to get established.

According to House (2002) 'Super's career stage model defined career development as dynamic, longitudinal and the career development process essentially evolves overtime with the implementation of the self concept' which is required for career today. Super's model links to the notion that continuous change is required to make an individual more employable and

Figure 3.1 Driver's (1982) Career Path Model

LINEAR Steady State ⟶ TRANSITORY Spiral

Figure 3.2 Super's (1957, 1980) – Career Stage Model

Stages	Use of Age	Category of Stage
1	0–14	Childhood Growth
2	0–25	Search and Inquiry
3	25–45	Establishment
4	45–56	Continuity or Maintenance
5	56+	Decline or Disengagement

according to House (2002) 'Super theorized that a person journeys through developing interests, skills and values, developing greater commitment to choice and adapting to changes in the world of work' which is required in today's labour market where organisational change is common. Career stage models are essential in today's labour market where job security cannot be guaranteed and Wrobel (2003) states 'career stages used to be linear and stable but Super has updated the concept of career stage to encompass modern, varied patterns of career development.' Super's model is based on career change however it was noted that this model could be limited as 'for the most part the stage theory has been applied to men' (Wrobel 2003).

It is more acceptable for an individual to change career and Super's model could be useful for the individual such as helping one identify where they are at and that they will move through different career stages. However it is not a useful tool as 'it does not guide the organisation in terms of what is needed to develop and establish individuals within the organisation' (House 2002). Also people are working longer according to CIPD (2007) 'retirement age can go beyond 65' therefore does this model need to be developed to take this into account as a 65-year-old may require a different career and skills to be employable at this age. The model does highlight that careers go through different stages and less of linear traditional career structure which links to how careers have changed.

Two theories that also support career in today's labour market are Schein's (1971) theory of 'Organisational Career' and Hall's (1996) 'Protean Career'. These theories are based on how individuals move through an organisation and 'Organisational Career' denotes a decision-making process based on variables of when to move, how and at what speed and does not rely on length of service or commitment to the organisation. Wrobel (2003) states that 'Schein's career anchors provide an understanding of individual career within the current reality of impermanent organisational ties' which highlights that security from organisations is no longer guaranteed.

Hall's theory also moves away from linear career as 'Protean Career' is 'the transition of the classic linear model of career stage to a modern view of careers as a series of interrelated experiences' (Hall 1996). Hall states that the individual is the main driver of career and not the organisation however this concept 'highlights increased frequency of change and less organisational commitment' (Wrobel 2003). These theories highlight lack of commitment to the organisation which does not help an organisation retain and build talent and could also hinder an individual's career as some degree of commitment might be required from a potential employer and length of service could actually help an individual's career instead of continuous change. Woodall and Winstanley's (2001) changing psychological contract model of career management also links to today's labour market as organisations can no longer offer security as 'organisations today are making changes to cope with a highly turbulent external environment' (Kenneth

Figure 3.3 Changing Psychological Contract – Woodall and Winstanley 2001

Category	Old Contract	New Contract
Change Environment	Stable, short-term focus	Continuous change
Culture	Time served exchange for security and commitment	Those who perform get rewarded and have contract developed
Rewards	Paid on level, position and status	Paid on contribution
Mobility Expectations	Infrequent and on employees terms	Horizontal and frequent
Redundancy Tenure Guarantee	Job for life	Job for now
Personal Development	Organisation's responsibility	Individual's responsibility
Motivational Currency	Promotion	Job enrichment, competency development
Promotional Basis	Expected, time served, technical competence	Less opportunity, new criteria for those who deserve it
Responsibility	Instrumental employees, exchange promotion for more responsibility	To be encouraged, balanced more accountability
Status	Very important	To be earned by competence and credibility
Trust	High trust possible	Desirable but expect employees to be more committed to project or profession

et al 2006).The changing psychological contract as referenced below shows the shift from the old contract expectations such as job for life and security to the new contract. This links to the notion that traditional career has phased out based on the new contract. The 'old' psychological contract of career management highlights 'the mutual understanding under the psychological contract is that employees work hard and confirm to their manager they will be rewarded in return from the organisation with good pay, advanced opportunities and a guaranteed lifetime employment' (De Meuse et al 2001) but guaranteed lifetime employment can no longer be offered in today's labour market.

Woodall and Winstanley (2001) base career today on the 'new' psychological contract with a more flexible approach that careers will go through continuous change and jobs are for now and not for life and it is more the individual's responsibility for career development than the organisation. This model is not specific in terms of what industry the model is based on as some industries might be able to offer job security based on the old psychological contract and some careers might also consist of both the old and new categories. The model is useful in highlighting the changes in career in today's labour market.

To think about...

1 Separate out the claims in this writing.

2 How well are the claims supported by evidence?

3 Does this work display knowledge? What sort of knowledge?

4 Does this writer display understanding and application?

5 Highlight the areas of the work that you think display analysis.

6 Highlight the areas of the work that display evaluation.

7 What overall mark would you award this work (remember it is just an excerpt)?

SUMMARY

This chapter has looked at techniques and approaches to develop the higher-level skills of: analysis, synthesis and evaluation. These skills are the key to very high grades in university work.

- Bloom's taxonomy presents the intellectual skills of university and work as:
  - knowledge
  - understanding
  - application
  - analysis
  - synthesis
  - evaluation.

- Analysis tends to focus on:
  - the study of the constituent parts and the interrelationship of the parts
  - the breaking down and separation of the whole into constituent parts
  - simplifying the whole into parts to display the logical structure
  - an explanation of a process and the parts of that process.

- Analyse arguments against the standard template of:
  - the claim
  - the premises that hold up the claim
  - the evidence that supports the premise
  - the warrant about how the evidence relates to the premise
  - the qualification of the warrant
  - the conclusion.

- Data analysis involves breaking down the data into the constituent parts and simplifying the whole to understand the parts better.

- Evaluating theory criteria:
  - scope
  - operationality
  - structure
  - empirical evidence
  - curiosity
  - balance and precision
  - simplicity
  - usability.

- Work projects are assessed and evaluated by:
  - hard outcomes, such as financial aspects and time
  - soft outcomes, such as improvement in feelings.

- Evaluate your own writing by ensuring it has:
  - sections that answer the question fully and completely
  - an introduction that sets out the argument
  - proportions of skills the same as the assessment criteria
  - a structure that mirrors the assessment brief
  - a clear and logical sequence
  - a balanced argument
  - evidence to support all premises
  - correct referencing
  - the appropriate formatting.

EXPLORE FURTHER

FURTHER READING

Kotter, J. (1996) *Leading Change*. Boston, MA: Harvard Business School Press.

Mahaney, R.C. and Lederer, A.L. (2006) The effect of intrinsic and extrinsic rewards for developers in information systems project success. *Project Management Journal*. Vol 37, No 4. p42.

Sansone, C. and Harackiewicz, J.M. (2000) *Intrinsic and Extrinsic Motivation: The search for optimal motivation and performance*. London: Academic Press.

Steers, R M. and Rhodes, S.R. (1978) Major influences on employee attendance: a process model. *Journal of Applied Psychology*. Vol 63, No 4. pp391–407.

WEB LINKS

Article on the Institute of Employment Studies concerning assessing soft outcomes:
http://www.employment-studies.co.uk/summary/summary.php?id=rr219

CHAPTER 12

Examinations and Assignments

What skills will I develop in this chapter?

- how to approach understanding the question
- how to avoid making mistakes when interpreting the question
- understand what type of assignments you will be set
- examples of different types of assignment
- the value of learning logs or diaries
- the characteristics of reflective learning
- how to deconstruct the question
- how to prepare for examinations
- how to lower examination stress
- how to find the personal motivation to complete assignments

12.1 INTRODUCTION

In this chapter I am going to consider examination questions and assignment questions to be very similar. I am mostly going to consider them together. You might at first think that this is peculiar and 'not right'. I would argue two points. First, the skills you are trying to display in both assessments are exactly the same. Second, most students achieve considerably lower grades for examinations than for assignments. If some of the actions and behaviours that are used for assignments are also used for examinations, you are likely to be able to increase your examination grades. There will be a section related to examination preparation and stress towards the end of the chapter. Many of the skills that are needed for completing examinations and assignments are covered elsewhere in this book. Notably:

- Chapter 1 – Organising Life and Work
- Chapter 4 – What are the Key Skills of University Life and the Workplace?
- Chapter 6 – Effective Reading Skills
- Chapter 7 – Developing Good Writing Skills

- Chapter 8 – Presentation Communication
- Chapter 10 – Critical Reading and Writing Skills
- Chapter 11 – Analysis and Evaluation Skills
- Chapter 13 – Thinking and Memory Skills

Understanding the question is a key element in successfully completing examinations and coursework. This chapter sets out some of the areas you will need to investigate if you are going to fully understand the question your tutors have set. Understanding the question may seem a rather long and involved process, but an early mistake related to misunderstanding the question will ruin the grade your work is awarded. The activities explained here are connected with understanding the question and are probably described better as early development activities related to your examination or coursework. Some will be directly related to understanding the question; others will be developing your understanding of the subject area within which the question is set. Finally, it will be necessary to understand your tutor and yourself.

I would advise you to read this chapter after you have received you first assignment brief, but also to return to it when you begin each new piece of coursework or in preparation for examinations. At the first reading, try to work systematically through the chapter and carry out all the exercises. I have used the term assessment to mean either an assignment or an examination. If I am referring to a specific element, I will refer to it as an assignment or an examination.

12.2 OVERVIEW OF A POSSIBLE APPROACH TO UNDERSTANDING THE QUESTION

As you complete university assignments and examinations you will develop an approach that suits your particular skills and preferred way of learning. However, when you first encounter university assessments you may not have developed an approach, and this section sets out a possible way of carrying out the necessary tasks to understand the question. You may have developed an approach to tackling assignments and examinations but feel you are not achieving the grades you could. This section may help in realigning your approach so that it is more successful.

A GENERAL APPROACH TO UNDERSTANDING THE QUESTION AND CARRYING OUT PRELIMINARY WORK:

- Attend the teaching session where the assignment is issued, and attend all teaching sessions for a period of three weeks after the assignment is issued.
- Attend the examination preparation lecture and seminars.
- Carry out all the assigned readings related to the assignment task or to the likely examination questions.

- Deconstruct the assignment question into the component tasks or use past examination questions to practise understanding the question.
- Carefully consider the language used in the question.
- Understand the learning experience that is being encouraged.
- Focus on 'my' purpose in completing this assignment or examination.
- Discuss the assignment or the upcoming examination with a study group, the tutor, and the year group above you.
- Spend time considering the academic background and the teaching approach used by the tutor.
- Identify what types of question have been set, or set in the past, and know the preferred form to answer it.
- Carefully check the assignment and examination criteria sheet, or discuss with the tutor the performance expectations if none are issued.
- Research the general subject area before investigating the specific question.
- Uncover the general debates around the question subject area from academic and professional associations.
- Look at completed assignments in the same subject area; other students or the tutor may help here. Look at the general examination feedback from previous examinations if any is available.
- Use your creative skills to brainstorm and mind-map the subject area.
- Build a research base of textbooks, journal articles and websites; keep detailed and accurate notes of these resources.
- Form an opinion on the topic, and then develop the outline of an argument.
- Use the university librarians as a source of help.
- Create a WBS chart (see Chapter 1) to ensure you complete the assignment on time or carry out all the revision you need before the examination.
- Create a time plan to control the tasks that must be completed.
- Check the technical aspects of the assignment, such as word count, writing form, bibliographic form.
- Check the technical aspects of the examination.

You may now be thinking this is an extraordinary amount of work to carry out before answering the question. All successful tasks require a large amount of groundwork; if the foundations of the answer are weak, your work will be weak.

12.3 TYPES OF QUESTION

Throughout your time at university you are likely to carry out a wide range of different types of assessment and examination. Each assessment will require different skills, attributes and outputs. The following sections discuss some of the main types of question. However, your tutors will be constantly looking for new and innovative ways to assess your performance, so in practice you will come across some not listed here.

ESSAYS

The essay is a very common form of university question. Essays normally take the form of a presentation of your argument and opinions in response to a question or proposition. Essays are a formal writing form that requires you to use sentences and paragraphs to build your response to the question in a logical, reasoned and evidenced manner. Essays must be planned carefully to ensure there is a natural flow to the argument you present. The essay you submit will be partially judged on the strength, coherence, logic and flow of your argument.

EXAMPLE: AN ESSAY-STYLE ASSIGNMENT QUESTION

Level 2 – Business Economics

With the aid of appropriate diagrams, explain how a firm would achieve profit maximisation. (50% weighting)

Discuss and evaluate other objectives that firms might pursue, supporting your answer with relevant theories and diagrams. (50% weighting)

Your answer should be presented in the form of an essay of approximately 2,500 words. Credit will be given for:

- excellent review of relevant models and theories
- a high level of critical analysis of theories and models
- use of appropriate diagrams
- excellent range and variety of sources of information
- the coherence, logic and flow of your argument.

SHORT-ANSWER QUESTIONS

Short-answer questions present a number of short, succinct questions requiring factual and analytic answers. The emphasis is less on a reasoned logical argument and more on knowing things and calculating answers. The challenge with short-answer questions often lies in the number that must be completed in the specified time.

MULTIPLE-CHOICE QUESTIONS

Multiple-choice questions consist of a question and a range of four or five answers. When you have decided which is correct, you indicate the correct answer on a grid. If no marks are taken off for wrong answers, then you should answer every question, guessing at the ones you do not know. If marks are removed for wrong answers, then do not guess answers that you do not know. These types of question are mostly only used at undergraduate level 1.

REPORTS

Reports ask you to prepare a response to a specific problem, process or task; they often require you to come up with reasoned conclusions and recommendations. Reports have a particular structure containing numbered headings and subheadings. They will often contain detailed factual information and diagrammatic representations of data. The writing style should be precise, concise and direct.

PRESENTATIONS

In business the skill of presenting is a vital communication medium. Your tutors will often set an assignment task that contains an element of presentation (Chapter 8). The task then becomes a two-stage process of researching and answering the question and then preparing the presentation.

EXAMPLE: PRESENTATION QUESTION

Level 2 – Public Relations

Assignment 2

Title:	Public relations
Type:	Group activity
Weighting:	30%

Introduction

In groups of no more than four you are required to make a formal presentation to your lecturer/s and peers. You may present with or without PowerPoint/overheads (if used, hand them in at the beginning of the presentation). You are permitted prompt notes but no other back-up. Everyone on the team must take an equal role. Marks will be awarded to the group, unless there is a dispute over team participation that is brought the lecturer's attention prior to the presentation.

The presentation

For a technology company of your choice, examine its public relations output and the range of techniques it employs. Explain Grunig and Hunt's four models of public relations and decide which model/s your company is using.

Content

This should include:

- an introduction to the team

- a summary of the company of your choice

- the messages it conveys

- the public relations techniques it uses
- a profile of the 'publics'
- a thorough exploration of each of the Grunig and Hunt models
- an explanation of your choice of relevant model/s and the effect you think this has on the company
- a closing summary.

Planning

You should keep a summary of time spent by each person and a planning document to ensure you are ready to present on the due date.

Timing

The presentation should last between 15 and 20 minutes.

GROUP ASSIGNMENTS

Working in groups and teams is another essential skill of business. Your tutors will set some of your assignments as group or team activities. This presents an added dimension to the task by requiring you to contribute, help manage, and ensure the success of the whole team. In team assignments, just as in real life, the grade awarded will be for all members of the team. This can be both frustrating and stimulating, and, as in the work environment, you will have to deal with these and other emotions. Sometimes group difficulties arise; tutors are aware of this and sometimes require a group self-assessment summary to be completed and handed in with the assignment work.

EXAMPLE: GROUP ASSESSMENT DIARY

Self-assessment diary

You may use as many sheets as necessary and each sheet must be signed by **all** members of your group. Hand them in attached to the back of your work. This diary can be handwritten or typed.

Name: ....

Subject: Level 2 – Public Relations and Sponsorship

Assessment: PR presentation

Date	Time	Student no.	Activity

Signed:

....

....

....

....

STUDENT COMMENT

When I first encountered group assessments I hated them. My groups were so not groups; they just argued, were lazy and were rubbish. The grades were always rubbish; we even failed one assignment. That was my first and hopefully last fail grade. Then I took some time to understand how groups should work.

Since then I have taken control and organised things; I've been really bossy. One useful spin-off is that lots of people want me to be in their groups. I have 'sort of' found my role – bossy organiser. The grades have really gone through the roof; it is always 'A' grades for the group assignments now!

ANALYSIS OF CASE STUDIES

Assignments that are based on case studies are another common form of assessment in business. The case study typically provides the context for a report-based assignment.

EXAMPLE: E-COMMERCE ASSIGNMENT BRIEF

Module Title: E-business

Assignment Title: Review of Blackwell's Nursery Case Study

Assignment No.: Coursework 1

Assignment: Blackwell's Nurseries Case Study

E-commerce is a fundamental part of e-business. This assignment gives you the opportunity to review the benefits to a small business of e-commerce, which forms part of e-business. In reviewing this case study, you should demonstrate your understanding of the impact e-commerce has on a business. This should prepare you for making your own recommendations for the adoption of e-business in Coursework Assignment 2.

Assignment

Read the Blackwell's Nurseries (BN) Case Study carefully, then answer the following questions. Present your answers in the form of a report.

1 In your introduction, evaluate the key elements of the BN business model. (25 marks)

2 Explain what you consider to be the *three* most important factors contributing to the success of e-commerce at BN. (60 marks – 20 marks for each)

3 As a conclusion, identify the opportunities for e-business at BN and explain which of these you consider should be BN's first priority. (15 marks)

CARRYING OUT BUSINESS TASKS

Business is essentially practical – carrying out tasks that can get something done. Assignments are often set around the practical tasks of business. This requires you to understand the task and its associated skills and be able to effectively carry out the task. There are so many of these tasks that your tutors will never run out of new ideas for your assessments. Tasks that you may be asked to complete include:

- prepare a budget
- solve an HR problem
- carry out business analysis, maybe STEP analysis
- create an advertising campaign
- plan a project
- create a marketing strategy

- design some aspect of an organisation
- create a business process, maybe a production process
- create an advertising story board for a TV commercial
- create a Dragon's Den pitch
- carry out some market research.

EXAMPLE: PROJECT MANAGEMENT ASSIGNMENT BRIEF

Module Title: Business Problem-solving

Assignment Title: Project Management Application

Assignment:

1. Describe a suitable business project that has a number of interdependent activities. Explain why the activities do depend on each other and how difficulties might arise in the management of this particular project. [20 marks]

2. Specify a list of activities and prerequisite activities with activity times. (You may well need to make up the numbers here.) Enter the data into Microsoft Project and produce a summary of suitable outputs, including network diagram, activity schedule, Gantt chart, critical path and so on. Explain what each output (apart from the Gantt chart, which is in the next question) tells you and what it is used for. [60 marks]

3. In particular, explain how you would use the Gantt chart to reschedule activities in the light of any project difficulties experienced. [20 marks]

EXAMPLE: MARKETING COMMUNICATIONS ASSIGNMENT BRIEF

This assignment requires you to work in groups of THREE. You are to produce a 30-second radio advertisement and written justification for one of the following four scenarios.

Häagen-Dazs new apple and blackberry flavoured ice cream
HD requires a radio campaign in conjunction with a print and TV campaign to launch their new apple and blackberry flavoured ice cream. The launch date is 7 July 2010. The launch is to coincide with the summer holiday season when people are more likely to try new flavours of ice cream. (You may make whatever assumptions you need to about the print/TV campaigns.)

Gerry Martins of Chephampstead
This high-quality local butcher is determined to run a locally based radio campaign to try to solve its annual dip in sales during the summer months. July and August are characterised by lower sales as customers go on holiday and eat salads.

Gillette 'The Best a Man Can Get'
Gillette requires a radio ad to boost sales over the summer months of their Fusion Hydragel Shaving product. They have relied on 'tie-ins' with football during the rest of the year but over the summer the absence of football has created a dip in sales.

National Deaf Children's Society Awareness Week

This London-based charity is running an awareness week during the third week of July. In awareness measurement studies they continually fall behind other children's charities, such as NSPCC and Children in Need. They cannot afford TV advertising and believe that radio may well be the most effective form of media for their campaign.

Deliverables:

30-second radio advertisement

You should submit one 30-second ad (timed exactly) on tape or digital media. The advertisement should be preceded by a tune of your choice. (Do not worry if the sound-recording quality is not as good as you would like but do ensure that the script can be heard clearly.)

Report

You should also submit a written justification for your ad in no more than 2,500 words. The report should make reference to the following:

- an explanation of the communications model
- clearly stated communication objectives
- target audience
- chosen media in terms of selected radio stations
- an academic argument regarding the creative aspect of your advertisement; this should revolve around the following theories:
  - strong and weak
  - four frameworks
- a timetabled plan and costs (for example burst campaign, number of times per day, number of weeks, cost of 30-second slot on that radio station)
- appendices:
  - secondary data explaining target audience, for example numbers, demographics, values, hobbies, and so on
  - advertising rates from chosen radio stations.

PORTFOLIOS OF EVIDENCE

Some assignments will ask you to produce a portfolio of evidence as part of the assessment regime for a module. Portfolio assessments originated in the arts and the performing arts, where it was common to 'build a portfolio' of evidence relating to your development as an artist or performer. In business, portfolios are most commonly used to present a body of evidence related to reflective learning. Whereas most assignments are focused on one point in time at the submission of the assignment, portfolios have a longitudinal element and require evidence to be gathered over a period of time, maybe the whole of a university year. In this respect they require a very different approach to more conventional assignments, the emphasis being placed on good organisation to trap and collate the evidence and on sound reflective practice to consider the learning that has taken place.

Portfolio assignments will become more common as they develop an important set of skills related to workplace professional development and lifelong learning. If you are asked to complete this type of assessment, you may feel it requires a huge amount of work. However, the time you spend developing business-related skills and reflective learning will serve you well in the workplace. This development will also be reflected in the skills you are able to bring to other assignments. Try not to resent the amount of work they require and focus instead on the important developmental aspects of your skills for university and the workplace.

EXAMPLE: PORTFOLIO ASSESSMENT

During level 2 of your course you will be expected to maintain a portfolio of evidence relating to your learning and skills development.

What is a personal development portfolio?

Your personal development portfolio (PDP) is a collection of information related to your own personal development planning that represents and serves as a record of your development and achievement. You may want to refer to it when you are preparing to move to the next level of study or when applying for a job. It will provide evidence of your experience or ability to a prospective employer or to someone who may offer you funding or a place on a course.

Why develop a personal development portfolio?

Your PDP helps you keep track and establish one central place in which to keep all relevant information relating to your personal, academic and career-related information. By progressively compiling a portfolio you will find it easier to review and reflect on your learning and development.

Portfolio building process

During level 1 personal development you started to compile your portfolio by collecting evidence of your skills and development. You also started to develop and use the skill of reflection.

During level 2 personal development you are going to modify and elaborate your portfolio so that you can use it to demonstrate a broad range of skills that will enhance your employability. In addition, you will be updating your online MyPDP.

It is essential that you make your portfolio-building a regular activity. Note that this year your portfolio attracts a **weighting of 50%** for the module. It is important to develop sound PDP practice; this will serve you well once you return to the world of work.

Portfolio content

The most important thing is to record and add evidence of your achievements to your portfolio as soon as you have them. We will not be as prescriptive about the content of your portfolio as we were for level 1. You can be rather more creative about what you choose to include. However, there are minimum requirements, which will be addressed during your personal development classes with both your academic tutor and specialist tutors. Remember, you may add any other evidence you feel appropriate to any of the sections. **Please note: to achieve a good grade for your portfolio you are expected to add a range of appropriate evidence that supports your skills and personal development.**

Contents page

Before you submit your portfolio in week 28, prepare a new contents page, clearly outlining the contents in each section.

Table 12.1 Typical elements that might be included in your PDP

Section	PD class week	Evidence	Evidence included
Front of Portfolio	1 27–28	Add name of Level 2 academic tutor Level 2 Personal Grade Sheet New contents page	
1 General Skills	2–28	Updated skills analysis from MyPDP Analysis of your learning style (VARK is available on MyPDP or questionnaire from Level 1) along with some evidence from your Level 2 studies to support this	
2 Action Plans	1–28	Updated action plans from MyPDP showing at least one entry per month, demonstrating links with your reflections on assignments and progress	
3 Assessment, Feedback and Reflection	3–28	Assessment feedback sheets and reflections on your assessments and your progress Include at least 10 carefully considered reflections demonstrating your progress	
4 Career Planning	8 10 16 17	Updated CV illustrating changes to Level 1 CV Printout from Careermanager Reflection on presentation Reflection on job interview	
5 Communication	4–8 26	Evidence of your ability to undertake Harvard referencing Evidence of your ability to think critically Evidence of your ability to evaluate Evidence of your ability to compile a questionnaire	
6 Information Technology	3–6 25–27	Evidence of personal webpage Analysis of research data	
7 Numeracy	2–28	Evidence from any Level 2 module demonstrating your skills with numbers	
8 Team Role	21–23	Business Game and Belbin team role reflection	

BECOMING REFLECTIVE PERFORMERS

Louise: 'Simon! Have you seen that portfolio assessment for Contemporary Issues in Management?'

Simon: 'Yes, that one that is likely to take about 100 hours and produce 50–60 pages of evidence for 15% of the module grade.'

L: 'Yes, that's the one, but what's with worrying about how big it is in terms of the whole module?'

S: 'You are so naive! Nobody is going to do that assessment! Too much work for too small an amount of marks.'

L: 'How can you be so confident that it is not worth the time to complete it?'

S: 'I have a friend in the year above us and he said that no one bothered to do that assessment. Everyone still got through the module alright.'

L: 'Don't be stupid. Why did they set it if no one is going to do it? Someone must have done it; a whole group of 400 students is not going to just forget an assignment.'

S: 'It was marked by peer assessment; your class group reads the work and gives it a grade. The tutor just checked and then confirmed the grade. Who wants other students marking their work? Madness!'

L: 'What, the students mark each other's work?'

S: 'Yes, you got it, brains!'

L: 'Wow! That is either brilliant or very dumb! I am not sure which.'

S: 'Well, you can see why no one wants to be bothered. Too much work and then the "swots" mark it, I am guessing really hard.'

L: 'There must be something useful in it or why do they set it as a task?'

S: 'No idea – just mad professors, I suppose.'

L: 'I've had a look at the assignment sheet and it explains that the portfolio is about developing good learning practice for your personal development.'

S: 'Great!'

L: 'It also says there is a module next year that has the same arrangement that is worth half the module marks. Also, it says it develops the skills you will need in the dissertation.'

S: 'Great, it's developmental! I may not get to the stage where it is any use. I'll pass and spend more time on the cricket pitch.'

L: 'It also says that it will develop skills that you will need in the workplace. Also that PDP is a normal professional activity in many professions like management, marketing, HR.'

S: 'That is useful to me – how!'

L: 'Didn't you say you want to go into a large organisation in a marketing job? Well, according to this your developmental portfolios will be useful to show employers.'

S: 'That "rings a bell" from an article I read the other week where some graduate in marketing was saying that without a portfolio of work you stood no chance of getting an advertising role. They said it was just like being an artist or a model; if you haven't developed a set of advertising-related outputs you would find it difficult to get a job.'

L: 'I am listening. But, you are the one that needs convincing it is a useful assignment.'

S: 'Yes, I am getting to the point of seeing the purpose of it.'

L: 'Let's get the study group to talk it through.'

S: 'I'll find someone in the year above us who did the assignment to come along and explain it and what they did.'

Result:

Louise's module grade: 74%

Simon's module grade: 82%

A short note about the types of assessment at the different levels of your course and the value of reflective learning logs

Most university degrees use a range of different assessments at the different levels of degree courses. There will be a natural progression from the more developmental assignments, such as portfolios and completing business-related tasks, towards the more analytic and evaluative tasks of essay writing. Your tutors will have planned this assignment progression, and it is important to recognise the learning opportunity of each assignment. Development of the skills required to complete the more challenging assignments at level 3 takes place in the level 1 and level 2 assignments. One way to 'trap' and use the learning experience of each assignment is to keep a reflective learning diary. Reflective learning diaries can be maintained in different ways but yours should aim to 'trap' the following information:

- What activity has been carried out? For example, researching the assignment.
- How did I feel about this activity? For example, 'seemed like I made no progress', 'waste of time'.
- How well or badly did this go? For example, 'poor use of my time'.
- What did I learn? For example, you cannot just randomly search the web for assignment stuff.
- What will I do differently next time? For example, create a more structured way of working.
- How will I do it differently? For example, think about the key words before I start clicking.
- What did I learn about myself? For example, I can be really scatterbrained and unfocused.
- Is there any help I can get? For example, the library runs effective searching courses.
- What skill level do I need to do this task well? For example, a structured mind and a structured process are needed.
- How can I develop this skill so that I am successful at level 3? For example, look back at the PDP notes on reflective learning, read about reflective learning.
- When should I review my performance on this again? For example, two weeks' time.

How you keep this information is very much up to you; a paper file is often used, but an electronic diary in Word makes it easier to manage and learn from the entries. If you read the section on Microsoft OneNote in Chapter 2, then this software would be most suitable.

12.4 DECONSTRUCTING THE QUESTION

In deconstructing the question into component parts you are aiming to understand the various elements more clearly and thereby address all the elements of the question more effectively. When you deconstruct an assignment question you can take your time and treat it as a skills development session. In an examination you must still deconstruct the question, but it must be done under the pressure of time. But before we deconstruct a question, let's look to see if there are any more clues about the assignment and examination questions:

- What textbook does you tutor recommend? Take a look at the chapter related to the question. Form a view about the style of the text: descriptive, analytic, well-argued, well-evidenced?

- What style of teaching does your tutor use? Evidence-based arguing? Description and examples? Analysis and evaluation?

- What types of assignment are usual for this subject area? See the examples above.

- Can you find examples of assignments or examinations that have already been set for this module? Try the e-learning site, or speak to friends in the year above you. Is there a theme to the assignments set over the last few years? Is the same assignment set every year? Do the examination questions follow a pattern?

- How do the assignments and examination questions relate to the readings and course materials?

- What are the learning outcomes ('university speak', but you will find reference to them in documents you have been given) for the module? What learning outcomes are being tested by this assessment?

Deconstructing and analysing the question

(This is based on an assignment, but you will need to carry out a similar set of activities for each exam question.)

One popular way to deconstruct the question is the three-step process:

Step 1 – Clarifying parts you are not sure of

- Check the meaning of any words, terms or phrases you are not sure of. Don't just think, 'I know roughly what that means.' If you are not 100% sure then take some time to check! You should find answers in lecture notes, the course handbook, a textbook or a dictionary.

- Some assignments use direct quotes from published material. 'Google' the exact phrase and you should be offered a number of places where you can obtain the source document. Tutors tend to use newspapers or journals as the source for quotes, so if you log onto Athens you should be able to look at the original source document. This will enable you to look at the context of the statement, and the wider argument that supports the statement. The reference list in a journal article will lead you to other theory and ideas connected to the statement.

Step 2 – Identifying the main parts of the question

In this three-step process there are also three main sections to identifying the main parts of the question.

Instruction – These are instruction or directing words that tell you what to do, such as analyse, compare, discuss, evaluate, critique. If you are not sure what the instruction word means, then look it up in on the web or in a textbook. A vague idea of what the instruction means will not do! You need a clear, precise, thoughtful and reflective understanding of what you are being asked to do. A little work here may save a lot of time and heartache later.

Topic – This is the general area of the assignment. Asking the 'what' question is a good way to understand the topic area. Analyse what? Evaluate what? By carefully thinking about the topic area you will develop a precise understanding of exactly what is being asked in the question.

Focus – This will qualify the topic area to a specific area – for example, the assignment topic may be diversity. The wording of the assignment may then focus on age diversity. Look out for words and phrases that focus the assignment – if you miss these explicit or implicit terms your answer will be too broad and wide-ranging and will lose marks for lack of focus.

Worked example

Question: Analyse the value of work–life balance practices to modern business.

At first glance we may separate the question into the following sections.

Instruction: Analyse

Topic: Work–life balance

Focus: Modern business

The instruction 'analyse' requires you to find a way, maybe theory, to separate the topic 'work–life balance' into its component parts so as to understand it better.

The topic 'work–life balance' is a large range of ideas, practices, policies and procedures designed to create some amount of balance in a person's life between work and home or social life.

The focus on modern business requires that you have an idea about what modern business is, and how it might differ from traditional business.

Step 3 – Internalise and contextualise the question

Internalising and contextualising the question is an important part of fully understanding the question. Internalising is a process that makes it personal to you. Rewriting the question in your own words can do this. Once you have done this, check carefully that you have not changed the meaning or focus of the question. Contextualising places the question into a context that you know. So if the question is concerned with learning you could place it into a context with which you are familiar, such as university. You then explore and think about the question in this context before rethinking it in other contexts that arise from your thoughts. Effectively you are 'testing out' the question idea in different circumstances.

Our three-step process has created more clarity, understanding and focus and should therefore ensure that your writing will have clarity and focus and display understanding.

However, there may be a problem. List the words in the question that we have not used in our analysis so far.

You should have identified that we have not considered:

- value, or the value
- practices
- to
- the
- of.

Value? Now that is an interesting word! What does it mean?

You might be surprised to know that academic conferences are organised around discussions and papers are written about the meaning of 'value' in various contexts. So this word is going to be a bit of a problem in this question. The tutor will have added the word to the question in the full knowledge that it is a poorly defined word and is open to interpretation. So one of your more challenging tasks will be to understand and carry out the instruction precisely.

Notice I am using the word as an **instruction**. It does not look like an instruction word! We already have one – analyse. This is a second instruction word. Failing to spot that would have created a real weakness in your answer. As an instruction, value may mean 'evaluate', express an idea about its 'worth', its 'usefulness', its 'monetary worth', its 'merit'.

Hopefully with this example you will see the usefulness of spending time carefully examining the words used in questions.

'Practices' is a little less troublesome for our analysis; this is another **focus** word meaning the practical ways that the idea of 'work–life balance' is used. This excludes discussion of aspects that are not commonly translated into organisational practices.

The three other words are linking words, 'to', 'the', 'of'. But, be careful, these words can change the meaning and required task in the assignment. Let's just look at the 'to' word. This is used in front of 'modern business'. The phrase is 'to modern business'. This means that your earlier analysis and evaluation (value) of work–life balance practices is to the business, not to the employees. Your answer will need to address the value to the business. It should not use many words discussing the value to the employees of that business.

But, notice there is still a problem, in that value to employees may become value to the organisation. If the work–life balance practices are seen as of value to the employees, new employees may want to join the company, assisting with recruitment.

LEARNING DIARY ENTRY

I am so angry, livid, livid, livid. I have just failed my work–life balance assignment, 25%. Stupid, stupid stupid. I am purple with rage, I could kill! What is worse is that it looks like it was all my fault. I obviously didn't pay enough attention to the assignment instructions and I produced an analysis of how useful if would be for family life and sport and leisure if companies used work–life balance procedures. I thought it was a rather good assignment; I put in loads of work, 40–50 hours. I really enjoyed it and was expecting a 70%+. What a shock, 25%. At first I took it back and said I had been given the wrong assignment – but no, it was mine. 25% – how stupid have I been?

Well it feels better just to let the rage out!

How could I have done this?

How can I avoid it in the future?

I have had a look at the assignment question again and it seems to turn the whole assignment around with just a couple of words. The phrase, 'to modern business' seems to be the bit I missed out on seeing,

reading – because I focused closely on the benefits to the family and employee, and brought in theory related to society and families, so most of what I wrote was wrong.

I guess the way to avoid this is to very closely look at the words in the assignment brief, and deconstruct them all into parts. I'll do this at the start. But, I will also return to the question once I have created my writing plan and check that my writing and the points I want to make will exactly answer the question set.

I might also look at it again when the whole thing is written. This might be overkill but I don't want to do this again. I am so mad!

I think I will in future also send the writing plan to the tutor and see if they will comment on what I am about to write. Some of the other students do this. Some tutors also have drop-in assignment sessions so I am in future going to use all these opportunities not to make the same mistake again.

COMPLEX ASSIGNMENT TASKS

Some assignments and examination questions will be more complex, and this may mean that you have to split the question into sections and then analyse each section. Some assignments at levels 1 and 2 will split the assignment task into parts for you; this is to make it easier to understand. This is helpful, but each part will need to be analysed and interpreted.

REFLECTIVE SUMMARY

- We have seen that even an apparently simple question needs analysis.
- The three main sections of any question are instruction, topic and focus.
- There is often more than one of each of these words in a question.

- Phrases must be analysed as well.
- Linking words can modify the meaning, focus and instruction.
- If any word or phrase is unclear, spend time reflectively thinking about the word or phrase and what it means in the context of the question.
- Carry out some background research on your tutor, course, subject area and any quotes used in the assignment.

INSTRUCTION WORDS

It is vitally important that you have a good working understanding of a range of instruction words. The following table shows a range of instruction words and their meaning.

Table 12.2 Instruction words and their meanings

Analyse	Display the main parts of something by breaking it down into its various parts and closely examining each part. Theory can help to define the parts.
Argue	Present a logical, evidenced case for and against a proposition.
Calculate	Use the standard method to ascertain the exact value.
Compare	Look for and express a range of differences and similarities between ideas, practices, theories or concepts.
Construct	Create or form by combining things.
Contrast	Place two or more things in direct opposition and show the differences between them.
Criticise	Prepare a detailed and evidenced judgement about the merit of a theory or practice, the validity of research or the strength of an argument.
Define	Set out the precise details of a thing or idea, so that its uniqueness is displayed.
Describe	Set out the detailed characteristics of a thing, or the detailed steps of a process.
Differentiate	Show the precise differences between two or more things, ideas or theories so that the distinctness between them is displayed.
Discuss	Debate or argue the merits or attributes of an argument or practice.
Enumerate	Specify a thing or idea in a step-by-step process.
Evaluate	Systematically appraise the worth of something, such as theory, policies or recommendations.
Explain	Present a clear, precise account of the detail of something, and the parts that make up that something.
Explore	Systematically inquire into something by examining and analysing all aspects of it.

Identify	Ascertain the origin, nature, character of something, or the possibilities of doing or achieving something.
Illustrate	Make clear the nature of something by using diagrams, graphs, data or examples.
Interpret	Explore the meaning of something, make clear and explicit, often interpreting data or statistics.
Investigate	Research, survey and explore all aspects of a subject, idea or theory.
Justify	Make evidenced argumentative claims about something.
Outline	Set out the main points or general principles, focusing on the structure and generic details.
Prove	Using evidence, make claims as to the truth or validity of something.
Relate	Display the connections between things and make estimates of the strengths of these connections; in the negative, display how things are not related.
Review	Explore an area or thing and state the important elements; make judgements about how useful these elements will be in particular circumstances.
Specify	Accurately set out the detail of a thing or idea.
State	Set out a position of a thing in exact detail.
Submit	Provide the complete and finished object.
Summarise	Provide a precise statement of the main points, omitting details and examples.
Trace	Accurately set out development of something.
Value	Express the worth of something.

12.5 MY PURPOSE IN COMPLETING THIS ASSIGNMENT OR EXAMINATION

This section is about clarifying your own motivations in completing a particular assignment or examination. Personal motivation is vital in completing successful examinations and assignments. Your motivation will vary based on your like/dislike of a subject area, your previous performance and the stage you are currently studying. In level 1 of a course you can expect early enthusiasm to motivate you. Level 2 is often a weakly motivating year, as the early enthusiasm has passed and the final finishing post is too far away. The following sections will provide some techniques to ensure your motivation remains high.

HISTORY

Every three months or so take some time to reflect on what situations have motivated you recently. Note the subject areas, the people, the tasks and your personal circumstances; from this try to determine the things that successfully motivate you. Then, try to recreate the circumstances and the characteristics of these motivated periods. If you have been keeping a reflective diary it will be easier to identify the detail of your motivation. Equally, reflect on the times when you were demotivated and try to avoid these situations.

> ## ❝❞ STUDENT COMMENT
>
> I found I was very unmotivated in the second year of my course. I could easily have 'dropped out', but I didn't and managed to get a 'first'. I motivated myself by the thought of finishing and getting a good job and by the horror of having to explain my 'dropping out' to my family. The fear of failure can be a big motivation. Practically I organised things like it was a job, every morning 10:30 (that's when I got up) to 1:30 I studied and did assignments, then from 6:30 to 8:30 in the evening I did uni work again. The reward was a trip to the pub or out to eat when I was finished. I kept the same habits in the final year and it worked well for me.

DON'T DEMOTIVATE YOURSELF

It is very easy to have demotivating thoughts. Try to avoid:

- negative people
- time-wasting distractions
- focusing on things you have failed at in the past; focus on the successes
- long, uninterrupted passages of boring, repetitive tasks
- attacking large, unstructured problems or messy problems without breaking them down into smaller, more manageable tasks
- working on a task without a clear goal
- not using SMART objectives
- not keeping calm and unemotional
- chaos and unplanned mess.

DEVELOP AND FOCUS ON CLEAR, ACHIEVABLE GOALS

Having clear goals is motivating. Why do you want a degree? You should have a specific answer to this question. If it is to earn lots of money, then post pictures of the things you will buy around your study area. If it is to help out in the Third World, or to assist in the battle for a sustainable environment, then post pictures of these in your study area. These are your long-term goals. A 'so that' mantra can be really helpful. I want to do really well in this examination 'so that' I get a good degree and can enter the graduate programme of this company. Post a picture of the company headquarters in your study area and post the 'so that' mantra near your computer screen. You can have lots of 'so that' mantras; in general the more you have the more motivated you will be. 'I must do well in this, *so that* I can reward my family's help.' You can take this idea to greater lengths, with computer backgrounds of your goal(s), music and videos of the goals.

You may also need some shorter-term goals. These are things you want to achieve today, this week, this month. The 'so that' mantra works for these as well. 'I want to complete that assignment early, *so that* I can go surfing at the weekend.' Keeping your personal goals visible and in your mind is a great motivator.

PLANNING AND ORGANISING

Large tasks and blank sheets of paper can be very demotivating. Assignments are completed in small steps. Focus on the first small step, maybe doing some background research; when this is complete, focus on the next step. In this way you will only have to do small and easily managed things, but they add up to a lot of work in a short while. Chaos and unplanned mess is very demotivating; try to plan tasks a day, week or month ahead. Use some of the planning ideas from Chapter 1 to help plan and organise assignments.

REWARD YOURSELF

Rewarding yourself encourages the right sort of achievement behaviour. From the ideas above you should always be planning the next steps in learning and assessments, and when you plan each step plan for a reward. Every small step needs a reward: 'When I have finished this bit of research I'll have a coffee and a cookie! When I have finished writing this page I'll take a break!' Rewards are powerful motivators and you should use them all the time to get things done. Have bigger rewards for the completion of large tasks, such as, 'I will have a night out at the cinema with my friends when the assignment is submitted.' What a huge reward you'll arrange for the successful completion of the course!

You can also use performance rewards. Here the reward is graduated against the performance outcome. 'If I get an "A" grade for that assignment I'll buy a new mobile – no "A" grade, no mobile.' If you are in a study group, small group rewards can be used for the top performer. The top grade in the assignment gets a free dinner and drinks from the rest of the group. Sales teams use this gift reward strategy to motivate their staff, and it really works – well, it would when a tropical holiday or a car is the prize. In study groups you can make a big show of delivering the prize to the top performer.

BE POSITIVE AND CONSTRUCTIVE

University life will have its problems and some of your work may be criticised by tutors. It is really important to remain positive when you have had poor results and feedback. Critical feedback is the way to improve what you do and the grades you receive. Your tutors are not being hurtful to you; they are just offering critiques of your work that are intended to help you to improve. Remember, when anonymous marking is used, they won't even know who wrote any assignment. Being able to accept criticism and use it constructively is part of growing up and very much part of the world of work. It is important to learn this early and see criticism of your work as an opportunity for learning.

USING MUSIC AS MOTIVATION

Music can be very motivating. If you normally work in silence, try having 'stirring' and motivating background music while you work.

FINALLY, CREATE A TOLERANCE LIST

We all have things in our lives that have to be tolerated. Things such as an old and difficult-to-use computer, lack of books, noisy neighbours, other students in your group that don't perform. These things drain our energy and demotivate us. Create a 'tolerance list' of all the things that are draining your energy and gradually work through the list solving the problems. If you solve one a day you soon find there is very little that is draining your energy. Any that cannot be solved must remain as a tolerated item.

12.6 EXAMINATIONS

I have argued that most of the actions required to understand and develop an assignment are the same processes and techniques that are required for examinations. This is, I believe, true in most respects, but there are at least three areas that will need special attention as you work towards an examination. First, the preparation for an examination is specific to that form of assessment. Second, you will need to commit some knowledge to memory. Finally, you will have to cope with general stress and time pressure stress. The memory elements required for examinations will be covered in the next chapter.

PREPARING FOR EXAMINATIONS

You will need to investigate the exact type of examination you will be taking. The following are some of the common forms of examination:

Unseen examinations – You do not see the examination paper before you sit the examination and you can take nothing into the examination room but pen and pencil (also a few other bits of stationery). All the knowledge you take in must be in your head. This becomes a test of memory and thinking performance in a time-constrained environment.

Open examinations allow you to see the examination at a designated point before the examination takes place; typically this is one week. This allows you to prepare specifically for the questions set. It removes some of the stress of not knowing if you can answer the questions. It normally allows answers to focus more on critique, analysis, synthesis and evaluation. If you answer open examinations with only knowledge, you will get a very low mark. The answers should contain large amounts of these higher-level skills. Typically, 30% critique,

30% analysis and evaluation. You may think it is a great idea knowing the question before the examination, but you will have to perform to a higher level to achieve a good mark.

Open book examinations allow you to bring a variety of specified sources into the examination. Sometimes this is the course book with your own notes added to the pages – annotated. More commonly you will be allowed to bring in a set number of pages of notes. Two sides of A4 paper is a typical allowance. The emphasis then moves from what you can remember to how well you understand things and can demonstrate the higher-level skills. In this type of examination you are essentially partially completing an assignment. You will know the general subject area but will not know the exact question. These types of examination are becoming much more popular in university assessments because they allow the student to demonstrate critique, analysis, synthesis and evaluation – the higher-level skills.

COPING WITH EXAM STRESS

Make sure you are not overly stressed before the examination period

Feeling stressed on the day before the exam and on the day of the examination is quite normal. A little stress will help you perform well. But, it is important that you are not at your stress limit before the examination period. If you have any of the following more than a week before the examination period, seek help from your doctor:

- onset of headaches
- sleeping badly
- loss of a normally healthy appetite
- being unusually bad-tempered
- feeling tired all the time
- feeling sick for more than a short period.

Planning to reduce stress

Stress can be caused by unknown and low-control environments. Being organised is a good strategy to reduce stress. Make sure you know the details of the examination and how to get there, including day, time, place, what you have to bring, such as ID cards, duration and the type of examination you will be sitting.

Ensure that you study and learn effectively throughout the course and keep accurate and useable notes from lectures and seminars. Effectively, make sure you are an efficient learner from day one. Plan a revision strategy that works for you and the time you have available.

Use past papers to reduce stress by carrying out 'mock' examinations using papers that are similar in subject and length to the actual examination. This will prepare you to operate in limited time situations where you must remember material and think clearly. Carry out any number of mocks until you are familiar with the timings and issues.

Plan your revision schedule so that you do not become overstressed before sitting the examination. Try to maintain a balance to your life in the run-up to the examinations. Don't work flat out on revision at the expense of a social life. However, try to remove unnecessary activities to provide more time for revision and relaxing; de-clutter your life for four weeks before the examination period.

How do I de-stress?

It is worthwhile learning some simple de-stressing techniques for university life, which can be quite stressful. These techniques really pay off when you come to exam time.

Breathing

Slow and controlled breathing will help reduce anxiety and stress. It is best to do this sitting upright but comfortably. Place your hand on your stomach; breathe slowly out and then slowly fill your lungs and gently tighten the stomach to the count of ten; then slowly breathe out to the count of ten. Carry this out about ten times and then sit relaxing for five minutes. As you wait for the examination to start you can carry out this breathing routine.

Relaxation

This is a yoga technique that can be adapted for general use. When done in a yoga class it is called the corpse pose and is done lying on the ground with your head on a pillow so that your spine is level. Lay on your back with your feet about 40–50cm apart and hands by your side about 10cm away from your body. Close your eyes and, moving around your body, tense each muscle group and then relax that group. So you could start by tensing and relaxing your feet and ankles, then calves, and so on, until you tense and relax your neck muscles. Then try to think of your body sinking into the floor. As your body becomes still and unstressed, lie quietly for 15–20 minutes. After this time turn onto your side, take some slightly deeper breaths and then stand up relaxed and de-stressed.

You can adapt this technique for use in the examination hall in the 10–15 minutes that you normally have to wait while the exam preparations are completed. Sitting with your eyes closed, tense and release muscle groups before sitting quietly until it is time to start the examination.

Physical activity

Physical activity is good for you at any time. The current recommendation for adults is to exercise 3–4 times per week for longer than 20 minutes where your heart rate is raised above normal. Physical activity is also a great de-stressor, so try to take a brisk walk for 20–30 minutes three or four times a week at stressful times. Of course you may do much more exercise than this in a normal week, so don't change that routine in the run-up to examinations.

Sleep

Exam time can be a worrying time and this may interfere with your sleep. Try to avoid stimulants in the last two to three hours before you go to bed (tea, coffee, alcohol). It is also important to unwind in the last hour before you go to bed; reading is very good for unwinding and creating that sleepy feeling.

Study groups

Knowing you are not alone in having fears and worries is very supportive. If you are feeling anxious about exams, try to discuss this with your study group or a friend. University skills tutors can also help you put your worries in proportion, so seek out and use whatever stress services are available.

CASE STUDY

STUDY GROUP EFFECTIVENESS

Jesse, Tom, Korolyi, Bubba and Yin have formed a study group. They have found this useful and supportive but they now want to 'move it on a bit' so the group can help with assignments. They all have to complete the following assignment:

Part A – 50 Marks

Select an organisation that is undergoing major strategic change.

Provide a background of contextual knowledge for the organisation you have chosen. Describe the change strategy that the organisation has adopted.

Evaluate the effectiveness of the change strategy in relation to:

- organisational structure
- organisational culture
- organisational politics.

Part B – 50 Marks

Recommend and evaluate an integrated change strategy based on the aspects above. In evaluating the proposed strategy, make sure you fully discuss all attributes of the proposal.

(Word limit 2,500)

Case study tasks

This presents the group with a number of things to consider:

- How do we choose a company undergoing major strategic change?
- Can we all use the same company?
- Is it possible to split up the task so that each of us researches one aspect of the assignment?
- If so, how would we split up the tasks?
- How would we report back on the area we researched?
- Will this be regarded as plagiarism?
- What can we do to help each other once we have all written our assignments?

Reflect on these problems and present a precise paragraph that deals with each of these problems.

SUMMARY

- Create your own personal process for understanding questions. Such as:
  - a careful deconstructing of the questions
  - attending lectures and seminars related to the questions
  - use a study group or tutorial to discuss the questions.

- Understand the differing nature and characteristics of different types of assessment.

- Develop a clear understanding of the role that words take in questions, particularly:
  - instruction words
  - topic words
  - focus words.

- Use learning logs or diaries to reflect on how you developed answers to the questions set.

- Keep a record of the learning and skills development process in a learning log. Reflect and learn from these experiences.

- Ensure your personal motivation is high:
  - Develop clear, achievable goals for all stages of your university study.
  - Create and use a tolerance list.
  - Plan and organise.
  - Don't demotivate yourself.
  - Use rewards.
  - Avoid negative people and situations.

- Develop a strategy for developing and using the materials you are allowed to take into open book examinations.

- Have a clear question-choosing strategy and stick to it.

- Understand your own personal stressors and develop approaches that can deal with them.

EXPLORE FURTHER

FURTHER READING

McMillan, K. and Weyers, J. (2007a) *How to Write Essays and Assignments*. Harlow: Pearson Education Limited.

Northedge, A. (2005) *The Good Study Guide*. 2nd edition. Milton Keynes: Open University.

Perry, A. (2002) *Isn't it About Time? How to stop putting things off and get on with your life*. London: Worth Publishing.

WEB LINKS

Grunig and Hunt's four models of public relations: http://iml.jou.ufl.edu/projects/Fall99/Westbrook/models.htm

CHAPTER 13

Thinking and Memory Skills

What skills will I develop in this chapter?

- develop a clear conception of what thinking is
- recognise the different types of thinking and where to use them
- use De Bono's six thinking hats approach
- develop an understanding of the role of systems thinking in business
- recognise and avoid thinking errors
- develop a clear understanding of how memory works
- develop a good memory

13.1 INTRODUCTION

Effective thinking and memory skills will make a huge difference to your performance at university. This chapter starts by considering the nature of 'thinking'; it is placed in juxtaposition with 'routine action'. Essentially, much of what we do is routine action and does not require thinking. However, there are many university and work tasks that require clear and precise thinking. This chapter looks at a range of categories of thinking and the characteristics of that type of thinking. Two common thinking systems, 'six thinking hats' and 'systems thinking', are explored. Finally, the thinking section looks at some common thinking errors and how to avoid them. The second part of the chapter looks at memory: what it is and how it works. Some strategies for developing a good memory are considered. As this is a developmental chapter, my advice would be to work through the chapter slowly and sequentially, carrying out the reflective exercises.

13.2 WHAT IS THINKING?

'I did it without thinking!' We have all probably said this at some stage in our university, social or work life. It is often said when something goes wrong or when there is an unexpected outcome. Many of our daily actions are performed without thinking. This is not a problem. Indeed, if we had to think extensively before we did 'things', we would get very little done. This raises two questions:

- How careful should we be before allowing actions to become routine?
- How do we know when we should be thinking and not behaving in a routine manner?

REFLECTIVE PERFORMING

KNOWING WHEN TO THINK!

Reflect on the two questions below. I would suggest you use a mind map to assist your thinking to capture it in a form that can be easily seen and understood. If you are completing this in a tutorial or seminar, compare your mind map with the maps of others in your group.

1 How careful should we be before allowing actions to become routine?

2 How do we know when we should be thinking and not behaving in a routine manner?

To get you started in developing your mind map, you might like to think about:

Question 1 – If you only operate in routine ways, how would you change your actions when circumstances change?

Question 1 – Would thinking in routine ways disadvantage some people or groups?

Question 2 – Do you only know after something has gone wrong that you should have thought about it?

Question 2 – What sort of cues would there be to warn you to think before you act?

Once you have thought about this, you may come to realise that most of our daily actions are performed in a routine manner. Routine is a powerful controller of behaviour. Not that people are dogs – but the basic training of dogs is all about routine and reward. Repeat sit commands, with some rewards, ensure that when we say 'sit' our dog responds by sitting. This is what is called stimulus–response theory. Stimulus–response theory is now not favoured by psychologists for explaining actions, but it is still a sound theoretical stance for our work.

Your behaviour at university and work will be subject to the same process. A stimulus is any event that a human is capable of sensing that produces a sensation. For example, you may sense the displeasure of your tutor when you arrive late for his or her lecture. That stimulus can be a very small look as you enter the room. A response is anything that a human does as a result of receiving that stimulus. These responses fall into one of two categories:

- any overt observable response – public
- a covert response occurs in the human but is not readily detectable or observable – private.

THORNDIKE'S STIMULUS–RESPONSE THEORY OF LEARNING

You should note that this is a contested theory and you should critically appraise its usefulness before including it in any work of your own. I include it here as an illustration of the connection between situation (stimulus) and action (response).

Thorndike was an American psychologist who worked extensively on a theory of connectionism in animals and humans. It is a learning theory that consists of actions that strengthen the relationship between the stimulus and the response. Thorndike proposed three laws:

1 The law of effect proposes that rewarding a certain behaviour will increase the probability that the behaviour will occur. Punishing a certain behaviour will decrease the probability that the behaviour will occur. So we would find that behaviours that lead to pleasant outcomes tend to be repeated.

2 The law of exercise suggests that the more frequently a stimulus and response occurs, the more likely it is that the stimulus will follow the response. This suggests that we learn our behaviours by doing them frequently. Thus, the tasks we do most frequently are the tasks we will do without thinking.

3 The law of readiness suggests that learning is dependent on the learner's motivation and readiness to act. Readiness facilitates the strengthening of the bond between stimulus and response. If we are motivated by lack of time to do a task, we are likely to carry it out in a routine manner without thinking.

Reflection

● Reflect on whether these laws could apply in the twenty-first-century workplace.

● Reflect on ways that these 'laws' could be broken to ensure that when needed, we do not act in routine ways.

When you are late entering a lecture the response may be to say 'sorry', hold up a hand as a sorry or to change your behaviour and not be late again. A covert response might be to think 'it doesn't matter'. It is possible to have both responses at once: the public 'sorry' and the private 'it doesn't matter'. We investigated the meanings of learning in an earlier chapter, and one view of learning is that it is a permanent change in behaviour. So if your normal response is to think 'it doesn't matter' and because of the stimulus you decide not to be late again, you will by our theory have undergone learning.

We communicate with other people in an effort to change their behaviour. Thus, if we run an advertising campaign for a new product we are trying to create a response to the stimulus of the advertisement and a change in buying behaviour. Leadership and management communications endeavour to do the same thing – change the behaviour of our work team.

So thinking can be patterned and routine but there will be times when patterned routine behaviour will not be suitable. Real thinking will be needed when you encounter:

- a difficulty with normal patterned behaviour – what you normally do does not work anymore
- a new or unfamiliar situation – you have no experience to call upon or the normal patterned behaviour does not work in that situation
- a changed situation – something has changed and requires a change in behaviour.

When we are confronted by a situation, difficulty or problem that we have not experienced before, we will need to engage a 'thinking process'. Your ability to think in an appropriate way and develop practical and effective solutions is a very valuable skill. Being able to use this skill will be rewarded both at university and at work. Thinking takes time, so although you may concentrate on solving a problem, the solution may not readily come to you. You may have experienced this when you strain and strain to solve a problem, either academic or practical; you then give up and do something else and then wondrously wake the next morning with a solution. Thinking is the purposeful and conscious action of considering. When the conscious work is finished, the unconscious mind will carry on. Effective solutions often come from hard, purposeful conscious thinking and leaving the problem for a while (time).

❝ MANAGER COMMENT

I learned a lot from my father about our family business. He had a saying that I still use today: 'the first thought is the worst thought'. By this he meant that thinking takes time and while a solution can be found quickly, it is often the solutions that are given more time to 'gestate' that work the best.

I always make a point of sleeping on any big decision. This sometimes annoys my team because they want a quick decision so that they can get on. However, I quite often find that by sleeping on something before acting I change the decision. Often this is not a major change, just some small points that make it a better decision. Occasionally a decision I would have made the previous day I won't make the next day after sleeping on it. I believe I have saved the company from some really stupid decisions over the years with this strategy.

There are very few decisions that won't wait overnight.

Thinking may be required to solve an academic problem such as an assignment. It may be required to solve a practical problem such as poor team performance. In business these two elements are always connected. Academic problems need to be solved with reference to practical outcomes for business. Practical problems need to be solved with reference to academic theory. Let's move on now to think about the different types of thinking you can employ in solving problems.

13.3 DIFFERENT TYPES OF THINKING

When you look at these different types of thinking, you may feel they are all the same or very similar. Clearly, they are all examples of thinking. But, you will need to recognise the fine differences between these ways of thinking. An indicator of an effective learner or manager is that they will be aware of and able to control their thinking. So if at first these ways of thinking make no sense, persevere because, with time (as with thinking), they will stand out clearly as different ways of thinking. There are more ways to categorise thinking and more categories of thinking than can ever be useful. The following sections categorise thinking in ways that I think are useful in business.

Practical thinking focuses on the processes of business. How in practice does the process of business happen? The underlying data for practical thinking is observation. The skilled manager can observe and diagnose a problem. The key criteria of practical thinking are experiences. A manager's experience provides an extensive library with which to compare the present. Practical thinking is also logical process thinking. This is the ability to link one process to another in effective ways so that a process is effective. Over time managers build up mental models of what a good business process will be like and they judge current processes by reference to those mental models.

Convergent thinking is a cognitive process bringing information and thoughts to a common point. It is integrative in that it brings known things to one point. It is effectively a condensing process of bringing together a synthesis of ideas. This type of thinking might be used when there are lots of ideas and opinions but very few agreed solutions.

Figure 13.1 Convergent thinking

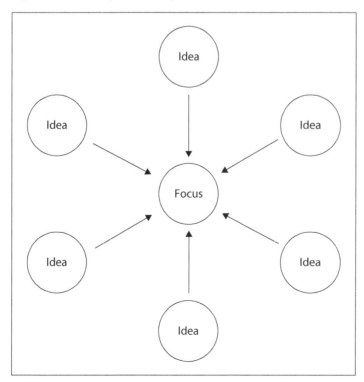

Divergent thinking starts from a common point and moves outward in a creative way to increase the diversity of thought. It is essentially creative in that it moves from what is known towards new ideas and perspectives. This type of thinking might be used with complex problems that have proved hard to solve for lack of ideas.

Figure 13.2 Divergent thinking

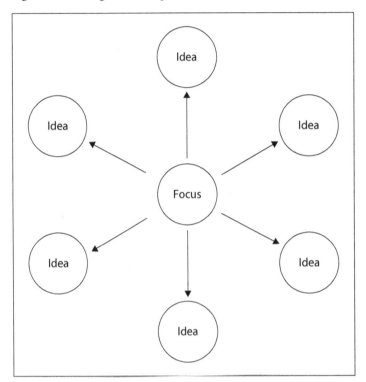

Critical thinking is convergent thinking that assesses the claims of something. This was covered extensively in Chapter 10.

Inductive thinking is a reasoning process that starts with the parts and cognitively works towards the whole. This type of thinking is most often seen in qualitative research where parts of a problem are researched and then the researcher argues how the parts create the whole.

Deductive thinking is a reasoning process that works from the whole to the parts. This is often seen in quantitative research where the whole of something is researched and the explanations are then made about the parts.

Evaluative thinking is thinking concerned with judging the value of something. It is closely tied to critical thinking and was extensively covered in Chapter 10.

Comprehension thinking is the cognitive process of understanding something. This process is often a case of understanding writing or situations. The techniques of comprehensive thinking are visualisation, contextualising and practice. In visualisation we make visual in our minds the ideas we read on paper. We imagine how the idea would take place. Drawing on paper or creating the image in your mind is an excellent way to comprehend something. We can also comprehend something by placing it in a familiar context. Finally, we comprehend by 'trying out' or practising. If we use the idea of speed reading, all three techniques could be useful. We read about speed reading then imagine how it will happen; we place it in context by thinking, 'I could use that idea here or here'; we will comprehend the idea better when we try it out.

Memorising thinking will be covered later in this chapter. It involves using strategies and approaches that allow the recall of information.

Reflective thinking involves careful and consistent thought about what you know and believe. The reflection requires that you weigh up the reasons for your beliefs. It also requires that you change your thinking dependent on the reasoned analysis of a situation or belief. Reflective thinking is the basis of all change and improvement.

Investigative thinking involves thinking and analysis of things that are incomplete or unclear. We could call this 'detective' thinking because it involves piecing together actions that have taken place. You will need to adopt this mode of thinking when investigating critical incidents at work. Managers often need to investigate some sort of failure, accident or complaint.

Social thinking concerns the emotions, beliefs, actions and thoughts of others. In most social situations you will have developed social thinking from an early age. But, conscious social thinking is required by managers, who must not only take the views, perspectives and desires of others into account but must also demonstrate that those views have been taken into account. Without active social thinking managers can easily overlook the perspectives of smaller groupings in their team or workforce.

Creative thinking involves measures and techniques that inspire new ways of thinking and acting.

The above section is one categorisation of thinking. There are infinite ways that thinking can be categorised. I would like to cover two more ways of thinking that are commonly found in the business community. The first involves the work of Edward de Bono (1986) and is derived from his book *Six Thinking Hats*. The second thinking schema belongs to the academic and writer Peter Senge (1990), where he explores 'systems thinking' in his book *The Fifth Discipline*.

Six thinking hats

This is a very brief introduction to this idea and is designed as an illustration of types of thinking. You can explore these interesting ideas further by following the link in the Bibliography. Six thinking hats is essentially a structured method of thinking that moves away from the predominant form in organisations of judgement thinking. By adopting the 'six hats' idea it is possible to provide more balance between different forms of thinking. The six hats represent six modes of thinking, and the idea encourages a proactive and pluralistic approach to thinking, where the expectation is that all the hats will be used equally when considering any problem or circumstance. The six thinking hats idea has changed over time, so you will find it explained in a variety of ways – the basic structural idea is as follows.

There are six hats and you can put on and take off one of these hats at a time to indicate the type of thinking being used. In group discussions it is helpful to have six coloured hats. So that someone may well say, 'Pass me the yellow hat because I want to do some logical positive thinking.' This also helps to control the group discussion because the only person speaking is the one wearing the hat. The different hats are listed below:

White hat is the information hat for delivering simple, objective facts and the source of those facts.

Red hat is the intuition, emotion and feelings hat. When you put on the red hat you can say what you feel without needing to justify what you say. This is very useful, because 'normally' you would have to justify your feelings with logic. As I am sure you are aware, sometimes we feel something and cannot justify it in the logical way.

Black hat is the judgement hat. The black hat is the critical evaluation hat that cautions against an approach or solution. It creates a balance with the logical positive yellow hat. Black hat judgements must always be logical and based in fact and evidence. So a statement such as, 'This won't work because of this or that…' is always followed by a logical premise and evidence.

Yellow hat is the logical positive hat that sets out the benefits that any action will accrue. It can look forward to proposed actions, but can also look back and find value in what has been done.

Green hat is the alternative change hat. Green hat thinking sets out the possible proposals and alternatives. It also sets out the challenges and provocations to the different solutions.

Blue hat is the process control hat. It introduces control and command steps into the process. It is also the reflective thinking about thinking hat and the chairperson's role hat.

How could you use the six thinking hats in a business meeting?

Let's imagine we are meeting together to solve or make progress with an organisational problem. This might be a typical opening sequence:

1 White hat gives the details and facts of the problem.
2 Green hat generates ideas and proposals for how the problem can be solved.
3 Yellow hat evaluates the benefits that might come from any course of action.

4 Black hat presents the drawbacks and cautions associated with each proposed action.

5 Red hat invites an expression of feelings about the proposals to solve the problem.

6 Blue hat summarises what is agreed and allocates actions.

REFLECTIVE PERFORMING

A SIX THINKING HATS MEETING

Obtain six hats and tie a 'six thinking hats' coloured ribbon around each hat. The rules of the meeting will be that only one person can speak at one time and they must be wearing a coloured hat. When wearing a hat they must restrict what they say to what is defined by the hat colour. They indicate their desire to speak by placing the appropriate coloured hat in front of them. The chairperson will decide the order of speaking. This exercise is ideally suited to a group of five to eight people.

You have 60 minutes to complete this exercise. The time should be apportioned in the following manner:

- 40 minutes – discussion of the problem
- 5 minutes – final blue hat summary – chairperson
- 15 minutes – reflective thought about the effectiveness and utility of the six hats meeting.

Choose one of the following problems:

- a complaint from a major customer about poor service
- a problem with an outsource supplier not meeting their service agreement
- a rising trend of manufacturing defects from 2.6% to 6.8% in three months
- a cash flow crisis looming in six weeks' time
- a group of female workers claiming that they have been discriminated against.

You will need to generate some basic facts as your meeting progresses. You can allow the first white hat speaker to do this as the first contribution to the meeting. Initially try to adopt the idealised progress of using the hats in this order:

1 White hat gives the details and facts of the problem.

2 Green hat generates ideas and proposals for how the problem can be solved.

3 Yellow hat evaluates the benefits that might come from any course of action.

4 Black hat presents the drawbacks and cautions associated with each proposed action.

5 Red hat invites an expression of feelings about the proposals to solve the problem.

6 Blue hat summarises what is agreed and allocates actions.

In reflection at the end of the hour, make sure to comment on how your actual process differed from this idealised process.

Now! You only need to have been to one business meeting to know that meetings do not progress in this structured and uniform manner. In practice it won't work like this, but planning the meeting to operate in this fashion does provide some balanced structure. In all likelihood the meeting will loop around and the contributions will be mixed up. But if each member of the meeting has to indicate which hat they are wearing before they start to talk, it does help balance and focus the discussion.

SYSTEMS THINKING

Systems thinking is a type of thinking originally suggested by very early writers relating to natural systems. Peter Senge (1990) popularised the idea in the 1990s and 2000s by relating the disciplines of systems thinking to the creation of 'learning organisations'. It involves considering four specific disciplines and how they relate to the fifth discipline of 'systems thinking'. One general practical approach advocated drawing out systems maps so the normally tacit system is exposed to scrutiny. It is argued that without a clear vision of the complete system, any solutions will be partial and ineffective.

The focus of the core disciplines is to understand and create awareness of:

- practices – what is done and how
- principles – what guides and controls actions and practices
- people – the skills and attributes that people bring to each of the disciplines.

The four core disciplines are personal mastery, mental models, building shared vision and team learning.

Personal mastery focuses on the notion that organisations only learn through individuals. Individual learning does not ensure that the organisation will learn. But without personal learning no organisational learning can take place. It involves the development of competence and skills but also goes beyond this notion of vocation. People with high personal mastery operate in a continual learning mode. This might be expected at university but can be absent in the workplace. This notion has been taken forward into business and life through the idea of 'lifelong learning'. Personal mastery also contains elements of reflective thinking and reflective practice.

Mental models are the deeply held assumptions and generalisations that influence and control how we understand the world around us. Often the effect of these assumptions on our behaviour goes unnoticed. Reflection can reveal these unspoken assumptions, and once revealed we are able to consider and adjust them. In group situations it is important to 'surface' the mental models in use so that the constraints and assumptions are explicit. It often turns out that a constraint can easily be turned into an opportunity once it is revealed.

Building shared vision focuses on developing a group image of the future. Where there is a 'genuine' vision of the future the people in the organisation understand, at a fundamental level, what needs to be done and their part in that process. The process of building a shared vision must unearth an organisational vision of the future that everyone supports. When this happens, the increased clarity, enthusiasm and personal commitment spreads throughout the workforce. Importantly, this will allow new and more effective mental models to be built.

Team learning is the process of building and aligning the skills and capabilities of the organisation's workforce. It partially builds on personal mastery and shared vision. But the people in a team need to operate as a team – they need to be more than the sum of the individuals. When teams learn the results can be exponentially better than when individuals learn. Effective team learning requires teams to understand the mental models and assumptions of all members, but also to accommodate them and allow them to 'think together'.

The fifth discipline, after which the Senge (1990) book was named, is **systems thinking**. Systems thinking concentrates attention on the whole system – the big picture, if you like. It focuses on patterns and behaviours of the whole system and proposes changes to the whole. It further considers and diagnoses relationships between the different parts of the system. Systems thinking will work on the interconnected whole and considers reactions in one part of the system to changes in another part of the system. Systems thinking integrates the other four disciplines.

THE THINKING PROCESS FOR PROBLEM-SOLVING

So far we have addressed a number of different types of thinking and now we must address the thinking process. No matter what the problem is – be it practical, academic or theoretical – the basic stages will be the same.

1   The thinker becomes aware of the problem. Without awareness there cannot be any thinking.

2   Parameter definition – the exact nature of the problem is defined. Importantly, the boundaries of the problem are also defined. At the end of this stage it should be clear what the problem is, what is excluded and the characteristics of the problem.

3   The approach to the problem and its analysis is defined. In many cases multiple perspectives on the problem will be formed. In business and academic problems, it is expected that theory will inform the perspectives. The conclusion of this stage will be a list of perspective and associated theories.

4   Solution generation phase uses the generated perspectives to produce possible solutions to the problem.

5   Logical reasoning is then used to consider the consequences of each action.

6   A proposed solution is selected.

7   This solution is tested in a small practice trial.

8   Adaptations are made and a final solution is put into place.

BECOMING REFLECTIVE PERFORMERS

Simon: 'Hi, how's your graduate job-hunt going?'

Louise: 'Well, it's hard work and pressure, isn't it?'

S: 'Well! I have been to a few but I don't seem to be getting anywhere. I don't know what I am doing wrong.'

L: 'It's a really tough job market. I think graduate opportunities are at an all-time low. What will you do if you don't get a graduate place?'

S: 'I am really not sure. I wanted to get a grad place in a top 500 company in a marketing role.'

L: 'No fallback position then! How about serving fries?'

S: 'Ha ha, you are cruel. I, like everyone else, have run up a lot of student loan debt so I need that weight off my back.'

L: 'You will need to think about it so you have a fallback position.'

S: 'I know that but when you have a little dream it is hard to let that slip. My dream is to work in marketing.'

L: 'Does serving fries count as marketing?'

S: 'Tread lightly on my dreams! If I spend time thinking about it there are only a few things I really like and enjoy and I would like to do something that I enjoy.'

L: 'How about general management? There are lots of jobs in that area.'

S: 'That's true but I really don't know that much about general management and it somehow doesn't appeal.'

L: 'I am going all out for a top 100 company in general management. I have written to them all asking to join as a graduate or to do an unpaid internship.'

S: 'What, you have sent a letter to every one of the top 100 companies?'

L: 'Sure thing; it only took about two hours with mail merge and about £30 in stamps.'

S: 'Really! Any replies yet?'

L: 'Yes. Five invites to graduate assessment centres and about six offers of unpaid internships. So I will probably be sorted.'

S: 'Well, I admire the spirit and cleverness of the approach. How did you think that one up? I have never heard of anyone doing that!'

L: 'It came to me one night when I was just thinking or dreaming about the future. It seemed like an easy thing to do so that I could get a job. Like you, I need a job to clear some of that student loan.'

S: 'They say that your lifetime earnings will be way more than a non-graduate but at this stage it takes some believing, doesn't it?'

L: 'At this stage I will settle for any job in a decent company.'

S: 'What's the fallback position?'

L: 'Would you believe I was thinking of teaching in university?'

S: 'Really! You're rubbish at presentations – how does the logic work on that one?'

L: 'Well, I am not sure there is any logic!'

S: 'So you're taught at university to think logically and you go for a totally illogical choice.'

L: 'Yea, odd isn't it? It's not logical but I think I might enjoy it. Not so much the teaching but the playing with ideas and thinking and researching.'

S: 'It does make you wonder if you should always make a rational and logical decision. Is there a place for "gut feeling" or taking a "mad" decision?'

L: 'I guess there is. Aren't some of the biggest companies based on ridiculous and non-rational decisions?'

S: 'What's the evidence for that one?'

L: 'Very funny!'

S: 'What about that really cool aquarium maker? The guy who started it up straight from university, what's his name? It's worth millions now! He must be worth millions.'

L: 'You will have to be really lucky to make millions in a paid job!'

S: 'Fallback position is now to start my own company.'

L: 'What will it sell?

S: 'Absolutely no idea!'

13.4 MEMORY

Memory is an important part of academic and business life. This section looks at the role of memory at university and work. It also looks at the characteristics of memory. Finally, it considers ways to improve your memory. You may at the moment think your memory is not very good – 'I can't remember a thing.' Understanding how your memory works and developing some helpful memory methods will soon improve your memory.

The most important reason to improve your memory at university is to do well in examinations. But improvements for this reason will also help with other university tasks and will certainly help you at work. It is not always your ability to recall facts and figures that is important; it is often that you need to recall where you can find those facts and figures. Modern computing can certainly help here in that organising information has never been easier. Well-organised information is also easier to retrieve and easier to remember. So part of having a good memory is to organise information in ways that are easily retrievable. In business the ability to remember your customers and their preferred purchases and some relevant personal facts is vital. If you are in sales, your customers will buy more from you if they think you know them personally and care about them. So how would you remember the details of each of your customers, their buying preferences and some personal facts? Modern handheld computers provide the answer. All the information you will need to successfully manage the sales relationship can be held on these devices. You only have to look up the detail five minutes before you make the sales contact. But you still have to be able to remember the detail for the length of the meeting.

Let's look at the nature of memory by considering what is easy to remember and what is hard to remember. I doubt you have any trouble remembering:

- the names of family members or friends
- your birthday
- how to read and write
- knowledge from school

- stories from your past
- skills, such as riding a bike
- routines and habits.

However, you might have more trouble remembering:

- things that you don't want to do
- things you believe will be difficult to remember
- information that you consider to be boring or trivial
- changes to your daily routine
- things you did when you were tired, bored or unwell.

Forgetting things can have some very unpleasant effects:

- embarrassment, frustration or anxiety
- a reduction in self-confidence
- feelings of being stupid
- avoiding participating in things – withdrawal
- apprehension once we have experienced the inability to remember.

HOW MEMORY WORKS

Memory is a process and that process is believed to follow these steps:

1 You perceive something by sight, sound, smell, taste or feel.

2 This information is filtered by the sensory registers and committed to short-term memory (STM) (also known as working memory).

3 STM can hold this information for up to 30 seconds and there is a limit of about five to nine items that can be held in STM, for most people.

4 If you choose to you can commit it to long-term memory (LTM); this is done by:

   - rehearsal
   - coding
   - imaging.

5 You need to retrieve it from LTM to STM if you want to use it.

As an example let's consider how you perceive information in a lecture using two different scenarios.

Scenario 1 – In the first lecture you are given extensive handouts that cover all the slides shown and the related information. You sit passively listening to the lecturer and at the end of the teaching session you can remember only one striking visual thing that was shown to you about halfway through the lecture.

Figure 13.3 Memory flowchart

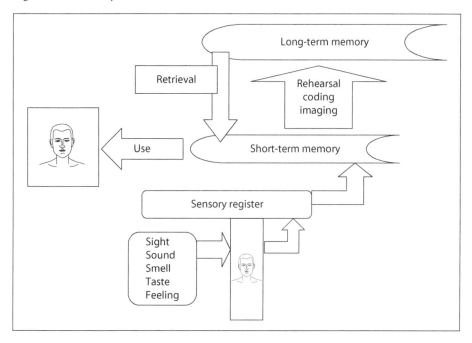

Scenario 2 – You are given no handouts and have to listen carefully and make your own notes. You do this by creating a visual mind map of the ideas presented. An hour after the lecture you can recall most of what was taught.

Memory in scenario 1 – The only stimuli you receive are a stream of sound that enters your STM; it is not encoded or otherwise transferred to LTM and is quickly forgotten. The visual stimulus is immediately transferred to LTM by imagery.

Memory in scenario 2 – The constant sound and visual stimuli are transferred by encoding and imagery – the mind map you created – to LTM as the lecture progresses. This is available to retrieve back into STM some time afterwards. If this LTM were reinforced, it would become relatively permanent in LTM and available to retrieve for years afterwards.

In memory scenario 2 there are simple techniques that will improve your ability to remember the mind map you created during the lecture. Common helpful techniques are:

- numbering and lettering – lists
- diagrams, pictures, tags and icons
- colours
- adding your own contextual examples
- linking and connecting

- logical structures and positioning – think about the clock index from Chapter 2
- top-level summaries.

You will need to reflect on the techniques of memory that will work for you. We are not all the same and some of the following work for some people and some do not. If you engage in developing your ability to remember, you will discover other new ways or adaptations of the following ideas that will help you remember. The first section looks at some general techniques that are very useful for studying and examinations. The second section considers some business-related techniques.

Pictures and images

We have already noted that pictures and images are easier to remember than words. Linking and visualising by drawing ideas will assist with remembering them. This is a two-stage process: the act of drawing fixes the thing in LTM and then the act of looking reinforces the thing in memory. For example, PESTLE is a form of business analysis that covers political, economic, social, technological, legal and environmental. Under pressure in an examination these can be hard to remember. So let's try some imagery (Figure 13.4). There is a man in a meeting sitting at a table with a laptop on the table – and he is handing out cash to other people at the table – while holding a banner saying 'vote for me' – into the room walks a policeman with a small raining cloud over his head – there is a large bee trying to sting him. It may work better if you draw this. The different parts are:

- man sat at table with computer – technological
- handing out cash – economic
- vote for me – political
- other people around the table – social.

These four things are another form of analysis called PEST analysis – hence the large bee.

Paying people to vote for you is illegal, so:

- in walks a policeman – legal
- with a small rain cloud over his head – environmental.

When using this technique it is important to create an image that is relevant to you personally. It also helps if the image is memorably eccentric or striking. It works best if you actually draw it!

Charts and tables

Complicated and complex data are easier to remember if they are structured into tables or charts.

Figure 13.4 PESTLE example

The Roman room

The Roman room strategy is an extension of the association and imagery approach. Here the things you need to remember are placed into rooms in your family home. In each room you will have furniture and furnishings that can also be linked to things you need to remember. This technique works because you are very familiar with your family home and you link new information to this familiar structure. While this will require some mental effort to link the items to the rooms and furniture, it does allow for excellent recall. If the links can be funny or odd, they will be all the more memorable.

Carrying on with our example above, we could place the six elements of PESTLE in rooms in our house. The policeman gets shown to the living room, where he places the following:

- current UK legislation in the armchair – small and self-contained
- European legislation on the settee, larger so needs more space
- future legislation is on the television screen
- industry-specific legislation shines over everyone so is the lampshade
- employment law statutes are the books in the bookcase.

And so on…

Once the information is organised in this way, revisit the room and try to recall what each room and each item represents. Reinforce the information occasionally and you should have created a memorable set of knowledge. You can use the same rooms for other information. In creating a good memory, connecting ideas together is important. So you could, for instance, use a mind map of the Roman room technique. If this technique is personally effective, you could use it to organise all your study notes. Using a blank mind map with only the rooms of your family home marked on it, you place the ideas of one lecture into the rooms.

Once the technique becomes familiar, you will soon have a very effective memory device for recalling lecture notes.

Acronyms

Acronyms are words made from the first letters of something you wish to remember. They allow recall of both the information and the order of information. One classic that most people will know is ROYGBIV, which is a way of remembering the colours of the rainbow – red, orange, yellow, green, blue, indigo, violet.

A more complicated one is BEDMAS for the order that maths operations should take – brackets, exponentials, division, multiplication, addition, subtraction.

Two business-related acronyms are:

- SMART – specific, measurable, achievable, realistic, timely
- TRACC – for business memos: timely, relevant, accurate, concise, clear.

And finally, a North American one for the quiz enthusiasts. HOMES – Huron, Ontario, Michigan, Erie, Superior – are names of the Great Lakes.

Acrostics

Acrostics are short phrases where the first letter of each word is the cue for something you need to remember. If we take a look at an acrostic that will help remember the planets in the solar system you will see how they work. The planets and the order they are from the Sun: Mercury, Venus, Earth, Mars, Jupiter, Saturn, Uranus, Neptune, Pluto. There aren't many useful acrostics in general and not many in business, so the essence is to build your own for remembering things.

Now to that acrostic that could be used to remember the order of planets from the sun is: 'My Very Excellent Mother Just Served Up Nice Pancakes.'

You will note that this works much better for this ordered list than an acronym would. This is because MVEMJSUNP doesn't actually mean much to most people. You can easily invent your own acrostics to cope with the specific knowledge that you need to remember.

Story-making

Story-making is a technique that associates the information you need to remember with a story. They can be quite complicated and involved, but here is a simple one for a marketing concept. 'Matt Price places promotion products in stores', is a way of remembering the marketing mix: price, placement, promotion and product.

Rhymes

Rhymes can assist with memory; it is possible you learned the alphabet by singing along to 'twinkle twinkle little star' as you recited: a b c d e f g, h i j k l m n o p, q r s, t u v, w x, y and z.

Chunking

Chunking is useful with numbers. If you remember, your short-term memory will be running out of space by the time you have heard or seen five to nine items. A ten-digit telephone number will be difficult to remember. Try remembering 0770525252 as a single digit sequence. This may be difficult because your mind will automatically chunk it to make it easier to remember. Wait 30 seconds and see if you can remember it. Now try remembering 0770 52 52 52. This should be easier and you will probably remember it tomorrow.

Chunking with familiar numbers is an even more effective method. If your birthday is on the 07 of August and your granny lives at number 70 and part of your car registration is 52 then this becomes a number you are unlikely to forget.

Reading aloud

This is essentially a reinforcement strategy. It involves reading your notes or the information you need to remember aloud. Normally this would be done several times. This is a slow process but it does provide for good recall of information. An extension to this technique is to read aloud and then try to recite what you have said – only getting help from the original source when you 'dry up'. This technique works well in conjunction with other techniques and is often used for information that you need to remember in presentation situations.

Remembering names and faces

There are two well-established strategies for remembering people's names. The simplest basically involves paying attention. Most of the time our memory for someone's name fails because we never created an effective memory code for it.

We can dramatically improve our memory for names simply by:

- **Paying attention** – taking a good look or consciously making an effort to remember a name.
- **Elaborate the information** – do something with it. Breaking and imaging a name is one method. Ruth Farwell could become roof on a far well – can you picture it?
- **Reinforce** the name by deliberately remembering it. Remember, the more you meet someone the less likely you are to forget their name. Artificially create this by reinforcing their name.
- **Face–name association** connects the name to one or more physical features. Despite the name of this technique, it probably works better if you associate with more general physical features like height, size, hairstyle.
- **Role association** involves thinking about the type of job or role a person may do. These can sometimes end up being derogatory, so think about any offence you might cause before you share them with anyone else. For example, 'she looks like a cleaner,' 'he looks like a rock musician,' 'she looks like a dancer.' If the name can be connected to the memorable role, you will have an enduring

record of the persona and their name. Phil Collins who looks like a rock musician – at least to older people.

- Finally the simplest technique of all – **write down the name**. Extend this with a small doodle or a few descriptive words.

In business, remembering names and faces is a frequent and essential skill. Apply one or all of the above techniques and you will quickly improve your ability to recall names and faces. The best place to practise these techniques is in meetings when you are a new person so don't know many of the people present.

Mind maps

Mind maps were considered in Chapter 2 when thinking about how to study. But it is worth thinking about the technique here in relation to memory. The mind map can be an amalgam of all the techniques we have just considered.

CASE STUDY

THE BILLIONAIRE BUSINESS IDEA WITH ETHICS

Bethany, Rachael and Katie sat down to a well-earned drink. They had just finished their final examination and they wanted to plan the rest of their lives. Bethany said, 'So, what are we going to do?' Neither of the others answered. Then they all laughed – 'This is not a good start,' said Katie. Rachael pointed out that they needed to think about this very hard because they were all in debt and with a recession there were no jobs. They all thought the same thing at once: 'This is not going to be easy.'

Then Bethany mentioned that they had all been trained to think effectively. They didn't know it, and wouldn't know it for some months, but they were much better at thinking than they realised. They would all be getting first-class degrees in a few weeks. But, they needed to make progress with the rest of their lives.

They gradually started to think about what they wanted to do. As with most thinking, they thought in terms of 'abstract wants and needs'. This is the agreed list of things they produced:

- They wanted to be entrepreneurial.
- They wanted their own company.

- It had to be ethical.
- They wanted to give a slice of the profits to good causes, maybe in developing countries.
- They wanted to create a healthy product that did not harm the environment.
- They wanted their company to become very large, turning over at least £1 billion per year.
- Between them they had £5,500 to start the company.
- They wanted their product to appeal to a young and middle-aged group of buyers.
- They wanted a brand that would add value to people's lives.
- They wanted to start now or as soon after now as possible.
- They realised they would have to start small and grow the business.
- They knew that other businesses had started this way and gone on to be huge brands.
- They had some catering experience and some marketing and IT experience.

To think about...

- Set out a thinking process that will work for this group.

- How could they generate ideas for their new company?

- How will they know which ideas will be best?

Then work through the process you have set out and develop that billion-pound idea!

SUMMARY

Effective thinking and memory skills will make academic and work life easier.

- Develop a systematic way to decide when to think and when to act in routine ways.

- There are different types of thinking:
  - practical thinking
  - convergent thinking
  - divergent thinking
  - critical thinking
  - inductive thinking
  - deductive thinking
  - evaluative thinking
  - comprehension thinking
  - memorising thinking
  - reflective thinking
  - investigative thinking
  - social thinking
  - creative thinking.

- Six thinking hats is one way to categorise thinking that can be useful in business environments. It involves adopting a particular thinking 'stance':
  - white hat – information
  - red hat – emotion
  - black hat – judgement
  - yellow hat – logical positive
  - green hat – change
  - blue hat – process control.

- Senge's (1990) systems thinking is based on five disciplines:
  - personal mastery
  - mental models
  - building a shared vision

- team learning
- systems thinking.

● Memory is divided into short term (STM) and long term (LTM). It is necessary to transfer things you want to remember into LTM; how you do that affects how well you remember.

● You can improve your memory by using the following techniques:
  - pictures and images
  - charts and tables
  - the Roman room
  - acronyms
  - acrostics
  - story-making
  - rhymes
  - chunking
  - reading aloud.

EXPLORE FURTHER

FURTHER READING

Boak, G. and Thompson, D. (1998) *Mental Models for Managers: Frameworks for practical thinking*. London: Imprint Random House Business Books.

A guide to mental models, frameworks and analytical techniques used by managers.

De Bono, E. (1986) *Six Thinking Hats*. London: Penguin Books Ltd.

Higbee, K. (1988). *Your Memory: How it works and how to improve it*. London: Piatkus.

Senge, P. (1990) *The Fifth Discipline: The art and practice of the learning organisation*. London: Random House.

CHAPTER 14

Word Processor Skills

What skills will I develop in this chapter?

- basic Word skills
- using the new features of Word 2007
- using keyboard shortcuts
- getting help in Word 2007
- saving different types of document
- using templates
- understanding and using styles and themes
- creating references and a bibliography
- creating an index
- creating a contents page
- using mail merge
- publishing documents on the web and blogs
- working together on Word documents

A note about computer instructions: Where there are instructions that should be followed, they will be presented in **bold type**. So to carry out the actions required, simply follow the words that are **emboldened**.

14.1 INTRODUCTION

Microsoft Word is probably the most extensively used word processing programme in academe and business. You will have encountered it at school and can probably carry out the basic tasks of creating, formatting and printing documents. There are some very useful extra features of Word that can help with your academic work. It will take a little time and application to learn these features, but the improvement in the speed, accuracy and presentation of your work will be marked.

In business you will need to be able to use the more advanced features of Word to carry out business tasks. In the business context it will be assumed that you, as a graduate, can function effectively with documents and business tasks.

Gradually the Word version that you can buy and will find on university and work computers is moving to Word 2007. This version has many more useful features that make handling documents easier. Unfortunately, the interface looks and operates quite differently from earlier versions. Don't be put off by this because the improvements far outweigh the time needed to familiarise yourself with the new layout. It is worth repeating the point made in Chapter 2; there are discounted prices for students that provide fully functional versions of Office 2007, of which Word 2007 is one programme. At the time of writing a fully functional version of Office 2007 is available for less than £40.

14.2 BASIC WORD SKILLS

In this section I will work through many of the basic actions required to open and operate Word 2007. I'll work through opening, setting up the quick menu, getting help, using and making templates, formatting a letter and setting up an assignment template.

STARTING WORD

You may think this is so basic that no comment is needed, but there are several ways to start the Word programme and some are more efficient than others. Let's start Word in the ordinary way:

Opening Word

1 Click the **Start** button on the taskbar (bottom left in green),

2 Then point to **All Programs**.

3 Click **Microsoft Office**.

4 Click **Microsoft Office Word 2007**.

You will now have Word 2007 open in full screen. Note: it does look very different from earlier versions.

THE MAIN WORD 2007 WINDOW DETAIL

1 This looks like a logo but is actually the Office Command Button and contains a number of important commands.

2 This is the ribbon; it is new to Word 2007 and contains all the main commands that you will need. If you look to the top of the ribbon you will see the tabs; these are covered in 3 below. The ribbon has commands grouped together; you can see the group names at the bottom of the ribbon: clipboard, font, paragraph, styles. This screenshot is of the home tab; it contains many of the most frequently used commands, such as: copy, cut, paste, font changes, paragraph set-up and styles.

3 Tabs run along the top of the ribbon and allow access to other commands. In this screenshot you can see the tabs: home, insert, page layout, references, mailings, review, view and add-ins.

4 This is the main document window where you add the detail of your document.

5 The status bar runs along the bottom of the screen. It is customisable so you can add the elements you need to see. This screenshot shows page number, word count, proof reading status and language. Right-click the status bar to add or remove elements.

6 This is the zoom control; you can '+' or '–' it or slide it. To the left of this are the page view commands.

Figure 14.1 Main Word window

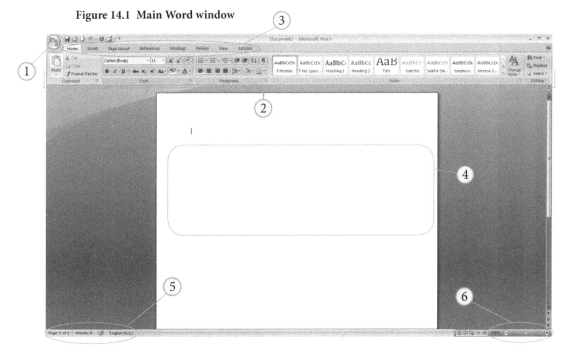

Opening Word alternative 1: You will find that opening Word as above soon becomes tedious. Another way to open Word and a better way is to use a desktop icon that is simply double-clicked to start the program.

Creating a desktop icon to open Word

1 Click the **Start** button on the taskbar – at the bottom of the screen.

2 Then point to **All Programs**.

3 Click **Microsoft Office**.

4 Right-click **Microsoft Office Word 2007**.

5 Point to **Send To** and then click **Desktop (Create Short cut)**.

You will now have a desktop icon that will start Word immediately with one double-click. You may have to close or minimise some of the files you have open to be able to see the desktop icon.

Opening Word alternative 2: There is one other useful way to start a specific document in Word.

Open a Word document from Windows Explorer

1 Right-click the Start button on the taskbar and then click Explore All Users.

2 In the pane, find and click on My Documents.

3 Find the file that contains the document you want to open.

4 Double-click the **required document file** and it will open Word with the document in the main pane.

Let's return to the new look of Word 2007 and investigate some of the new areas.

USING THE OFFICE BUTTON

Many new users of Word 2007 open the program and then get a little stuck by not knowing where or what to click. The Office logo in the top left corner is a main command button. Click it now and you will see it opens a set of important commands.

Figure 14.2 Word 2007 Office button

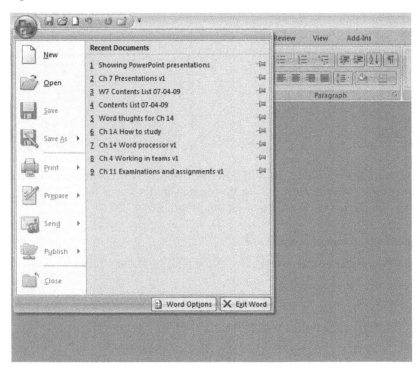

The Office button in detail

1 These are the main commands: new, open, save, save as, print, prepare, send, publish, and close.

2 Word Options allow access to the detailed options that allow you to customise the way Word looks and operates.

3 Exit and close Word.

4 In this section the documents you have used recently are displayed and can be opened by clicking them. Notice the pin icon if you click this; the document will be permanently stuck to the recent documents list, that is, it will not drop off when many more documents have been opened. This is useful for documents you need to have quick access to but do not open frequently.

Quick access toolbar

Using the quick access toolbar will considerably speed up the tasks you do frequently, such as saving, undoing, opening files, closing files. It is, by default, positioned at the top left of the screen next to the Office button. In this screenshot it contains the commands: save, open, new document, undo, redo, and close. This is a customisable toolbar so you can add and remove elements. The screenshot shows the main toolbar selection window that is opened by the small down-arrow on the right. You can then select commands that you want to add or remove.

Figure 14.3 Quick access toolbar

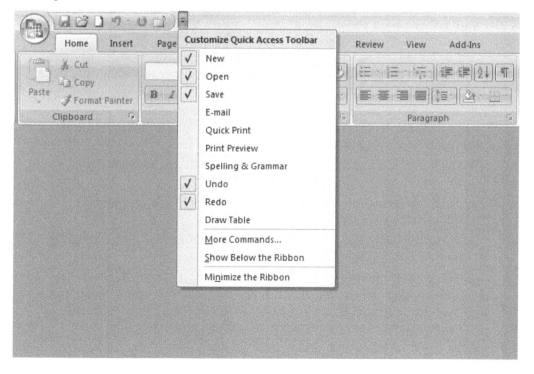

1 In the toolbar showing icons, click to activate.

2 The down-arrow for opening the selection pane.

3 Tick main commands to include on the toolbar; unclick to remove them.

4 More commands button provides access to all commands.

If you do one thing to make Word 2007 work better for you, customise this toolbar to include the commands you frequently use. It saves a lot of time, stress and finger energy.

USING THE RIBBON

The ribbon is a band of instructions at the top of the screen. It replaces all the menus, toolbars and taskbars that were found in Word 2003. You will note that the ribbon contains tabs that are organised by work task.

Figure 14.4 Word 2007 ribbon and tabs

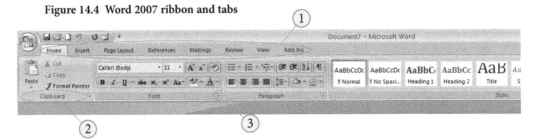

1 The ribbon tabs – Looking closely you can see that the tabs are labelled: Home, Insert, Page Layout, References, Mailings, Review, View and Add-Ins. Click on each of them now and see the types of task they contain. You should have noted that the ribbon tabs are associated with activities. The first four tabs are the ones you are most likely to need when creating university documents, such as assignments.

2 Now click on the home tab and we will investigate that some more. Word opens with the home tab showing on the ribbon; it contains four parts – the names are at the bottom of the ribbon:

- 'Clipboard' contains the cut/copy/paste commands that you probably know already.

- 'Font' contains all the commands related to the size, style, position and colour of the text in the document.

- 'Paragraph' controls the way that paragraphs are formatted, including bullet lists, paragraph marks, indenting, text positioning.

- 'Styles' control the formatting of designated parts of the text. The first style box is 'normal'. If you right-click this you can modify the appearance of the style. The third style is Heading 1 followed by Heading 2; this can be used by inserting the cursor in a line of text and clicking the style button.

KEYBOARD SHORTCUTS

People use keyboard shortcuts for a variety of reasons. Some because using a mouse is difficult or painful. But most businesspeople use the keyboard shortcuts in Word because it saves time by not having to remove your fingers from the keys to use the mouse. There are two types of keyboard shortcut. Key combinations perform specific commands for the set key combination. They involve holding down one key and pressing another at the same time. An example that most people know is holding down the Control key (bottom left of most keyboards, marked Ctrl) and pressing the C key for 'Copy'. Access keys are the other shortcut method and give you access to the ribbon commands.

Key combinations

Key combinations are a very fast way of accessing commands associated with text. However, there are many more that you will learn over time. The most commonly used shortcuts are:

- Ctrl + C = Copy
- Ctrl + X = Cut
- Ctrl + V = Paste
- Ctrl + S = Save

Text-related shortcuts include:

- Ctrl + I = Italics
- Ctrl + B = Bold
- Ctrl + U = Underline

Table 14.1 Word keyboard shortcuts

Apply Heading1	ALT+CTRL+1
Apply Heading2	ALT+CTRL+2
Apply Heading3	ALT+CTRL+3
Apply List Bullet	CTRL+SHIFT+L
Bold	CTRL+B or CTRL+SHIFT+B
Bookmark	CTRL+SHIFT+F5
Cancel	ESC
Centre Para	CTRL+E
Change Case	SHIFT+F3
Clear	DELETE
Close or Exit	ALT+F4
Close Pane	ALT+SHIFT+C

Copy	CTRL+C or CTRL+INSERT
Copy Text	SHIFT+F2
Cut	CTRL+X or SHIFT+DELETE
Date Field	ALT+SHIFT+D
Delete Back Word	CTRL+BACKSPACE
Delete Word	CTRL+DELETE
Dictionary	ALT+SHIFT+F7
Double Underline	CTRL+SHIFT+D
Find	CTRL+F
Font	CTRL+D or CTRL+SHIFT+F
Font Size Select	CTRL+SHIFT+P
Grow Font	CTRL+SHIFT+.
Grow Font One Point	CTRL+]
Hanging Indent	CTRL+T
Help	F1
Indent	CTRL+M
Italic	CTRL+I or CTRL+SHIFT+I
Justify Para	CTRL+J
Left Para	CTRL+L
Mark Citation	ALT+SHIFT+I
Mark Index Entry	ALT+SHIFT+X
Mark Table of Contents Entry	ALT+SHIFT+O
Move Text	F2
New	CTRL+N
Next Misspelling	ALT+F7
Normal	ALT+CTRL+N
Normal Style	CTRL+SHIFT+N or ALT+SHIFT+CLEAR (NUM 5)
Open	CTRL+O or CTRL+F12 or ALT+CTRL+F2
Outline	ALT+CTRL+O
Page	ALT+CTRL+P
Page Break	CTRL+ENTER
Page Down	PAGE DOWN

Page Down Extend	SHIFT+PAGE DOWN
Page Up	PAGE UP
Page Up Extend	SHIFT+PAGE UP
Para Down	CTRL+DOWN
Para Down Extend	CTRL+SHIFT+DOWN
Para Up	CTRL+UP
Para Up Extend	CTRL+SHIFT+UP
Paste	CTRL+V or SHIFT+INSERT
Print	CTRL+P or CTRL+SHIFT+F12
Print Preview	CTRL+F2 or ALT+CTRL+I
Proofing	F7
Redo	ALT+SHIFT+BACKSPACE
Redo or Repeat	CTRL+Y or F4 or ALT+ENTER
Replace	CTRL+H
Save	CTRL+S or SHIFT+F12 or ALT+SHIFT+F2
Save As	F12
Select All	CTRL+A or CTRL+CLEAR (NUM 5) or CTRL+NUM 5
Shrink Font	CTRL+SHIFT+,
Shrink Font One Point	CTRL+[
Small Caps	CTRL+SHIFT+K
Style	CTRL+SHIFT+S
Subscript	CTRL+=
Superscript	CTRL+SHIFT+=
Thesaurus	SHIFT+F7
Underline	CTRL+U or CTRL+SHIFT+U
Undo	CTRL+Z or ALT+BACKSPACE
Word Underline	CTRL+SHIFT+W

Access keys are another way to access commands and are operated from the 'Alt' key; when you press it small labels appear on the ribbon called 'badges'. Once you choose an option you then get more options until you get to the command you want. Let's try it:

1 Press **Alt** and the badges appear (make sure you are in the Home tab).

2 Press **P** to move to paragraph.

3 Press **O** to go to page orientation.

4 Use the arrow key to select Landscape.

5 Then press **Enter** (the large key on the right of most keyboards with a left line and arrow head).

Your page is now in landscape format.

The quick access toolbar can be accessed in the same way: **Alt** then the numbers 1 to however many commands you have.

HOW TO GET HELP

Even the most experienced Word users need help from time to time and the Microsoft suite has an excellent help facility. You can access Help using the small '**?**' on the right just above the ribbon or press the shortcut **F1**.

Figure 14.5 Word 2007 help page

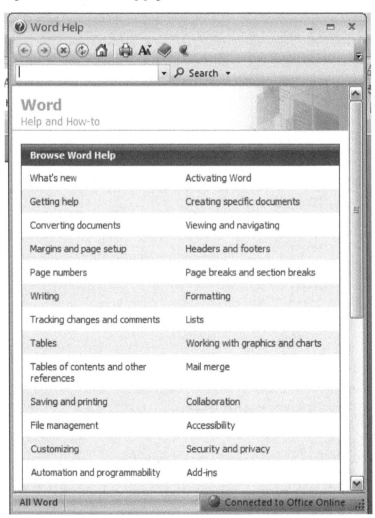

1 When the help window opens you can add a search term to locate the information you need. Type in the term and press 'enter' and Word will search for an appropriate topic. You will then be presented with a list of possible help items. Select one of these by clicking on it.

2 You can also use the main window to browse topics.

3 If you are connected to the Internet, Help will automatically connect to Microsoft Office Online, which will provide access to updated information. You can check the connection status here at the bottom of the task pane.

4 When you have finished, close the task pane with this X.

OPENING A NEW DOCUMENT

I will deal with opening a new document here and in a later section we will look at opening documents from templates. The main **New** command is on the Office button menu. To open a new document:

1 Press the **Office Button**.

2 Press **New**.

3 Default is **Blank Document** so press this.

(You can add 'New' to the quick access toolbar; when you use it a new blank document will open.)

You will now have a new blank document open on the screen. If you already had an existing document open you may wonder where it has gone. If you look at the bottom of the screen you will see two Word icon boxes; one will contain the name of the previous document and one will contain the name Document 2 (this may be a different number). You can navigate between the documents by clicking the appropriate icon. When you have lots of documents or other applications open, the icon will revert to one icon and a small white down-arrow will appear to the right of the icon. Using this you can select the document you want. The title of the document you are working on will appear at the very top of the Word window.

SAVING DOCUMENTS

After you have added things to your new document you should save it. Don't wait more than a few minutes to do this because if there is a power interruption you will lose the work you have done. The process of saving is slightly different from the first time you save. To save a new document:

1 Press the **Office Button**.

2 Press **Save As**.

3 Select the type of document:

- **Word document** – is the normal document type for Word 2007; it will not be compatible with earlier versions of Word Software. This uses a file format called '.docx'.

- Word template – we will deal with this later.
- Word 97–2003 – this format will be fully compatible with earlier versions of the Word software. Use this if you are working between computers and one of them has the earlier software. This uses a file format called '.doc'.
- Ignore the last two formats for now.

4 Check the detail in the 'Save in' box to ensure the document is being saved where you want it.

5 Add a file name and then press **Save**.

(You can add 'Save As' to the quick access toolbar, but because it is not used very frequently you may want to ensure you have the 'Save' icon but not the 'Save As' icon.)

Once you have saved the document using 'Save As' you should frequently save the document using either the save command on the quick access toolbar or the keyboard shortcut Ctrl+S. Try to save every five to ten minutes and always press Ctrl+S when you go away from your computer.

AUTORECOVER

As you work with computers, occasionally things will go wrong. The computer might lose power, the software may stop responding, you may have equipment failure or someone may just turn off your computer. If you set Word options to AutoRecover you will have some protection when things go wrong. To set AutoRecover:

1 Press the **Office Button**.

2 Press **Word Options** – at the bottom of the task pane.

3 In the left pane click **Save**.

4 **Tick the AutoRecover box** and then set it to **5 minutes**.

5 Check out and adjust where the AutoRecover will save the file.

6 Then press **OK**.

After a problem the AutoRecover task pane will appear and you can select the document you wish to recover.

14.3 FURTHER WORD SKILLS

USING TEMPLATES

Templates are prepared Word documents that contain text, styles and formatting. These mean you can create a professional look quickly and easily. At work many organisations use a set of corporate templates for business communication. Creating an organisational brand and a brand image involves creating a suite of professional and effective documents for communication. At university these templates can be useful. But do beware that while tutors like professional-looking documents, your assessments are evaluated mostly by what they contain. Style is not a substitute for content. But effective professional styles make excellent content look even better.

Letter template

So let's create a letter. You have probably done this before but we will start by using a template. It is worth noting that a lot of the Microsoft templates have an American approach.

To open a template:

1 Press the **Office Button**.
2 Click **New**.
3 In the left-hand pane select **Installed templates**.
4 Then select **Employment**.
5 Then select **Oriel Letter**.
6 Then click the **Create** button.

(It is possible that this template will not be available to you; if so, just choose any basic letter template.)

You should now have a Word document that contains some text, some visual elements and some detail insertion points. Now add the details you need to create the letter: pick the date, add recipient's details, a salutation greeting and address and the letter is complete. You can also add more information to the right-hand side. Remember to save the letter before you close it.

This particular letter template would not be suitable for UK-based organisations. The expected layout for organisational letters is more formal and would need to contain the type of style and structure in the following example.

Assignment template

Let's try to find something a bit more exciting and useful:

1 Press the **Office Button**.
2 Click **New**.
3 Type in the search box '**school report**', then **Enter**.
4 Find School Report (Butterfly Design).
5 **Select it** and then **Download**.

I am not suggesting that you complete and submit your university assignments in this template. I just want something that shows the possibilities of templates better. Let's see what we have:

EXAMPLE: FORMAL LETTER STRUCTURE

Tom Sawyer
16 Just Street
Neverland
NV13 6JS
7th August 2009

Mr David Simple
Noble & Noble
Pension Road
London
W14 5SX

Dear Mr Simple,

I am writing to request a meeting to review my salary. My responsibilities have grown significantly since I joined the company 18 months ago, and I believe that this fact and the quality of my work warrant a pay rise.

As a new employee, my responsibilities included completing individual tasks associated with the Zeeborg Works account under your supervision. For the last six months I have managed several aspects of the account and have supervised other team members working on those tasks.

I have also implemented new procedures for managing and scheduling resources that have saved more than 500 employee hours. These changes allowed for the completion of Milestone 1.231 ahead of schedule and saved the company nearly £15,000 in contractor salaries.

In addition to these significant contributions, I have greatly improved my technical knowledge and the skills critical to my work.

Based on the feedback that I have received, I believe that you and your manager have been pleased with my work. I hope that you will give my request serious consideration.

I look forward to hearing from you.

Yours sincerely,

Tom Sawyer
Mr

- Cover page is a large, colourful picture – click into it and you can change aspects of it.
- There are text placeholders for document title, student name, class name and teacher's name.
- On page 2 – there is a table of contents, a page border and a page number.
- On page 3 – we have the use of headings, more art, smart art and the use of styles.
- Page 4 – more text and pictures.
- Page 5 – contains the bibliography.

HOW CAN I USE THESE IDEAS TO IMPROVE MY ASSIGNMENTS?

Take another look at the Butterfly School Report and reflect on how the ideas and concepts could be used to improve your own assignment presentation.

Think about...

1 Do pictures and artwork add to the substance of my work?

2 Should I use headings, styles and themes?

3 Should I structure my work in sections and have an index?

4 Do I need a striking cover page?

5 How will I produce a bibliography for my work?

6 What other insertion elements might I need in assignments?

MAKING A TEMPLATE FOR A UNIVERSITY ASSIGNMENT

We have considered an American-style assignment template. Let's now develop a well-structured and effective assignment template for a UK university. This should save you time by being available for a number of assignments. We need to know a bit more about some of the features of Word 2007 in order to achieve this task. These next sections will look at templates, styles and themes.

Templates

Templates start out life as Word documents. It is not obvious, but all Word documents are templates. When you open a new document, it is a template that has very little formatting. The pre-existing templates available in Word use styles, themes, formatting, page layouts and some pictures to create a document built for a specific purpose. The Microsoft designers have given a lot of thought to the colour and visual combinations that will make a striking and effective document.

There are many good examples of templates available from online sources. The first place to search for a template is the Microsoft website. Google 'Microsoft Templates' and you can quickly find the site – it is then worth bookmarking the page. Find some interesting templates and download them to your computer – file the instructions that appear on screen.

Opening a template:

1 Click the **Office Button**.

2 Then **Open**.

3 In the left-hand pane click **Trusted Templates**.

4 Select a template and then double-click to open, or **Open** at the bottom of the pane.

So it is as easy as that to use existing templates.

Create a template:

Start with a blank new document and add all the features you want to the document. It is important to ensure that all text, paragraphs and borders are formatted. Any pictures, graphics or other items must also be consistently formatted. Remember that a template is just a set of formatting; if you do not format some aspects of the document they will not be controlled.

Then to save the template:

1 Press the **Office Button**.
2 **Save As** then click **Word Template**.
3 Give the template a memorable name.
4 Then **Save**.

What we have done covers the basic mechanics of creating and saving a template. We need to know about some other elements of Word to create really impressive templates that stand out from the average Word document.

Styles

A style is simply a set of formatting settings saved with a distinct name. Using styles makes your document more consistent and often clearer. Let's try adding a style:

Type in some basic text – about two or three lines will be fine.

1 **Highlight** the text you want to style.
2 **Home** tab.
3 Select a style from the styles grouping; scroll down for more styles. It will be styles at the click of the mouse.

You can change any style to exactly match your workplace or university formatting instructions.

1 **Home** tab.
2 Styles group.
3 Right-click the style you want to change, then **Modify**.

The pane then allows you to set name, style following the paragraph, line spacing, indents, distance between paragraphs, text alignment and text size and colour. As you modify these settings, the preview panel will display the settings you have made.

There are two radio buttons at the bottom of the pane:

- Add to quick style list.
- Only in this document or new document based on this template.

Select these as you desire.

There are further formatting options under the **Format** button.

Then click **OK** to finish.

There are only a limited range of styles on the default menu, so you may quickly want to change some or create new ones. Keep the text you typed earlier for testing out changes and new styles. The styles you used above are just the default ones; there are quite a few other style sets.

To change a style set:

1 **Home** tab.

2 Styles group (on the far right of the group).

3 **Change Styles** then **Style Set** – choose one from the list (try out quite a few to see the differences).

Note: If you hold the cursor over any style set it will preview in your document.

Note: Once the style set is changed, the styles gallery shows the new styles ready for you to select.

At university you will have to print and submit your documents for assessment, so styles based on black and white will be best; colour printing is costly and unnecessary. If, however, you are submitting your assignment digitally, then the colour styles may be useful. Your university may well have formatting requirements for assignments and dissertations, so you will need to use these as a guide to the styles to use.

As a minimum, you should create styles for:

- Normal text or body text – Arial 11 point
- Title – Arial 26 point, centre aligned, underlined, followed by normal paragraph
- Subtitle – Arial 18 point, centre aligned, followed by normal paragraph
- Heading 1 – Arial 14 point, Bold, left align, followed by normal
- Heading 2 – Arial 12 point, Bold, left align, followed by normal
- Heading 3 – Arial 11 point, Bold, left align, followed by normal

Using the Format drop-down menu you can set:

- tabs
- border
- frame
- language
- numbering
- shortcut keys.

Themes

Themes are used to create professional and consistent-looking documents. Themes consist of text colours and background colours, accents like shadows and fills, and hyperlink colours. They would normally apply to the whole document. Let's try it out:

Make sure you have a document with a range of style elements, such as title, heading 1, heading 2, bullets, normal text.

1 **Page Layout** tab.

2 **Themes**, then select a theme (as you point to a theme it will preview in your document).

3 Select the theme you want.

You select fonts using the fonts drop-down arrow.

In this section you have covered templates, styles and themes; by combining these ideas and with a little time and imagination, from you, it will be possible to create some useful and great-looking templates.

14.4 ACADEMIC-RELATED WORD SKILLS

REFERENCES AND BIBLIOGRAPHY

In writing assignments you are creating an academic argument. Your argument will need extensive support from the work of other authors. Managing these sources can be difficult but Word can help in this respect. To create references and a bibliography in your assignments, you need to use the citation and bibliography commands. Once you are familiar with how this works, you will be amazed at how easy it is to keep track of your references.

To create a reference and bibliography:

1 At the point where you want to add the reference.

2 On the **References** tab.

3 Click the reference style that you want choose – use **GOST – Name Sort**.

4 Click **Insert Citation** button.

5 Click the **Add New Source** button.

6 In the new task pane that appears, choose Type of Source – **Book**.

7 Add the author name, title, year, city (place of publication), publisher, volume (if any).

8 Click **OK**.

Figure 14.6 Word 'create source' box

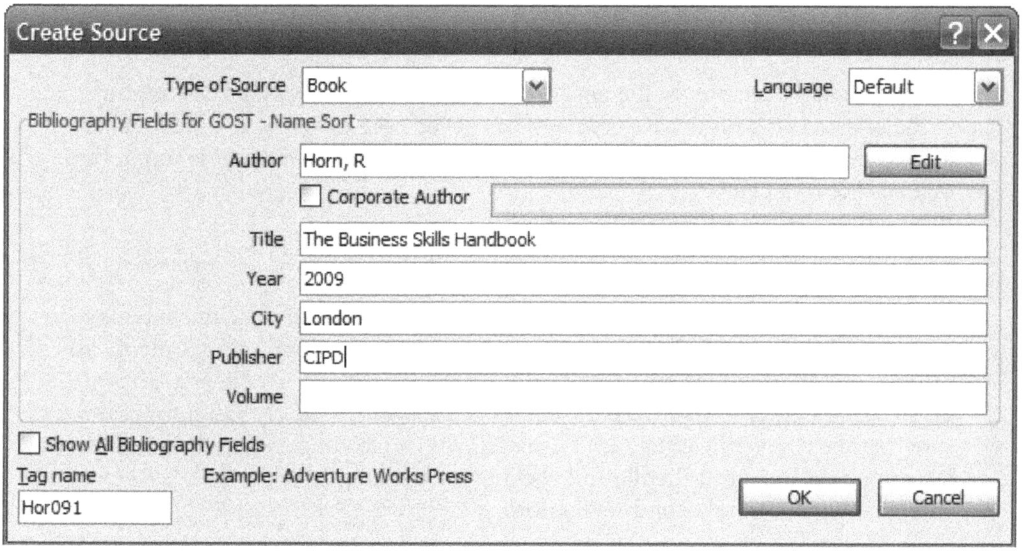

A reference will be entered at the text insertion point. A note of warning: GOST – Name Sort is as close as Microsoft can get to Harvard referencing, and you do need to change the style when you insert the bibliography. It does not, however, conform to the British Standard for referencing using the Harvard format. Most universities will accept that the system is sound and accurate if not totally correct, but do check with your tutor.

It is quicker to add a reference or citation by using the access key shortcuts **Alt, S, C, S. Note: shortcuts are quick and accurate and mean that you do not have to take your fingers off the keyboard.**

Once you have entered a citation or reference it will be available to use again from a list of citations once you press the **Insert Citation** command.

When your assignment, project or dissertation is written, it is easy to add the bibliography at the end:

1 **References** tab.
2 Change the style to **APA**.
3 Click **Bibliography**.
4 Insert **Bibliography**.

Your bibliography is added at the insertion point in the correct alphabetical order. If you make a mistake in a reference or just want to add more and then build a new bibliography, just delete the old one and insert it again. There is one added advantage to this method. You can make your references or selected references in one document available in another document. This saves a lot of time and stress. To do this:

1 Click the **References** tab.
2 Click **Manage Sources**.

3 In the Master List pane copy the references you want into the Current List pane.

4 Click **Close**.

When you add a citation in the new document the copied citations will appear in the selected citation list. Referencing has never been easier. If you are looking for just one or two sources in a long list, there is a search facility at the top of the Manage Sources pane.

TABLE OF CONTENTS

Longer academic documents such as dissertations will need a table of contents to make navigation easier. This can be done automatically in Word. The contents list is based on the use of the Heading 1 style and the second-level entries are based on Heading 2 entries. To ensure the contents list works properly you must make sure that the chapter headings are formatted with a Heading 1 style. This is done by placing the cursor in the tile and clicking on Heading 1 for the first-level entry and Heading 2 for the second-level entry.

To create the table of contents, place the insertion point where you want the list, then:

1 Click the **References** tab.

2 Then **Table of Contents**.

3 Choose the required style.

The table of contents will appear at the insertion point. You can update the table of contents at any point by the update table button on the References tab.

INDEX

Longer academic documents and many larger business documents must have an index. Indexing is a skilled and time-consuming activity, but Word can help manage and create an index. The first phase is to mark each of the index entries in the text. You can mark individual words, phrases or whole sections and chapters.

Mark individual word entries by:

1 Go to **References** tab.

2 Click **Mark Entry**.

3 The main entry can be changed and a sub-entry added.

4 The page number format can also be changed.

5 Then click **Mark**.

Carry on marking all the index entries you want.

To create multiple-page entries, do the following:

1. Select the text that is to form the index entry.
2. Go to **Insert** tab.
3. Click **Bookmark**.
4. Enter a name and then click **Add**.
5. Place the cursor at the end of the text that has just been marked.
6. Go to **References** tab.
7. Click the **Mark Entry** button.
8. Add a name for the entry.
9. Click the radio button **Page range** and select the bookmark you have just entered.
10. Click **Mark**.

Carry on in this manner until all the index entries have been marked.

TO CREATE THE INDEX

1. Place the cursor at the point of insertion.
2. Go to **References** tab.
3. Click **Insert Index**.
4. Choose the format of the index and the number of columns and any of the other options.
5. Click **OK**.

Your index is entered into the document. If you need to add more entries, delete the existing index then mark the additional index points and then insert the index again.

14.5 BUSINESS-RELATED WORD SKILLS

MAIL MERGE

Mail merge is a process that merges a standard letter (or any other document) with a list of data to personalise it. Using this method it can appear to the recipient as if the letter has been sent to them alone. This technique is used extensively in business for communications, marketing and sending specific data. It would then become a simple matter to send out bulk letters addressed to individuals and to their correct addresses. Your tutors could send you individual feedback that relates to just the issues or problems you had experienced with an assignment or examination.

The mail merge function needs two documents: first, a form letter that contains the text you want to send; second, a data document that contains all the specific information relating to the individual. The form letter contains the detail of the document and also the **merge fields** for the personal information. The data document contains the information that goes into the merge field.

For example, imagine you are inviting friends to a wedding that has two separate parts: an informal drinks and canapés part, and a formal dinner. Not all guests will be going to the same parts; let's say that 100 guests have been invited and 36 will be attending the formal dinner. You want to send a personal note to each one.

The form letter would look something like this:

Dear <name>,

I would be really pleased if you would come to the wedding of my daughter on Thursday, 15 July 2010 at 2:30pm at Cliveden House in Buckinghamshire. We will be having a <eventtype> at <time> in <place>.

I look forward to seeing you there.

RSVP.

The data table would contain a list of guests and what event they had been invited to:

name	eventtype	time	place
Katie	formal dinner	7pm	Waldo's Restaurant
Ross	informal drinks party	4pm	The Terrace Restaurant
Simon	formal dinner	7pm	Waldo's Restaurant
Louise	informal drinks party	4pm	The Terrace Restaurant
Glenys	formal dinner	7pm	Waldo's Restaurant

When the letters are printed they will substitute the merge field for the personal details contained in the data table.

So the first two letters will look like this:

Dear Katie,

I would be really pleased if you would come to the wedding of my daughter on Thursday, 15 July 2010 at 2:30pm at Cliveden House in Buckinghamshire. We will be having a formal dinner at 7pm in Waldo's Restaurant.

I look forward to seeing you there.

RSVP.

Dear Ross,

I would be really pleased if you would come to the wedding of my daughter on Thursday, 15 July 2010 at 2:30pm at Cliveden House in Buckinghamshire. We will be having an informal drinks party at 4pm in the Terrace Restaurant.

I look forward to seeing you there.

RSVP.

As you can see from my example, mail merge is not just a way to add someone's name and address to a letter. It is a very effective way to control elements of your business or social life. If you are sending out marketing information, you can make comments about products the customer has already purchased.

So a letter could go out saying something like:

Dear Joanne,

I hope you like the blue floral dress you purchased for your aunt's wedding. Frocks r Us has a limited sale on similar items at the moment…

Employers will expect you to be able to operate this powerful business tool with little or no supervision.

Let's look at how it is done in practice using the Mail Merge Wizard:

1 **Mailings** tab.
2 **Start Mail Merge**, select the type of document (letters in this case).
3 Then click **Step by Step Mail Merge Wizard**.
4 At the bottom of the right-hand pane, click **Next: Starting document**.
5 Choose radio button **Use the current document,** then **Next** at the bottom.
6 Radio button, **Type a new list**.
7 Then click the symbol below **Create**.
8 Type in the detail of four or five recipients, then **OK**.
9 **Save As** this new file, name it something like 'Data for form letter'.
10 Then **Save**.
11 When the recipients list shows, unclick the radio button; tick if you don't want any particular person to receive the letter.
12 Then **OK**.
13 You are on stage 3 or 6, click **Next**.
14 Complete the detail of your letter.
15 Add the detailed data showing in the right-hand pane by placing the cursor in the letter at your chosen spot and then clicking one of the details to add. Repeat this step, adding all the details.
16 In our example you only need to add 'Greeting line' and 'Address line'.

Note: When you add the data detail, Word inserts <<Greeting line>> or <<Address Line>>.

17 Then click Next.

18 In this stage you can preview the letters using the << or >> arrow keys.

When you are happy that they are correct:

19 Click **Complete the merge** and choose either **Print** or **Edit**.

Print does just this and prints out the letters. Edit merges the data into one large letter – each letter is a page – in a new Word document that you can individually edit before printing.

There are many options in terms of the form outputs and the data sources.

Outputs:

- letters
- email messages
- envelopes
- labels
- directory – a single catalogue of details.

Data sources:

- database
- spreadsheet
- Word table
- Outlook contacts.

PUBLISHING DOCUMENTS ON THE WEB

Webpages are based on a simple coding language called Hypertext Markup Language (HTML). Word can help you create these pages by adding various web elements and saving the document in HTML format. If you have created a Word document and wish to publish it as a webpage, you can do the following:

1 **Office Button**.

2 **Save As**, then **Word Document**.

3 In this pane change the Save as type box (drop-down towards the bottom) to **Web Page**.

4 A new box appears on the pane called '**Change Title**'; use this to change the title of the webpage – this is what will appear at the top of the webpage – then **OK**.

5 Select the location of the save in the top drop-down box.

6 Then **Save**.

An alternative format is to change the Save As type to Single file webpage. This saves all the webpage information in one page using the format MHTML. This binds all the graphic and text elements into one file.

BLOGS

A blog is a website that provides a personal or organisational journal site where people can post thoughts and actions. The word blog is derived from a shortened version of 'weblog'. Business and student blogs are becoming ever more popular. If you want to start blogging you will need to register an account with one of the many free services:

- Wordpress
- Typepad
- Blogger
- Yahoo 360
- Windows Live Spaces
- Vox
- Squarespace.

Once you have set up an account with a blog service, you will need to tell the Word software about it by registering it.

Create a blog posting by:

1 **Office** then **New**.
2 Under the listing blank and recent click **New blog post**.
3 Then **Create**.
4 Either Register now or Register later if there are no accounts registered.
5 Add a title in the placeholder.

Note: the conditional tab of Word 2007 is now headed Blog Post.

You can now write the blog and on the Insert tab add elements to the page, such as:

- pictures
- clip art
- shapes
- smart art
- charts
- hyperlinks
- tables.

Then, when you have completed the post, click on **Blog Post** tab, **Publish**.

14.6 USING WORD IN TEAMS

There are times at work when more than one person needs to contribute and work on a Word document. This joint working on one document is becoming more common in universities where you might send your draft work to one of your tutors and it will be returned with comments added. When more than one person is working on and contributing to a Word document, it becomes crucial to track and approve changes carefully. Multiple users of a document can also bring problems with identifying which version of the document is the current version. You may find similar problems when you work together as a student group.

INSERTING COMMENTS

It is useful for other people when they read your documents to be able to add comments at exact positions in the text. You can then review these comments and make changes or review them and then delete them.

TO ADD A COMMENT TO A DOCUMENT

1 Click on the **Review** tab.

2 Then click **New Comment**.

3 Type your comment in the balloon that appears.

4 Click outside the balloon when you have finished.

TO RESPOND TO A COMMENT

1 Click the **balloon** of the first comment.

2 Click the **Review** tab.

3 Then **New Comment**.

You will notice from the illustration that the new comment about the first comment is added as code R1 – meaning revision 1 of that comment. In this way you can keep track of the comments made about comments.

In this way you can read a document and add comments about the content or formatting that the author of the document can then review and make changes.

The comments can be formatted in balloons or as comments in a reviewing pane. The illustration below shows both formats at once. In practice this is not normally needed because one version will be sufficient.

When you save the document, the comments will be saved. The document can then be sent back to the author.

A note about naming files after revision. When a document is sent to which you add comments, you need to rename it before sending it back to the author. If you do not do this the author will be sent an amended file with the same name as the original document and this draft version may overwrite the original with some loss of content. When you are transferring documents with comments added, save the file as: [The original name] RGH comments added.

Figure 14.7 Inserting comments in Word

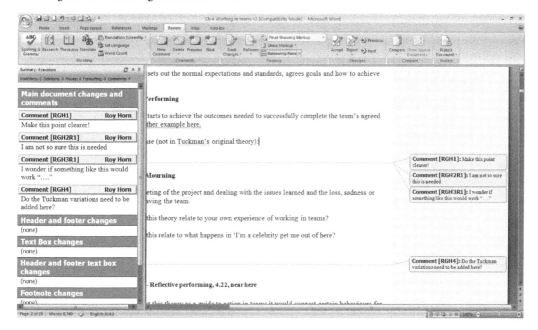

READING COMMENTS

In some documents you will not be able to immediately see the comments, so you will need to:

1 Click the **Review** tab.

2 Then **Show Markup**.

3 Then **Comments**.

4 Use the previous or next buttons to navigate between comments.

When you have reviewed and acted on all the comments in the document, you will need to delete them.

DELETE COMMENTS

1 Click on the **Review** tab.

2 **Show Markup** button.

3 **Reviewers** (at the bottom) [choose all or an individual].

4 Then **Delete** button.

5 Confirm all of individual.

TRACK CHANGES

Another useful option when more than one person is working on a document is to track any changes that are made. Once 'track changes' is turned on it will highlight the changes in different colours and add balloons to the side of the document. You can then review all the changes, accepting and rejecting them.

To track changes

1 Click on the **Review** tab.

2 **Track Changes**.

3 Then **Track Changes** (this will turn on track changes).

Reviewing changes

1 Click on the **Review** tab.

2 **Next** and **Previous** buttons to navigate.

3 Then **Accept** or **Reject** each of the changes.

SENDING A DOCUMENT BY EMAIL

If you have an email account set up on your computer, you can send a document to someone else directly from the Word program.

STRUCTURE AND STYLE

CASE STUDY

Geeta had been set a really unusual assignment and she was not at all sure how to proceed.

The assignment brief indicated that training was an important aspect of being an HR professional and that the assignment was devised to provide experience of designing and delivering training. The outcome was to be a 20-minute training event where some learning took place. The design of the training must include a way of determining if any learning had taken place. The group would evaluate the training event and this group evaluation would form 60% of the grade awarded. A report must also be submitted setting out how the learning method was chosen and a justification of why this would be successful (40%).

To think about...

- What is learning?

- How will you determine if any learning has taken place?

- Because the group marks the training event, what special arrangements will you need to make in preparing the training?

- How will you structure the report? Set your structure out in a Word document in outline mode.

- Ensure the report uses as many features of Word as you can practically add:

  - styles

  - themes

  - tables

  - insert pictures / clipart

  - contents list

  - index

  - full referencing and bibliography.

SUMMARY

Word 2007 is becoming the default version of Word you are likely to encounter at university and at work. It has many improved features and will greatly help you to survive at university.

- Learn the basics of Word 2007; many of these features will save time and stress:
  - opening Word and specific documents in an efficient manner
  - customise the quick access menu with items you use frequently
  - learn to save documents in different formats if some of your computers use Word 2003 or earlier
  - become familiar with the ribbon commands
  - use keyboard shortcuts
  - use the help command when you get stuck
  - set the options in AutoRecovery.

- Use templates, styles and themes to create terrific-looking documents.

- Develop academic and work-related skills:
  - create references and a bibliography
  - create a table of contents
  - create an index
  - learn how to mail merge
  - learn how to publish documents on the web or blogs.

- Learn the skills of working on documents in teams:
  - inserting comments
  - tracking changes
  - sending documents directly from Word using email.

EXPLORE FURTHER

FURTHER READING

Basham, S. (2007) *Word 2007 in Easy Steps*. Southam, Warwickshire: Computer Step.

Gookin, D. (2006) *Word 2007 for Dummies*. New York: John Wiley and Sons Ltd.

Matthews, M. (2007) *Microsoft Office Word 2007 Quicksteps*. Maidenhead: McGraw-Hill Education – Europe.

WEB LINKS

Microsoft Office – Education for £35: http://www.software4students. co.uk/?gclid=Clizr_rUoJsCFZkA4wodVHg6Jg

Word 2007 site: http://office.microsoft.com/en-gb/word/FX100487981033.aspx

CHAPTER 15

Being Effective with Spreadsheets

What skills will I develop in this chapter?

- the basic use of Excel
- being effective with the quick toolbar
- entering data and formula
- formatting numbers and text
- using tables and conditional formatting
- entering data and creating business outputs
- creating and using pivot tables
- sorting and filtering
- research analysis using Excel
- creating visual outputs
- validating data input
- using data forms
- statistical measures in Excel

A note about computer instructions: Where there are instructions that should be followed, they will be presented in **bold type**. So to carry out the actions required, simply follow the words that are **emboldened**.

15.1 INTRODUCTION

The main processes of business involve organising, accounting and monitoring things. Many of these processes will be carried out using a spreadsheet. As with earlier chapters, I will focus on Microsoft software; the spreadsheet software is Excel™ . The Office 2007 version of Excel, as with Word 2007, looks very different from earlier versions. This will mean that at first you will find the new interface slower, but as you become familiar with it the increased functionality will become apparent. On your first day at work, your new employer will assume that you can use Excel to carry out the professional processes of their business.

An extensive working knowledge of the software is vital. When you attend interviews and graduate centres, you may find that some of the selection tasks involve Word or Excel.

If you are new to spreadsheets, I would advise that you work systematically through the chapter. If you have some experience, you can start your reading in the middle of the chapter.

15.2 BASIC EXCEL SKILLS

STARTING EXCEL

Excel can be started in several different ways. As this is a program you are likely to use every day at work, it will be useful to understand the benefits of using the different methods. Let's start with the basic method.

Excel in the ordinary way:

Opening Excel

1 Click the **Start** button on the taskbar.

2 Then point to **All Programs**.

3 Click **Microsoft Office**.

4 Click **Microsoft Office Excel 2007**.

You will now have Excel 2007 open in full screen. Note: it does look very different from earlier versions.

Figure 15.1 Excel main window

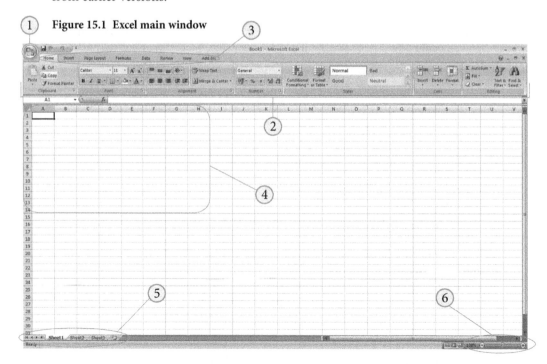

The main Excel window contains the following elements:

1 This is the Office button. It looks like a logo but it is a command button. Click this for the main commands: new, open, save, save as, print, close. You will also see a list of recent documents; you can use this to open a document. The Excel exit button is in the bottom right-hand corner of this box.

2 This is the **ribbon** and is the main new feature of Excel 2007. It contains the main commands set in groups that you will need. In this example you can see commands for (left to right on the ribbon):

- paste, cut, copy, format painter – grouped as **Clipboard** (the group name is at the bottom)
- font, font size, font format, borders, cell fill colour, font colour – grouped as **Font**
- cell alignment, text alignment, text orientation, indent size, text wrapping, cell merge – grouped as **Alignment**
- number formats – grouped as **Number**.

There are further groups to the right for:

- **Styles**
- **Cells**
- **Editing**.

You may have noticed a small 'x' in the right-hand corner of the group name box. If you click on this you will get a full range of options for this grouping.

3 You may not have noticed these tabs (like the dividers in a ring binder); they give access to other commands. The page is currently on **Home** with the most frequently used commands listed above. The other tabs are called:

- Insert – for tables, pictures, graphs links and Word Art
- Page Layout – for themes, page setup and sheet options
- Formulas – for access to formulas and calculations
- Data – for finding and opening data, filtering, sorting and grouping
- Review – for spelling, research, thesaurus, comments and workbook protection
- View – for page layout, zoom, split screens and macros
- Add-ins – for any extra tools you have downloaded.

4 This is the main spreadsheet window and work area. It consists of cells arranged in rows and columns. The rows are numbered and run horizontally and the columns are labelled with letters and run vertically. This is the area where you enter text, data or formulae.

5 Excel workbooks contain by default three worksheets. You can arrange your work more easily and clearly by separating out the important parts on different worksheets. For instance, if you were keeping all your banking transactions

in a spreadsheet you might have a different worksheet for each bank account: current account, savings account, rent account. You can add a new worksheet by clicking on the small icon to the right of the last sheet.

6 This is the zoom control. You will need to increase the size of the view to see the fine detail and decrease the zoom to see the overall layout.

You will find that opening Excel from the program files is a tedious method, and a better way is to use a desktop icon that is simply double-clicked to start the program.

Creating a desktop icon to open Excel

1 Click the **Start** button on the taskbar – at the bottom of the screen.

2 Then point to **All Programs**.

3 Click **Microsoft Office**.

4 Right-click **Microsoft Office Excel 2007**.

5 Point to **Send To** and then click **Desktop (Create Short cut)**.

You will now have a desktop icon that will start Word immediately with one double-click.

There is one other useful way to start a specific document in Excel.

Open an Excel document from Windows Explorer

1 Right-click the **Start** button on the taskbar and then click **Explore All Users**.

2 In the pane find and click on **My Documents**.

3 Find the file that contains the document you want to open.

4 Double-click the **required document file** and it will open Excel with the document in the main pane.

Figure 15.2 Excel quick access toolbar

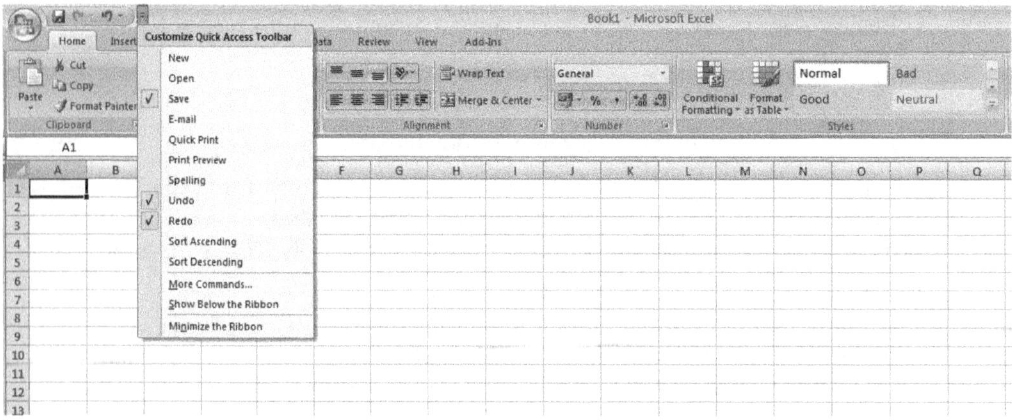

Quick access toolbar

1 You may not have noticed the very small toolbar at the top of the main window. This is the quick access toolbar and contains commands you are likely to use frequently. Spending some time setting this up will greatly increase your productivity. When you first start Excel it will probably contain three small icons: first is the save icon, second is the undo icon, and third is the redo icon. These are useful but may not be the commands you most frequently use.

2 The toolbar is customisable; if you click the small down arrow to the right of the toolbar this command screen will appear. Simply tick the commands you want on the quick access toolbar.

3 This is the more commands button and will give you access to all of the Excel commands.

My preference for the commands I include on this toolbar are, in order: open file; undo; redo; save; new; and close.

PRACTICAL TASK: STARTING TO USE EXCEL

This is a practical task to allow you to get started using Excel for something useful. Keeping track of your finances can be done in several ways, but this exercise will focus on the income and spending in your main bank account. It will allow me to illustrate many of the basic skills required to operate with Excel.

You should be able to open the software now and you will have a blank spreadsheet to work in.

Adding basic titles and headings

First, we need a title, so position the cursor in cell A1 – then just start typing.

I'll title my sheet 'Current account'. The title is too small, so in the font box on the ribbon change the font from Calibri to something else; I have used 'Times New Roman' and the size to '36'.

Note – a new feature of Excel 2007 – as you started to select a new font type and size, this was previewed. You may have missed it, so try it again.

We will need some column headings and we will add these to row 3 in columns A, B, C, D, E and F. I have used 'Date', 'Item Detail', 'Trans No.', 'Item £', 'Balance £' and 'Notes'. It is important to use gaps and spaces in a spreadsheet to aid readability, so that is why I have not used row 2. Now we have the column titles but they are too small and the columns have cut off some of the writing.

You know how to change the font and the font size, so do that now. Place the cursor in A3 and drag the box that forms across all the cells; this will highlight them. Now, when you change the font it will change in all the cells. I have used Times New Roman 14 point and bold. You will note that this looks a bit of a mess with the words cut off.

First, look in column E and note that 'Balance £' is cut off. Follow the right-hand gridline of that column upwards until it meets the column labels, in this case E. Place the cursor over the right-hand column line and double-click. The column will automatically adjust to allow the whole word to be seen. This double-click command auto-resizes the column to fit the largest item. We could do this to all the columns but we can guess that many of the details in the subsequent rows will be longer than the heading. We have the whole sheet to display this bank data, so let's spread things out a bit manually. We do this by single-clicking into the right-hand side of a column and dragging it to the size we want. I have set mine to these sizes:

- column A – 10.29 or 77 pixels
- column B – 50.29 or 357 pixels
- column C – 14.86 or 109 pixels
- column D – 10.43 or 78 pixels
- column E – 10.43 or 78 pixels
- column F – 48.00 or 341 pixels.

Having the pixels size indicated is new to Excel 2007.

There is still a problem with column E because it is cut off. But this is how I want it to be, so let's adjust it a bit more to improve the way it looks. Highlight the cell E3; it has 'Balance £' in it. On the **Alignment** group on the **Home** tab of the ribbon, click **Wrap Text** button. The '£' sign will have dropped down but will still be in the same cell. To improve this further, click the centre button on the same Alignment group. We now have the word 'Balance' with the '£' sign below it and both items centred in the cell. To achieve the same thing on 'Item £', you wrap text and align centre, but you will need to add some spaces in the gap between 'Item' and '£'. Now we have the money columns D and E set up on centre alignment and the text columns set up on left alignment.

We can make these headings stand out more if we put a border around them. Highlight cells A3 to F3 and then on the font group click the small down arrow on the border symbol; it is in the middle on the lower half. When the menu opens, click **All Borders**. Click the menu open again and click on **Line Style** (towards the bottom) and click on the first double-line border, then **All Borders** again. The headings now stand out from the page. Notice that now the symbol for borders in the font group has changed to All Borders. Highlight any cells now and click this symbol and the same border will be applied.

Saving

We have now done enough work to require that we save the workbook. When you first save a new workbook, you will need to use the 'save as' command. Click the **Office** command logo and from that menu choose **Save As**. You will be offered six possible formats; choose the first one, **Excel Workbook**; choose a file name and browse to a suitable file location, then click **OK**. If some of the computers you use do not have Excel 2007 or a compatibility pack, then choose the Excel 97–2003 Workbook. This loses some features but will be compatible with older software.

From this point onwards you can save the changes you have made by clicking save in the quick access toolbar.

All Office software has keyboard shortcuts that save time and, importantly, save you from removing your hands from the keyboard and using the mouse. For instance, you can save your work by holding down the control key (bottom left on most keyboards and marked with 'Ctrl') and pressing 'S' at the same time. This is normally shown as Ctrl+S. You should save your work every five to six minutes and always get in the habit of hitting Ctrl+S when you get up from your computer.

TOP TIP – There are keyboard shortcuts for many of the main commands in Office software. Six really useful ones are:

- Ctrl+C = Copy
- Ctrl+X = Cut
- Ctrl+V = Paste
- Ctrl+B = Bold
- Ctrl+U = Underline
- Ctrl+I = Italics.

If you want to know if a command has a keyboard shortcut, the easiest way to find out is to hover the mouse over the command and a small window will provide detail of the shortcut. Operating speedily at work requires that you know most of the keyboard shortcuts. It is far quicker and easier than having to stop and use the mouse.

Adding some detail and a little maths

Now we need to add some detail to our bank worksheet and ensure that it functions correctly mathematically.

First line of detail – use cell A5 and enter today's date. Then:

- B5: Opening Balance
- C5: OB
- D5: 1200 (do not add a £ at the front – just the number)
- E5: 1200
- F5: Opening Balance confirmed with the bank on 26 May 2009.

Note the F5 detail is too large, so reset the column width.

In many cells Excel will arrange the formatting of the cell depending on what you type into it. This works quite well but will sometimes need your intervention. Take a look at cells D5 and E5; they show 1200. This is correct but because this is a cell that can only have pound and pence represented in it, we should format it so that it is accurate and consistent.

Highlight the two cells D5 and E5 and in the number grouping select **Number** from the dropdown menu. You will then see that the 1200 changes to 1200.00; this is 1200 to two decimal places. You might have been tempted to click on currency and this would have worked just as well, but every number is prefixed by a £ sign. In detailed spreadsheets this soon becomes a nuisance. If you want to change the number of decimal places shown, use the two small symbols below the number format box to increase or decrease it. But we want to have two decimal places. We also need to centre the number in the cell, so in **Alignment** click centre.

Now at this stage you might want to add your own personal bank detail into this first row. Then add about ten more items into the detailed section. Remember to use a minus sign in front of negative numbers (costs or spending). Income will be a positive number; there is no need to add a sign to these as Excel will assume it is positive.

Use the arrow keys to move between cells as you add detail. You will quickly become annoyed at having to use the arrows to get back to the beginning of a row – this can be achieved more easily by using the 'Home' key. There are many quick ways to navigate around a spreadsheet; here are a few:

- Home – returns to the left-hand side of the spreadsheet in the same row
- Ctrl+Home – returns to A1 cell
- Ctrl+End – goes to the right-hand side of the last used row in the spreadsheet
- Ctrl+Page Up or Down – scrolls though the worksheets.

While we are thinking about worksheets, ours is still called Sheet 1. You can change it to something more meaningful by right-clicking on the name, then **Rename**, then type in the new name; in my case 'Current Account'.

Figure 15.3 Excel current account

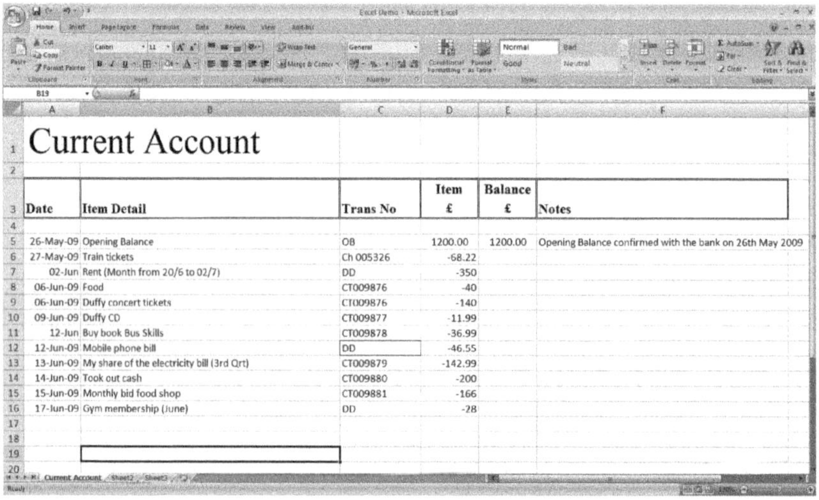

Our current account spreadsheet still has a few problems. We can sort out the formatting problem in 1 by doing the following:

Highlight D5 and E5 and open the number menu using the small cross in the bottom right corner. Then **tick** 'Use 1000 separator', then **OK**.

Make sure cells D5 and E5 are still highlighted and click **Format Painter** on the Clipboard group. Highlight the cells D6 and D7 down to D26 and E26. The number format in the first two cells will now be copied to all the money cells in the column down to row 26 (this allows for more entries to be made with the correct formatting).

Let's turn our attention to using a simple formula to keep a running balance in cells E6 down to E16. To calculate the balance left after each transaction, we need to start with the opening balance E5 (1200) and deduct the next transaction; this is in cell D6 (remembering that cell D6 is –68.22).

So we need to enter this formula in cell E6: '=E5+D6' – click the green tick when this is done. Now you should have 1,131.78 in cell E6. By default Excel shows the result of the calculation in the cell. But look at the formula bar just above the column headings and you will see the formula '=E5+D6'.

We will need this calculation in all of the E column cells: highlight cell E6, then **Copy**, highlight the cells E7 to E26 and then **Paste**. The balance in your current account will be shown as each transaction is made. Note: if you click on cell E16 you will see in the formula bar '=E15+D16', that is, the formula has been changed in each cell to make the correct calculation for each cell. This is called 'relative addressing' – the formulae are changed relative to the position on the worksheet.

You can carry on adding transactions and the balance will be calculated until cell E26 – the last cell we copied to.

Add one extra transaction, which is your wages being paid into the account. This will be a positive number, so just enter the number. That will remove the overdraft figure in cells E15 and E16.

So our basic spreadsheet can now do the job of keeping track of our current account. But it is not very visual and we have to look closely at a lot of figures to clearly see what the state of our account is like. We can do something about this by adding formatting, colour and art.

Improving the visual look of the spreadsheet

First, let's make the different lines stand out more clearly. First, highlight the cells A5 to F5; then under the font group let's add a light green fill colour to make the opening balance stand out. Then let's add colour contrast lines to make each line stand out from the next. Highlight A6 to F6 in the fill colour of the lightest blue; then A7 to F7 in a fill colour one shade of blue lighter. You could carry on like this one row at a time, but if you highlight the cell A6, then double-click the format painter, the pointer will have a small paint brush next to it; you can then paint the format across all the cells that you want. Click the format painter again to turn this off.

You could make the spreadsheet clearer by arranging for the font colour to change when the transaction was either spending (red) or income (green). This is called conditional formatting in that the colour is dependent on the detail of the cell.

Highlight the Column cells D6 to D17: then on styles grouping click **Conditional Formatting**, then **Highlight Cell Rules**, then **Greater Than**, enter the number 'o', and change the colour to **Light Green Fill with Dark Green Text**, then **OK**. Then, keeping the same cells highlighted, click **Conditional Formatting**, **Highlight Cell Rules**, **Less Than**, enter 'o' and use **Light Red Fill with Dark Red Text**, then **OK**.

The spreadsheet will now show outgoings as a light red cell with dark red text and income as light green cell with dark green text.

We can improve this more by highlighting the cells E6 to E26; then **Conditional Formatting**, **Icon Sets**, click the **three traffic lights** one down from the top in the right-hand column. If you repeat this and click **More Rules** at the bottom, you can set up the boundaries for when the traffic lights change from green to amber to red.

To finish off the sheet, place a thin black border around each cell.

In Figure 15.4 you can see:

1 traffic light icons that change as the balance in the account changes

2 conditional cell formatting that changes the colour for income and expenditure

3 light border added to every cell for clarity.

By working through this section you should be fairly familiar with most of the basic aspects of Excel. In business spreadsheets there will be more data and they are likely to need the more complex functions of Excel.

Figure 15.4 Excel current account (finished)

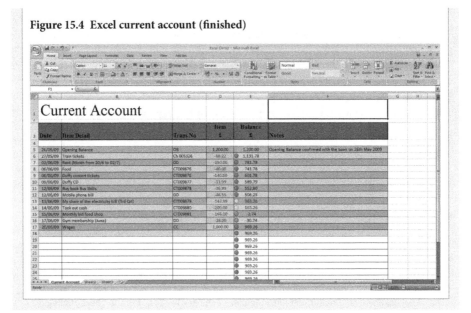

I cannot believe what universities are doing with students these days! Nothing, I imagine; they are mostly useless. They can't do anything business-related. They all come out with degrees in business, but even the simplest thing is beyond them.

They generally spend 12 weeks with use in inventory control as part of a general first year. Everything here is done in spreadsheets and databases. I often sit them down to do a simple input task, such as adding stock-take data to a spreadsheet, and they cannot even open the file. They just sit there looking blank for a long period and then disturb someone else to show them how to do it. Even when they have got it working they soon complain that it is boring. What do they expect? It is work!

I don't know what universities are doing but it is nothing that is useful to business.

15.3 EXCEL BUSINESS SKILLS

Businesses do at least three things with spreadsheets that you might not do at university. First, they keep track of money and things. For instance, a spreadsheet will be used to analyse the company sales ahead of the monthly sales meetings. They also carry out and analyse research using spreadsheets, such as absence reporting, asset tracking, market research, analysing defects or staff attitude surveys. Third, they use spreadsheets for projections of future positions, such as projecting sales for a year ahead or staffing needs. While I have placed a lot of business tasks into three categories of activity, businesses use spreadsheets for anything and everything. Excel skills will be highly prized at work. In many ways spreadsheets are used for many things that would be better done in a database. But two distinct advantages of spreadsheets often 'win the day'. Most staff are skilled and effective using a spreadsheet and the output options in terms of graphs, pictures and colour visualising are far superior in a spreadsheet.

In this section we investigate some of the business tasks that are commonly completed using spreadsheets. First, let's take a look at those sales figures. As we go along I will introduce aspects of Excel that we need to carry out the task.

QUARTERLY SALES ANALYSIS

The data needed for this analysis may well be contained in a sales and finance database; each month the data required for our activity will be exported to a spreadsheet. We will tackle the problem in a smaller and simpler way to illustrate some aspects of this task. In this exercise we will use more than one worksheet. It is often clearer and easier to have the raw data on one sheet and the analysis on another. We will start by entering some sales data. This data sheet does not need to look brilliant; we just need accurate data.

Open a blank Excel Workbook. In default mode it will have three worksheets. The first of these worksheets we will use for the output of our analysis, so we will rename it 'Output'. The second worksheet will contain our data, so we will name it 'Data'.

On the Data worksheet head up the columns as follows:

- column A: Product
- column B : Customer
- column C: Salesperson
- column D: Qtr 1 – 09
- column E: Qtr 2 – 09
- column F: Qtr 3 – 09
- column G: Qtr 4 – 09

Line by line you need to add data to the data table. Each entry will be: Product – Customer – Salesperson – Q1 total sales, Q2 total sales, Q3 total sales, Q4 total sales.

'Pisces Sales' is a fish wholesaler selling the following products:

- cod
- hake
- lobster
- crab
- prawn
- tuna.

'Pisces Sales' has ten customers:

- Babridges
- Best Northern
- The Best Fisher
- The Pea Pod
- The Fat Dog
- The Italian Sausage
- The Stream Inn
- The White Fish Room
- Prawn Shack
- Aeroles.

'Pisces Sales' have six salespersons:

- Alison
- Tom
- Ross
- Peter
- Susan
- Rosie.

I have entered 60 lines of data into my spreadsheet spread over all the products, customers and salespersons. You can add as many lines of data as you like, but 60 rows should be sufficient for our demonstration. Now we must ask: what information will the quarterly sales conference need to know? I would suggest they would be interested in data relating to:

- products
- customers
- salespersons.

So how do we go about analysing this data? If you look at the top 30 rows of my data, you will see that it is ordered by product. But with four quarters of data showing for each product and customers, it is hard to discern any patterns in the data. We can create a pivot table, which is a two-dimensional table that can place the sum of the products into a table showing the quarterly sales.

Create a pivot table by: **Highlight** the data columns and rows in the data table; then **Insert Tab, Pivot Table, OK** the pivot table box. In the Pivot Table Field list tick **Product**, then tick each of the **four quarters**. The pivot table is created on a new worksheet. See Figure 15.6 below. Rename the sheet to 'Sales by Product'. Then sum all of the rows not already summed using auto sum.

Figure 15.5 Raw sales data in Excel

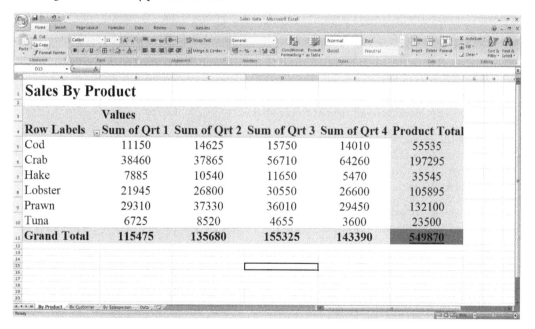

Figure 15.6 Sales by product in Excel

Sales By Product

	Values				
Row Labels	**Sum of Qrt 1**	**Sum of Qrt 2**	**Sum of Qrt 3**	**Sum of Qrt 4**	**Product Total**
Cod	11150	14625	15750	14010	55535
Crab	38460	37865	56710	64260	197295
Hake	7885	10540	11650	5470	35545
Lobster	21945	26800	30550	26600	105895
Prawn	29310	37330	36010	29450	132100
Tuna	6725	8520	4655	3600	23500
Grand Total	**115475**	**135680**	**155325**	**143390**	**549870**

What you see in Figure 15.6 is each of the products listed on the left, the quarterly sales across the page and a product total at the end. This pivot table has summarised the data for product sold by quarter quite well, but it is still not very clear which are the bestsellers and which sell less well. Highlight the product name and the annual sales and you can quickly produce a pie chart of the data: go to **Insert Tab,** click **Pie Chart.** In Excel 2007 the legend and titles can be formatted from the chart by clicking into the legend or title box.

Figure 15.7 Pie chart of annual sales

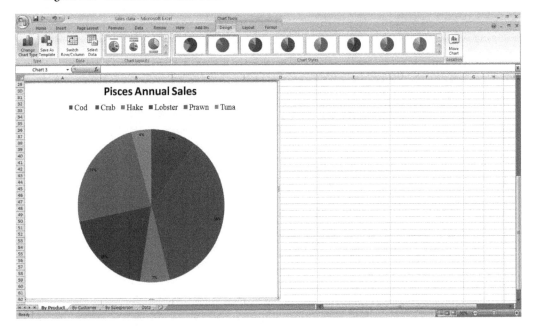

The pie chart screenshot displays another feature of Office 2007 software –the ribbon commands are context-specific. When you are formatting a pie chart, pie chart options will be shown. You can see this in Figure 15.7 at the top, where the ribbon commands are all related to pie charts.

Using the same raw sales data, we can also generate a pivot table of the performance of the sales staff. The procedure is the same until the point of ticking the Pivot Table Field, when you tick **Salesperson** and each of the **four quarters.** The pivot table output is featured in Figure 15.8.

The table is sorted by the total sales for each salesperson, giving us a rank order of sales performance. Using the total sales you can make some rough judgements about the best and worst performers.

SOME OF THE EXTRA SKILLS YOU WILL NEED TO FUNCTION WITH SPREADSHEETS

Sorting

Business spreadsheets often contain very large quantities of data and there will be occasions where this needs to be sorted into order. For instance, in the table of product sales by salesperson I sorted the data on the total column so that Alison was first in the table and Tom was last. Data is often easier to understand and make sense of when it is in some sort of order. Some statistical measures require data to be in rank order.

Figure 15.8 Product sales by salesperson

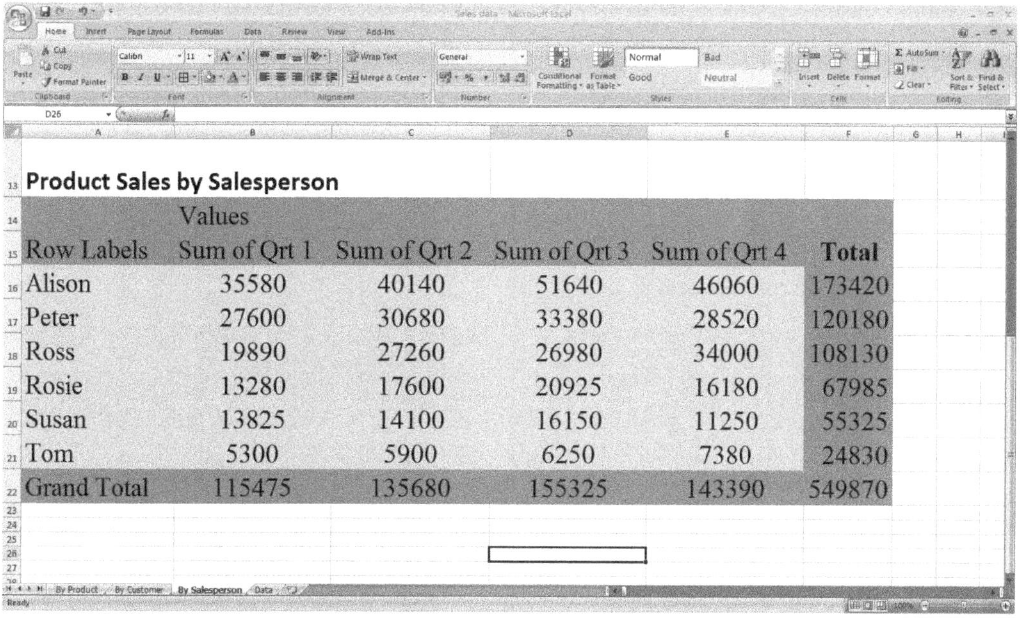

Product Sales by Salesperson

	Values				
Row Labels	Sum of Qrt 1	Sum of Qrt 2	Sum of Qrt 3	Sum of Qrt 4	Total
Alison	35580	40140	51640	46060	173420
Peter	27600	30680	33380	28520	120180
Ross	19890	27260	26980	34000	108130
Rosie	13280	17600	20925	16180	67985
Susan	13825	14100	16150	11250	55325
Tom	5300	5900	6250	7380	24830
Grand Total	115475	135680	155325	143390	549870

You can sort data by highlighting the cells containing the data. It is important to highlight complete rows of data; if you miss some of the rows the result will be a jumbled set of data not connected to the correct key field. If you inadvertently do this, don't panic: click the undo button and it will be put back to its original form. Microsoft will give you a warning and ask if you want to expand the selection to cover the data not highlighted. Highlight all the data in a worksheet by clicking the corner cell between column A and row 1. Then, on the **Data Tab**, **Sort**, select from the dropdown boxes, Sort by, Sort on, Order. An initial setting for the sales data might be to choose:

- Sort by: Product
- Sort on: Values
- Order: A to Z.

When you click **OK** the data will be sorted alphabetically A to Z on the product name.

In the sort box you can add extra sort levels so that in the sales data it is sorted by product first, but could also then be sorted by customers and if you add another level by salesperson.

Table styles

In the early part of this chapter we formatted the cell styles manually a few cells at a time. Excel has a command that can do this by creating a table and formatting the table. Highlight all the data in the data worksheet for Pisces Sales; then on **Home Tab**, **Format as Table**, then choose a design (note the live preview as your mouse passes over the options). Your data has now been formatted into a more professional-looking table and each column has a dropdown arrow.

Using the dropdown arrows you can select some data and hide other data. For instance, if you want to see only lines of data that were sales to The Fat Dog, you would untick all the other customers; then when you click **OK** you have only the sales to this one customer. You can use multiple column options to filter the data further.

Figure 15.9 Filtered sales data

	Product	Customer	Salesperson	Qrt 1	Qrt 2	Qrt 3	Qrt 4
1	Product	Customer	Salesperson	Qrt 1	Qrt 2	Qrt 3	Qrt 4
5	Cod	The Pea Pod	Susan	£500.00	£600.00	£700.00	£900.00
9	Cod	The White Fish Room	Susan	£1,200.00	£1,500.00	£1,400.00	£2,300.00
15	Crab	The Pea Pod	Susan	£850.00	£850.00	£700.00	£400.00
19	Crab	The White Fish Room	Susan	£2,800.00	£1,900.00	£1,500.00	£1,400.00
25	Hake	The Pea Pod	Susan	£450.00	£500.00	£650.00	£800.00
29	Hake	The White Fish Room	Susan	£2,500.00	£3,400.00	£4,000.00	£1,500.00
35	Lobster	The Pea Pod	Susan	£125.00	£250.00	£300.00	£450.00
39	Lobster	The White Fish Room	Susan	£2,000.00	£1,500.00	£3,000.00	£1,000.00
49	Prawn	The White Fish Room	Susan	£2,400.00	£2,800.00	£3,000.00	£1,100.00
59	Tuna	The White Fish Room	Susan	£1,000.00	£800.00	£900.00	£1,400.00
62							
63							
64							
65							

Conditional formatting

The message in data can be seen far more clearly if cells are of different colours. If you return to the pivot table we created for product sales by salesperson, you can get an idea of which salesperson is doing well and which are doing less well by sorting the table. However, if the sales target for the first quarter for all staff was £25,000, it is not immediately clear who has met the target and who has not.

Let's make this clear so that those salespeople making and missing the target are clearly visible.

Conditional formatting is the technique to do this. Highlight the cells B5 to E10, the quarterly sales figures by salesperson, then:

1 **Home** tab

2 **Conditional Formatting**

3 **Highlight Cells Rules**

4 **Greater Than**, enter **24,999** and with **Green Fill with Dark Green Text**

5 Then **OK**.

Follow the procedure again; this time choose:

1 **Less Than**, then enter **25,000** and with **Red Fill with Dark Red Text**

2 Then **OK**.

Click outside the table and you should be able to clearly see who made the target each quarter.

You can repeat these instructions and add more formatting. For instance, you could add a red border around the cells that miss the target.

There are lots of other rules for formatting, so investigate those that will work well with the data you have. For example, in larger groups of data you could highlight the top 10% or the bottom 10%. Another useful format is the above-average elements and the below-average elements.

Figure 15.10 Line graph of annual sales

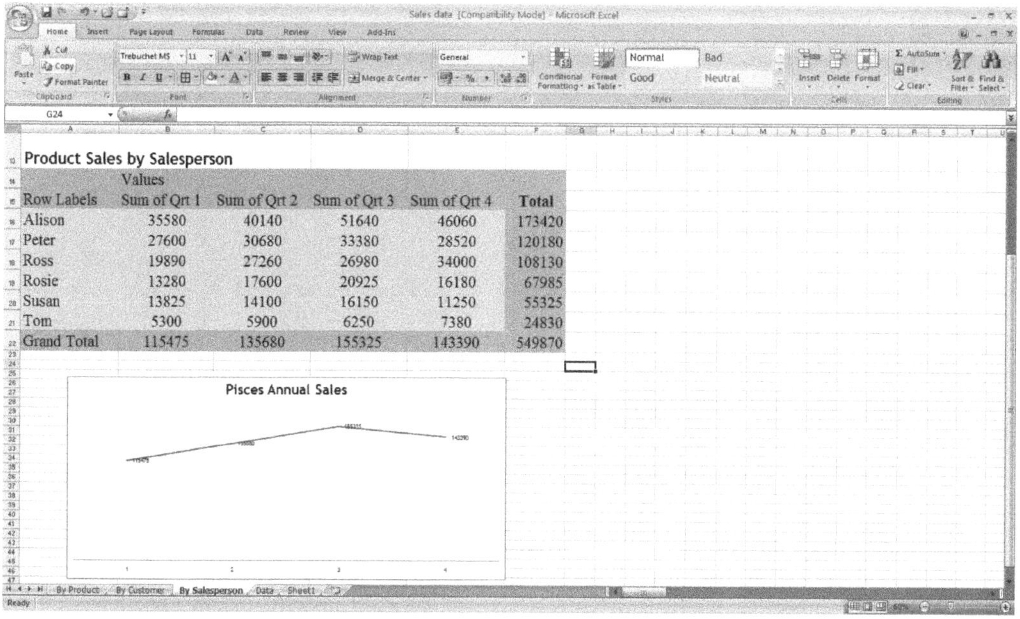

Trend data

For a lot of business data you will need to know the trend. For example, are sales rising or falling; if so, by how much? Let's create a simple illustration with the total sales data. In the product sales by salesperson, highlight the four quarterly sales totals – B22 to E22 in my data example.

Then:

1 **Insert** tab

2 **Line graph**

3 Choose the **first line graph** in the icon list.

15.4 RESEARCH AND ANALYSIS WITH EXCEL

One of the key uses of Excel is for recording and analysing the results of research. This section will provide a basic understanding of the process and should then prove useful when you complete a dissertation. At work all manner of surveys and research will be carried out using Excel or specialist survey software like SNAP.

Kasia works part-time for a large book publisher in London, and the Director of Research has asked her to devise a questionnaire that will find out how much money university students spend on books each year. She sets out to do this creating a questionnaire in Word and adding the data to an Excel spreadsheet.

The questionnaire in Word is seeking the following data:

- first name
- family name
- age
- gender
- course of study
- university
- year of study
- income from loans
- income from part-time jobs
- income from family assistance.

These items are called biographical data. They explain aspects of the person to which the data about book-buying relates. Biographical data is important so that when the analysis is carried out, it is possible to distinguish which parts of the cohort behave in certain ways. For example, it may be possible to say that the average spend on books by university students is £230 for women and £167 for men. A further example might be that the spend on books is in some way related to income.

The questionnaire then explored the following areas:

Q1. Do you buy the recommended text for modules?

A1. Always (1), Sometimes (2), Never (3), Tutors do not recommend books (4)

Q2. How many modules do you study each semester?

A2. Quantity – the actual number specified is the data entry.

Q3. How much do you spend each year on university books?

A3. Quantity – the actual number specified is the data entry.

Q4. How many books did you buy last year?

A4. Quantity – the actual number specified is the data entry.

Q5. Do you think that books are good value for money? Answer 1 for 'very good value' to 5 for 'very poor value'.

A5. data entry 1 to 5.

Q6. Where do you mainly buy your books?

A6. The university bookshop (1), High Street bookshop (2), Online (3), Other (4) please specify.

This represents a range of questions and biographical data that needs to be entered into Excel so that analysis can be carried out. Wherever possible the data will be coded using numbers. So the data that we store will be in the following forms:

- first name – enter as text
- family name – enter as text
- age – number
- gender – codes as number (1) for male, (2) for female, (3) for mixed, (4) do not wish to be categorised in this way, (9) no answer
- course of study – enter as text
- university – enter as text
- subject studied – enter as text
- level of study – use new university categorisation 1st year UG Level 4, 2nd year Level 5, 3rd year Level 6, postgraduate Level 7. Enter number 4–7.
- income from loans – enter number
- income from part-time jobs – enter number
- income from family assistance – enter number
- **Q1**. Always (1), Sometimes (2), Never (3), Tutors do not recommend books (4)

- Q2. How many modules do you study each semester? Enter number.
- Q3. How much do you spend each year on university books? Enter number.
- Q4. How many books did you buy last year? Enter number.
- Q5. Answer 1 for 'very good value' to 5 for 'very poor value'.
- Q6. The university bookshop (1), High Street bookshop (2), Online (3), Other (4) please specify.

Some of the data entries will require extra columns to record other things. For instance, the three income questions relating to loans, part-time work and family will be added to create an entry for total income. Question 6 has an answer called 'other'; this requires a text column to record this other data. The normal convention in Excel is to have each row as a record of one person's answers and columns to store the answers.

So let's start by adding the headings to the columns starting at A1 then continuing until we have all the required columns for each answer. For confidentiality reasons the names of participants are often kept in a separate and secure file so each participant in the data sheet is recorded by a record number only – the first column in the illustration. Add the column headings as in the illustration and format in a manner that stands out. Change the name of the worksheet to 'Data'.

Figure 15.11 Data table with headings

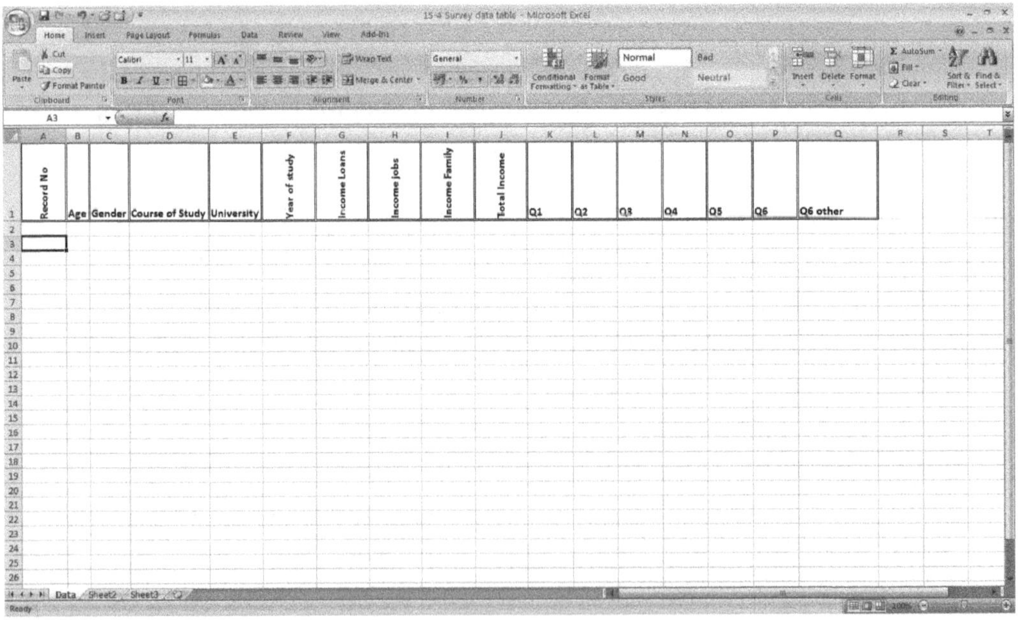

Let's add some data to the table. I have added 30 records of data.

Figure 15.12 Data table with data added

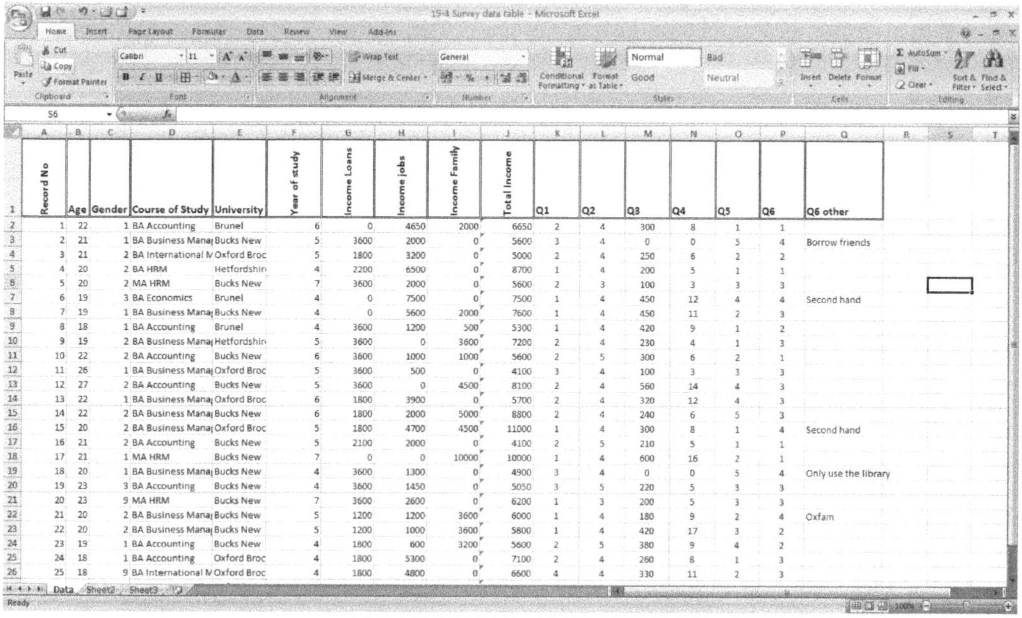

Record No	Age	Gender	Course of Study	University	Year of study	Income Loans	Income jobs	Income Family	Total Income	Q1	Q2	Q3	Q4	Q5	Q6	Q6 other
1	22	1	BA Accounting	Brunel	6	0	4650	2000	6650	2	4	300	8	1	1	
2	21	1	BA Business Mana	Bucks New	5	3600	2000	0	5600	3	4	0	0	5	4	Borrow friends
3	21	2	BA International M	Oxford Broc	5	1800	3200	0	5000	2	4	250	6	2	2	
4	20	2	BA HRM	Hetfordshir	4	2200	6500	0	8700	1	4	200	5	1	1	
5	20	2	MA HRM	Bucks New	7	3600	2000	0	5600	2	3	100	3	3	3	
6	19	3	BA Economics	Brunel	4	0	7500	0	7500	1	4	450	12	4	4	Second hand
7	19	1	BA Business Mana	Bucks New	4	0	5600	2000	7600	1	4	450	11	2	3	
8	18	1	BA Accounting	Brunel	4	3600	1200	500	5300	1	4	420	9	1	2	
9	19	2	BA Business Mana	Hetfordshir	5	3600	0	3600	7200	2	4	230	4	1	3	
10	22	2	BA Accounting	Bucks New	6	3600	1000	1000	5600	2	5	300	6	2	1	
11	26	1	BA Business Mana	Oxford Broc	5	3600	500	0	4100	3	4	100	3	3	3	
12	27	2	BA Accounting	Bucks New	5	3600	0	4500	8100	2	4	560	14	4	3	
13	22	1	BA Business Mana	Oxford Broc	6	1800	3900	0	5700	2	4	320	12	4	3	
14	22	2	BA Business Mana	Bucks New	6	1800	2000	5000	8800	2	4	240	6	5	3	
15	20	2	BA Business Mana	Oxford Broc	5	1800	4700	4500	11000	1	4	300	8	1	4	Second hand
16	21	2	BA Accounting	Bucks New	5	2100	2000	0	4100	2	5	210	5	1	1	
17	21	1	MA HRM	Bucks New	7	0	0	10000	10000	1	4	600	16	2	1	
18	20	1	BA Business Mana	Bucks New	4	3600	1300	0	4900	3	4	0	0	5	4	Only use the library
19	23	3	BA Accounting	Bucks New	4	3600	1450	0	5050	3	5	220	5	3	3	
20	23	9	MA HRM	Bucks New	7	3600	2600	0	6200	1	3	200	5	3	3	
21	20	2	BA Business Mana	Bucks New	5	1200	1200	3600	6000	1	4	180	9	2	4	Oxfam
22	20	2	BA Business Mana	Bucks New	5	1200	1000	3600	5800	1	4	420	17	3	2	
23	19	1	BA Accounting	Bucks New	4	1800	600	3200	5600	2	5	380	9	4	2	
24	18	1	BA Accounting	Oxford Broc	4	1800	5300	0	7100	2	4	260	8	1	3	
25	18	9	BA International M	Oxford Broc	4	1800	4800	0	6600	4	4	330	11	2	3	

This is the basic arrangement for adding data into a spreadsheet for data analysis. There are a few variations and improvements that can help with accurately adding data. I'll cover the analysis and output a little later.

RESTRICT DATA ENTRY IN CELLS

Accurately adding data at the input stage can save a lot of work later looking for and correcting errors. If you have a question like Question 5, which has only five possible answers – 1 to 5 – it is useful to restrict the possible data that can be entered to that range only.

1 Highlight the entries in column O.
2 Click on the **Data** tab.
3 **Data tools.**
4 **Data validation.**
5 Click the **Settings** tab.
6 In the Allow box, select **Whole Number**.
7 In the Data box add the lower limit as 1 and the upper limit as 5.
8 Then **OK.**

Now if you try to enter the number 6 in one of the cells in column O you will get a warning message: 'A user has restricted values that can be entered into this cell.' This is particularly useful if someone other than the designer of the spreadsheet is adding data as they do not always know the precise meaning of the data. An assistant will just be entering numbers from paper sheets. You can set data validation for all the cells in the spreadsheet.

DATA FORMS

A data form provides an easier way to enter data relating to one record. You can see from the illustration that one record is displayed and the entries are 'tab' through. It is easier to create a new record and populate it with data.

Figure 15.13 Data form in the data table

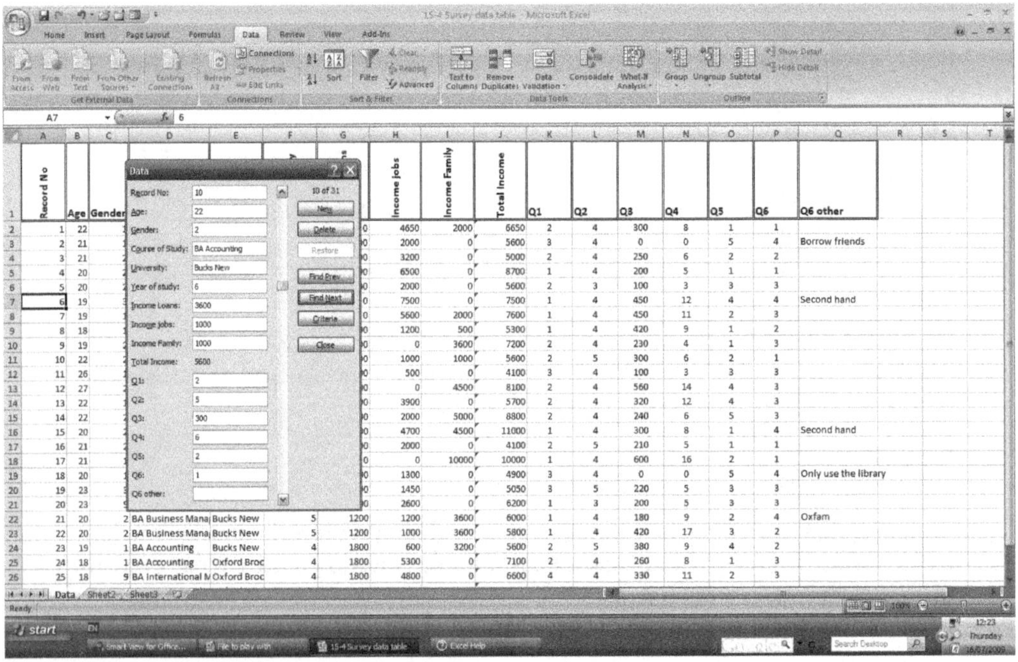

You enter the data in each field and then use the 'tab' key to move between fields. It is quicker to enter numeric data using the numeric keypad. When you have entered similar data to the example we can move on to carry out some analysis.

DATA ANALYSIS

Analysis, as we learned in an earlier chapter, is concerned with investigating parts of the whole. Research data can be investigated using a set of calculations and statistical tests.

The average

This is more correctly called the **mean**. It is the first statistic that you generate and it is the most commonly used statistic to find the centre of your data. The mean is calculated by adding all the values in your data and dividing by the total number of values. So if we add all the age values together in our data sheet (634) and then divide by the number of values (30), this gives us 21.13.

This is a simple statistic, easy to calculate but also very useful for describing your data and is essential for calculating other statistics.

Excel uses the following function to calculate the mean: AVERAGE(B2:B31) for our book-buying data.

The median

The **median** literally means a line dividing something down the middle. In statistics that is the middle value of a set of values. If we reorder the book-buying data (the amount spent on books in a year) into a rank order lowest to highest we will be able to see the middle value.

1 Highlight the cells **A2:Q31** (all the data).

2 Click **Data** tab.

3 **Sort**, then set Sort by: Q3, Sort on: values, Order: Smallest to Largest.

4 Then **OK**.

The median of this set of values is halfway between cells M16 and M17 = 245.

The median is easy to find in a set of data with an odd number of values because it is an actual value in the table.

The median can be calculated using a function:

1 Place the cursor in cell **M33**.

2 Then click the insert function symbol '*fx*' just above the main worksheet and to the right of the cell address that reads M33.

3 From the pane that appears, select the category **Statistical**.

4 Then scroll down to **Median**.

5 Then **OK**.

6 A function arguments pane will appear; click the cursor into the first cell M2 and drag a box down to M31; the cell address will be entered.

7 Then **OK**.

8 The median is displayed in cell M33 as 245.

(Note that using the median function means that you do not have to sort the spreadsheet.)

The median is just as acceptable as the mean for describing the centre of your data. You would use the median if you wanted to know the typical age of a group in a data set. You would use the mean if you wanted to know the average.

The range

The **range** expresses the lowest and the highest value of a data set. Using our example above (spending on books) the range is 0 to 600.

The range is often forgotten as a way of expressing the spread of the data, but it does convey useful information.

The inter-quartile range

Don't be put off by this rather grand and confusing name; it merely means separating the data into quarters. The statistic is normally calculated for ranked data (values in a list in ranked order). The main number that is returned is the inter-quartile range. Don't worry about the name; it means the middle two quarters, in other words, the middle half of your data ignoring the upper and lower quarters. This is useful as it removes 'outlying' data. That is the very large and very small data items.

In Excel this can be calculated using the quartile function:
QUARTILE(M2:M31,1).

The first numbers inside the brackets are the values in the range of cells M2 to M31. The number at the end should correspond to whichever quartile you want: remember to put the data in rank order (smallest to largest) – this is easy in Excel using the sort command.

1 First quartile (25th percentile)

2 Median value (50th percentile)

3 Third quartile (75th percentile).

To calculate the inter-quartile range you would subtract (in Excel's terms) the third quartile from the first quartile, or the upper quartile from the lower quartile:

QUARTILE(M2:M31,3) – QUARTILE(M2:M31,1) = Inter-quartile Range

BECOMING REFLECTIVE PERFORMERS

LOUISE AND SIMON

Louise: 'Have you been doing that survey case study in the skills book?'

Simon: 'No. I can't really be bothered – too much work.'

L: 'Really! I looked on it as a great dry run for the dissertation.'

S: 'Yes, maybe. But hey, I have better things to do.'

L: 'Like what? Most dissertations have a survey or something like it so you need the skills.'

S: 'I suppose so. But, I'll manage when the time comes.'

L: 'Well! I am having real trouble doing the basic maths. I never did understand statistics.'

S: 'I don't know either!'

L: 'Did you get a GCSE?'

S: 'Yes, grade B, but that doesn't mean I know anything.'

L: 'Yes, I got an A and I still don't have a clue.'

S: 'I mostly guessed all the answers; you never had to do the maths.'

L: 'Or indeed do anything with it.'

S: 'Why don't you do a qualitative study? Then there isn't any maths or statistics.'

L: 'Well, that is what I intend to do. But I still feel like I am ducking something I should know about and will need to know about at work.'

S: 'Yes, you're right about work in marketing; there is tons of this statistics stuff.'

L: 'I really don't understand even the basics and it all puts me off when I start to read about it.'

S: 'The statistics tutor is a dead loss. As soon as he speaks I fall asleep.'

L: 'Yes, he makes it so boring. ZZZZZ...'

S: 'You could get a book out and work through it.'

L: 'I don't think it is that sort of subject. Reading is no good; you have to do it to be able to do it.'

S: 'As I need to be able to do this, why don't I work with you and complete the skills book case study?'

L: 'Good idea. We can also ask my boss at work; she is really good with spreadsheets.'

After the case study is complete:

S: 'Well, that wasn't so bad. We managed it and I think I might be able to do it again.'

L: 'That's true. The maths wasn't the problem in the end.'

S: 'Too right. I never thought it could be so difficult to think up precise questions that could get precise answers.'

L: 'That is a real skill. I guess you get better with time.'

S: 'Amazing how many different ways you could analyse data. There must be hundreds of spreadsheet functions and they all do something different.'

L: 'Well, we can chalk that one down to experience.'

S: 'I stand a better chance of completing my dissertation now.'

L: 'At least I am not afraid of statistics anymore.'

S: 'Yeah, they're doable and actually mean something and are useful.'

The standard deviation

The standard deviation expresses the data spread in a slightly different and more useful manner. Each value in a data table is compared with the mean value for all the data.

So, for the range of values for book spending, the mean is 260.33.

Record 1 shows that the person spent £300 on books in the year.

The standard deviation calculates how far 300 is away from the mean:

300 is 39.67 from the mean of 260.33, so the deviation is 39.67.

Record 2 value for spend is 0, so that is −260.33 away from the mean.

Record 3 is 250 − 260.33 = 10.33.

And so on for all the values of spending books.

To avoid negative numbers being generated, the difference is squared (multiplied by itself), so that we now have:

- Record 1: 39.67 × 39.67 = 1573.70
- Record 2: –260.33 × –260.33 = 67771.70
- Record 3: 10.33 × 10.33 = 106.70

Then the amount of each squared deviation from the mean is added together and then averaged; finally the square root of the number is calculated and this is the standard deviation.

Don't worry about the maths; Excel will do that for you:

STDEV(M2:M31) = 149.52

In the research setting the standard deviation and the mean are useful in understanding if the data has a **normal distribution**. A 'normal' distribution is one where the data displays a 'bell-shaped' frequency curve. The **empirical rule** states that 68% of the data will lie within one standard deviation either side of the mean. Also, 95.4% of the data will lie within two standard deviations either side of the mean. Finally, that 99.7% of the data will lie within three standard deviations either side of the mean.

Figure 15.14 Standard distribution curve

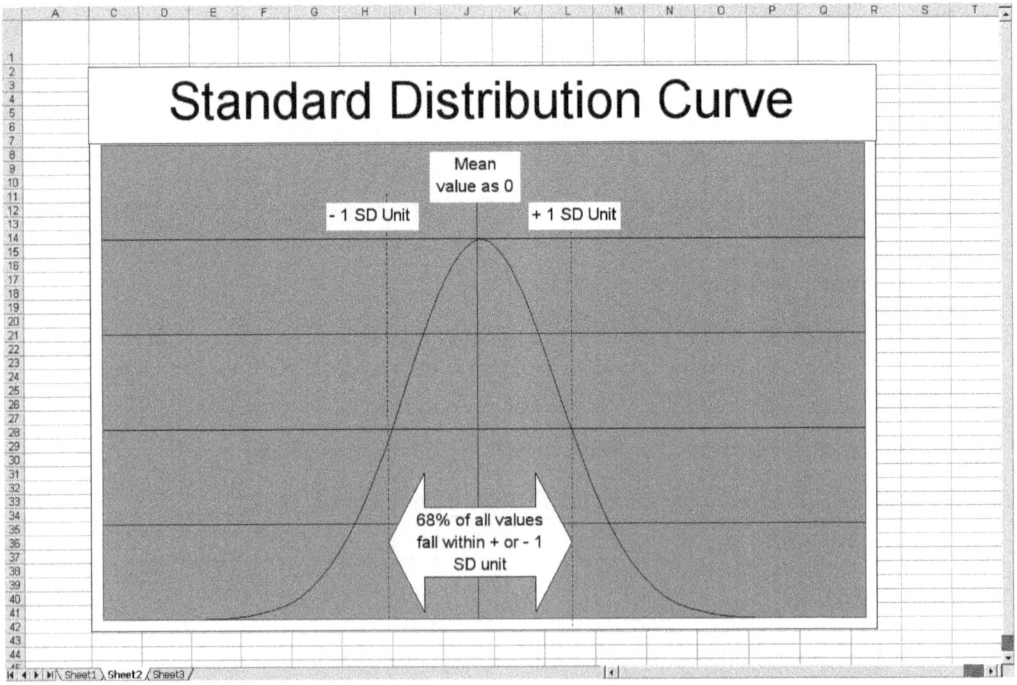

Frequency tables

Frequency tables and frequency distributions summarise the number of respondents that gave a certain answer; in statistical language this is the number of cases in each category. The output can be varied by the settings you make in Excel, but the minimum output will be the categories of answer and the number of respondents that so answered. You would normally include an entry for missing data, as this is an important consideration in relation to the validity of the question and the answers.

In Excel 2007 these charts are called histograms. The tools to do this are not normally loaded with the software and you have to load them manually:

1 Click the **Office** button.

2 **Excel options**, at the bottom of the pane.

3 **Add-ins** in the left pane.

4 In the **Manage box** at the bottom, use the dropdown menu to go to **Excel Add-ins**.

5 Then **Go**.

6 Tick the Add-in marked **Analysis ToolPak**.

7 Then **OK**.

When it has loaded you will have an extra box on the data tab of the ribbon.

To create a frequency distribution for Question 5, 'Do you think that books are good value for money?', I have hidden some of the columns I don't need in the illustration below – this is to aid clarity. Before you create the table, add a title for each answer in a range of adjacent cells:

- S3: Very Good Value   T3: 1
- S4: Quite Good Value   T4: 2
- S5: Neutral   T5: 3
- S6: Not Very Good Value   T6: 4
- S7: Very Poor Value   T7: 5

Create a frequency distribution (histogram) for the answers to Question 5:

1 Click the **Data** tab.

2 **Analysis** tab, the last on the ribbon.

3 Data Analysis.

4 From the dropdown box, **Histogram**.

5 Set the input range to O2:O31.

6 Set the bin range to T3:T7.

7 Set the radio button to output range and to the cell S11.

8 Then **OK**.

The table will appear starting at S11.

To create a more visual graph of this data:

1 Highlight cells T12 to T16.

2 Insert tab.

3 Pie or column.

4 Then place the chart where it is needed.

Figure 15.15 Frequency table with charts

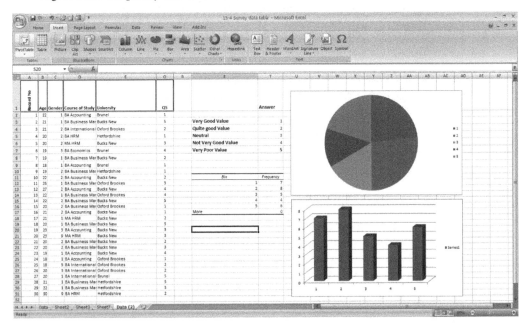

Correlation between variables

One key relationship that researchers want to explore is the correlation between variables. This allows analysis output that suggests one variable is related to another and displays the strength of that relationship. It is very tempting to say that one variable causes the other to change, but this is wrong. This section is a very brief introduction to creating charts that display correlation. There is a considerably more accurate and full treatment of this important aspect of research in *Researching and Writing Dissertations* (Horn 2009).

In our data table we might suspect that the more income at the student's disposal, the more they spend on books. The illustration below shows the two variables of income to spend set out in a scatter chart with a line of best fit added. If the relationship between spending and income were 100% correlated, the data points would all lie along the line of best fit. As these data points are scattered a long way from the line of best fit, we might conclude that while some relationship between these two variables exists, it is not a very strong relationship.

Figure 15.16 Correlation of income to spend

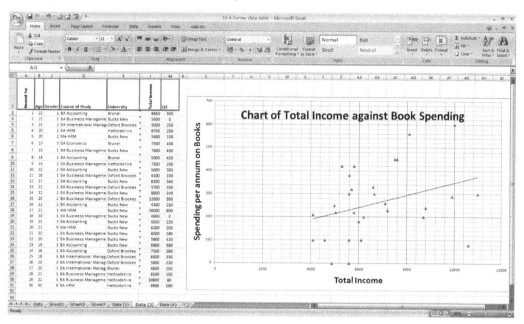

If spending on books was perfectly correlated to income, the chart would look like Figure 15.17.

Figure 15.17 Perfect correlation of income to spend

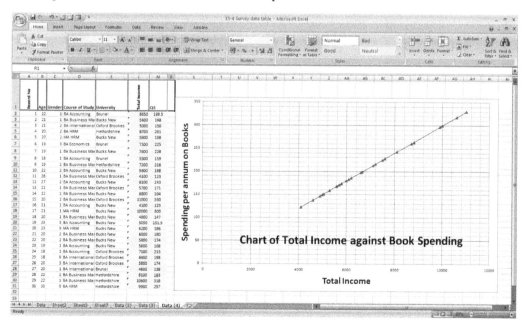

Excel is an excellent tool for storing and analysing data. This section has covered a very small amount of the possible ways to analyse data and produce charts that communicate important outcomes. One of the most effective ways of improving your skills with Excel is to explore and experiment. If you carry out quantitative research for your project or dissertation, the skill and experience you have built up carrying out these exercises will be very valuable.

CASE STUDY

THE BOOK-BUYING SURVEY

Creating, exploring and analysing the book-buying survey

This case study is designed to give you experience of completing a small survey. It is designed to prepare you for completing your dissertation. There is very little research or data about the book-buying habits of higher education (HE) students. Your role is to develop a quantitative survey, collect data from 50 students and analyse that data in Excel before producing a short report about the findings. This will take about 10–14 days of intermittent activity or, if you are completing the case study as a seminar activity, about four weeks of seminars.

Look back at section 15.4 to make sure you understand the nature of biographical data. Then consider what data will be required to understand why students buy books.

Activities:

1 Prepare a paper-based questionnaire for administering to participants face to face.

2 Conduct the survey with approximately 50 students at your university.

3 Enter the data in an Excel spreadsheet using data validation of the input fields.

4 Carry out the following types of analysis:

- descriptive analysis of the data

- use frequency tables or histograms to analyse all the questions

- create pivot tables of pairs of variables and discover which seem to be most significant

- investigate possible correlations of variables to discover the significant variables

- produce a range of charts and outputs to explain your analysis.

To think about...

- Reflect on the questions you asked and at the end of the process how you would change these if you were completing the tasks again.

- What problems did you encounter in conducting the face-to-face research?

- On reflection, how would you go about carrying out the analysis if you did it a second time?

- What do your outputs of data, analysis and charts tell the reader about the nature and extent of book-buying by HE students?

SUMMARY

Excel is a powerful tool for business and academic life. Excel 2007 is somewhat different from earlier versions, but once you are familiar with its new look and features you will appreciate the improvements.

- Explore and develop effective ways to carry out the most commons tasks of Excel.

- Understand and use the customisable quick access toolbar.

- Use the keyboard shortcuts and the numeric pad to speed up data entry.

- Develop your skills in the commonly used elements of Excel:
  - entering data and filling cells with data
  - entering formulae
  - using basic functions such as sum and average
  - know how to format cells for different types of entry
  - use tables, formatting and styles to improve the visual clarity of the data
  - use conditional formatting to highlight important aspects of the spreadsheet.

- Businesses use spreadsheets for:
  - accounting for things
  - analysing research
  - projecting data forward.

- Use pivot tables to summarise data and display data.

- Excel can be used to analyse and display trend data.

- Excel can store, analyse and display quantitative research data:
  - Columns are used for individual questions.
  - Rows are used for the results from each subject.
  - Descriptive statistics include:
    - mean
    - median
    - range
    - inter-quartile range
    - standard deviation.
  - Analyse data using:
    - frequency tables
    - histograms and charts
    - correlation between variables
    - scatter graphs.

EXPLORE FURTHER

FURTHER READING

Holden, G. (2009) *Microsoft Excel 2007 in Simple Steps*. Harlow: Prentice-Hall.

Horn, R. (2009) *Researching and Writing Dissertations: A complete guide for business and management students*. London: Chartered Institute of Personnel and Development.

Stephen, M. (2007) *Teach Yourself Excel 2007*. London: Teach Yourself Books.

Strawbridge, M. (2006) *Spreadsheets: The ECDL Advanced series*. Oxford: Pearson Education.

WEB LINKS

Microsoft online Excel tutorials: http://office.microsoft.com/en-us/training/CR100479681033.aspx

Google Docs free office software: http://www.google.com/google-d-s/tour1.html

Statistics tutorial: http://www.meandeviation.com/tutorials/stats/

CHAPTER 16

Project Management Skills

What skills will I develop in this chapter?

- understanding the whole project process
- understanding the project lifecycle
- using the project triangle to manage projects
- developing an awareness of project scope and how to manage it
- how to define a project
- how to plan the detail of projects
- how to develop and use work breakdown structure charts
- creating timelines with Gantt charts, network diagrams and critical path analysis
- using communication matrices
- choosing project management software

16.1 INTRODUCTION

Project management skills are vital to business. When you come to carry out your dissertation, they can be vital to you. Project management is fundamentally a defined process. Not everyone will agree on the exact detail of the process, but to be successful, a well-defined process must be in place and predominantly followed. Project management is a discipline separate from business but also vital to business. The demand for skilled project managers always seems to be high and employment in a project management role can be exciting and well paid.

This chapter first looks at the project management process. Second, some parts of the detailed process are investigated. If you are new to project management, then I would advise that you work sequentially through the chapter, carrying out each of the activities and tasks. The skills you will learn in this chapter can be put to good use when you complete your final-year project or dissertation.

16.2 OVERVIEW OF PROJECT MANAGEMENT

There are many ways to describe the project process. The project lifecycle is one of the most enduring approaches. To complete a project it is necessary to carry out all the stages. All the stages will have more detailed actions contained under them. At this stage I will investigate the project lifecycle and later sections will address the detail of each stage.

Figure 16.1 The project lifecycle

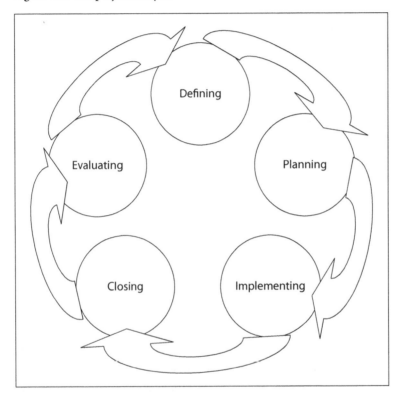

The stages of the project lifecycle are:

Defining – This is also called the initiating stage; it sets out the basic elements of the project at a high level. The first act is normally to make a business case for the project. Then a project manager is appointed, whose initial work includes:

- Select a project team and office.
- Liaise with stakeholders.
- Carry out a feasibility study.
- Define the terms of reference (the proposed scope of the project).
- Set up a communications matrix.

Towards the end of this phase, the project manager will:

- Define the agreed scope of the project.
- Set out the agreed high-level deliverables.
- Complete a stage review.

Planning – This involves creating a suite of planning documents that will guide the project implementation stage. The planning is carried out at various levels, and normally the higher-level plans are created first and then lower and more detailed plans are produced for each area. The range of plans required varies with each project, so there are no hard and fast rules, but most medium-sized or larger projects will need the following:

- a work breakdown structure showing all the tasks required to complete the project
- a team and organisational structure showing who is responsible for what
- a task estimation plan showing the detail of each task in terms of time, expertise and duration
- a time schedule showing the duration of each phase and task
- plan 'milestones', which are important and measurable points in the progress of the project
- a budget plan showing the details of cost and the flow of cash
- detailed specifications for 'deliverables' showing what will be completed, to what standard and by when
- a risk assessment prioritising and detailing risks to the project
- contingency plans showing how to deal with the high-priority risks.

Planning can be carried out in several ways. The most logical and most frequently used is top–down planning. This is where the major tasks to complete the project are detailed and then ever more detailed plans are created until each small task has been planned. Bottom–up planning starts with the detailed tasks and then clusters the tasks into larger groups until there are a small number of large tasks. Time planning is a technique to plan backwards from the required point of completion.

Building the stages of the plan involves discussion and communication, so this planning phase will take some time. You can record the agreed stages in any way that you like, but an Excel spreadsheet is a good starting point that allows for different levels of task.

Implementing – Once you have clear and agreed plans, you can move into the implementation stage. This is the point at which the project begins to produce the agreed outputs. While the 'deliverable' is being created, there will need to be a suite of monitoring actions to ensure that the project implementation is going to plan. Not all projects are the same, but the following areas are normally included for monitoring:

- time and progress for tasks and phases
- procurement of resources
- financial performance against budget
- quality against specification
- communication.

Towards the end of the project there will be a process of acceptance of the deliverables by the end-user. This is normally a formal process where the users accept parts of the whole project and sign an acceptance form.

Closing – Project closing involves releasing the final deliverables to the user. There is normally a formal signing-off on the project. At the finish of the project any project documentation will be handed to the user and formal closure will take place. Closing also involves terminating agreements with suppliers and subcontractors. There will be a final communication to all stakeholders.

Evaluation – This can take various forms and be carried out at various levels. The user evaluation will involve a structured evaluation by the end-user of the deliverables. There will often be a project team evaluation. Supplier evaluations are also carried out and recorded. A reflective record of learning, knowledge and experience is a useful activity, both during the project and at the end. In a project management environment it is important that the learning from one project is systematically communicated and used on later projects.

❝ MANAGER COMMENT

I am a senior manager in a packaging manufacturer and I mentored Sally, a young graduate trainee. She was assigned a small project to develop some prototype packaging that reduced the amount of card used by 33%. This was her first project management experience. She had run into problems and came to see me for help. She was about halfway through the agreed project timescale and the project had made no real progress; she was under pressure from her manager to report progress.

We sat down together to run through what had happened. They had clearly had a lot of meetings and had generated a lot of ideas for how to improve the packaging. If anything, they had too many ideas and some were very radical. I asked to see the project plan – Sally was rather alarmed. After going back to her office, she came back with a very short and not fully completed project plan. She said

that she had tried to follow the company's guidelines on producing project plans but had got confused and didn't like to ask. She said, 'If I'm honest, I didn't see why I needed to go through all these steps just to produce some new designs.'

I pointed out all the stages and parts of a project process that the project plan was meant to cover. Sally just sat there amazed! I helped her to work through the project cycle and we produced all the paperwork that was needed. I especially pointed out that if she had done this in the beginning it would have produced 'milestones', which would have alerted her to the problems earlier. It took us two very full days to complete all this and she then had to take the team backwards quite a way so that she could go forward.

In the end the new designs got an eco design award.

PROJECT SCOPE

In this section I would like to consider just one important aspect of managing a project. Traditionally it is thought that a project manager must 'juggle' with three things: cost, scope and time. My version of the project triangle recognises more fully that people deliver the project and have to be managed and controlled.

Figure 16.2 The project triangle

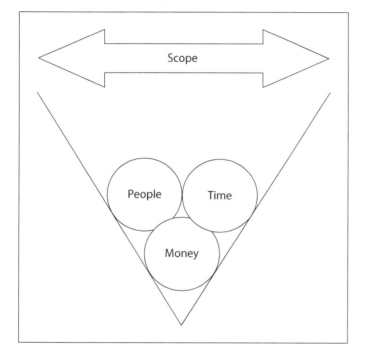

In Figure 16.2 you can see three main aspects to a project depicted as three circles. They are:

- people
- time
- money.

By drawing two lines touching the sides of the circles, we create two sides of the project triangle. The top line completes the triangle and represents the scope of the project. Projects change over time and the scope always tends to increase. This is called 'scope creep'. Scope creep is a major cause of project failure. Scope is what a project manager agrees and commits to deliver at the completion of the project. It is normally specified in documentation, discussed with stakeholders and then signed off. The project manager's job is then to deliver what has been agreed at the right time and at the right cost and to 'specification'. But, when you run your first project commercially you will find that within days of agreeing the scope you are getting calls to change some small thing, or perhaps a slightly larger thing. This is dangerous, and when you consider that only about a quarter of projects complete on time and in budget, you can see the magnitude of the problem of scope creep.

If I depict the problem graphically it may make more impact. In Figure 16.2 the area of the three circles represents the amount of people, time and money available to complete the agreed project. The scope at the top of the triangle is that agreed before the start of the project. If the project is forced to make small changes to the scope, then what the project manager agreed to deliver grows a little. No problem, you may say! The scope has only increased a little; let's say 10%. Look at Figure 16.3.

Figure 16.3 The project triangle – 10% increase in scope

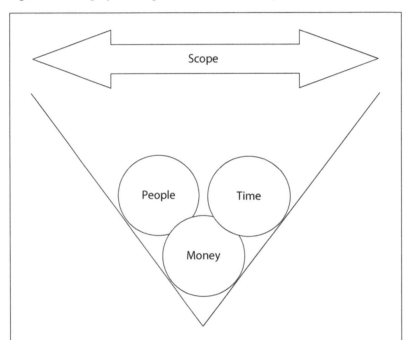

The scope has indeed increased by 10%. But the area of the circles that represent people, time and money have increased by 20%. Small increases in scope will quickly push projects over time and over budget and more people will be needed to complete the project.

What are the main causes of scope creep?

- poor specification of requirements at the planning stage
- not including the stakeholders early and controlling their expectations
- underestimating the complexity of the project
- poor change control
- 'gold-plating' – involves creating top specifications for aspects of the project when a lesser specification would be sufficient.

All projects will encounter some scope creep. In most projects there are procedures to counteract the problem, for example providing contingency allowances – some money not allocated to existing requirements – to account for overspending. Slack is designed into the timescale to allow recovery of some overrunning. Slack is a term used to indicate spare time in the project timescale. Often it is impossible to avoid scope creep, especially when there is a business case for the changes or the changes are required to overcome unforeseen problems. When scope creep does occur, it is important to have a robust system to manage the changes, attribute the cost and time overruns, and communicate the consequences to stakeholders.

LEARNING DIARY

MATHS – I HATE IT

I have just been to a project management lecture where the lecturer explained that by increasing the scope of a project by 10% it would increase the resources required by 20%. But I cannot see it. Is my maths rubbish or is he wrong? I don't normally fixate like this but it is really irritating not to understand how the math works.

I have made an entry here because I am annoyed. Not sure if I am annoyed with the lecturer for not explaining it well enough or with myself for not understanding it.

I am not going to let this one rest. I will ask him to go over this again next week until I understand the point he is making. There must be a moral here somewhere.

Maybe, 'Don't let things you don't understand pass', or if you do, just forget about it. I cannot get the idea out of my head that this could come up in the examination and I would be lost or struggling.

16.3 THE PROJECT PROCESS IN DETAIL

DEFINING THE PROJECT

Successful projects are well designed so that they know in detail what is to be achieved. Projects can have many aims and it is important to specify all of them and the priority of each. An example of a project you will be faced with is the organising and completing of a dissertation.

Take a moment to think about what your aims are in completing a dissertation.

I can think of a few: you can probably think of more, and more-specific ones.

- to pass your degree
- to research something interesting and worthwhile
- to get a first, or 2:1
- to survive this gruelling and unpleasant process.

What order would you place these items in if you had to prioritise them?

I think many people would place them in this order:

1 to survive this gruelling and unpleasant process

2 to pass your degree

3 to get a first, or 2:1

4 to research something interesting and worthwhile.

The example of a dissertation is a simple project with you as the only stakeholder. In 'real-life' projects there will always be multiple stakeholders. Every project has a set of stakeholders. Stakeholders are the people or organisations who are connected to the project and who can influence the aims and outcomes of the project. In the dissertation example I said you were the only stakeholder. This is wrong! Who else do you think is involved and can influence the outcome?

My list would be:

● your supervisor

● the university

● the research methods lecturer

● the research participants

● others you may get help from, such as family and friends.

The expectations of the stakeholders will alter the scope of the project. In completing your dissertation, what do you think will be the expectations of the stakeholders listed above?

In real-life projects we might recognise a wider set of stakeholders:

Project manager – As a key stakeholder in any project, you will need to explore and define your expectations carefully. If you don't 'surface' your real expectations, they will remain under the surface and affect the project without being visible. Take some time before you meet other possible stakeholders to reflect on your expectations. You can prioritise these so that if you need to compromise on some of them, you will know if an expectation is crucial or desirable.

Team members – Team members invest their time and emotions in a project; they must get something out of it. The success of your project will be in the hands of the team members. If they do not understand what is required and cannot see how the project benefits them, they will not perform at the required level. It can be quite difficult to get team members to express their personal expectations of a project, but you will need to take time to explore and 'surface' this area.

Team leaders – In larger projects there will be project areas run by team leaders. This group is vital to the delivery of the project and their aims and expectations need to be explored and taken into account. Extensive separate meetings with this stakeholder group will be needed to not only bring out their expectations, but also to clearly communicate the agreed scope and expectations of the project.

Resource managers – These people are a part of larger projects; they acquire and control a lot of resources. The most frequently occurring role is that of project accountant, especially as cost overruns are a frequent way for projects to fail. Having an effective project accountant who understands the expectations of other stakeholders will be vital to the successful completion of any project.

Senior managers – These are the people who manage the project manager. Their expectations must be surfaced and integrated with the sponsors' and users' expectations. Progress is communicated to them and, when things go wrong, they will be the ones who have to become involved to get the project back 'on track'.

Sponsors and users – Sponsors provide the resources and will have a set of expectations about the project. The user, or end-users, will also have a set of expectations about how whatever it is that is being produced will work and be used when it is complete.

Advocates – This group does not have a formal power to influence the project but they may have an interest in the outcome of the project. We might call this group 'distant stakeholders'; they don't have formal connection but they may be powerful and interested in the outcome of the project. Mostly advocates are interested in the success of the project, but sometimes advocates are interested in the failure of the project and so will need careful 'managing'.

Your role as project manager is to understand the expectations of each group. The expectations of each of these different groups will often be in conflict, so your role is to balance the expectations and agree precisely what will be achieved. This cannot be achieved in one round of discussion. It is what we would call an 'iterative' process. It takes a number of rounds of discussion, specification and reflection before all stakeholders will agree to the defined deliverables. This can be a frustrating phase of project-managing but it is vital to its success.

Stakeholder management

Stakeholder management is a suite of specific processes and procedures that allows for the discussion and agreement of the aims and thereby the scope of a project. In the next chapter we will look at social skills – these are vital to managing stakeholders. As expressed above, the first phase of stakeholder management is to explore and manage expectations. It is vital to understand the values and beliefs of each stakeholder group so that you can fully understand what they want from the project.

The next phase is to build stakeholder commitment. You need to realise that the stakeholders are in a relationship with you as the project manager. Commitment is the glue that binds the project together and allows it to succeed. Commitment is something that develops over time; we could think of it in terms of a ladder.

Figure 16.4 Commitment snakes and ladders

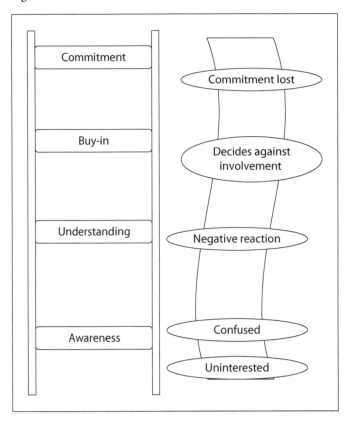

The idea behind Figure 16.4 is that commitment must be consciously developed in phases but can also be easily lost. You need positive actions to build commitment: making people aware, allowing them to understand, encouraging buy-in and then gaining commitment. But you need to guard against them being uninterested, confused, having a negative reaction to the project, making a decision to withdraw or pulling out their commitment late on in the project.

Building commitment is a slow and developmental process, and I would suggest the following steps:

- education activities to understand the project group, the expectations and the benefits of the project
- small group and one-to-one activities to develop trust in the project team and understanding of the emerging project
- meetings to connect the project's proposed outcomes with the stakeholders' 'wants and desires'
- activities to 'sell' the outcomes of the project to stakeholders
- final commitment and sign-off meeting to raise any outstanding issues and formally agree the deliverables and other aspects
- ongoing communication meetings to maintain commitment.

DEFINE THE DELIVERABLES

A successful project must deliver the things it set out to produce. We call these outcomes deliverables, and they will need careful definition at the start of the project process. In many projects, these are things that are built or made. If your organisation has a project to build a new office centre, that will be the deliverable. It will be specified in detail and the standard will be agreed. Mostly deliverables will be by a certain time. It is not uncommon to have diagrams and plans, and written documents to define the deliverable in sufficient detail. Inaccurate specification or insufficient specification of the deliverable is a common reason why projects go wrong and cannot be completed on time or in budget.

If your project is to deliver a short film, the actual deliverables may be:

- a final script
- the film
- a set of extra resources such as stills shots and outtakes.

These may be further specified with times, so that they become:

- a final script – February 2010
- the completed film – January 2011
- a set of extra resources such as stills shots and outtakes – January 2011.

You can carry on specifying the deliverables more closely until all the stakeholders agree that the detail is sufficient and they agree the details of each deliverable. For instance, the second bullet point above may be too risky for the stakeholders and they may ask for an extra deliverable of a first edited cut of the film in September 2010. The film itself may well be specified quite closely in terms of length, quality, media used, number of scenes, cost, number of breaks for adverts, and so on.

PLANNING THE PROJECT

The work breakdown structure (WBS) is the foundation of all project planning. WBS charts define all the tasks that are required to complete the project. In Figure 16.5 you can see that the WBS is defining the task for creating a short film. The defined section in the illustration is the writing and delivering of a final script. This is defined as Script Writing Task 5. Organisations define levels in a WBS chart so that teams deliver the higher-level activities and one person often delivers the lower-level activities, but these can also be assigned to a small team. You can see an example of a three-level WBS in Figure 16.6.

WBS charts break down the deliverables into the component tasks. Each small element is specified by:

- a task description: a detailed description of the task to be completed
- preceded by: the task that must be completed before this task

- responsible: sometimes referred to as 'owner', this is the person responsible for carrying out the task or ensuring that the task is carried out
- role: is the specified role of the responsible person; this helps when people or responsibilities change
- monitored: is the person responsible for ensuring the task has been completed to the required standard
- % complete: this indicates the progress of the task from 0 to 100%
- start/finish dates and number of days allowed to complete the task.

Then come a range of financial columns dealing with:

- hour cost
- day cost
- total cost
- budgeted cost
- actual cost
- variance from budgeted cost to actual cost – this shows if this task has been completed under or over budget.

Figure 16.5 Standard WBS chart

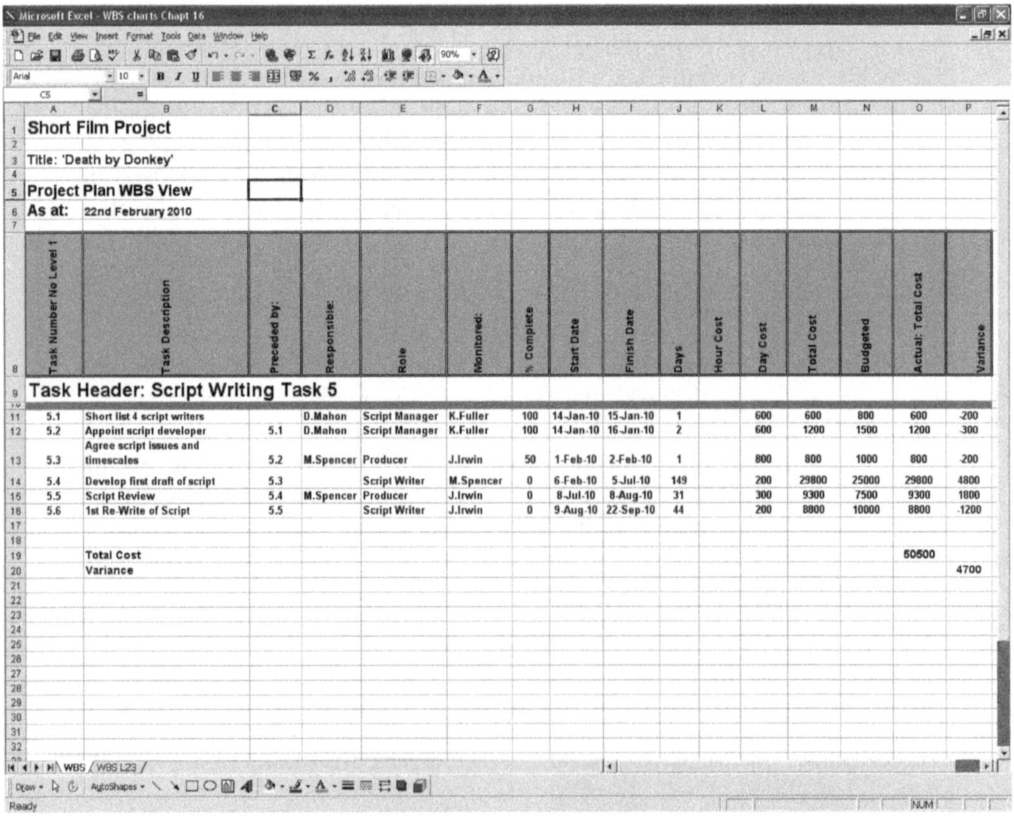

Short Film Project

Title: 'Death by Donkey'

Project Plan WBS View

As at: 22nd February 2010

Task Number No Level 1	Task Description	Preceded by:	Responsible:	Role	Monitored:	% Complete	Start Date	Finish Date	Days	Hour Cost	Day Cost	Total Cost	Budgeted	Actual: Total Cost	Variance
Task Header: Script Writing Task 5															
5.1	Short list 4 script writers		D.Mahon	Script Manager	K.Fuller	100	14-Jan-10	15-Jan-10	1		600	600	800	600	-200
5.2	Appoint script developer	5.1	D.Mahon	Script Manager	K.Fuller	100	14-Jan-10	16-Jan-10	2		600	1200	1500	1200	-300
5.3	Agree script issues and timescales	5.2	M.Spencer	Producer	J.Irwin	50	1-Feb-10	2-Feb-10	1		800	800	1000	800	-200
5.4	Develop first draft of script	5.3		Script Writer	M.Spencer	0	6-Feb-10	5-Jul-10	149		200	29800	25000	29800	4800
5.5	Script Review	5.4	M.Spencer	Producer	J.Irwin	0	8-Jul-10	8-Aug-10	31		300	9300	7500	9300	1800
5.6	1st Re-Write of Script	5.5		Script Writer	J.Irwin	0	9-Aug-10	22-Sep-10	44		200	8800	10000	8800	-1200
	Total Cost													50500	
	Variance														4700

The WBS chart is the major planning tool in projects, and this detailed breakdown is necessary to carry out some of the more visual planning tools. WBS charts can also be created as a hierarchical diagram, where each deliverable is connected backwards to each sub-task until the deliverable is fully specified.

Figure 16.6 Three-level WBS chart

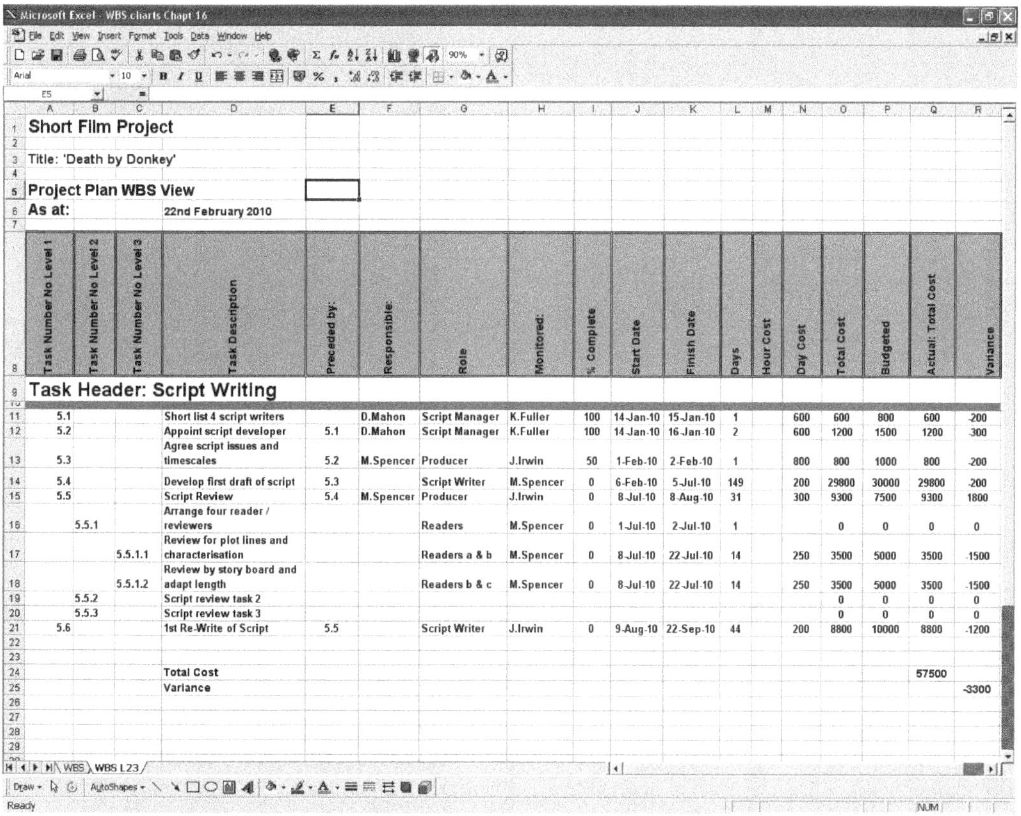

OTHER BREAKDOWN STRUCTURES

Breakdown structure charts can be produced for other resources and also for risks. A commonly used chart is the resources breakdown structure (RBS), which lists and defines all the available resources and allocates those resources to the tasks in a WBS. Some projects will not need full-time personnel for some tasks. For example, if you are carrying out building projects, you would not need a solar engineer full-time on one project but you might need one full-time person to work across six or eight projects. Using an RBS chart will allow you to allocate the solar engineer to each of the projects at the correct time. Where there are numerous personnel to carry out one task or function, the RBS can be used to allocate the resource to the tasks in an effective manner. For example, if you have six electricians you can use the RBS chart to allocate them to tasks either singularly or in pairs or in small groups. The RBS is just another type of planning chart.

Another commonly created breakdown chart is the risk breakdown structure (RiBS). All projects can be affected by outside risks. Planning what possible risks might affect a project and the likelihood of those risks occurring is vital to the success of the project. An example of an RiBS is shown below.

EXAMPLE: RIBS CHART FOR A GENERIC BUILDING PROJECT

Risk Description	Risk factor P × I	Impact (1–5)	Probability (1–5)	Contingency
Planning permission is refused and the proposal has to be appealed to the Secretary of State	15	5	3	Extensive relationship management with local residents before planning application meeting
Inclement weather during the construction phase causing delays	20	5	4	Five slack periods built into contract. Contingency plan (12.36) prepared for 24/7 working. Monitor at 12/7, 6/8, 2/9, 12/10.
Major accident causes closedown of construction. Typically 10 days lost from data evidence (7.81)	9	3	3	Health and safety team to monitor 'near-misses' or low-level accidents. Accident recovery plan in place (24.13).

Risk breakdown structure (RiBS) charts come in many and varied forms but the example above sets out the common elements of most charts. The first column describes the risk and may, as the example does, link to evidence. The numbers in brackets refer to other documents. The risk factor is a calculation of the impact x probability. A risk that has a large impact on the project and is likely to occur would be rated at 25; a low-impact risk that is unlikely to occur would be rated as 1–5. Each project will set guidelines for actions and contingencies related to risks. Risks above 15 would, in many projects, have an associated contingency plan that sets out in detail what actions will be taken if the risk occurs. Impact is used in the calculation of the risk factor and is the effect on the project if the risk occurs – high impact 5 through to low impact 1. Probability is used in the calculation of the risk factor and is the likelihood of the risk occurring, 5 being very likely and 1 being unlikely. The final column lists the contingency actions. This will often include a reference, the number in brackets, to a detailed contingency plan.

BECOMING REFLECTIVE PERFORMERS

Simon: 'How's the new job going?'

Louise: 'Good; very good, but full-time work is so tiring.'

S: 'Tell me about it! Such long hours and pressure!'

L: 'What are you on at the moment?'

S: 'I started my first PM role about five weeks ago.'

L: 'You're the Prime Minister already?'

S: 'No, project manager!'

L: 'Yes. Got it now. What is the project doing?'

S: 'Well, it is only small but very important. It is a celebrity client. I am not even allowed to say who it is.'

L: 'Oh go on, do tell.'

S: 'No, I would be sacked if I did. I had to sign a confidentially agreement before I was given the project brief.'

L: 'Serious celebrity then.'

S: 'Well, not really a celebrity. A bit above that.'

L: 'Intriguing.'

S: 'It is a project on the River Dart to create energy from the tidal areas of the river on land owned by... Sorry, confidential.'

L: 'Oh give over; it cannot be that confidential; it's an energy scheme.'

S: 'Well, I do have to meet a certain someone and feel like I have to bow.'

L: 'Anyway, the scheme sounds interesting. What's it about?'

S: 'I thought you would never ask. The River Dart has a daily rise and fall of 5.6 metres and the project is designed to generate power from that sea level rise.'

L: 'You can get power from the rising tide?'

S: 'Yes you can. The project with its celebrity connection is really stressful and I don't really know if I can do it.'

L: 'Tell me more!'

S: 'Well, it is project management but nothing like we learned at university. The basic process is the same and we create WBSs and critical paths and all that stuff, but the real pressure comes from getting the workforce to do it.'

L: 'I think I see.'

S: 'The people side of project management is completely underplayed at university. There are rows and politics and "huffishness". People seem to be nothing but trouble.'

L: 'But they are also the way the job gets done.'

S: 'That is so right! But it is all so slow and painful.'

L: 'You never really were a people person; you were a good technical and logical person.'

S: 'Well now I am learning very fast about people.'

L: 'Do you see much of the sponsor? He who cannot be named with the initials...?'

S: 'Yes, that just adds more pressure. He visits about once a week and I have to stop managing and spend about half a day walking around and showing him stuff.'

L: 'So he is really interested in what's going on then.'

S: 'Yes, so enthusiastic and committed to it. It is like his force of personality is driving it forward. It just adds so much pressure.'

L: 'You're not at breaking point, are you?'

S: 'No, I don't think so, but I never would have imagined how hard I have had to work to stay afloat. Eighteen-hour days are not so unusual.'

L: 'I thought there was a Working Time Directive that limits working hours.'

S: 'There is, but it doesn't seem to apply to me.'

L: 'How well are they paying you?'

S: 'Oh that bit is really good. They pay me loads and I am so busy I have no time to spend any of it. I should be able to buy a house very soon.'

L: 'Oh well, not all bad then.'

S: 'No, not too bad, just not how I imagined work would be. It sort of takes over your life.'

L: 'Tell me about it!'

16.4 PROJECT TIMELINES

Managing time and delivering on time is a major outcome of any project. There are several ways to plan the timeline of projects. I will look at just two Gantt charts and critical path analysis (CPA). Both of these tools allow for the graphical communication of timelines. The Gantt chart is descriptive and the CPA is analytic.

GANTT CHARTS

The Gantt chart is named after Henry Gantt and is widely used for planning and communicating the timeline of simple projects. The horizontal or X axis represents time and the scale will vary depending on the project. The vertical or Y axis contains the detail of each task in the project ordered so that the progression bars move from left to right. Where one task must come before another, the progression bars follow sequentially. Where two of more tasks can occur together, the progression bars can be one on top of the other.

In Figure 16.7 you can see a simple Gantt chart detailing the process of producing a dissertation. On the left is the task number. Larger tasks can be broken down into more detail by adding a row and using the task number 2.1, indicating it is task 1 of a higher-order task 2. In large projects you might find four or five levels of task numbering. So that you might have a small task with the number 2.1.12.18, indicating it is at the fourth level of task 2. The task description will need to be specified sufficiently to carry out the task. In the example the progression chart is marked off at two-week intervals, but any time interval that allows for the right level of planning is acceptable. A small time-dependent task may have one week as the whole timescale. This is a fairly basic Gantt chart; you can enhance it by adding extra elements. The following are all useful additions to the basic chart:

- a vertical marker indicating the present time
- change the colour of the progression bar as the work is completed
- connect tasks with arrows and lines to indicate when one task is dependent on another
- use comment boxes to indicate when an important resource is required
- use extra charts at different levels to plan the progress of sub-tasks
- add vertical lines to indicate important milestones.

Figure 16.7 Gantt chart of dissertation time plan

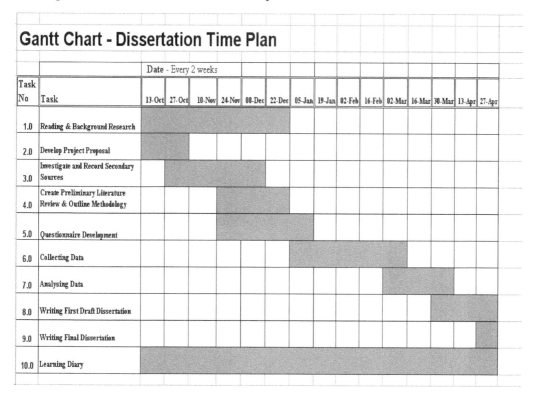

These charts can easily be produced in Microsoft Excel, as in the example. You can also produce a more visually appealing chart by adding the data of task, start time, duration, then using the stacked bar chart form to represent it.

If you are using Microsoft Project, the Gantt charts will be produced automatically by the software. This is exceptionally easy in that you have two panes: a spreadsheet look-alike pane for entering tasks and a Gantt chart pane that represents what you enter. Once you have tasks in the Gantt chart view, you can drag and drop them and link one to another. You can add milestones and control resources and risks.

Figure 16.8 Example Gantt chart in Excel

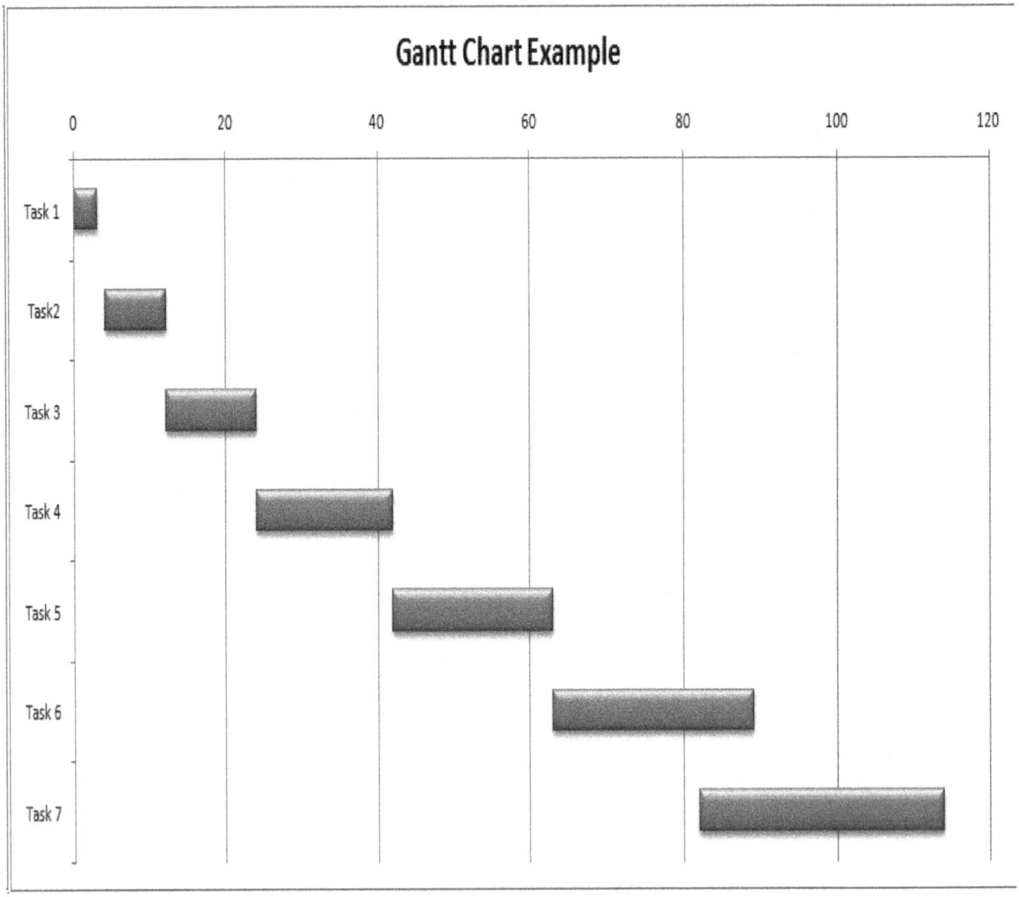

Gantt Chart Example

CRITICAL PATH ANALYSIS

Critical path analysis (CPA) is an analytic planning tool for projects. It sets out the tasks that are required for the whole project. It shows the order and dependencies of tasks. The key component in CPA diagrams is an estimate of the time each task will take. Once the detail is programmed into the diagram, the critical path can be determined. The total time along the critical path is the minimum time to complete the project. CPA allows you to control the float or slack time in a project. Often the planning is designed to minimise the total time taken. But projects can introduce slack time as a contingency. It is important to remember that the times in a CPA diagram are estimates and can and will change as the project progresses.

REFLECTIVE PERFORMING

GANTT CHART IN EXCEL

Open a worksheet in Microsoft Excel 2007 and add the following data.

	A	**B**	**C**
1	Task	Start	Duration
2	Task 1	0	3
3	Task 2	4	8
4	Task 3	12	12
5	Task 4	24	18
6	Task 5	42	21
7	Task 6	63	26
8	Task 7	82	32

Highlight the cells A1 to C8. Then follow the instructions:

- On the Insert tab, click **Bar, 2D Stacked**.
- From chart styles choose Style 27.
- Click on the legend on the right, then right-click **Delete**.
- On the Layout tab, second from last, click chart title and add a title.
- Double-click on the first part of the stacked bar then right-click **Format Data Series, Fill** in the left-hand pane, then click **solid fill**, then **no fill**.
- Finally, to turn the chart around so that the earliest is first, click the Y Axis that lists the tasks, right-click **Format Axis**, then click the radio button **Categories in Reverse order**.

You can experiment with the chart to change various elements.

1 You might like to add a clear timescale and a better task numbering system.

2 You might also want to experiment with making the numbers in the table more like the correct start times. At the moment it works visually but not in date terms.

3 You might also want to experiment with sub-tasks of a different colour.

The elements of a CPA

Nodes are the points where activities start and finish. Nodes are represented by circles and identified with a number: an earliest start time and a latest start time.

- CPAs must begin and end with a node.
- Paths in the diagram should not cross.
- Lines represent activities or tasks and each should be labelled with a name or a letter.
- Each activity line will be marked with the time to complete.

Figure 16.9 CPA diagram (annotated)

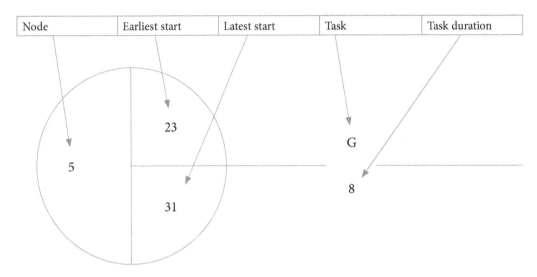

Nodes are then connected together with tasks or activities to represent the complete process.

Figure 16.10 CPA diagram

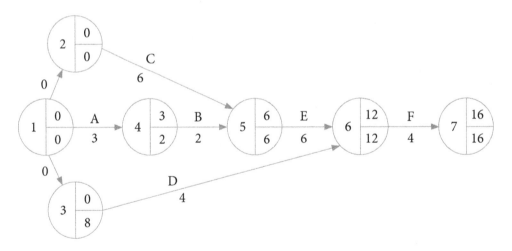

Let's say that Figure 16.10 represents a project such as building a large shed, with the following tasks to be completed:

- A – Order shed and arrange delivery (3 days).
- B – Paint panels before construction (2 days).
- C – Build concrete base (6 days).
- D – Arrange for delivery of special safety glass (4 days).

- E – Erect shed (6 days).
- F – Fit roof and weather-proof (4 days).

The numbers in the nodes for the earliest start times are worked out as follows:

- Nodes 1, 2, 3 are starting points.
- Node 1 to 4 has activity A between it, which takes three days, so the earliest node 4 can start is three days; that number is placed in the upper quarter (the bottom latest start time will be dealt with later).
- Node 4 to 5 have activity B between it, but it is also dependent on activity C from node 2, which takes six days – so the earliest that node 5 can start is six days.
- Activity E leads on to node 6 and that takes six days; it is also dependent on activity D, which takes four days from the start – so the earliest that node 6 can start is 12 days.
- Finally, activity F takes four days to the finish node 7 – so the earliest that the project can finish is 16 days.

The numbers in the nodes for the latest start times are now calculated by working in reverse order. The earliest finish time is assumed to also be the latest finish time:

- Node 7 – receives the earliest time as 16, the same as the latest finish time.
- Node 7 to 6 has activity F, which takes four days, so 16–4 = 12. This number is placed in the bottom quarter of the node to represent the latest finish time.
- Node 6 to 5 has activity E of six days, so the latest time to this node is 12–6 = 6; place this number in the bottom quarter.
- Node 6 to 3 activity D takes four days, so the calculation is 12–4 = 8.
- Node 5 to 4 takes two days, so the latest node 3 can start is 6–2 = 4.
- Node 5 to 2 takes six days, so 6–6 = 0; so Node 2 latest start time is 0.

We now have the earliest and latest times for each node. The critical path runs through the nodes that have earliest and latest times equal.

Our critical path for our shed is therefore:

- Nodes 1, 2, 5, 6, 7.

In activities it is C, E, F.

To effectively manage a project, it is important to know the critical path because it defines which are the most important tasks. In our example the project manager would concentrate on ensuring the following three activities started and progress to plan: the concrete base, the building of the shed and the roofing of the shed. Conversely, if there was a slight delay on getting the safety glass, it would not be crucial, just as it would not matter if the delivery of the shed was one day late. You can see that knowing the critical path allows the project manager to be relaxed about some things and vigilant about others.

STUDENT COMMENT

It had never dawned on me the significance of the critical path of a project until I made a complete mess of my dissertation. The tutors were telling us all to make progress early and that students sometimes fail because they run out of time. But I didn't see it.

Then my tutor invited me in to see him and he said I was probably going to fail if I didn't do something drastic. He sketched out my project on a bit of paper as a critical path and showed how I did not have enough time to finish by the deadline. That was a real shock to me. But the shock jolted me into action and I really adjusted things and worked on a new and quicker critical path. After the panic I did manage to sort it out and finish on time. But, I feel sure I could have got a better grade if I had applied a few project management principles in the first place.

16.5 COMMUNICATION

Planning and organising is wasted if it is not communicated effectively. Larger projects will require complex webs of communication. During the execution phase if a change is made to one of the tasks, it needs to be communicated quickly and accurately to the team. If a change to the specification of an item needs to be made, the request and approval needs to be fast and precise. Reporting progress is a specific type of communication that needs to be planned and executed effectively. As a project manager it is difficult to remember what needs to be communicated to whom, so a communications matrix is often used.

Projects need to communicate with different groups using different strategies. In most projects you will have to communicate with the following:

- project team
- team leaders
- your senior managers
- stakeholders
- sponsors
- the media
- the public
- advocates
- the end-user
- suppliers.

One way to manage communications is to use a communications matrix. This is a list of actions and against those actions a list of who is to be communicated with when this action takes place. I will use a simplified form to illustrate how this works. In the matrix below you will see some common actions and the communication that needs to follow the action.

Table 16.1 Communications matrix

Actions	Team	Team leaders	Senior management	Stakeholders	End-users	Company SMT contact	Media	Sponsors	Method
Changes	✓	✓				✓			Change docket
Milestones	✓	✓	✓	✓	✓	✓	✓		Press release
Progress reports internal			✓			✓			KPI and progress document, variance on budget
Progress reports external				✓	✓	✓			Press release
Task assignments	✓	✓							Weekly allocation document
Project aims			✓	✓	✓	✓			Project document variance statement
Topping out			✓	✓		✓	✓	✓	Press release
Cost overrun		✓	✓						Variance statement
Resource allocation	✓	✓	✓						RBS chart

The matrix can be adjusted to show the group or person to be communicated with on the left and the actions that will trigger that communication.

16.6 PROJECT MANAGEMENT SOFTWARE

Microsoft Excel

The main advantage of Microsoft Excel is that you probably already have the software, so it will cost you nothing to manage your project by using it. The second advantage is that you will probably know how to use it. If the project is relatively simple, such as an undergraduate project, Excel will be an effective tool. Once a project becomes more complex it becomes difficult to manage all the elements in an integrated manner. Workplace projects are often managed using Microsoft Project.

MICROSOFT PROJECT

Microsoft Project is designed to assist you with the processes of managing a project. It is software that can help with:

- developing plans
- allocating resources
- tracking progress
- creating and managing budgets
- assigning and analysing workloads
- creating critical paths
- producing Gantt charts and network diagrams
- producing reports
- analysing activities.

Figure 16.11 Gantt chart in Microsoft Project

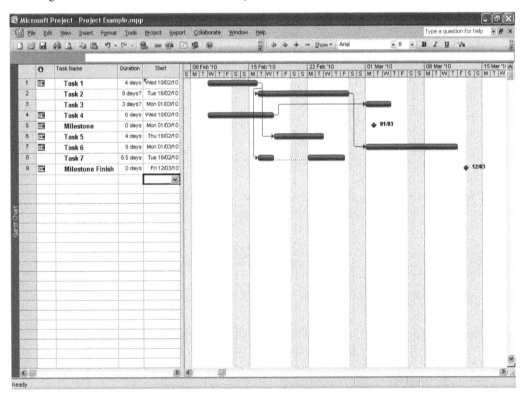

Using any software will present advantages and disadvantages. There are two main disadvantages of Microsoft Project. It is expensive to purchase and it takes quite a while to learn to be effective at using it. This second point means that you will spend a considerable amount of time learning how to use the software. For simple projects it really is a large sledgehammer to crack a small nut.

However, when managing large and complex projects, it is a powerful and effective tool for planning, controlling and communicating.

Figure 16.12 Example network diagram

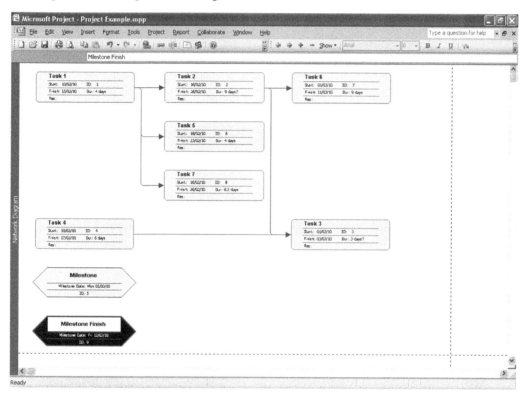

PRINCE2™

PRINCE2 is a process-based project method used by many organisations in the UK and globally. The acronym stands for **PR**ojects **IN** **C**ontrolled **E**nvironments. PRINCE2 is a developed version of earlier project systems PRINCE and PROMPT. PRINCE2 is a process method that has eight major headings. It is well established and is often specified in tenders for works related to large businesses and government departments. You can undertake training in the process and become qualified.

The eight top-level headings are:

1 Starting Up a Project (SU)

2 Planning (PL)

3 Initiating a Project (IP)

4 Directing a Project (DP)

5 Controlling a Stage (CS)

6 Managing Product Delivery (MP)

7 Managing Stage Boundaries (SB)

8 Closing a Project (CP).

Each stage is defined in the process as follows.

SU – Starting Up a Project addresses the vital tasks of getting a project up and running. These include:

- appointing a project team
- preparing an outline proposal
- defining aims
- preparing a business case.

PL – Planning begins by analysis and determination of the detailed aspects of the product or service.

IP – Initiating a project concerns the detailed documentation of the business case and the aims of the project. Planning the nature of the quality outputs and the controls of quality also occur in this stage. The finale of this stage is a full and complete set of project documentation.

DP – Directing a project focuses on the control of the project. It carefully defines the authorisation and control processes.

CS – Controlling a stage defines the procedures and practices to control the individual stages of the project. There will be many and varied stages to even the simplest of projects. Projects don't always go to plan and so corrective actions will be planned and controlled in this stage. The finish of this stage is when the planned and corrective work is complete.

MP – Managing product delivery is concerned with acceptance and operation of the completed project.

SB – Managing stage boundaries precisely defines and controls the tasks that should be contained in the various stages of the project. It also concerns the maintenance of project records, such as log files and amendment tools.

CP – Closing a project itemises how the project will be wound up and the evaluation of the project.

If you carry out a project or a stage or phase of a project in a large contractor, business or government department, you will probably find it is being controlled by the PRINCE2 methodology.

CASE STUDY

KATSU'S STUNNING GARDEN BUILDING

Katsu has been successful in her role as project manager for a large IT company. This has brought her responsibility and a six-figure salary. She now feels that she has worked hard enough for long enough and would like to relax and spend some time developing other interests. To help her relax and enjoy a slower pace of life, she is going to have a large and very stunning building built in her large garden. The neighbours are a bit worried about this proposal for such a large building in Katsu's garden.

The building will require planning permission, which will take about six to eight weeks to achieve. It is going to be built of Swedish cedar and is pre-assembled in large sections in a factory in Gavle in Sweden and then shipped to the UK and transported by lorry. The manufacture takes about six to eight weeks and the shipping will take 10–14 days. The sections are too large to get into Katsu's garden other than by crane and the road outside is quite small. The total weight of the building is 54 tonnes. The foundations for the building are circular 600mm concrete pile foundations driven 3,500mm into the ground; there will need to be 32 piles. Concrete takes 28 days to harden to full strength and develops 82% of its full strength in seven days. The building is L-shaped consisting of two rectangles 10 metres by 6 metres and 8 metres by 6 metres. The roofing material is Swedish cedar shingles, which will need a specialist roofer to supply and fit; it is not clear how long this will take. The building requires the following services:

- electricity
- gas
- water
- waste removal
- fast broadband
- satellite television.

The manufacturers claim that the building can be erected in four days by a team of six people in fine weather. Katsu wants the building to be painted with a very light garden green paint on the outside and a pale cream on the inside.

Katsu has planned a grand opening of the building on 4 May.

To think about...

- Who will be the stakeholders in Katsu's building?
- Create a WBS chart to account for all the activities needed to create Katsu's stunning garden building.
- Create a Gantt chart to visually display the progress of the building.
- Create a critical path diagram that ensures Katsu's building is ready by 4 May.
- Create a communication matrix to manage and control the necessary communications.

If you have access to project management software, you can use that to help manage the build.

SUMMARY

Project management skills are vital to business. Try to develop these before you carry out your dissertation.

- Understand the project lifecycle:
  - defining
  - planning

- implementing
- closing
- evaluating.

- Understand the nature of project scope and how an increase in scope increases other areas of the project. The project triangle helps to control the scope of the following elements:
  - people
  - time
  - money.

- The project process consists of various stages:
  - defining the project
  - stakeholder management
  - definition of deliverables
  - planning the project
  - using other breakdown structures, such as resources and risk.

- Develop accurate and visual timelines using:
  - Gantt charts
  - critical path analysis.

- Communicate to all interested parties using a communications matrix.

- For larger and more complex projects use project software:
  - Microsoft Project
  - PRINCE2.

EXPLORE FURTHER

FURTHER READING

Biafore, B. (2007) *Microsoft Project 2007: The missing manual.* Sebastopol, CA: O'Reilly Media.

Reed, J. (2008) *Project Management with PRINCE2 Best Practice Handbook: Building, running and managing effective project management – ready to use.* Brisbane, Australia: Emereo Publishing.

Slack, N. (2000) *Operations Management.* London: Prentice Hall.

WEB LINKS

Project Management Institute: http://www.pmi.org.uk/

The Association for Project Management: http://www.apm.org.uk/

Project Management Today: http://www.projectnet.com/

CHAPTER 17

Social Skills

What skills will I develop in this chapter?

- six key social skills for work and university
- emotional intelligence
- good listening
- excellent networking

17.1 INTRODUCTION

Social skills are as important in business as technical and transferable skills. This chapter explores and develops some of the important social skills, starting with a look at six social skills to make you effective in the workplace. Social skills are about getting on with your university and workplace colleagues. They make a huge difference to how much you like and respect yourself and how much other people like and respect you. The six key social skills are my creation from my experience in teaching and working in organisations. Since the mid-1990s and the publication of a book by Daniel Goleman, emotional intelligence (EI) is a familiar term in business and at university. Emotional intelligence is now a huge field of study and I present a limited introduction to the theory and ideas. A later section takes a look at two of the most important skills in business: listening and networking. You might think everyone can listen, but it is a more demanding skill than it might at first seem. Business and business success thrives on networking and you will need to develop skills to squeeze the most out of your networking opportunities. Business networks will get you jobs, lose you jobs and allow you to make sales and seek help. You cannot overestimate the importance of being a good networker.

17.2 SIX SOCIAL SKILLS AT WORK

Having an appropriate set of general social skills is vital to your survival in a business environment. Later in the chapter we will look at more specific skills, but in this introduction to social skills I will consider the basic range of skills that anyone would need to survive at work. When you are selecting candidates to join your organisation, or being interviewed for a job, you will be assessing or will be assessed on some or all of these skills. As with many aspects of social skills, there are very few reliable and widely agreed 'maps' of what is required. In many respects you would expect the emphasis placed on each of the following skills to vary by organisation.

Humans are social animals and business is a social process. So it is hardly surprising that businesses are looking for social skills as well as technical skills. Quite frequently they do not appear as specific skills listed on an employee specification, but most recruitment processes will be testing that candidates will 'fit in'. How much you enjoy working for any particular organisation will depend on how well your social skills align with the organisational culture. Social skills will also determine how quickly and how far you are promoted. Like most skills, learning, reflection, change and practice can improve social skills.

1 COMFORT ZONE

To function in social settings you need to remain relaxed and to control your anxiety levels. You may have experienced the anxiousness of new and pressured social settings. It is quite normal to feel a little anxious when faced with unknown or new social settings. However, you have to be able to control this anxiety to a level that you feel comfortable with, that is, stay within your comfort zone. Very few people can operate effectively when they are constantly outside their comfort zone. If you are too anxious, your mind is working too hard in controlling this anxiety and it means you are less inclined to listen carefully and respond appropriately. You will be sending out non-verbal communication signals that will indicate this to those around you. It is very difficult to build rapport with those around you when you are anxious.

How can you control anxiety? Remember, there will be short periods when anxiety is a perfectly normal response, but there will also be times when you need to think positively about controlling your anxiety. The first area to think about is avoiding foods and drinks that may increase anxiety. Caffeine and junk food are two things that can make you more anxious. In Chapter 8 we thought about controlling your breathing during presenting anxiety. Making a conscious effort to control your breathing will help to avoid feelings of anxiety. Shallow breathing is a response to anxiety; try to change to abdominal breathing. This consists of breathing deeply, in through your nose and filling your abdomen, then breathe gently out of your mouth. Don't do more than three or four of these deep breathing cycles because you can feel a bit dizzy.

If you find that being anxious at work does not pass in a short time, contact your doctor or the occupational health adviser at your university or place of work.

2 LISTENING SKILLS

Listening skills are vital at university and work, but listening is not just 'not talking'. You can easily develop your listening skills and, once learned, you will hear and understand much more of what people are saying. You need to listen carefully before you can understand someone or have empathy with his or her feelings and circumstances. There is a larger section on listening later in the chapter.

3 EMPATHY SKILLS

Empathy means to feel the same things as someone else. Empathy consists of understanding someone's feelings and also being able to share them. Empathy is a vital social skill so that groups, teams and even just two people can fully understand and jointly 'feel' situations and circumstances. There is an old saying about not judging someone until you have 'walked a mile in their shoes'. This warns about making judgements about someone's work, position, actions, beliefs or feelings until you know what those feelings are. Once you understand in an empathetic manner, you will be able to help them to deal with whatever feelings they have.

Understand that to empathise is not soft management – Encourage your staff or peers to express their emotions, thoughts and feelings. Remember de Bono's six thinking hats from Chapter 13. Encourage your staff to wear the red hat. An emotional workplace is not one of tears and tantrums; it is one where all members of the team understand where the other members are coming from. It may take a bit longer to make decisions and agree strategy when emotion is involved, but you will get better decisions that allow the organisation to make better progress.

Listen to feelings, not words – Listening to feelings requires you to interpret the words that are spoken. They have said 'this or that'; how must they be feeling? When someone says, 'I just can't believe they would do this to us' – what does this mean? It can mean many things, but you might be able to determine that they are feeling: worthless, unloved, betrayed. By interpreting the feeling behind the words you can be in a better position to empathise.

Read body language if you want to know feelings – By reading body language you can better understand the feelings that the person may have.

Know your own feelings and compare them with others – Use your learning diary to record your emotions in various circumstances. In OneNote, have a separate 'emotions diary' page. Knowing about your own emotions helps you to perceive them and understand them in other people. You can compare your emotions in any given situation with other people. One technique is to have an emotions debrief. This allows all the participants in an emotional event to put their feelings on the table.

Mirroring – This involves copying all the visual cues of someone else to assist in understanding their feelings. Recent research has led to the understanding that there are parts of the brain that have neurons especially adapted for empathy.
A warning – be careful with this technique because in face-to-face encounters mirroring can look like you are mocking. To mirror someone's behaviour, copy

all the visual cues; if they are frowning, frown; if they are hunched up, hunch up. You are trying to copy as many visual aspects as you can. You will be surprised how effective this technique is in allowing you to understand what the other person is feeling.

> ## 〞 STUDENT COMMENT
>
> I work for a small advertising agency part-time while I do my degree. Just the other day we had some shock news that the agency was being sold to a larger rival. We were all shocked! We were invited to a 'meet the new owners meeting' – they did a lot of talking and we all sat in stunned silence.
>
> After the meeting one of the group suggested we go to the pub to unload our emotions. I hadn't heard it put like this before and said 'What?' She said it would be a good idea to have an emotional debrief. I thought, 'Well, I'll give it a try.' It turned out to be very liberating and amazingly useful. There were nine of us and we all took three minutes to unload our emotions onto the table. Debbie, who suggested it, used a large piece of paper to record everything.
>
> I found that I was not alone in feeling very scared about this takeover. But I was quite surprised by some of the fears and feelings the others came out with. After our session I felt a lot less sorry for myself; when I understood what the others were going through I found I had a great deal of empathy and worry for them.

What are you trying to mirror? Things such as:

- posture
- breathing
- tone of voice
- type of language
- eye contact
- eye movements
- hand expressions
- head posture
- verbal approaches.

As you become more experienced in mirroring, you will find it not only improves your ability to understand the other person's feelings but it also improves your rapport with that person. See the section below.

Role-play – Role-play is useful for understanding another person's feelings but is most useful in helping groups to understand the feelings associated with groups and individuals. Business role-plays can assist in many areas of the business process. For example, if a group role-plays the buying decision for any particular product, they are in a stronger position to understand the unique selling point and the key blockages to closing a sale. Role-playing the recruitment process will allow trainee interviewers to understand the feelings of candidates. There are numerous possibilities for understanding better the feelings of individuals and groups using role-play.

Practise empathetic narratives – If you can practise using empathetic narratives, such as 'how are you feeling?' 'what is it that makes you feel this way?' and 'I expect that creates a vivid feeling', you can build confidence in speaking about empathy. Practising these types of words will soon allow you to speak them to others. You do need to become comfortable with the words and the emotions of empathy.

Building empathy skills is vital to modern business. The more you can engage with feelings and emotions, the more you will be in touch with an important aspect of doing business.

4 RAPPORT SKILLS

Rapport is about matching your communication to other people's behaviour. When you do accurately match then communication is easy and flowing and outcomes are easy to agree. Essentially it is a mirroring process, because people like people that are like themselves. Rapport is a vital social skill and is valuable in so many situations, such as dealing with complaints, interviews, selling, pacifying angry people, getting decisions, negotiation, controlling meetings and getting colleagues to work together.

Mirroring and matching needs to be subtle and just below the point where another person would find it obvious. Remember it is mirroring and not copying. If you just exactly copy what the other person is doing it will soon become obvious and the rapport will be lost. You need to use similar actions, not exact copies of actions. So if someone crossed their arms, cross your legs. If someone is fiddling with their pencil, use a similar action with your ear. When you first start to use mirroring it can seem very contrived and silly – keep developing and you will soon be able to subtly mirror other people's behaviour. Mirroring requires that you match the rhythm of their movements. When rapport is building, the conversation will build.

You will note that to build rapport using mirroring you will need to closely observe the other person. One of the main areas that you will quickly notice is their preferred sensory approach.

Visual people – Visual people use terms such as 'I see what you mean' and 'It appears as if that will work'. The main cues of people who prefer visual communication is that they speak quickly, breathe shallowly and look upwards. You can build rapport with these people by communicating in visual ways.

Auditory people – Auditory people use terms such as 'that rings a bell' and 'I have got that loud and clear'. The main cues of people who prefer auditory communication is that they speak more slowly, make rhythmic movements with their body or arms, such as swaying gently, and they tend to look sideways. You can build rapport with these people by matching their rhythm, posture and eye movements.

Kinaesthetic people – These people use terms like 'I feel it would be best to do this' and 'I will be in touch'. The main cues to people who prefer kinaesthetic communication are speaking slowly and ponderously, looking down and breathing slowly. To build rapport with these people, match their movements and speak about actions and events.

Remember, just as you can skilfully build rapport, there will be situations when you want to break it down. In this situation you simply display mismatches to break the rapport. This is useful when you want to end a conversation or meeting. Typical mismatch activities include:

- showing impatience, pen-fiddling, sighing, looking away
- exclusion posture, like leaning back and folding your arms
- turning away and looking to other things
- touching your face and covering your eyes suggests withdrawing
- removing eye contact for long periods.

Telephone rapport is a very different skill, as your voice has to do all the work of mirroring. For telephone conversations it might be better to call this reflecting rather than mirroring. Reflecting is a sound word and mirroring is a visual word. The principle is the same in that people like people who are like themselves. The first point is to reflect the pacing of the conversation so that if your caller speaks slowly, you would speak slowly as well. An individual's pattern of pausing is often quite distinctive, so reflect that pattern back to them. If you pick up on an accent, move your tone to a similar accent. If the caller's phrasing suggests something about them, such as age, try to match that phrasing. Visualising the other person can help you to reflect their actions and approach.

5 MAINTAINING AND DISPLAYING REASONABLE SELF-ESTEEM AND SELF-WORTH

Self-esteem and self-worth are two terms that are what we might call near-synonyms; they mean almost the same. There are some more terms you will know, such as self-regard, self-respect, self-love. It is the difficulty of 'bounding' the term that leads to so many near-synonyms. I will use the term self-esteem as a global term that might be characterised as meaning:

- the value we place on ourselves
- our feelings of inherent worth – over and above our skills
- our innate abilities, values and beliefs
- our competence in life
- our life comparator with others.

Having sustainable or reasonable self-esteem is a social skill. It is socially debilitating to have too high a level of self-esteem just as it is debilitating to have self-esteem that is too low. When people are seen by others to have excessively high self-esteem, there is a tendency for people to avoid them or to set out to 'bring them down a peg or two'. When people have very low self-esteem there is a tendency for others to think they are worthless and to ignore them. Members of the social circle we call business have responsibilities to maintain a reasonable self-esteem for ourselves and to be responsible for the self-esteem of those around us.

It is worth making a warning note here about the concept of self-esteem in global organisations. The concept of self-esteem is a Western phenomenon that developed earliest in the USA and then found favour as a concept in Western Europe. In some parts of the world, where social organisational principles are stronger, it is an alien concept. In Western business it is thought of as something that needs to be managed, developed in some and lowered in others, the desire of business being to harness the positive effects of self-esteem without the problem of people with excessively high or low self-esteem.

Maintaining your self-esteem

Business and university environments can be tough on your self-esteem, easily causing it to lower. This is because many of the outputs are what we might call 'hard'; they are objective outputs. If you get 32% for your assignment, it is difficult if not impossible to avoid the conclusion that the work was not good enough. If your sales figures are the lowest in the region, it is difficult to avoid feelings that you are not good enough. One of the main reasons this book was written was an attempt to build better skills and more effective action at university and at work. If your performance at university or work is not what you want, by focusing on the skills that are needed you will improve. One thing to avoid is the negative and self-defeating feeling that *you* are not good enough. If you fail at university and business-related things, it is not *you* that is not good enough, it is *your skills*. Working on these skills will improve your performance.

Your self-esteem will have developed as a child, and if you have either low or high esteem, it is worth looking back to your childhood to diagnose issues. However, your self-esteem is under your conscious control. If you choose to value yourself more highly, then you can. In maintaining reasonable levels of self-esteem it is worth grounding those feelings in some objective outcomes and feelings. Self-esteem is grounded on your actions. Focus on your successes and you will feel better about yourself. Don't dwell on the things that went wrong; diagnose what skills you can develop from the experience and positively work to improve those skills.

Many business and university processes focus on comparing you with someone else. This is the reality of life in these environments, but it is important to realise that the comparison is one of performance, not of people. When things go well, learn to receive compliments with a 'thank you'. Use images and affirmations to keep your self-esteem at a high level. If you have pictures of your successes, graduation being a common one, make sure they are visible. Use affirmations such as 'I accept myself and will be the best that I can be today.' In your learning diary regularly review your successes and learn from your failures.

6 BODY LANGUAGE

Your body language speaks much louder than you do. The visual cues you give off are very important to your social interaction. It's so important that the wrong visual image may ensure that you never even get to speak. Everyone develops their own preferred body language elements over time, so don't take the sections that follow as prescriptive; just be aware that these are the well-researched elements of body language. It is actually quite important to make an impression in business and an unusual feature is a memorable feature that may help you to be remembered. Razor-cutting stripes in your hair and standing on the boardroom table is not the way to do it.

Eye contact – This is probably the most important aspect of your non-verbal impact. If you don't make regular eye contact with someone when you are speaking to them, they will assume that you:

- are ignoring them
- are untrustworthy
- don't like them
- lack social skills
- are rude and difficult.

How much eye contact would be correct? In the UK in a one-to-one conversation, you would be expected to make eye contact for around 60–70% of the time. Any more than this and you will make them feel uncomfortable and any less and they will think one or all of the above.

Posture – This is context-specific. If you are attending a formal interview, sit up straight but not rigid. If you are in an informal interview, it is as well to sit back and relax without being horizontal. Good posture also benefits you in terms of breathing and expression.

Head posture – To give the air of confidence, stand straight and keep your head vertical and level horizontally. You can also use this vertical and horizontally straight alignment when you are trying to be authoritative. If you want to convey friendship and sympathy, tilt your head slightly to one side. Remember, if you are mirroring, hold your head in a similar but not exactly the same position as the person you are talking to. Don't forget to nod your head for silent agreement and shake your head from side to side for disagreement. Use your head tilting to one side with a hand to your chin for thoughtfulness.

Arms – The classic 'no-no' is arms crossed, which is deemed to indicate that you are a closed person who keeps out the world. Crossing your arms when you are normally showing open positions indicates your displeasure or disapproval. Arms by your side or slightly behind your back indicate you are confident and ready to accept the world. The larger your arm movements, the more comfortable and confident you are deemed to be.

Legs – Your legs tend to be under the least conscious control so may give away your true feelings. Legs tend to move a lot when we are nervous, under pressure or being deceitful. A classic sign of nerves is when someone is bouncing their foot and leg up and down on their toes. A natural and comfortable position is to have your feet placed lightly on the floor. When you cross one leg onto the knee of the other, it is the defensive equivalent of crossing your arms.

Leaning – We don't always stand upright at all times. The angle of lean can indicate your attitude to people. When you lean gently towards them we are indicating that we like them. The reverse is also true.

Hands and hand gestures – The possibilities here are endless and very culture-specific, so use hand gestures carefully. Palms up is always taken as a warm, open and friendly gesture, whereas palm-down gestures are taken as aggressive and dominant. You might like to try presenting for a handshake with your hand in different positions. The neutral position is to present your hand in a vertical position. But try presenting palm up or palm down to see the different effect you get. All aggressive hand gestures should be used with care or not at all. Finger pointing and shaking means, 'don't do that, I will punish you.' Clenched fist gestures mean aggression. Two hands raised palms away means, 'slow down and back off.'

Personal distance – How far you stand or sit away from someone means a lot and is very different in different cultures. In Western cultures, standing too close is a mark of being pushy or too intimate. Be careful with distance because many people will feel you are invading their space and become frozen, move away or ask you to back off. If you stand or sit too far away from others, you will be seen as aloof and stand-offish.

Remember that the meaning of these 'feelings indicators' will vary in different cultures. One aspect of international assignments is to understand the culture you are joining. When operating in a new culture, be sure to seek out local knowledge about the meaning of body language.

By way of summary for this section I would offer the following advice on improving your social skills:

- Become conscious of your own effect on other people. Until you are aware of your own effect, it is difficult to consciously improve your social skills. Use your learning diary to keep a record of social situations that make you uncomfortable so that you can consciously change your behaviour in those settings.

- Actively analyse all the points we have covered so that you have a clear 'view' of the 'social canvas'.

- Learn to accept positive feedback with grace. Learn to use negative feedback to change and develop. Be open to the giving and receiving of feedback and feelings.

- Pay close attention to the non-verbal elements of social situations. Actively manage and adjust your own non-verbal behaviours.

- Plan techniques and approaches that allow you to maintain a healthy level of self-esteem. Develop a grounded approach to judging yourself and your feelings.

- In social situations use the skills of social rapport and develop them to suit your own style and personality.

- Remember you have one mouth and two ears. Do more listening than talking. Learn to listen to feelings.

17.3 EMOTIONAL INTELLIGENCE

In starting our look at emotional intelligence we need to answer the question, 'What is intelligence?' This proves to be like many academic areas – debatable. If you look for definitions and research you will find a wide range of ideas. I would like to present a précis of the ideas of Sternberg (1996). Sternberg uses a three-part theory of intelligence:

1 General intelligence consists of the ability to think about ideas, analyse problems and solve problems. This general intelligence can be measured using IQ tests.

2 Creative intelligence is the ability to use previous experience to solve new problems.

3 Practical intelligence is the ability to cope with everyday situations.

These are primarily cognitive or thinking abilities. Early studies of intelligence focused on IQ and measures of mental ability. Other researchers argued that IQ was not a good indicator of life success and sought other measures to explain how people with low IQ could still be very successful. There were many studies of life success and IQ, and there was little consistent correlation between the two measures. This led research to enquire about other indicators or measures that would correlate to life success. In business the main output measure is job performance, where it turns out that IQ is a poor predictor of job performance.

A whole range of multiple intelligences emerged, but one has since taken a more central role in business. Emotional intelligence is now regarded as an accurate predictor of job performance and leadership performance in particular. This does not mean that it is the only predictor; in one study by Hunter and Hunter (1984) IQ was estimated to account for 23% of the variance in outcome.

WHAT IS EMOTIONAL INTELLIGENCE?

I would define it as 'a form of intelligence driven by emotions focusing on the ability to be aware of one's own emotions and the emotions of others'. This is my synthesis of the many and varied definitions of emotional intelligence (EI). Mayer et al (1997) favour the following definition: 'the ability to perceive emotions, to access and generate emotions so as to assist thought, to understand emotions and emotional knowledge, and to reflectively regulate emotions so as to promote emotional and intellectual growth.'

Their most quoted definition is: 'Ability to monitor one's own and other's feelings and emotions to discriminate among them and use this information to guide one's thinking and actions.'

Driven by the structure of research into emotional intelligence and the normal reflective cycle after carrying out research, a model has developed that contains four branches. These four branches are:

- perceiving emotion
- using emotions to facilitate thought
- understanding emotions
- managing emotions.

Perceiving emotion – We have already covered some aspects of perceiving emotion, but this is the starting point for emotional intelligence. Accurate perception of non-verbal cues from face, voice and body postures requires that you observe carefully these aspects. This area requires conscious effort and practice to reach accurate perceptions. In skills terms, this aspect can be learned and improved with practice.

Using emotions to facilitate thought – Having perceived emotion, it has to enter your thinking process. Emotion will get our attention. Someone who is angry, sad or frustrated, to name a few emotions, will grab our attention. In thinking about emotions, the first step is often to ask why. Why is that person crying? Why did he get so aggressive? Why was she defensive? We have to engage with the feelings behind the emotion before we can understand the root of the emotion.

Understanding emotions – Emotions can tell us something about the person displaying the emotion. But it is not always easy to understand what is behind the emotion. Is the person who is crying happy, sad or hurt? The skill of understanding emotion arises from experiencing emotions in ourselves and having experience of other situations where emotion has occurred. I suggested earlier that keeping an 'emotion' diary would help you to understand when emotions occur and what the person is feeling. Emotions are closely associated with relationships, so that a colleague who is threatening is feared. The relationship is cognitive, in your mind, and so can be real, remembered or imaginary. Once we understand the emotion and the relationship between it and actions, we can reason using emotion. I make it sound easy, but it is not. We often learn to understand emotions by trial and error, and so can expect to encounter many awkward social occasions where we do the wrong thing before we are skilful enough to do the right thing.

Managing emotions – Emotions can be managed within certain individual limits. You can not only control your own emotions but you can also control the emotions of others. This is a valuable skill when leading in business.

Understand and express your own feelings in positive, non-confrontational ways. As a leader, create a culture that allows for the expression of feelings, but also in a non-confrontational way. The involuntary outburst of feelings may be an instinctive reaction but it cannot be described as managing emotions. One of the roles of leadership is to manage emotions for the productive good of the organisation.

WHY IS EMOTIONAL INTELLIGENCE USEFUL?

The simple answer is that it makes you more effective in social situations. University and work are social situations. Mayer et al (2004) describe the 'high EI individual' in these terms:

> The high EI individual, most centrally, can better perceive emotions, use them in thought, understand their meanings, and manage emotions, than others. Solving emotional problems likely requires less cognitive effort for this individual. The person also tends to be somewhat higher in verbal, social, and other intelligences, particularly if the individual scored higher in the understanding emotions portion of EI. The individual tends to be more open and agreeable than others. The high EI person is drawn to occupations involving social interactions such as teaching and counselling more so than to occupations involving clerical or administrative tasks.

> The high EI individual, relative to others, is less apt to engage in problem behaviours, and avoids self-destructive, negative behaviours such as smoking, excessive drinking, drug abuse, or violent episodes with others. The high EI person is more likely to have possessions of sentimental attachment around the home and to have more positive social interactions, particularly if the individual scored highly on emotional management. Such individuals may also be more adept at describing motivational goals, aims, and missions. (Mayer et al 2004, p210)

Work and business is an environment full of emotions. Some of it is expressed and some of it is suppressed. In an emotional environment the person who is most skilful will be the most successful. It is argued that high emotional quotient (EQ) managers are more successful at managing conflict, negotiating and leadership. In business environments where most managers have an MBA qualification, it can be assumed that they will all have similar IQ and technical skills. Research is beginning to suggest that their social skills and their EQ score explain the significant difference between successful and less successful managers.

17.4 IMPORTANT SKILLS IN BUSINESS

LISTENING SKILLS

Improving your listening skills will help you succeed at university and in the workplace. Listening is not hearing. Listening is an important skill that, with practice, you can develop. Most people seem to be very poor listeners. They talk to be heard at the expense of listening to others. They often hear selectively by noticing the things that support their view and not perceiving the things that contradict their view. If you can start to be an excellent listener you will become a better student, worker or manager.

Some characteristics of excellent listening include:

- Concentrate on giving full attention to the person speaking. This must be a conscious and sustained effort to hear and understand what is being said.

- Do not plan what you will say next. When you are planning your next sentence, you are not listening to the speaker's next sentence. Good listeners focus on and soak up every word.

- Avoid being distracted by outside events.

- Do not jump into the conversation. Allow the speaker to finish and then pause one… two… three… then speak.

- Do not respond to the speaker immediately; let their words sink in. Think about what they have said. Think about what the words mean. Do not be afraid of silence in conversations. Silence is the point when people are thinking.

- Make a brief review of the conversation so far before extending the discussion. For example, if we accept Sam's point about using the money as effectively as possible and agree with Petra's position about investing in the staff skills then… make your point. This serves several purposes in that it shows you were listening. It confirms the main points and allows challenges to those points. It creates legitimacy for the point you wish to make.

- Ask questions of what has been said. These can clarify the point or extend the point.

- Give feedback to let the speaker know the effect their words are having. Nodding the head is a form of feedback supporting the points the speaker is making. Shaking the head gives feedback that you disagree with the points being made. You can also give verbal feedback of support or disagreement.

- Record what is being said. Writing is a reflective and thought-provoking activity.

- Speak less, think more and remain relaxed.

- Display empathy for the speaker. By understanding the feelings behind the words, you will better understand the words.

- Concentrate on non-verbal cues. Maintaining eye contact is the most effective way to indicate you are listening. It also allows you to understand the emotion of what is being said.

- Allow other people to shine.

- Moderate the quantity of your spoken contribution.

BECOMING REFLECTIVE PERFORMERS

Simon: 'Hi, sorry about that show in the tutorial.'

Louise: 'You can be so arrogant!'

S: 'Sorry – as I said.'

L: 'Sorry doesn't nearly redeem that!'

S: 'I don't know what came over me.'

L: 'Your insensitive stupidity really upset the lecturer.'

S: 'Yes, sorry. I know, I'll go around to her office and apologise.'

L: 'And so you should, go do it now.'

A bit later...

L: 'What did she say?'

S: 'Well, she accepted the apology and then told me I ruined the seminar with my loutish behaviour.'

L: 'And do you accept that?

S: 'Yes, I really don't know why I did that. I am not usually insensitive.'

L: 'Well! I agree you are normally pleasant to be around or I wouldn't be around you. What caused this one?'

S: 'I quite like that lecturer. I guess I was just showing off.'

L: 'Well, it is a strange way to show someone you like them; you could have just been pleasant.'

S: 'I agree. I need to practise my social skills at bit more.'

L: 'While we are talking about that, you do have a tendency to jump into seminar conversations and talk over other people, particularly the girls.'

S: 'I don't mean to. I just find it difficult to time my entry into a conversation. It's really difficult. I think someone has stopped talking and then as I start to talk I realise they were not stopping.'

L: 'Yes, and it makes you look really pushy. Wait a bit longer to get your point in.'

S: 'You're not perfect; you don't seem to listen very much. You're not always talking but I can tell you are not listening either. You seem to be working on something else instead of listening.'

L: 'I am writing down the next point I want to make. I think it makes for a better seminar.'

S: 'Except by the time you make that point the conversation has moved on and you look like you are a bit slow.'

L: 'Really! That is terrible. I never realised that is how it came across.'

S: 'Well, it does. Your timing and skills in groups are not perfect. So can we end the lecture there, please?'

L: 'Sure! But let me know if I do that again in a group. I hate to think people see me as slow.'

NETWORKING

My definition of networking is: 'systematically building mutually useful long-term relationships'. Why bother with networking? Networking is a common business activity that can bring benefits to you personally and to your organisation. Networking is a communication process and that process can vary, but in a lot of instances it will follow the paths set out in Figure 17.1.

Figure 17.1 The networking process

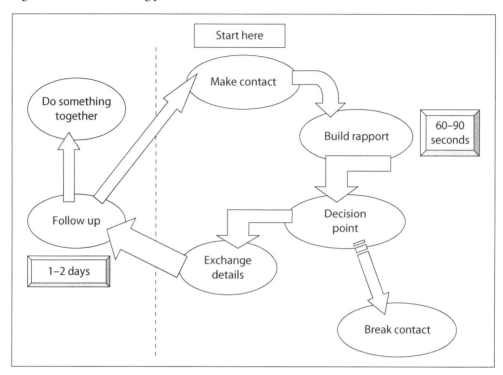

The networking process in Figure 17.1 represents the basic process. The context of where the networking is taking place can vary it. Starting at the top of the diagram:

Make contact – If you are shy or new to networking, this can be the most difficult part. In social gatherings choose someone who is on their own – they may remember the kindness of your conversation long after you have forgotten it. Scan the room to see who is on their own, then walk up to them making eye contact as you approach. An alternative approach is 'side entry' into a group; just join in at the side and listen to the conversation. Experienced networkers will be curious and ask you who you are and who you work for.

Build rapport – In most circumstances you will have 60 to 90 seconds to chat in the rapport-building stage. It is important to manage this and have a few opening sentences ready. A good starting sequence might be:

- 'Hi I am…' pause for the return introduction.
- 'What is your interest in this gathering?' pause for reply.
- Then focus on their answer followed by a question about what they have said.

Other useful and safe questions are:

- Where are you from?

- What company...?

- What do they make or do?

In no time the 90 seconds are up. You will either have built rapport or not.

Decision point – After 90 seconds or two minutes at the most, you must make a judgement to exchange contacts or to part and move on. The business card is the traditional way to exchange contact information. Mobile numbers and text details are becoming more common. As a networking professional, your aim is to work the room, so you must not stay too long with one person.

Follow up – Within one to two days make contact with the person again. A simple email will work, saying something such as, 'Hi, it was good to meet you at the BAM Conference. If I can be of any help in any of your future projects, please let me know.'

Do something together – If your follow-up works and the person has an interesting project that they want you involved in, the outcome of your networking could be some sort of action. Alternatively, you may meet them again at another function or event. The procedure when you make contact the second time is slightly different in that you will need to remember the details of who the people are and what they do. In these circumstances there is no substitute for keeping good records of the contacts you have made by networking.

Remember, at events designed for networking, every person will be actively networking. Don't be put off by people coming and talking for a minute or two and then moving on. Think of it as professional speed-dating – you are looking for new and interesting partners with whom to build a relationship.

LEARNING DIARY

I AM WAY TOO SHY FOR NETWORKING

I have just been to a small networking event at work. It was only about 12 employees and about 12 more customers from three companies. I hate these things. I only went because my boss made a fuss and said she wanted me there. Well, I got a drink and stood in the corner hoping no one would talk to me. This worked okay for a while. A couple of colleagues were the only ones who spoke to me.

Then my boss brings someone over and introduces me and said I was just the right person to discuss this 'thing'. Well, I was so embarrassed; I hate talking to strangers. This bloke was okay, but it is all way too

stressful for me. I cut the conversation pretty quick and went back to the corner with another Pepsi.

Then my boss came over and gave me a talking to, saying I was not here to socialise with work colleagues, I was here to work. She said I was to get out in the main grouping and start networking. She took my drink and pushed me out and said I would be okay. I was mortified and just stood still, almost in shock. Like a rabbit in the headlights.

I am not going to any more of these – I'll throw a sickie if they try to make me. I am not cut out for networking!

NETWORKING EVENTS

If you are serious about networking, you will need to research and select which events to attend. Business and networking events are numerous, but the following is a list of some of the more common ones:

- business lunches
- conferences
- briefing meetings
- company social events
- action learning sets
- management development activities
- launch parties and other external social events.

BUSINESS CARDS

In face-to-face networking, your business card is the vital link in the above process. Make sure that you have one because you cannot network without cards. For larger network events, you will need quite a few cards so take plenty. It is possible to create a specific networking card. The face of the card contains all the normal titles and contact information. But, the rear of the card contains a short précis of your interests and skills.

EXAMPLE NETWORK BUSINESS CARD

Mobile: 07785 42154

murder_bucks@yahoo.co.uk

Address:
5 Strangler's Lane
Marlow
SL18 9SX

Skills:
Script creation
Script editing
Script development
Genre:
Horror
Murder mystery
Credits:
3 episodes of *Midsomer Murders*
3-part radio play *The Daughters of Lethe*
2 episodes of *Lewis*

STUDENT COMMENT

One of the coolest things the university ever did was to provide us with a networking event towards the end of our third year. It was called a 'Mocktail Party'. We had to do the whole deal of black ties and cocktail dresses. The party was in a large ballroom with about 100 local businesspeople, alumni of the university, tutors and some overseas guests from Thailand. We all had business cards and really looked the part. There were prizes for who could make the most contacts – a contact being defined by getting the business card of the person with whom you were networking. The winner, not me, had made contact with 61 people. Amazing! I managed 32. It was a great experience and, as my tutor said afterwards, experience builds confidence.

I learned so much about these types of alcohol and minimal dresses parties. I now understand the practical things, like how do I hold a glass and write at the same time. I also learned not to drink too much. The wine was free, so after a while I couldn't speak. All my friends were spilling drinks and food all over the place. I did start to feel comfortable just walking up to complete strangers and introducing myself. We had to create a job role and I made myself Managing Director of 'Slick Ads', a specialist advertising agency for the oil industry.

All in all a great night and I really loved it.

NETWORKING PREPARATION

Taglines – Create one or two taglines. These are quick introductory sentences to initiate conversation. You can normally deliver these as you shake hands. Create taglines that are specific to the event you are attending. Don't just stick to the same old thing. Think about the event and mentally go through who is likely to be there; try to make the tagline appeal to the likely audience.

Think about the non-verbal cues you are communicating – People will read a lot into your clothing, stance, shoes, makeup, hair and every other aspect of your appearance and behaviour. Think these points out before the event and take advice from colleagues and friends. Even where you place your name tag will mean something to some people.

Plan your objectives before the event – A simple set of networking objectives will help you to stay focused on doing networking and not socialising. At a typical large networking event you might set yourself the target of collecting 25 business cards, arrange three follow-up coffees and agree to do three small favours.

Arrange a way to record information as you work the room – This is difficult but you cannot rely on having their business card alone. You need to record a small amount of information about each person you meet. A small notebook that you keep out of sight works quite well.

Follow up the contacts quickly after the event – Don't follow up immediately after the event, but be sure to send a follow-up communication within two days. Include a small amount of information so that the person is aware that you have remembered something about them.

Remember not to ask directly for a business card – The important guests expect to be well known enough that they don't need a card. If you ask for one it implies that you don't know who they are and they will very likely feel insulted. The passing of a business card is the assent that you can follow up the contact. People who want to withdraw from the interaction will not offer you a card – asking for one then appears too 'pushy'.

PROFESSIONAL NETWORKING ON THE INTERNET

Social networking for business occurs on specialist sites. You can set up a profile just as in Facebook and then start communicating with your current colleagues and acquaintances. As with all social networking, it is the extended connection and communication that is so very valuable. The most well-known site is LinkedIn; it has a simple interface not dissimilar to Facebook. Once you are registered you can invite friends to join you and link with their contacts.

Networking is not just about being noticed and included in future events or jobs. By networking you are also attracting future talent to the organisation.

REFLECTIVE PERFORMING

THE OBSERVER

There are a lot of very experienced and clever networkers in the world of business. When you next attend a networking event, go as an observer. Take a notepad and focus on what the various active networkers are doing. Particularly note:

- how long they spend with each person
- how they use non-verbal cues to interact with people even before they shake hands
- how they break an interaction to move on.

When you have observed a networking session, reflect on your own networking skills and how they could be improved.

CASE STUDY

SOCIAL OUTCAST

Jay was an MBA graduate from a prestigious university; he was witty and intelligent. When he landed a job at NetLands, a large supplier of networks and cabling to business, his new colleagues really liked him. However, as they got to know him better, they didn't like him quite as much. He would generally turn up for work hours late and take long lunches. He told the most offensive and rude jokes to everyone. He would argue with everyone except his boss. He had a really nasty trait of being very friendly with his boss and then saying really nasty things behind her back. He was flirtatious and came way too close for many of the women in the office. When things went wrong, he was furious with his staff and did a nice line in blame to his bosses. It was so unethical that no one wanted to work with him.

In conversation with his boss she clearly thought he was very good at his job. In reality everyone knew he was useless.

Colleagues started to avoid him and most of his staff left. If you worked with him on a project, it was a Herculean task to get any deliverable out of him. When he was on the project you knew the project was doomed. But he always managed to shift the blame to someone else. On the last project he managed jointly, he got the other project manager the sack. He was useless but ruthless.

If his colleagues were honest, everyone was afraid of him and the effect he could have on their careers.

To think about...

- Is Jay emotionally intelligent?
- Analyse his behaviour using the four aspects of emotional intelligence.
- If you were one of his colleagues, what would you do?

SUMMARY

Developing your social skills will help you fit in and be effective at work and university.

- My six social skills at work are:
  - staying in your anxiety comfort zone
  - listening skills
  - empathy skills
  - rapport skills
  - display and maintain reasonable self-esteem
  - control body language.

- Emotional intelligence is based on:
  - perceiving emotion
  - using emotions to facilitate thought
  - understanding emotions
  - managing emotions.

- Two of the most important skills of business are:
  - listening
  - networking.

EXPLORE FURTHER

FURTHER READING

Goleman, D. (1996) *Emotional Intelligence: Why it can matter more than IQ*. London: Bloomsbury.

Goleman, D. (1999) *Working with Emotional Intelligence*. London: Bloomsbury.

Hunter, J.E. and Hunter, F. (1984) Validity and utility of alternative predictors of job performance. *Psychological Bulletin*. No 96. pp72–98.

Mayer, J., Salovey, P. and Caruso, D. (2004) Emotional intelligence: theory, findings, and implications. *Psychological Inquiry*. Vol 15, No 3. pp197–215.

Sternberg, R. (1996) *How Practical and Creative Intelligence Determines Success in Life*. New York: Simon & Schuster.

WEB LINKS

Light-hearted test for Emotional Quotient at iVillage: http://quiz.ivillage.co.uk/uk_work/tests/eqtest.htm

A more valid and longer EQ test can be found here: http://www.queendom.com/tests/access_page/index.htm?idRegTest=1121

CHAPTER 18

Leadership, Coaching and Mentoring Skills

What skills will I develop in this chapter?

- understanding and using management
- the characteristics of management work
- practical management skills
- understanding the nature of leadership
- trait leadership skills
- behavioural leadership skills
- contextual leadership skills
- transformational leadership skills
- development skills
- coaching – how to get it and give it
- mentoring at work
- management development skills

18.1 INTRODUCTION

One of the key skills of business is leadership. In this chapter we look at the difference between leadership and management. There are many ways to lead organisations and teams, and we investigate some of the well-researched areas of leadership. Essentially you will have to develop your own style of leadership. No two leaders lead in the same way. However, having a portfolio of possible leadership styles makes a good starting point when you are first thrust into a leadership role. Modern leading requires coaching and mentoring skills, so this is covered as well.

Management is the function that runs the business of today. Leadership is the process that takes a business to the future. Good management will create effective businesses. Great leadership will create fantastic businesses of the future. But leadership can be on a much smaller scale; leading a small team well will allow the team to contribute to the future of the larger organisation. Leadership can seem a very distant and difficult-to-grasp concept, especially in modern high-performance businesses. The good news is that with knowledge and skill you will be an effective leader. Experience and reflection will improve the skills you learn and then, you never know…

18.2 MANAGEMENT

The two terms leadership and management are often used as if they are the same thing – they are not. You will need to have the distinction clear if you are to lead groups and teams effectively. Let's look at management first. Management is the control and direction of people and resources to achieve the agreed vision and objectives of the organisation. This is a very important function of business, but it is different from leadership. In your business career your first steps are very likely to be as a manager. So what do managers do? What should managers do?

Henry Mintzberg has had a major and enduring impact on the nature of management since his book, *The Nature of Managerial Work*, in 1973. There have been numerous add-ins to the basic ideas over the years. There has also been extensive research and investigation looking at the nature of the manager's work. One of the basic building blocks of Mintzberg's beliefs, and a major driver for this book, is that management is the applying of human skills to organisational systems. His much-published and reiterated paper, *The Manager's Job: Folklore and fact* (1975), exposes the constant pressure managers feel, the push to do too much work, respond too quickly and deal with interruptions.

Mintzberg expresses the manager's job in six characteristics and ten roles.

THE CHARACTERISTICS OF MANAGEMENT WORK ARE:

- Management tasks are a mixture of regular, programmed jobs and unprogrammed tasks.
- Management tasks require both generalist and specialist skills.
- Managers seek information from all sources but show a preference for that which is orally transmitted.
- Managerial work is made up of tasks and activities that are characterised by brevity, variety and fragmentation.
- Management work is more an art than a science and is reliant on intuitive processes and a 'feel' for what is right.
- Management work is becoming more complex.

The ten roles that make up the content of the manager's job are:

INTERPERSONAL

- figurehead – performing symbolic duties as a representative of the organisation
- leader – establishing the atmosphere and motivating subordinates
- networker – developing and maintaining webs of contacts both inside and outside the organisation

INFORMATION

- monitor – collecting all types of information that is relevant and useful to the organisation

- disseminator – transmitting information from outside the organisation to those inside

- spokesman – transmitting information from inside the organisation to outsiders

DECISION-MAKING

- entrepreneur – initiating change and adapting to the environment

- disturbance-handler – dealing with unexpected events

- resource-allocator – deciding on the use of the organisation's resources

- negotiator – negotiating with individuals and dealing with other organisations.

You can probably see from Mintzberg's early work that management is a function that organises and executes the organisation's effort. Traditionally we teach management rather like it is a science. Indeed, we will teach subjects such as management science, but then we also teach social skills that are far more like art. So management is neither pure science nor pure art; it requires the skills to manage using science and the application of art.

We can define science a little more easily than art, so let's start there. Science is the application of systematic knowledge. Systematic knowledge is knowledge derived from a systematic research process. We can say that science has at least three facets:

- It uses systematic and organised knowledge that is based on scientific methods of research.

- Inferences are arrived at after extensive research and analysis.

- It operates on clear logical principles.

The science of management uses the collectively organised, extensively researched and logical knowledge to make management decisions. The art of management uses skill, expertise, wisdom and instinct to make decisions. The science of management skilfully uses past experience to execute the present. But on occasions the art of management comes to the fore when 'gut instinct' is the basis for action. Sometimes managers just get lucky and 'art' decisions work out better than could ever have been expected. Sometimes 'art' decisions work out badly. As a world-famous golfer once said, 'The more I practise the luckier I get.' We could turn this around so that we have a saying, 'The more skilful I am the luckier I get.' The point here is that as a manager most of the decisions and actions you take will be based on science, logic and evidence, but some proportion of decisions will be made by instinct.

Management skills are acquired by training, education and practice. Management skills are applied by understanding vision, people, team dynamics, creativity and empathy. Practical management involves using scarce resources and

MANAGER COMMENT

I manage 42 people in six teams so my job is pressured and fast-moving. I make maybe 100 decisions a day; any one of these can lead to major problems. Having a system that makes it easier to know which decisions have the most potential to go wrong is very important.

I use a traffic light system:

Green decisions I make 'on the hoof', so to speak. They are decided there and then and I live with the consequences. I know from experience which day-to-day decisions are unlikely to be trouble. There are maybe 65 of these a day.

Amber decisions have potential to go wrong but the consequences will not be too serious if they do. I give myself an hour or two to make these decisions, but I always make them the same day. Time is money, and if a team needs a decision, I don't want them waiting around for too long.

Red decisions are the ones that have the potential to go wrong and cost money or lives, so I take a few days to make these. I always carry out a risk assessment and do some financials on these decisions. I will also normally consult with other directors or the CEO, even if it is only a short telephone conversation. Some of them have to be made by the board anyway.

By using this method I prioritise speed for the easy and non-risky decisions but prioritise accuracy for the ones that are dangerous or expensive.

making the most of those resources. In modern business there are always scarce resources. There is never enough time, finance, people, expertise, raw material or knowledge. How you argue for and use the resources that are made available to you will be the measure of your success.

MANAGEMENT IN PRACTICE

If you are new to management you may wonder what you will do all day. The following is a list of managerial activities that I have put together from my own experience and the experience of managers I have known.

- **organising** – designing processes, procedures and practices for others to follow
- **analysing** – investigating things and discovering the various aspects of those things and how they currently fit and work together
- **evaluating** – assessing whether people, processes, resources and other things are operating effectively
- **planning** – setting out the steps that individuals and teams need to take to get something done; this includes short-term planning of activities covering days, weeks, months, and long-term planning covering months and years

- **financial aspects** – arguing for resources, budgeting for those resources, and accounting for what has been spent and what has been produced; also, costing goods and services

- **motivating** – talking to teams and individuals to inspire and motivate them

- **monitoring** – checking the progress of products and services to ensure targets are met; also checking on the actions and outcomes of people

- **negotiating** – discussions and actions that resolve conflict, agree ways forward, sort out problems and so on

- **providing** – all teams and employees need things to do their work; as a manager you will spend a lot of time negotiating what is needed and arranging for the necessary things to be provided at the right time

- **paperwork** – recording and requesting actions required by the organisation in paper or electronic form; as one anonymous airline manager remarked, 'I never knew how much paper it took to get a plane in the air.'

This is a very general idea of the types of activities you can expect to do when you become a manager. As with all assertions, challenge and probe my version of what management involves. You will quickly find it is a general characterisation of management and the reality is often quite different.

❝ MANAGER COMMENT

Straight from university I was really lucky and got a job managing a small team of people in a retail stationer. On my first day I turned up and the regional manager showed me my office, did some quick introductions and left me to it. I went back to the office, someone made me a cup of tea, the door shut and I sat there not having a clue what to do next.

The phone did not ring (thank goodness) and no one came to see me. I couldn't even access my computer. So I sat there all day doing absolutely nothing – I think I was afraid to ask anyone about anything. At the end of the first day I was ready to quit. I wasn't sure what I was doing and no one seemed to care if I was there or not. I fretted about this all night. I nearly didn't turn up the next day. But I thought, 'This is ridiculous; I am starting out in a managing career and I don't know how to do anything.'

On the second day I made myself go around and talk to every member of the team. I spent about 30–40 minutes just shadowing them and talking to each one when their work allowed for this. This made me feel a bit better, and I understand from the team later that they were really impressed that I had bothered to come round and understand what each of them did. I was then able to ask them about logons to the computer and how the systems worked. By the end of the first week I felt I had worked there for ages.

But I never forgot the horror of that first day. I now make sure that all my new managers get a full and detailed induction, and I plan out their first day, week and month in detail before they arrive.

18.3 LEADERSHIP

Leadership is about creating a vision and direction for people. This is in contrast to management, which is concerned with organising and directing individuals and teams to achieve agreed organisational objectives related to an organisational vision. The two roles of leader and manager are nearly always intertwined. One cannot exist without the other. So while you will be expected to manage the day-to-day aspects of getting things done, you will also need to create some vision, focus and direction for your staff. This can be on a small scale where small teams need to understand, to see, what has to be done. It can also be on a grand scale, where you are leading a whole organisation or group of organisations. Leadership styles can vary greatly and there is no 'right' and 'wrong' way to lead. You will develop your own leadership style in time, but to begin with I will consider some of the well-known approaches.

TRAIT LEADERSHIP

Trait leadership approaches are grounded on the idea that leaders contained a set of traits and behaviours that could be studied and emulated by others. You may have already noticed at university and work there are some people that seem to have natural leadership qualities. People just seem to accept them as leaders and want to be led by them. So we seem to know leadership when we see it. However, if I ask you to set down what it is that makes a good leader, you might struggle to come up with a clear list of things.

REFLECTIVE PERFORMING

WHAT MAKES A GOOD LEADER?

Think of someone you know personally who you regard as a good leader. Write down what it is about them that makes them a good leader. From this list refine it to make two lists:

- the traits that this leader has
- the behaviour that this leader exhibits.

Reflect on the connection between these two lists, that is, do any of the traits create or help to create the behaviours?

When it comes to studying leadership traits we could adopt the approach of looking at great leaders and then seeing how the majority of leaders measure up. Alternatively we could look at everyday leaders and see what traits they have that make them effective. The problem with great leaders is that they are often individual and the traits they display are rather rare in practical leading. So let's try to come up with a list of traits that could make you an effective leader.

REFLECTIVE PERFORMING

TRAITS OF GOOD LEADERS

Spend about 60 minutes investigating the traits of good leaders. I would suggest that you use:

- the web in general – 'Googling' may work
- Athens portal for searching journal sources
- professional leadership and management websites, such as the CIPD and Chartered Institute of Management.

As you work, keep a list of traits. At this stage, don't exclude any.

If you performed the reflective performing exercise, I think you will have found a massive number of traits that indicate a good leader. I also expect there was little agreement between different authorities. If you focus on the more researched and evidenced sources, you may have found a similar list of traits to what follows.

Traits of leaders – a synthesis

- energy, vitality and enthusiasm
- honest and trustworthy
- able to see the big picture – vision
- good at doing things – task competence within specialist areas
- understands and accepts team and individual needs, wants and desires
- skilful person-handler, negotiator and conflict-handler
- effective decision-maker
- inspires and motivates
- courage and 'stickability'
- values diversity
- achievement-driven
- intelligence
- accepts responsibility and remains calm under pressure

- self-confident and self-aware, but also balanced, humble and modest
- assertive and can lead from the front
- supportive and can lead from the rear
- adaptable, flexible and can handle change
- consistency
- a good listener.

Your research and findings may agree with these traits of leaders or indeed may differ. This is the nature, and one of the weaknesses, of trait theory. Much of the theory and ideas are generated without context. So traits of army generals appear to be the same as traits of headteachers. Future research in this area should address the traits of leaders in well-defined environments – just in case you were thinking of looking at leadership in your dissertations. A common criticism of these lists of traits is that they appear to be very male-oriented. My synthesis above has been designed to be as gender-neutral as I can make it.

The focus of this book is on the skills of business. How useful is trait theory in developing the skills of leadership? Some of the traits in the list above have connections to areas of this book and the skills that are developed in different chapters. Others are personal attributes and are not very easy to change and develop. But, I have to believe that anyone can change and develop different skills and personal attributes.

BEHAVIOURAL LEADERSHIP

Behavioural leadership moves on from the traits of leaders to the behaviour of leaders. The focus of this approach is how leaders behave towards those they lead. The different patterns of behaviour are grouped together into styles of leadership. The most popular of these styles is the managerial grid (Blake and Mouton 1978).

The managerial grid is based on only two dimensions; these are:

Concern for people – this represents the degree to which the leader considers the needs and wants of the team. 'Low' implies that the leader gives no concern for the people in the team and 'high' implies that the leader considers and acts on the needs of the team.

Concern for production – this is the degree that the leader is concerned with achieving concrete outcomes. 'Low' implies little concern for the productive output and 'high' means the leader is fully focused on achieving agreed outcomes.

If you plot any one person on these two dimensions you come up with one of Blake and Mouton's five leadership styles. Working from the bottom left corner of the figure, we have:

IMPOVERISHED LEADERSHIP – LOW PRODUCTION/LOW PEOPLE

The leader has little concern for either production or people. The work environment is neither personally pleasant and satisfying nor high-achieving.

Figure 18.1 Managerial grid

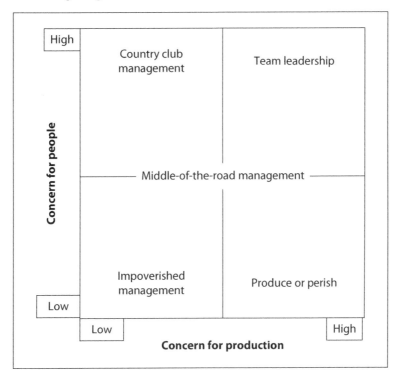

This style of leadership is likely to create a demotivated workforce that achieves very little. If this characterises your work group, you make need to look at and change your leadership style.

PRODUCE OR PERISH – HIGH PRODUCTION/LOW PEOPLE

This style is also known as leadership compliance style, 'do what you are told'. This style of leader believes that people are just like any other resource and are there to produce output. This style of leader is autocratic with strict rules about working; there will be very little social interaction between team members during work hours. Their management style will punish inappropriate work behaviours as the way to motivate staff.

MIDDLE-OF-THE-ROAD MANAGEMENT – MEDIUM PRODUCTION/ MEDIUM PEOPLE

This style of leader balances the needs of the people carrying out the work with the need to achieve and produce. The compromise of balancing the two foci means that leaders using this style will not produce high-performance teams. The compromises create this middle ground position where teams are satisfied and production is average. When you first search for your own leadership style, it is this position that is often taken until you develop more experience. This middle ground position is not a bad style to adopt for new leaders because they can build on the people and task focus to improve the performance of the team.

COUNTRY CLUB MANAGEMENT – LOW PRODUCTION/HIGH PEOPLE

The leader using this style puts the greatest emphasis on the well-being, needs and feelings of the team. The basic managerial assumption is that if the team is happy then the productive output will be high. This is often wrong! The team is happy and interacts well but it is at the expense of production. So the team likes working under this style of management but does not work as hard as they could.

TEAM LEADERSHIP – HIGH PRODUCTION/HIGH PEOPLE

This is the most desired leadership style because it produces happy teams that produce high outputs. Employees' views and needs are canvassed and acted upon but in the context of producing high outputs. Team members are likely to be fully involved in the management process. The leader maximises both the people focus and the productive output by skilled interventions. While you may desire to use this leadership style, it is not easy to achieve. The main difficulty is to balance the team needs and involvement with maximum output. Teams operating under this style of leadership are likely to trust the leader and the leader will trust the team. The team will be happy, motivated and focused on production.

The managerial grid is a practical and useful way to focus on your own leadership style. A weakness is that it only focuses on two dimensions of a very complex process. It does, however, allow you to diagnose your own style and work towards something more desirable. It is not too difficult to create other two-dimensional tables that focus on your own precise leadership context. Indeed, it makes good reflective sense to think about the possible dimensions of your own leadership position. Exploring other dimensions of leadership in various contexts would make an interesting dissertation topic.

One further criticism of this approach is that it assumes the leader is free to change the focus of their attention. How much freedom a leader has to adopt people-centred or production-centred leadership is not clear, but it is unlikely to be a totally free choice. It is important to recognise that team leadership style may not always be the most appropriate aspirational style. If an organisation is in the midst of a merger, then a refocus on to the concerns and issues of the people is acceptable. Also, if you have a large production deficit and delivery time issue, a focus on production for a short period is acceptable. The main skill to develop is the ability to change focus and use whichever leadership style is most appropriate.

CONTEXTUAL LEADERSHIP

Contextual leadership is an approach that changes depending on the context. So in one situation you lead in one way and in another you lead in a different way. I might argue that this is a move from the best way to lead (behavioural and trait) to the best fit of leadership to the situation. Teams often change leader; another way to view contextual leadership is as a selection process where project team leaders are chosen according to the context of team operation. Fiedler (1997) suggests that leadership effectiveness depends on the relationship between leaders and their teams. If leaders are well liked and respected, they will get more support to complete tasks. Another dimension is how structured the task is that must be achieved. Some tasks and processes are clearly defined while others are less clear and have a more messy character. The final dimension is the leader's position power; this relates to whether they have high authority and influence to 'get the job done' using rewards and punishments.

So in Fiedler's contingency theory we have three dimensions:

1 leader–team relations

2 task structure

3 leader position power.

The outcome of these three dimensions is an indication of the leadership approach required to be effective. The outcome for any given set of circumstances is an indication of the appropriate approach to leadership, either task-motivated or person-motivated (also called relationship-motivated). These are similar to the two dimensions in behavioural leadership.

Example 1

The easiest situation to use as an example is a forces or services-related example. Let's imagine we have a station officer of a fire station who is well liked (leader–team relations – good). The team might be carrying out a structured task – most tasks are in this area (task structure – high). The leader person power is likely to be high with a station officer (leader person power – high). According to Fiedler's research and argument, in this situation the most appropriate leadership approach is task-motivated.

Table 18.1 Most effective leadership approach in certain contexts

No.	Leader–team relations	Task structure	Leader position power	Effective leadership approach
1	Good	High	High	Task-motivated
2	Good	High	Low	Task-motivated
3	Good	Low	High	Task-motivated
4	Good	Low	Low	Person-motivated
5	Poor	High	High	Person-motivated
6	Poor	High	Low	Person-motivated
7	Poor	Low	Low	Task-motivated
8	Poor	Low	Weak	Task-motivated

Contingency approaches help you to realise that the skill in leading is to be able to change and adapt to the circumstances. The approaches to leadership that have been considered all look at very specific parts of the leading process. In organisations, there are a lot of other 'influencers' on performance, for example:

- organisational culture
- organisational politics

- the availability of resources
- the skills of the workforce
- distraction or noise activities
- the nature of employee relations with the organisation
- pay and reward structures
- economic constraints.

LOUISE AND SIMON

BECOMING REFLECTIVE PERFORMERS

Louise: 'Well, the course is almost over!'

Simon: 'Yes. Are you looking forward to getting out to work?'

L: 'Well, I am looking forward to being treated like an adult again and not a pseudo kid.'

S: 'I hadn't really noticed that!'

L: 'I do have some worries about work.'

S: 'What are they? You're normally super confident.'

L: 'I have to lead a small team in my new graduate job and I am worried that I might not be up to the task.'

S: 'You've led tasks at uni and that all went well. Why worry now?'

L: 'It's just different and they are paying me a good wage so they probably expect me to be good at everything.'

S: 'Any particular bits of leading that worry you?'

L: 'I think they might all resent me as a leader and not do anything I say.'

S: 'If you start telling them what to do in one of your bossy moods, you will soon be in trouble.'

L: 'How do you mean?'

S: 'No one wants people who are leading to be bossing about from the back of the group. Most people like their leaders to be out in front in the battle zone. Lead by example.'

L: 'Now that is what I mean. I wouldn't have thought about that. I would have just issued orders and expected action.'

S: 'If you do just fire off orders, you won't get much action.'

L: 'You can see my point, though – leading is a tricky thing and I don't have much if any experience.'

S: 'Everyone starts leading with no experience.'

L: 'Anything bothering you about work?'

S: 'Yes – getting some.'

L: 'You've still not got a graduate job then.'

S: 'As you said, I'll be serving up fries…'

L: 'Don't go getting depressed. Chin up and stick at it. You always had trouble with sticking at things.'

S: 'There are a couple of small firms that want some part-time help with a marketing campaign, so I might try that just to tide me over.'

L: 'It's all experience and getting some is the catch-22 when you don't have a job.'

S: 'A couple of other guys in my year are going to Africa with a voluntary organisation to get some experience.'

L: 'That's a really good idea. There is also this site on Facebook for internships; they are a good way to gain experience. I think it is called recruitment[2].'

S: 'I'll take a look as I am getting desperate.'

TRANSFORMATIONAL LEADERSHIP

Transformational leadership is a form of leadership that moves beyond the transactional to elevate team members above their own interests to work for and towards the organisation's interests. Transactional leaders operate by recognising what the team wants from work and providing it for appropriate performance. It recognises and rewards self-interest in team members. Team members in a transactional environment are there to get the things they want and need. Transactional leadership requires central control and the management of rewards and punishments. Transactional leaders make the decisions and control precisely what happens.

Transformational leaders in contrast create environments where team members can act independently for the good of the organisation. The relationship is one of trust and respect. Team members are likely to feel more valued and satisfied with their jobs and are likely to suffer less stress and improved well-being. How do transformational leaders behave? Transformational leaders:

- develop and communicate a clear and desirable vision of the future
- communicate this vision using stories and symbols
- develop a collective mission
- convey optimism and confidence in achieving the organisation's goals
- create environments that engender trust and co-operation
- value diversity
- develop systems that appreciate each employee's contribution
- make decisions that are morally and ethically sound
- base actions on sound values and beliefs.

Transformational leadership looks and feels quite different from more traditional approaches. However, as with all leadership, the qualities required to adopt a transformational approach can be learned. The principal ways that transformational leadership is learned are by:

- coaching
- mentoring
- shadowing
- interactive workshops.

Later sections in this chapter cover some of these points.

OTHER LEADERSHIP APPROACHES

Authoritarian leadership

This is leadership based on the power behind a formal role. We obey, agree to be led, because we see their power as legitimate. But we also obey because we fear the consequences of disobeying. These consequences can range from not getting a small reward to getting sacked. Leaders who rely solely on formal authority give orders and expect them to be obeyed. That is, they make no attempt to personally influence or persuade those they lead to follow this or that path. You will experience authoritarian leadership and sometimes it is necessary in leading in dangerous situations. However, as a day-to-day business style of leadership it has limited potential and some major person-centred consequences. Authoritarian leadership styles used in day-to-day business tend to create a cowered and grudging workforce that does what it is told and no more.

Charismatic leadership

Charismatic leaders lead by virtue of their personality, character and charm. They tend to have the skill to present clear, simple visions of the future even in complex situations. They create environments full of energy, trust and positive reinforcement. Charismatic leadership is not an approach you can simply choose; it is based so heavily in your own personality and character that you are either lucky enough to have a charismatic personality or you are not. Having said this, it is useful to try to emulate some of the characteristics of charismatic leaders, such as:

- self-confident and self-aware, inspiring confidence in those they lead
- able to create compelling and apparently achievable grand visions
- eloquent and emotionally expressive
- capable of a wide range of expression – calm and cool, and passionate and expressive
- inspires great loyalty and commitment
- displays unique or unusual behaviour or appearance.

Who do you consider to be a charismatic leader? Think of one person who you would describe as charismatic. How do they compare with the bullet list of characteristics?

SUMMARY

We have now looked at leadership and management, and I would like to summarise those two sections. As part of an old song goes, 'you cannot have one without the other.' Businesses with strong management and poor or non-existent leadership can function well in the existing environment. But when the environment changes, they can struggle to carry out the necessary changes to survive. When the leadership skills of a business are stronger and the management is poor, the business will struggle to deliver products and services and may also fail. What is required is good leadership with strong and effective management; different people within the organisation often provide these two things. At the lower functional levels, such as team leader or section manager, the two skills are vital and must be developed together. Some managers and leaders can cope with being either weak managers or weak leaders by running teams, sections, regions, sub-business units or whole organisations by working with complementary colleagues. So a good manager but poor leader may seek out a colleague who is a good leader but a poor manager. In business you don't have to have all the skills, but you need to understand all the skills and be able to analyse your strengths and weaknesses.

LEARNING DIARY

MY MANAGER HATES ME

Well, today is a really bad day. My manager left about four weeks ago and the new manager arrived today. I thought they took an instant dislike to me. He seemed so hostile.

I really liked my old manager and got on with her – I think she liked me. So I think my career is over. I felt sure he was saying that he thought I was incompetent and that I would need to go. I can't remember the exact words.

This sort of change is really unsettling and upsetting. I don't know what to do now.

18.4 DEVELOPMENT

In business there are many forms of people development that take place almost continuously. Some of these are informal and effective on a small scale, such as asking a colleague or your supervisor for help in completing a task. Other forms are more formal and structured and are backed up by organisational processes and support. This section will look at three of these: mentoring, coaching and management development.

MENTORING

Mentoring is a long-standing form of support and training that helps to develop people in the workplace. Essentially it is a one-to-one relationship where one experienced person passes on knowledge, advice, guidance and support to another less experienced person. When you get your first job after you graduate you will, in many organisations, meet up with your mentor on the first day of work. In this early period the mentor's aim is to help you settle into the new organisation and job role. It is surprising how effective a mentor can be in the first few weeks in just letting you know how the place operates – from where and how to make tea to how to work the photocopier. You may have already experienced this mentoring arrangement at university, because it is now quite common for universities to appoint 'academic buddies' for new students. The mentoring process in many organisations stops after one year. But this does not have to be so. More and more organisations are gaining considerable advantage from mentoring all staff with more experienced colleagues. For example, when you take up your first manager role, you might be appointed a mentor. Mentoring is a valuable one-to-one learning process. My advice would be to treat it like any other learning process and record your systematic thoughts and reflections about the process in your learning diary and make it a feature of your continuing professional development portfolio.

A typical mentoring arrangement should have the following characteristics:

- mentor and mentoree are mutually agreed
- the arrangement is for mutual support and guidance based on personal need
- the relationship has a limited life span (less than a year) but further new mentorship arrangements are often made
- meetings are often informal and on an 'as needed' basis
- the support and guidance is focused on career and personal development rather than technical skills.

LEARNING DIARY

MENTORING

Day 1: This is the first day of my mentoring career. I have been asked to mentor Susie, a new girl who has started in our section. I am so pleased and proud – also a bit worried. What does a mentor do? I will meet her tomorrow, so I guess I will find out.

Day 2: Susie is lovely; she is really, really nice and pleasant. We had a great first day; I spent the morning with her showing her all the areas that we use. Then I showed her some of the general processes that run our section.

Day 9: Susie seems to be flying on her own now. She has made a few friends and seems to be settling in really well. She doesn't seem to need my help much now. Amazing really, as she has only been here just over a week. I am a bit sad.

COACHING

Coaching is a development intervention designed specifically to improve a person's skills and knowledge with the aim of improving their work performance. It differs from mentoring in that it is aimed at organisational performance whereas mentoring is focused on personal and career development. Coaching can be informal – when one person coaches and helps another to improve – and it can be formal – when a person's performance is deemed to be lower than required, a coaching plan is put into place to improve their performance to the desired level. Coaching can sometimes have a stigma attached to it, but you should avoid feeling this way about coaching. If you play tennis or golf, using a coach to improve performance is a normal activity. Most of the more complex physical, mental or social skills are very difficult to learn and to improve without using a coach. It is much easier and quicker to learn skills from an experienced expert than to try to learn them by experimentation.

When I first started at the Gift Box Company I knew I would be expected to run large sales meetings. After all, I was the regional sales manager, even if I was straight out of university and only 22 years old. These were meetings of about 16 sales reps with more experience than me and all very pushy and talkative. I have to say I was frightened and apprehensive. The first meeting was a real disaster and the second was no better. I knew I needed help.

I sought out another, older regional sales manager and asked for help. He pointed out we could make a formal coaching arrangement with HR that registered the development and provided time and other support. What we agreed was that I would shadow him for three similar meetings and after each we would debrief the activity. He would then sit in on my next three meetings and coach me after each one. We also arranged a couple of formal skills training events: one dealing with assertive people and the other on structuring and running meetings.

I was mortified that I needed help, but in the end I was very glad of the arrangement and I now have no problem with running all kinds of meetings. HR described what we actually agreed as a hybrid coaching arrangement because it contained coaching and some formal skills development.

The characteristics of a coaching development arrangement are:

- often one to one, where a more experienced person coaches the less experienced
- it focuses on a specific aspect of work performance
- coaches can come from outside the organisation and be experts in the required skill
- it is a closely defined process and specifies timescale, output measures and the path to performance
- it can be personally instigated or organisationally instigated
- it should not deal with counselling, health or well-being issues
- it is a short-term development activity lasting weeks or months, not years.

The CIPD's annual *Learning and Development* survey report 2009 indicated that:

- 69% of organisations in the survey use coaching
- nearly half of respondents provide coaching as part of a leadership development programme
- a quarter of organisations have coaching written into the formal learning and development strategy
- two-thirds of respondents see coaching as a positive development opportunity rather than a remedial process.

EXECUTIVE COACHING

Executive coaching has become a popular way to improve the performance of top executives and organisations. It is a rapid development process for individuals in senior roles. It is normally facilitated by a professional coach and tailored to fit in with the senior executives' lifestyle and work patterns. It has many of the characteristics of coaching but also some unique features in that it:

- is time-limited – short term
- is expensive, provided external to the organisation and often confidentially
- is specific and action-oriented
- focuses closely on assisting the executive to deliver the required performance
- is a rapid development process.

Executive coaching is often branded under programmes of need, so that executives can seek help and development from coaches dealing with things such as:

- board-level coaching
- first 100 days coaching
- senior women coaching
- top talent coaching
- transition coaching
- leadership coaching
- soft skills coaching
- high-performance team coaching.

MANAGEMENT DEVELOPMENT

Management development is an umbrella term that covers every formal process by which managers learn and improve their skills. As you enter paid management work you will encounter the term and the practical experience of being part of a management development programme. This formal development programme will cover all the organised and accepted learning processes. What it will not cover and focus on is the manager's informal learning process. There is a fair bit of debate about which is the most important development process: the informal day-to-day learning that occurs during the managing process or the formal, structured and organisation-led process of seminars, workshops and other interventions.

Informal learning

You will have learned in this book that if learning is not captured and reflected upon, it does not form part of a learning process. A Microsoft OneNote workbook set up as a learning diary might have the following sections:

Chronological diary – This records all of your reflections, actions and thoughts just as in a normal diary. But, you can smart-tag the workplace learning events that need reflection. You can also capture pictures and documents. So if you have your photo taken with a small group at a conference, you can add this to the diary. Remember, you can also add video and audio entries. Using the first section as a chronological diary is an excellent start to capturing your workplace learning.

Workplace reflections – This section would contain a copy of the items you smart-tagged in the chronological section but with a reflective comment or statement and maybe a learning action. Smart-tag the learning actions and these can be copied to another section that just contains learning actions.

Self-analysis and evaluation – This section is a repository for all the work and personal analysis and evaluation items, such as health records and workplace appraisals. It can also store your own skills appraisals, online skills test or workplace skills analysis and tests.

Learning actions – Remember, for learning to take place, some permanent change needs to have happened. You can ensure these changes get made and not forgotten by having one section for learning actions.

You can add other sections that suit your lifestyle and working arrangements.

This is one way that you can focus on the informal learning that can take place from experience. If you don't have a formal, systematic process to capture this learning, much of it will be lost. Using OneNote has the added advantage that you can communicate your learning and share your learning and the learning of others.

Formal learning

Management development is normally a process owned and administered by the organisation you work in. You will contribute to the process by being part of the groups that determine the policy and approach. What sorts of things are included in a management development programme?

Qualifications – These are extra qualifications provided off-site or on-site, such as MBAs, MA HRMs, supervisory qualifications, and technical qualifications.

Coaching and mentoring – These include formal coaching and mentoring arrangements.

Learning sets – These are meetings of groups of people from various organisations who come together on a regular basis to discuss and solve organisational problems. Experienced managers with formal facilitation skills facilitate them. These provide an external organisation perspective that is hard to achieve by other means.

Conferences – These are the annual and intermittent conferences for professional organisations, such as the CIPD annual conference held every year at Manchester. These provide formal learning opportunities to hear speakers and join in industry-related discussions. They also provide excellent networking opportunities.

In-house training events – These are externally run training events run at the organisation's premises and using the actual organisational context as the subject of the training event. For instance, if a 'controlling absence' event is planned, it will use the problems and data from the organisation rather than random data.

Action learning – Many people prefer to learn by doing. Action learning creates structured learning activities that solve real problems using real data and contexts.

Outward Bound events – These residential events are often undertaken in the natural environment. The Lake District, Wales, Scotland and the New Forest are all common venues. Their primary aim is to build stronger and more effective teams. This is facilitated by placing the teams in difficult environments, often cold, wet, windy, and then requiring them to perform a task to a high level. Navigational challenges and route marches are commonly used.

Project working – Involvement in cross-functional project teams is seen as a form of management development. It exposes managers to new environments and new relationships, broadening their experience and skills. Leading project teams is also seen as a development activity.

Secondments – Secondments are another management development activity designed to broaden the perspective of managers and develop new skills. The secondments can be to other parts of the organisation or to other organisations. A popular secondment arrangement is to second commercial managers to the voluntary sector, thereby providing a broadening experience for the manager and much-needed commercial skills to the voluntary sector.

Development centres – Development centres are intensive training and assessment events that rapidly develop skills and assess participants for promotion. They are commonly used when a new suite of skills is needed quickly or when organisational developments need to be trickled down through management. Cultural change programmes are often developed and assimilated in this manner. Managers attend development centres for training and learning about the new desired culture and then they subsequently train and develop their own staff.

E-learning and blended learning solutions – These are a fast, efficient and cost-effective way to deliver management training. They can be used to assess competence using interactive questionnaires and diagnostics.

ZULU COMPUTERS

Zulu Computers produces bespoke computers to customer specifications. It is an Internet business and uses e-commerce for sales. One innovation is that the website has arranged for video content that literally talks potential customers through the available options for their new computer. This service is not cheap, but as it is only about 15% more expensive than an off-the-shelf computer, it is not expensive either. Zulu Computers was built from the ground up by Barry Tsaki and Emma Whitehouse. They have grown rapidly and now have five divisions and employ around 90 people. The five divisions are:

1. Research and Development
2. Marketing
3. Production
4. Post-production – delivery and service
5. Business functions – Finance, HR, and so on.

Performance as indicated by turnover and profits has been increasing at a rate of 22% per annum until the current year. The financial forecasts are showing negative profit growth. The directors think this a bit strange because the turnover is still increasing 32% per annum but the profit has changed to a loss. Zulu employs 22 more staff this year than last year, and some of the directors of divisions think that while headcount has gone up, production has not.

Zulu had never seen the need for training and development; most staff just learn the job as they do it. There is no budget for training or development. There are very few processes for any support and development activity. There is no systematic induction process. A recent incident has brought some of these issues into sharp focus. The Research and Development Team became aware of a 'hard bug' problem in one of the motherboard circuits that freezes the computer. They made provision for this in the design of the next-generation motherboard due out in eight months' time. At the same time the Production Team were unaware of this problem. They continued to produce and deliver computers with this fault. The fault was known to the Research and Development Team but unknown to the Production Team.

The Service Team started to responded to an increasing service problem with computers freezing. They were trying to solve the problem with software 'patches' because they believed it to be a software problem. Remarkably, this situation carried on for five months with the Service Team being 'run off their feet' and unable to cope with the level of the returns and call-outs.

The whole problem only became apparent when three of the divisional directors happened to sit at the same table at lunch. Later analysis showed that the problem had inflated costs by a staggering £2.6 million.

To think about...

- How would you categorise the training and development of managers in this company?
- Diagnose the underlying problem with Zulu Computers.
- Why did this problem take so long to recognise and address?
- How would you advise them to proceed in terms of leadership and development?

SUMMARY

As a business manager, leadership and management skills will determine how effective you are at work. In time you will develop your own personal style, but this chapter should help you with the basics.

- According to Mintzberg, management involves the following roles:
  - figurehead
  - leader
  - networker
  - monitor
  - disseminator
  - spokesman
  - entrepreneur
  - disturbance-handler
  - resource-allocator
  - negotiator.

- Management in practice carries out a range of functions similar to these:
  - organising
  - analysing
  - evaluating
  - planning
  - financial monitoring
  - negotiating
  - paperwork.

- Leadership can be approached from different theoretical positions:
  - trait leadership
  - behavioural leadership
  - contextual leadership
  - transformational leadership
  - authoritarian leadership
  - charismatic leadership.

- Development activities in organisations can take many forms, including:
  - mentoring
  - coaching
  - executive coaching
  - informal learning
  - formal learning.

FURTHER READING

Blake, R. and Mouton, J. (1978) *The New Managerial Grid*. Houston, TX: Gulf.

CIPD. (2009) *Learning and Development [online]*. Annual survey report. London: Chartered Institute of Personnel and Development. Available at: http://www.cipd.co.uk/surveys [accessed 27 August 2009].

Fiedler, F.E. (1997) Situational control and a dynamic theory of leadership. In K. Grint (ed.) *Leadership: Classical, contemporary and critical approaches*. Oxford: Oxford University Press.

Fiedler, F.E. and Garcia, J.E. (1987) *New Approaches to Effective Leadership*. New York: John Wiley.

Grint, K. (ed.) (1997) *Leadership: Classical, contemporary and critical approaches*. Oxford: Oxford University Press.

Mintzberg, H. (1973) *The Nature of Managerial Work*. London: Joanna Cotler Books.

Mintzberg, H. (1975) The manager's job: folklore and fact. *Harvard Business Review*. Vol 53, No 4. pp49–61.

Sadler, P. (1997) *Leadership*. London: Kogan Page.

Senge, P.M. (1990) *The Fifth Discipline: The art and practice of the learning organisation*. London: Random House.

Wright, P. (1996) *Managerial Leadership*. London: Routledge.

WEB LINKS

The Association of Coaching: http://www.associationforcoaching.com/home/index.htm

CIPD site for management development: http://www.cipd.co.uk/subjects/lrnanddev/mmtdevelop

Edward de Bono and Robert Heller's Thinking Managers site: http://www.thinkingmanagers.com/business-management/leadership.php

EXPLORE FURTHER

CHAPTER 19

Careers and 'Futuring' Skills

What skills will I develop in this chapter?

- the skills required to manage a traditional career
- the skills required in modern careers: protean and portfolio
- understand career theory
- strategies for making the transition into a career
- the employer's view of graduate skills
- the skills to survive and thrive in interviews and assessment centres
- behavioural skills during interviews and assessments
- the skills of 'visioning' the future

19.1 INTRODUCTION

You have completed a lot of hard work to get to the last chapter of this book. Creating a fulfilling and worthwhile career is now your life goal. Your university degree is just the ticket to get into the ball – it is how you dance that will make an impression with employers. This book has been written to address what employers say are deficiencies in the skills that graduates show when they enter work. When employers select candidates for jobs in their organisations, you can be sure they will look closely at the areas they say are deficiencies. If you can display good skills in the areas that interest employers, you will soon be on the career slope and moving upwards.

This chapter explores the traditional career approach and the contextual pressure to move away from traditional careers. It investigates more modern notions of careers and the skills needed to succeed in this new environment. It also develops some of the important aspects of working and success. This chapter considers the research that underpins the graduate skills debate and what employers want from employees. It also looks at the selection and interview process.

19.2 CAREERS

Careers and the notion of 'a career' can be characterised in many different ways. I will look at three possible characterisations and associate these with the skills needed to succeed. Before we do that, let's spend a few moments reflecting on the nature of careers.

Spend some time thinking about the following:

- What is the difference between a career and a job?
- In reality, is there such a thing as a career or is it just a succession of jobs?
- If a career exists, do you own it and control it or does the organisation you work for own it and control it?
- If you don't work in paid employment, can you have a career?

We often use the term career without ever exploring what it means. Different groups have defined the word 'career' in many ways. Psychologists would define it as 'the pattern of organisational experience throughout someone's life'. A career coach might define it as 'a work-related dream that is defined by goals and milestones'. An experienced manager might define it as 'the upward progression or job roles within a single industry'. You can see from my few examples that it has been and can be defined in numerous ways. So does that mean it is a meaningless term that is of no use when thinking about the skills needed to enable you to have a successful working life?

The main benefit in considering the notion of a career is that it creates an entity, something that exists. If a career is something, if it exists, it can be managed. So to my way of thinking the term 'career' is useful because it creates something important that you have to manage. This leads to the notion that being successful involves having a 'good' career and, further, to have a good career you need to manage it and bring skills to bear on that career. Careers are not all the same and the skills you need to succeed vary with the different types of career.

ORGANISATIONAL OR TRADITIONAL CAREER

Traditional careers, also called organisational careers, will be played out in only one or two organisations. People would enter organisations at a young age and by progressive promotion rise up the corporate ladder, achieving status and pay increases as they progress. The organisation supports employees and maps out their career paths. They provide a safe and secure working environment where time served is more important than outright performance. In some circumstances an individual career would change organisations, but this was often only among two or three employers. The locus of control always lies with the organisation, and techniques like manpower planning, succession planning, job rotation and overseas assignments are the means of organisational control.

Traditional careers still exist in large organisations but this career path is available to fewer and fewer people as organisations become smaller and leaner. If you enter an organisation through a graduate recruitment programme you can expect to see some elements of traditional careers. Modern businesses are much flatter organisations, where the number of layers of management is considerably reduced. Therefore, even in large organisations the inexorable rise up the corporate ladder is not often seen. Career paths tend to take zig-zig routes that go upwards, sideways and sometimes down. Sometimes these careers paths will change dramatically to different professions even if they do stay within one organisation. One other trend away from traditional careers is the move to part-time and flexible working.

The term psychological contract had been used since the 1960s to describe the mutual, but mostly unexpressed, obligations of employee and employer. These obligations are mostly informal, imprecise and developed by custom and practice. But, both parties are expected to abide by this unwritten and informal contract. If the employer breaks the contract the employees feel betrayed and often leave the organisation or stay and operate in an unwilling manner. If the employee breaks the contract, they are often ostracised or feel the pressure from peers or management to leave the organisation. The psychological contract covers a wide range of actions and behaviours by employers and employees. Table 19.1 considers some that might apply in relation to careers.

Table 19.1 Responsibilities under the traditional career contract

Employer psychological contract elements	Employee psychological contract elements
Pay salaries in relation to performance	Work hard to achieve the organisation's objectives
Provide security in old age by providing a pension scheme	Remain loyal to the organisation
Provide structured promotion prospects	Attend work when not ill and attend punctually
Recognise the value of employees both in reward and respect	Carry out work in an efficient and innovative manner
Provide interesting and varied work	Work harder and for longer periods when the organisation is busy
Provide an attractive benefits package	Be flexible and adaptable in completing the work of others
Treat all employees with respect and courtesy	Conduct yourself in a professional manner at all times
Provide reasonable security of employment	Behave honestly at all times
Provide training and development	Develop new skills

The traditional career is not dead, but you are less likely to experience it in the way your parents would have done. The majority of your parents would have been employed full-time in a few organisations throughout their working lives. Your experience is more likely to be one of mixed career approaches during your life after making the transition to work from university. Alternative career approaches, at least in the early stages of your careers, are likely to be needed.

MY CAREER

I had always assumed I would just get a job and then progress up the ladder of success until I had my perfect job. But I am beginning to doubt if this will ever happen. I have had two jobs since university – I am 28 years old now. The first was the usual graduate entry job with a bit of this and that. Then I changed companies and became team leader of a small production team assembling gas valves for boilers – my employer is one of the largest gas boiler makers in Europe. I like the team I was working with and the money was okay even though I'd prefer to work in retail or fashion. I may in a few more years get some promotion. I feel stale and I don't feel the job is a challenge any more.

I could stay here; it is comfortable and okay, but I want more. I like the security of this paid work and the company looks after all the employees. Okay, I can't carry on doing this for any longer. I need something new, exciting, challenging.

I wonder if I should chuck the job and start something of my own?

PROTEAN CAREER

Protean careers place the emphasis for managing the process onto the individual. They are essentially a twenty-first-century self-managed career. Protean is named after the Greek god of the sea who could change form at will to match the environment; the term 'protean' is often applied to something flexible or ever-changing. Protean careers were first suggested by Hall (1976) and the term came to be used more extensively during the latter part of the 1990s. As economic change required organisations to de-layer and outsource functions, the hierarchical structures of bigger organisations were slimmed down. The traditional career relies on having many organisational layers to provide the progression steps upwards. Once these were removed by de-layering and downsizing, the concept of traditional careers was undermined. This was further eroded as the practice of working with one employer for a whole working life gradually disappeared. So, protean careers are likely to have frequent changes of organisation, job role, work setting and contractual arrangement. It may be that the traditional psychological contract as exemplified above is now broken and will not be seen again in the Western world. If we follow the format of the table above and use it to explore the protean career, you will begin to see the differences. There will naturally be more elements for the employee than the employer as the control of careers passes to individuals.

WHAT SKILLS WILL BE NEEDED TO MANAGE A PROTEAN CAREER?

Using this book will help you to focus on developing skills that transfer well between workplaces. But more-specific actions will help you manage your protean career:

1   Keep a skills inventory in a form that you can use when you network or are interviewed for roles in organisations.

2   Keep an up-to-date portfolio of your achievements so that you can show potential new employers.

Table 19.2 Responsibilities under the protean career contract

Employer psychological contract elements	Employee psychological contract elements
Pay salaries in relation to the market rate	Meet contractual obligations
Provide communication and networking possibilities	Adopt continuous learning approach
Provide intrinsic rewards related to skills and development	Loyalty based on profession, not organisation
Training for statutory elements only, such as safety and diversity training	Focus on developing marketable, transferable skills
	Personal career management
	Self-analysis of strengths and weaknesses
	Project focus, not a job focus
	Develop risk-taking behaviours
	Using personal planning techniques to manage skills and career

3   Maintain an up-to-date CV.

4   Become a member of your professional association.

5   Scan the employment market in your sector so that you know:

   – the major employers

   – the salary rates

   – new projects that are being developed

   – network contacts

   – the desired skill set for any areas you are interested in.

6   Make sure that your key skills, those we have been studying in this book, are up to date.

7   Focus on and record all learning opportunities.

8   Make sure that you have an up-to-date and well-developed CPD file in an appropriate form for your professional association.

9   Develop meaningful relationships with peers, employers, customers and competitors.

10   Organise and prioritise your wants and needs.

11   Actively manage your work–life balance.

12   Invest in yourself, setting aside time and money to develop marketable skills.

13   Take every opportunity to network.

Management authors have always looked for a definitive set of skills and competencies to indicate the effective manager. This has proved an elusive concept, but Pedler et al (1994) developed a competency classification system reflecting the successful manager. Their research indicated that there were three levels of competencies and qualities an effective manager possessed.

In order, these are:

1 basic knowledge and information
2 skills and attributes
3 meta-competencies.

Hall (1976) also makes reference to 'meta-competencies' in terms of managing protean careers. They list the two meta-competencies as:

- self-awareness
- adaptability.

A further set of skills that would allow for the effective management of protean careers are:

- planning, organising and priority-setting
- self-assessment of skills and attributes
- focus on and development of saleable skills
- relational skills
- social skills
- reflective learner skills
- personal management skills of work–life balance
- coping with change skills
- networking skills
- sense of security and identity – self-worth skills
- stress-control management skills
- retraining and development skills.

Protean careers are likely to be far more common than traditional careers as business adapts to global competition.

PORTFOLIO CAREER

Portfolio careers, as the name suggests, consist of a portfolio of jobs. These can include full-time or part-time jobs, paid or unpaid. They will normally be with a range of employers in a range of places. They may well be completely different types of job. For example, a professional HR practitioner on a fractional appointment may also have a hobby organisation producing plants in a small nursery. Portfolio careers exist most commonly for the newly graduated or young person and, at the other end of the spectrum, for the newly retired or partially retired person.

For the newly graduated it is a way to make some money and gain some experience. For the newly or partially retired person, it is a way to top up a pension and keep active and involved. For the young portfolio careerist, it is often a transition stage to a protean or traditional career. For the retired, it is often a permanent change of approach that allows them to be in more control of their lives and to some extent, when working voluntarily, to give something back to the local community.

There is a further group of portfolio careerists who choose the approach for work–life balance reasons so that they are more in control of when and where they work. It is also a chosen option for those who want some security but also want the freedom to create their own enterprise.

Portfolio careers are built around a collection of skills and experience. The skills required for managing a portfolio career are very similar to those needed for a protean career. These feature the meta-skills of self-awareness, adaptability, self-organising and networking.

An example of a transitional portfolio career might be the new graduate who works voluntarily one day a week in a conservation area, but also has two days' paid work at a marketing agency and works two evenings in a bar. The balance of the portfolio will start off biased towards making some money but should develop into a more strategic experience-gathering portfolio. The main aim for many people is to secure a full-time paid job in one organisation.

SUMMARY

I think we can now talk about career strategy. Your approach to it will depend on your personality and skills. How much time and effort you spend managing it will depend on whether you are following a traditional career, a protean career or a portfolio career. What is important is that you understand the career environment and apply the appropriate skills and management:

- Understand your own skills.
- Actively dream about the future.
- Turn your dream into goals and milestones.
- Actively manage the steps of your own career.
- Network at every opportunity.
- Market your skills and experience.

19.3 THE TRANSITION INTO A CAREER

The economics of the second decade in the twenty-first century will make the transition from university to the career ladder harder than ever. For many students there will need to be a transition stage that gives them a 'leg up' onto the career ladder. This transition step could take one of many forms. This section considers some of the better-known ways to make the jump from student to career ladder.

INTERNSHIPS

Internships for graduates are not new; they have existed in the USA for a long period and they are being used in the UK and throughout the world more frequently. Work experience is a major success factor in getting on the career ladder with a well-paid permanent post. Internships are designed to give you practical experience and provide an environment where you can practise business skills. They may be paid, unpaid or partially paid. It can seem unfair to think you have worked hard for a degree and then have to take unpaid work. However, it is better to view this as the vital finishing aspects of your degree before you enter the career environment. In law this process is more formalised because all law graduates have to undergo pupillage as the final step in becoming barristers. To become a solicitor you have to undergo two years' practical training in what is now known as a 'training contract', but used to be known as 'articles'. So the idea of having practical experience after graduating is fairly common in some areas of enterprise.

One of the recurring problems for new graduates is their lack of work experience. You often hear them say, 'How can I get any experience without a job?' Internships will fill this gap and make you more likely to be recruited at a job interview or assessment centre. Work experience not only provides you with valuable 'real' experience, it also gives you the opportunity to experience your chosen job before you enter into a career in that area. Many, many graduates have taken an internship in their desired and dreamt-about business area only to realise after just a day or two that it is not the job for them. So it gives you a chance to try out the 'nuts and bolts' of a job, thus avoiding a miserable major career mistake or blind alley.

There are other benefits to internships:

- enhancing your CV with business-related experience
- networking contacts for your future career search
- provide an environment to practise and hone your business skills
- learning specific work-based skills
- experiencing the working environment and developing coping strategies
- improving the important business-related skills such as presentations, management, communication and sales
- understanding organisational culture and workplace politics
- engaging with organisational training and development to further enhance business skills
- experience of operating in project teams.

PORTFOLIO CAREERS

A portfolio career is one where your income comes from a range of sources. When transitioning from university it normally consists of a number of small,

STUDENT COMMENT

I did two internships after my graduation. One was with a company in France that made textiles; I helped out in the marketing area. They wanted my detailed knowledge of English and I wanted some experience and to learn a little French. The south of France was just a great, warm and easy-going climate. That lasted, as planned, six months – I was very sorry to have to come back to a cold English winter. Then a few months after that I worked for an IT company in southern England. I did a lot more generalist, short roles here: accounts, transport, service centre and marketing.

After six moths they offered me a full-time permanent post as an advertising officer with special responsibility for media advertising. I loved that job and it was well paid. They wanted me so much that they gave me a golden student loan introduction of £10,000. I didn't actually pay off the loan with that; I put it towards a deposit on a small flat.

I have no doubt that I would not have even got an interview for that job – as my experience was still limited. It was just that they knew me and I was partially doing the role.

part-time jobs. You take a small role for four hours a week here and another small role somewhere else for six hours and maybe two evenings a week on something else. The main point is that you are earning money and getting a diverse range of experience. It is important to try to gain experience in your chosen area rather than take any small job. In economic recessions companies cannot often afford to employ full-time specialist workers. But they may well create a role for an HR, accounting or marketing person for six hours per week. New graduates often have limited experience but they still have specialist knowledge and enthusiasm.

There are benefits to portfolio careers:

- They are flexible and fit in around other commitments, such as childcare or sport.
- They provide a diverse range of experience quickly.
- They provide a wide range of networking opportunities within the companies and with the company's suppliers and customers.
- You are in control of the roles you choose to take.
- There is very little chance that the roles will get boring and repetitive.
- There will be many opportunities for learning and development.
- Above all, they show potential employers that you are willing and able to find work and make a success of it.
- They place you in the work environment so you are well placed if a job role does come up.

ENTREPRENEURIAL CAREERS

Entrepreneurial careers involve starting and running small organisations to provide products or services. It is very easy and quick to start a small company. It costs practically nothing to start a small service company because you can operate from your home base and work for clients at their premises or at home. So if no one will employ you, employ yourself. Entrepreneurial careers provide independence and the boss will never sack you. You never know, once you have tried it you may not want a 9–5 career. But, if you do, the experience will allow you to stand out from other candidates.

AGENCIES OR INTERIM MANAGER POSTS

Working for an agency can provide valuable experience. As an alternative, if you have a small amount of experience in management you can become an interim manager. See the website for interim managers at the end of the chapter.

SOCIAL NETWORKING JOB SEARCH

The new trend in recruiting is to use social networking sites such as Second Life and Twitter. In Second Life you will find companies like Microsoft, Dell, Toyota, Adidas and Cisco Systems. Twitter job search has about 250,000 jobs added each month. It has a job search map where you can search for jobs in your local area. Recruiting using social networks will continue to grow, so if you are looking for that first job – start networking.

19.4 GRADUATE SKILLS

What skills will your future employers want you to have? If you are able to focus on these skills along with the academic skills you will need at university, you should find your route into work easier. The Council for Industry and Higher Education (Archer and Davison 2008), in an international employer barometer study of 233 employers, found in a list of the top ten most important skills and capabilities that communication skills were ranked top by 86% of organisations. The top ten important skills are shown in Table 19.3 on page 486.

At employment interviews you would be well advised to have supporting material, examples and evidence of the skills in this table. Some are clearly easier to demonstrate and provide examples of than others. Clear communication at the interview may be evidence enough. But how do you provide evidence of your integrity? A common method of assessing candidates' skills and behaviours is to use an assessment centre event.

WHAT HAPPENS AT A GRADUATE ASSESSMENT CENTRE?

Assessment centres are processes that rigorously assess whether candidates have the skills required to carry out a job. They also assess future potential in the context of what the organisation will need from employees as they progress within an organisation. Between four and 12 candidates will come together to compete individually and in teams a range of activities and tests. There may be several groups of 12 attending at the same time. Assessment centres typically last

LOUISE AND SIMON

BECOMING REFLECTIVE PERFORMERS

Simon: 'How is the job-hunting going?'

Louise: 'Yes, really well!'

S: 'I am not having so much luck. I have been to a lot of graduate assessment events but only got past the lunchtime selection barrier once and then didn't get to the interview stage.'

L: 'That's a shame. I'm sure you deserve better. But, it is really, really competitive; this year of all years.'

S: 'I was wondering whether to go and see someone about careers and see if I am right for the sort of things I want to do.'

L: 'Are you going to go the careers service?'

S: 'Well... I thought of something a bit different and heuristic.'

L: 'What can that be – a life coach?'

S: 'No. I was going to see Gypsy Rose May, you know, the university clairvoyant!'

L: 'The university has a clairvoyant?'

S: 'Yes, she is a professor in the Psychology Department, doing research on futuring and psychic readings. She has a couple of drop-in sessions every week. I understand the Vice Chancellor relies on her for determining the strategic direction of the university.'

L: 'I think I will stick with the careers service.'

S: 'Nothing ventured, nothing gained.'

Some days later...

L: 'How was the reading with Gypsy Rose May?'

S: 'Brilliant but confusing.'

L: 'So nothing really helpful then?'

S: 'She talks in riddles. It's a bit confusing but she constantly came back to tell me to be in touch with the environment. I took that to mean I needed a job in marketing green products. But it wasn't much help. I'll try the careers advice service.'

L: 'You should try Assessment.com – they have a motivation-driven career test that is really useful. It's called MAPP.'

S: 'I might give it a try. What did it suggest you should be – bossy?'

L: 'My three top jobs were: promotion/ publicity, teaching, consulting and business. So it looks like I might be in the best job area for me. It is not just a readout of the jobs I might think about doing. It is also a skills matrix for aptitudes.'

S: 'I'll definitely give it a try. But I think you need to be lucky to get a job at the moment and I don't seem to be lucky.'

L: 'That has to be rubbish. You need to be skilful to get a job. Skilful and persistent – stickability gets you the job and makes you good at the job.'

S: 'Maybe – we'll see.'

between half a day and two days. These aim to measure competencies. Typical activities can include:

- psychometric tests
- technical exercises related to the role – for a sales area you may be asked to role-play making a sale

Table 19.3 Top ten important skills and capabilities when recruiting graduates (extracted from the full table)

Skill or capability	% of employers
Communication	86
Teamworking	85
Integrity	83
Intellectual ability	81
Confidence	80
Character/personality	75
Planning and organising	74
Good writing skills	71
Good with numbers	68
Analysis and decision-making skills	67

Source: Council for Industry and Higher Education (2008)

❝❝ MANAGER COMMENT

We want graduates who have the skills and ability to join us quickly, understand the role we give them and then to contribute quickly. We want them to settle in quickly and then improve the role and the performance. We look for two sets of skills: social skills such as empathy, communication, natural authority, and the ability to lead teams and contribute to teams. But we also want to see that they have mastered some technical skills such as finance, engineering and marketing. We provide them with training to carry out the technical skills of our business, but they need to be able to associate with carrying out a technical task to a high level.

We put great emphasis on the simple functioning skills of reading, writing and working with numbers. The other important area is the ability to communicate in a range of situations. Universities know what employers want but these simple skills seem to be forgotten. We often have to put our new graduates into an intensive training scheme to show them how to write a clear sentence, add up and handle simple data.

- written exercises
- thinking exercises
- physical exercises
- interviews
- presentations
- in-tray and e-tray exercises
- team activities
- physical challenges.

STUDENT COMMENT

When I went to my first graduate assessment centre I was so nervous. I actually had to go in the toilets and be sick. I have never been so unsettled and nervous before or since. I was very tense and a bit uptight so I couldn't perform very well. Naturally I wasn't selected to go forward to the recruitment stage. The second one I went to was a bit better but I was still too nervous to do myself justice. It was not until the third one that I could settle and really perform to the best of my ability.

My advice is to put yourself through a few of these for areas for companies you don't really want. Do a few tryouts that don't really matter. Then, when you really want a company or a job, you stand a chance of performing at your best.

The university set up a dummy assessment centre, but I didn't bother going. I wished I had after my first two days because I think the learning curve would have been easy and more supportive. Learning as you go at live events is just too stressful and difficult.

These activities are designed to test competencies. Competencies are often divided into two groups. Competencies that relate to actual tasks are called technical competencies or hard competencies. Competencies that relate to how you approach a problem and how you carry out a job are called behavioural competencies or soft competencies. I am sure if you look back, you will see which chapters of this book relate to the hard and soft competencies. When you attend a graduate assessment centre you will probably be called on to demonstrate some or all of the following:

- the ability to manage the time available for tasks
- the ability to communicate in writing, one-to-one and one-to-many
- the ability to organise yourself and others
- the ability to solve problems with information and data
- the ability to make decisions
- the ability to demonstrate drive, enthusiasm and initiative
- the ability to solve problems in creative and innovative ways
- the ability to lead and be led
- the ability to adapt and be flexible
- the ability to be a team member and a team leader
- the ability to influence a situation and persuade others.

The format of the assessment event will vary from company to company, but the following might be regarded as a typical one-day assessment centre.

08:00   Meet and greet over a coffee and a light breakfast
08:30   Formal welcome to the organisation and the event followed by a chance to ask questions

IBM'S STATED COMPETENCIES FOR GRADUATES

Adaptability – You're flexible when dealing with changing demands.

Drive to achieve – You're committed to success and actively seek to acquire new knowledge and skills.

Client focus – Your rapport with clients means you can see their point of view, anticipate their needs and respond to their queries.

Creative problem-solving – Your alternative solutions to problems are always supported by logical methods and appropriate analysis.

Communication – Not only do you listen carefully to others, you also match your communication style and method to your audience and situation.

Passion for the business – Your enthusiasm and pride in your work inspires others.

Taking ownership – You identify and take responsibility for tasks and decision-making.

Teamwork and collaboration – You work well with others to achieve shared goals.

Trustworthiness – Your customers and colleagues are impressed by your integrity and professionalism.

(Source: IBM website at: http://www-05.ibm.com/employment/uk/media/graduate_brochure_08-09.pdf)

09:00	Writing and numeracy tests
09:45	Psychometric tests
10:30	Break for light refreshments
11:00	Three 20-minute case studies – one individual presentation – one paired case study – one group case study
12:00	Case studies debrief
12:30	Morning debrief – general
13:00	Lunch and an opportunity to network with other candidates and staff members
14:00	Individual morning debrief – only candidates that impressed in the morning activities will be asked to remain. The deselected candidates get an intensive debrief and then leave.

For selected candidates:

14:00	Cycle interviews with three managers on a one-to-one basis, 10 minutes for each one
14:30	Group discussion – role-play meeting
15:00	Decision-making exercise followed by in-tray and e tray exercises
15:45	Light refreshment
16:00	Team physical challenge (tracksuits provided and showers after)

Assessors select those who will attend the panel interviews.
(debrief the unsuccessful)

17:15   Panel interviews with a short presentation and decisions
18:00   General and specific debriefs
18:30   Candidates depart

This is a fairly intensive programme for one day. You might find a programme
like this spread over an evening and a day. These are intensive and stressful events
where you are 'on show' all the time. Even when you are taking a break, you are
being assessed. In business networking skills are paramount, so it is important to
use the lunch and refreshment breaks to actively network with the staff members.

HOW TO PREPARE FOR AN ASSESSMENT CENTRE EVENT

You need to know the organisation, so research what they do, their products
or services, their cultural values and their vision for the future. It helps to have
some facts and knowledge at your fingertips, such as the company mission and
where they operate in the region or world. Investigate the graduate skills they
are seeking. As in the IBM example above, organisational websites often contain
valuable details about the competencies they are looking to recruit. It also helps
to understand the assessment process. Many organisational websites contain
vignettes of successful graduates; these can be useful in understanding the type of
people they have recruited recently.

Prepare 'potted' examples of the sort of behaviours and skills that assessment
centres test. Carry out some reading around how psychometric tests are used in
assessment centres. Being prepared for the format and conduct of the tests will
help. But don't try to second-guess the answers you think the recruiters want – be
yourself and answer honestly. If your university offers training and preparation
for assessment centres, go along and absorb all you can from them.

Plan your transport arrangement and timing with care. Aim to arrive at least 30
minutes before the activities start; 60 minutes if you don't like being rushed. You
will need a strategy to combat nerves:

- Arrange travel so that you have a very large time contingency – being late
  makes you nervous and stressed.

- Avoid stimulants or alcohol the night before and on the morning of the event.

- Eat an early and simple breakfast.

- Be as well prepared as you can be – practise, practise and practise.

- Investigate as much detail of the process as possible – uncertainty makes you
  nervous.

- If you have time, do a 20–30-minute exercise activity before you leave for the
  event – if you are staying at a hotel this won't be a problem.

- If you cannot exercise beforehand, arrive early and go for a 20-minute stroll.

- Take some relaxing 'I music'.

- Don't 'put all your eggs in one basket' – arrange to attend lots of events. This removes the stress that this is your only chance. You will become an experienced pro at these things after a completing a few.

HOW SHOULD I BEHAVE AT THE EVENT?

The simple answer is to be your normal self. But this is not so easy in a new, stressful situation. Remember, when you try to give the answers you think the assessors want to hear, you will often sound rather shallow and one-dimensional. So relax and let your personality shine out.

Things you should try to do

- Relax and smile; it will make you feel more relaxed and make the assessors think you are a quiet and confident person.

- Maintain your usual polite and considerate demeanour – this is quite hard to do in a stressful situation.

- Make appropriate eye contact with assessors and fellow graduates.

- When you speak, do it clearly and distinctly – remember to calculate your share of the speaking time. For example, if there is a 20-minute session and five people, you should aim to speak for no more than four minutes.

- Contributing too much is as bad as not contributing, so use the rule above.

- You only have so long to speak; don't waste words. Aim to make a quality, thoughtful contribution. Remember quality, not quantity.

- Time your intervention into discussions carefully so that you don't talk over other people, but you may have to push into the conversation if lots of people are talking.

- When you are not talking, listen actively and show all around you that you are listening actively. Use small gestures and eye contact.

- Make sure when you do contribute that it is relevant to the current discussion.

- Stay calm and collected even when things seem to be going against you or other people are annoying you.

- Try to subtly introduce the research you have done in clever and thoughtful ways.

Things you should try not to do

- Use humour because it nearly always goes wrong in these situations.

- Address the assessors directly except when you are being interviewed.

- Be overawed and shrink into the background – you need to make a favourable impression.

- Raise your voice, shout, get angry or annoyed.

- Dominate the conversation or actions – team players bring the whole team into play.

- Think you are 'off-camera' at any point.

- Sit quietly on your own away from the group.

- Use blunt leadership tactics such as telling everyone what to do – remember persuasion, not instruction.

What to do after the assessment event is finished

You will need to take on board the feedback given by the assessors if you are going to learn from the assessment event. This can be difficult in the highly charged and stressful atmosphere of the event. Remember, you have probably put your heart and soul into impressing the assessors and, unless you are offered a job, your efforts will have been unsuccessful. However, you may not have got a job offer from your efforts, but you can get useful learning from the effort.

These are my tips for receiving critical feedback:

- You will want to respond and defend your performance – don't. Your job at this stage is to listen and record what is said. Make short notes about the feedback. Do not speak to defend yourself.

- Show the assessors that you are actively listening with eye contact, small head movements and short, compliant comments such as, 'That is interesting. I hadn't realised I did that.' This will diffuse any adversarial feel and make it more effective.

- Once a non-adversarial approach is established you can engage in exploring your performance in the eyes of the assessors. Such comments as, 'Yes, I can see your point there. Did the assessors take into account that I was trying to lead by authority and not just boss people around?'

- Try to accept the criticism in the positive way it is undoubtedly intended. The assessors are taking time to explain how you came across to them so that you can change and improve.

- Remember to say thank you and be gracious – you may yet be asked back to this organisation or apply to them again in the future.

Finally

An assessment event is a big, stressful day full of new and life-changing experiences. As soon after the event as you can, record your thoughts and observations in your learning diary. It is good to 'shake off' the experience, good or bad, on the journey home. So take a small pad of paper and reflect on the journey home. Then when you get home you will be ready to relax and enjoy your free time rather than rerun the events of the day.

19.5 VISIONING THE FUTURE

Well! We have come to the end of this book. I hope it has been interesting and has developed skills that you can use throughout your life. As you finish university or study, exciting possibilities will lie before you. How will you know which direction you want to travel?

FINDING INSPIRATION FOR THE LIFE AHEAD

See if you can find this YouTube clip: **http://www.youtube.com/ watch?v=PAC1lyasoPs** If you cannot find this exact clip, search for others using the search terms 'personal', 'vision', 'future' and 'YouTube'.

YOUR INSPIRATION

In your learning diary try to answer the following questions:

- What are my five greatest strengths, attributes and values?
- What five things have I been good at in the past?
- What five things do I want to be good at in the future?
- What are the ten things I most enjoy doing in life?
- What five things must I do every day to feel fulfilled?
- If I won a large amount on the lottery, so that I never had to do a paid day's work again, what five things would I do?
- What five strengths have other people seen in me?
- What five weaknesses have other people seen in me?

Use the thinking and reflection you have done in relation to these questions to write your personal vision statement. Write this vision statement in the first person, 'I will be…' Write at least one important goal for each of the following areas:

- my physical future
- my work future
- my family future
- my intellectual future
- my financial future
- my leisure future
- my fun future
- my community future
- my dream.

Hopefully, you now have the inspiration and the dreams. Now use all the skills you have learned to make them reality.

SUMMARY

- Careers can be conceptualised in many different ways. But thinking about a career creates something that can be managed.
- There are different types of career and each needs different skills:
    - the traditional career

CAREER SURPRISE

Glenys Mahoney got into work at 8:10am as usual and was surprised to find many more people than usual around. 'Strange,' she thought, 'at this time I usually have the place to myself for half an hour.' If truth be told, she was a bit angry because she had some important things to do before a meeting at 9:00am. She couldn't know it, but she would never get to that meeting. She had been sat at her desk for about ten minutes when her manager asked her to come to the office – this angered her even more because she wanted to prepare.

Her manager Helen explained that her rather pushy style and aggression were not what the company was looking for at the moment and, before she had the chance to say anything, Helen said her job no longer existed. Helen said she must clear her desk and leave the office within ten minutes. At 8:40am she was standing outside with a small cardboard box and a rather confused look on her face. She stood there for a full 15 minutes just trying to take in what had just happened. Now a deep and very dark anger was taking over her. She had worked in this job for 16 years and never once had a bad appraisal. She had a limited set of skills but they perfectly matched her job as outsourcing manager. She hadn't done any training for 15 years and was not very good with computers. She accepted that she might be 'stuck in a rut'.

As part of the redundancy package Glenys was referred to an outplacement service. She was very sceptical about this. Most of Glenys's time since the redundancy was spent going over and over the things that had happened in the weeks before her dismissal. She was living in the past and could not get back to the future. The first outplacement meeting was just setting the agenda and dealing with these feelings of rejection and anger.

In the second outplacement meeting the attention of her advisor turned to what skills and motivations she had.

To think about...

- In the twenty-first-century business world, these sorts of setbacks are quite common. How would you advise Glenys to assess her situation and move on?
- What likely issues will Glenys have with finding another job?
- What career path has Glenys been following?
- What career path is she likely to need to follow in the future?
- What skill issues will she have if she followed a protean or entrepreneurial career path?

– the protean career
– the portfolio career.

- Managing the transition from university to work can be difficult, but the following will help you to secure a well-paid job:
  – internships
  – portfolio careers
  – entrepreneurial careers
  – agencies
  – interim manager jobs
  – social networking.
- Graduate skills that employers are looking for:

- communication
- teamworking
- integrity
- intellectual ability
- confidence
- character/personality
- planning and organising
- good writing skills
- good with numbers
- analysis and decision-making skills.

- If you are going to attend graduate assessment centres, be sure to prepare for:
  - psychometric tests
  - technical exercises related to the role – for a sales area you may be asked to role-play making a sale
  - written exercises
  - thinking exercises
  - physical exercises
  - interviews
  - presentations
  - in-tray and e-tray exercises
  - team activities
  - physical challenges.

- When visioning your future, reflect on:
  - What are my five greatest strengths, attributes and values?
  - What five things have I been good at in the past?
  - What five things do I want to be good at in the future?
  - What are the ten things I most enjoy doing in life?
  - What five things must I do every day to feel fulfilled?
  - If I won a large amount on the lottery, so that I never had to do a paid day's work again, what five things would I do?
  - What five strengths have other people seen in me?
  - What five weaknesses have other people seen in me?

FURTHER READING

Archer, W. and Davison, J. (2008) *Graduate Employability: What do employers think and want?* London: Council for Industry and Higher Education.

Brown, P., Hesketh, A. and Williams, D. (2005) *How to Get the Best Graduate Job: Secret insider strategies for success in the graduate job market.* Harlow: Prentice-Hall.

Hall, D.T. (1976) *Careers in Organisations.* Pacific Palisades, CA: Goodyear Publishing Company.

Hodgson, S. (2009) *A–Z of Careers and Jobs.* London: Kogan Page Ltd.

Pedler, M., Burgoyne, J. and Boydell, T. (1994) *A Manager's Guide to Self Development.* 3rd edition. London: McGraw-Hill.

WEB LINKS

Career finder website: http://science.education.nih.gov/LifeWorks.nsf/CareerFinder.htm

Careers guidance website: http://www.careers.ed.ac.uk/STUDENTS/Careers_Guidance/Careers_guidance.html

A Manpower report on graduate skills: http://www.manpower.co.uk/news/Graduate%20Report%20FINAL.pdf

Interim Management Association: http://www.interimmanagement.uk.com/pages/home.aspx

MAPP career assessment test: http://www.assessment.com/MAPPMembers/Welcome.asp?accnum=06-5210-000.00&gclid=CLSe2qD495sCFUoB4wodnnsw_A

EXPLORE FURTHER

Bibliography

AMIR, A. and SOUNDERPANDIAN, J. (2004) *Business Statistics*. London: McGraw-Hill Education – Europe.

APPLEGARTH, M. and POSNER, K. (2008) *The Project Management Pocketbook*. Alresford: Management Pocketbooks.

ARCHER, W. and DAVISON, J. (2008) *Graduate Employability: What do employers think and want?* London: Council for Industry and Higher Education.

BASHAM, S. (2007) *Word 2007 in Easy Steps*. Warwickshire: Computer Step.

BELBIN, M. (2004) *Management Teams: Why they succeed or fail*. Oxford: Elsevier Butterworth-Heinemann.

BIAFORE, B. (2007) *Microsoft Project 2007: The missing manual*. Sebastopol, CA: O'Reilly Media.

BLAKE, R. and MOUTON, J. (1978) *The New Managerial Grid*. Houston, TX: Gulf.

BOAK, G. and THOMPSON, D. (1998) *Mental Models for Managers: Frameworks for practical thinking*. London: Imprint Random House Business Books.

BOUD, D., KEOGH, R. and WALKER, D. (1985) *Reflection: Turning experience into learning*. London: Kogan Page.

BOWELL, T. and KEMP, G. (2005) *Critical Thinking: A concise guide*. London: Taylor & Francis Ltd.

BRADLEY, T. (2008) *Essential Mathematics for Economics and Business*. 3rd edition. Chichester: John Wiley and Sons Ltd.

BROWN, P., HESKETH, A. and WILLIAMS, D. (2005) *How to Get the Best Graduate Job: Secret insider strategies for success in the graduate job market*. Harlow: Prentice-Hall.

BUZAN, T. (2004) *Mind Maps at Work: How to be the best at work and still have time to play*. London: HarperCollins.

CIPD (2009) *Learning and Development [online]*. Annual survey report. London: Chartered Institute of Personnel and Development. Available at: http://www.cipd.co.uk/surveys [Accessed 27 August 2009].

DE BONO, E. (2000) *Six Thinking Hats*. London: Penguin Books Ltd.

FAIRBAIRN, G. and FAIRBAIRN, S. (2001) *Reading at University: A guide for students*. Milton Keynes: Open University Press.

FIEDLER, F.E. (1997) Situational control and a dynamic theory of leadership. In K. Grint (ed.) *Leadership: Classical, contemporary and critical approaches*. Oxford: Oxford University Press.

FIEDLER, F.E. and GARCIA, J.E. (1987) *New Approaches to Effective Leadership*. New York: John Wiley.

FISHER, A. (2001) *Critical Thinking: An introduction*. Cambridge: Cambridge University Press.

FORSYTH, P. (2006) *How to Craft Successful Business Presentations and Effective Public Speaking*. Berkshire: Foulsham.

GOLEMAN, D. (1996) *Emotional Intelligence: Why it can matter more than IQ*. London: Bloomsbury.

GOLEMAN, D. (1999) *Working with Emotional Intelligence*. London: Bloomsbury.

GOOKIN, D. (2006) *Word 2007 for Dummies*. New York: John Wiley and Sons Ltd.

GRINT, K. (ed.) (1997) *Leadership: Classical, contemporary and critical approaches*. Oxford: Oxford University Press.

HALL, D.T. (1976) *Careers in Organisations*. Pacific Palisades, CA: Goodyear Publishing Company.

HELLER, R. (1998) *Managing Teams*. London: Penguin Books.

HIGBEE, K. (1988). *Your Memory: How it works and how to improve it*. London: Piatkus.

HIGHER EDUCATION ACADEMY. (2005) *Guide for Busy Academics No. 1: Personal development planning*. York: Higher Education Academy.

HINDLE, T. (1998) *Making Presentations*. London: Penguin Books Ltd.

HODGSON, S. (2009) *A–Z of Careers and Jobs*. London: Kogan Page Ltd.

HOLDEN, G. (2009) *Microsoft Excel 2007 in Simple Steps*. Harlow: Prentice-Hall.

HORN, R. (2009) *Researching and Writing Dissertations: A complete guide for business and management students*. London: Chartered Institute of Personnel and Development.

HUNTER, J.E. and HUNTER, F. (1984) Validity and utility of alternative predictors of job performance. *Psychological Bulletin*. No 96. pp72–98.

JELPHS, K., DICKINSON, H. and MARKIEWICZ, L. (2008) *Working in teams*. Bristol: Policy Press.

KOLB, D.A. (1984) *Experiential Learning: Experience as a source of learning and development*. Upper Saddle River, NJ: Prentice Hall.

KOTTER, J. (1996) *Leading change*. Boston, MA: Harvard Business School Press.

LEVI, D. (2007) *Group Dynamics for Teams*. London: Sage.

LEVIN, P. (2006) *Perfect Presentations!* Milton Keynes: Open University Press.

MAHANEY, R.C. and LEDERER, A.L. (2006) The effect of intrinsic and extrinsic rewards for developers in information systems project success. *Project Management Journal.* Vol 37, No 4. p42.

MATTHEWS, M. (2007) *Microsoft Office Word 2007 Quicksteps.* Maidenhead: McGraw-Hill Education – Europe.

MAYER, J., SALOVEY, P. and CARUSO, D. (2004) Emotional intelligence: theory, findings, and implications. *Psychological Inquiry.* Vol 15, No 3. pp197–215.

McMILLAN, K. and WEYERS, J. (2007) *How to Write Essays and Assignments.* Harlow: Pearson Education Limited.

McMILLAN, K. and WEYERS, J. (2007) *The Smarter Student: Study skills and strategies for success at university.* Harlow: Pearson Education Limited.

MINTZBERG, H. (1973) *The Nature of Managerial Work.* London: Joanna Cotler Books.

MINTZBERG, H. (1975) The manager's job: folklore and fact. *Harvard Business Review.* Vol 53, No 4. pp49–61.

MOON, J. (1999) *Reflection in Learning and Professional Development Theory and Practice.* London: Kogan Page.

MOON, J.A. (2007) *Critical thinking: an exploration of theory and practice.* London: Routledge.

NEVILLE, C. (2007) *The Complete Guide to Referencing and Avoiding Plagiarism.* Milton Keynes: Open University Press.

NORTHEDGE, A. (2005) *The Good Study guide.* 2nd edition. Milton Keynes: Open University.

OLSSON, S. (2000) Acknowledging the female archetype: women managers' narratives of gender. *Women in Management Review.* Vol 15, Nos 5/6. p296.

PEDLER, M., BURGOYNE, J. and BOYDELL, T. (1994) *A Manager's Guide to Self Development.* 3rd edition. London: McGraw-Hill.

PERRY, A. (2002) *Isn't it About Time? How to stop putting things off and get on with your life.* London: Worth Publishing.

PREPPERNAU, J., COX, J. and FRYE, C. (2007) *Microsoft Office Home and Student 2007 Step by Step.* Redmond, WA: Microsoft Press Inc.

RAWLINSON, G. (1986) *Creative Thinking and Brainstorming.* Aldershot: Gower Publishing Ltd.

REED, J. (2008) *Project Management with PRINCE2 Best Practice Handbook: Building, running and managing effective project management – ready to use.* Brisbane, Australia: Emereo Publishing.

SADLER, P. (1997) *Leadership.* London: Kogan Page.

SANSONE, C. and HARACKIEWICZ, J.M. (2000) *Intrinsic and Extrinsic Motivation: The search for optimal motivation and performance.* London: Academic Press.

SCHON, D. (1991) *The Reflective Practitioner: How professionals think in action.* London: Avebury.

SEELY, J. (2005) *Oxford Guide to Effective Writing and Speaking.* Oxford: Oxford University Press.

SENGE, P.M. (1990) *The Fifth Discipline: The art and practice of the learning organisation.* London: Random House.

SINCLAIR, C. (2007) *Grammar: A friendly approach.* Milton Keynes: Open University Press.

SLACK, N. (2000) *Operations Management.* London: Prentice Hall.

STEERS, R.M. and RHODES, S.R. (1978) Major influences on employee attendance: a process model. *Journal of Applied Psychology.* Vol 63, No 4. pp391–407.

STEPHEN, M. (2007) *Teach Yourself Excel 2007.* London: Teach Yourself Books.

STERNBERG, R. (1996) *How Practical and Creative Intelligence Determines Success in Life.* New York: Simon & Schuster.

STRAWBRIDGE, M. (2006) *Spreadsheets: The ECDL Advanced series.* Oxford: Pearson Education.

TIETJEN, M. and MYERS, R. (1998) Motivation and job satisfaction. *Management Decision.* Vol 36, No 4. pp226–31.

TUCKMAN, B. (1965) Developmental sequences in small groups. *Psychological Bulletin.* No 63. pp384–99.

VENOLIA, J. (2001) *Rewrite Right! Your guide to perfectly polished prose.* Berkeley, CA: Ten Speed Press.

WEYERS, J. and McMILLAN, K. (2007) *The Smarter Student: Study skills and strategies for success at university.* Harlow: Prentice-Hall.

WOOD, F. (2008) *Business Accounting.* 11th edition. Harlow: Financial Times Prentice Hall.

WRIGHT, P. (1996) *Managerial Leadership.* London: Routledge.

ZELAZNY, G. (2008) *Say it with Presentations: How to design and deliver successful business presentations.* Maidenhead: McGraw-Hill Education – Europe.

Index

The CIPD would like to thank the following members of the CIPD Publishing editorial board for their help and advice:

Caroline Hook, Huddersfield University Business School
Edwina Hollings, Staffordshire University Business School
Pauline Dibben, Sheffield University Business School
Simon Gurevitz, University of Westminster Business School
Barbara Maiden, University of Wolverhampton Business School
Wendy Yellowley and Marilyn Farmer, Buckinghamshire New University School of Business and Management